D0095302

MOTHERS *And Such*

MAXINE L. MARGOLIS

UNIVERSITY OF CALIFORNIA PRESS

MOTHERS And Such

Views of American Women And Why They Changed

BERKELEY · LOS ANGELES · LONDON

University of California Press
Berkeley and Los Angeles, California

University of California Press, Ltd.
London, England

Library of Congress Cataloging in Publication Data

Margolis, Maxine L., 1942–
Mothers and such.

Bibliography: p. 309
Includes index.
1. Women—United States—Attitudes—History. 2. Women—Employment—United States—History. 3. Mothers—United States—History. 4. Housewives—United States—History. 5. Sex role—United States—History. I. Title.
HQ1410.M36 1984 305.4'0973 83-12639
ISBN 0-520-04995-0

Printed in the United States of America

1 2 3 4 5 6 7 8 9

FOR NARA

WHOSE MOTHER DID NOT PLAY THE MOTHER ROLE VERY WELL WHILE SHE WAS WRITING THIS BOOK

CONTENTS

PREFACE AND ACKNOWLEDGMENTS

This book had its inception in 1976 when I published an article in *Ms. Magazine* analyzing the housekeeping tips offered to women by Heloise, a syndicated advice columnist. It seemed to me that most of her hints encouraged mindless make-work activities designed to keep the full-time housewife/homemaker as busy as possible. The article suggested that one of the reasons women were spending so much time on housework, despite the plethora of modern appliances in the middle class home, was the high housekeeping standards advocated in women's magazine articles and television and print advertisements for various domestic products.

I also became interested in the depiction of working women in the popular media at different periods in American history. In a 1977 article in the journal, *Michigan Discussions in Anthropology*, I examined the material correlates of these changing attitudes toward women in the labor force and concluded that they were not fortuitous but were molded by such material factors as the demand or lack of demand for women's labor.

Three years later in the same journal I published an article that applied the concept of "blaming the victim" to women. Although the concept had been widely used by social scientists in relation to minority groups, there had been no systematic attempt to analyze how it was employed to "explain" women's inferior position in employment and in other areas.

By this time I realized that I wanted to expand my research on these topics and include them in a book on the perception of American middle class women in the prescriptive literature of different historical eras. Certainly such a volume had to include chapters on how the advice-givers depicted motherhood if it were to be a well-rounded analysis of women's major roles. As such, I devoted my sabbatical year 1980–81 (as well as the following year) to researching and writing the chapters on the maternal role and housework and to expanding, updating, and rewriting the chapters on women in the labor force and on blaming the female victim.

During the very long haul of transforming a few short articles and half-formed ideas for additional research into a final book-length manuscript, I received help and advice from a number of friends and colleagues. Foremost among them is Marianne Schmink whose tireless reading of the various versions of the chapters and whose penetrating comments clarified my thinking and contributed greatly to the final form of this work. Marvin Harris, H. Russell Bernard, and Helen I. Safa also read a draft of the manuscript and made useful suggestions. Conrad P. Kottak and Sue-Ellen Jacobs will recognize the incorporation of their ideas and I thank them for them. Needless to say, the responsibility for any shortcomings in the book are entirely my own.

The staff at the libraries of the University of Florida were always helpful and I greatly appreciate the efforts of those in the Office of Inter-Library Loan who were able to obtain the few rare and obscure sources unavailable in the library's otherwise excellent collection on American women.

Before I discovered the delights of writing on an Apple II Plus Computer, Phyllis Durrell expertly typed early versions of three of the chapters.

The photographs in the volume come from a number of sources. I thank Dr. Benjamin Spock's office for his photograph, the Tribune Company Syndicate for the Don Wright cartoon, as well as the National Archives and the Schlesinger Library at Radcliffe College for the historical photographs. I am particularly indebted to Michael Kappy, M.D., who generously offered to take photographs especially for my book and to Susan Johnson, Ph.D., Nora Dalton, Jane Keister, and Farhat Moazam, M.D., for graciously agreeing to be photographed.

Throughout the long and often frustrating process of writing and publishing this work, the love and encouragement of my husband, Jerry Milanich, has been boundless. When my belief in this project sometimes flagged, his never did. And to my daughter, Nara, to whom this volume is lovingly dedicated, I owe not only its title but the joy of being her mother.

Gainesville, Florida
August 1983

M.L.M.

Helmer: "Before all else you are a wife and mother."

Nora: "That I no longer believe. I believe that before all else I am a human being."

Henrik Ibsen, A Doll's House, 1879

1 THE ANTHROPOLOGICAL PERSPECTIVE

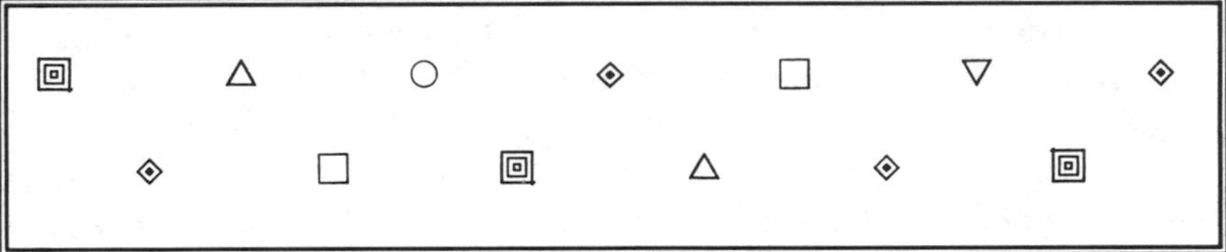

Genuine research seeks explanations, not just examples; its goal is understanding, not reassurance.

Robert Asahina, "Social Science Fiction," 1981

This book about women in the United States is written by an anthropologist. Why an anthropologist? Given the outpouring of scholarship on American women over the past ten or fifteen years, why would an anthropologist, often erroneously stereotyped as a person interested only in "exotic" peoples in remote jungles, write a book on women's roles in the United States? What can anthropology contribute to our understanding of changes in women's roles over the course of American history? A good deal, I believe.[1]

Anthropologists, because of their broad cross-cultural perspective, take little for granted in the way of human behavior. For most generalizations about the way people live, anthropologists can cite exceptions to the rule. This does not mean that there are no regularities in human behavior and culture but only that anthropologists are usually more careful than most people about making generalizations that people in "all cultures" behave in this way or that. For example, the claim that women everywhere are the primary caretakers of children is readily disputed by anthropologists, who can provide examples of cultures in which older children have the principal caretaking responsibility. The assertion that women are universally "domestic," that in all cultures they keep the home fires burning while men go out to "make a living," also is easily challenged. Anthropologists can point to dozens of foraging and horticultural societies in which there is no distinct domestic realm and in which women as well as men contribute to the work of earning a living.

Anthropologists recognize then that women's roles and beliefs about women's "natural" propensities differ from one culture to another. They recognize that the roles of women in western industrial societies and their supporting ideologies are simply variants of a diverse human picture. Moreover, anthropologists insist that their own culture's beliefs about women's roles are neither more natural nor more rational than the practices and beliefs of other cultures.

An important question can now be raised: How do we explain the various roles that women play in societies around the world and how do we explain the attendant ideologies about women's "true nature" and "proper place"? Why is it that at some times and in some places women are viewed as innately domestic and nurturing and are thought to be the only persons who can properly care for children, while at other times and in other places this belief is absent? Why is it that in some societies women carry heavy loads of water and firewood and engage in the back-breaking activities of planting and harvesting crops while in other societies women are said to be too "delicate" for such heavy work? Why is it that tasks labeled "women's work" in some cultures are assigned exclusively to men in others?

Although no one has the final and definitive answers to these and myriad other questions, some anthropologists have made considerable headway toward explaining them. I believe that those who have been most successful have adopted a theoretical approach and research strategy called cultural materialism, which assumes that explanations for cultural similarities and differences lie in the material conditions of human life: how people make a living, how they relate to their environments, and how they reproduce themselves. These conditions are termed the infrastructure of a society. In the words of anthropologist Marvin Harris, cultural materialism is "based on the simple premise that human social life is a response to the practical problems of human existence."[2]

Cultural materialism rejects the time-worn adage that "ideas change the world." Instead, it holds that *over time* changes in a society's material base will lead to functionally compatible changes in its social and political structure along with changes in its secular and religious ideology, changes that enhance the continuity and stability of the system as a whole. The ultimate goal of this approach is to explain, not simply describe, cultural variations in the way people live.

This type of analysis has been fruitful in explaining certain aspects of human sex roles. Previous studies using a cultural materialist orientation have shown that variations in men's and women's roles are related to environmental, technological, and demographic factors, to a people's way of making a living, and to social and political arrangements. An important assumption of cultural materialism is that biology is not destiny. Quite to the contrary. The diverse roles that women play in different cultures, along with varying ideologies about women's nature, are linked to and molded by such mundane factors as subsistence strategies and population pressure.[3] From a materialist point of view women's roles are neither grounded in biology nor indeterminate in nature, fluctuating through time for no apparent reason. Ideas about women's capabilities and proper place in the scheme of things do not change at random; they are ultimately shaped by a society's sexual division of labor, which in turn is causally related to its productive and reproductive imperatives.

A caveat is in order here. While cultural materialism looks to the productive and reproductive modes in a given society in order to account for its structural and ideological components, it does not postulate a simplistic, mechanistic correspondence between material conditions and structural and ideological phenomena. There may be a time lag before an ideology evolves that is compatible with changed material conditions. A relevant example of such a lag is the case of the "feminine mystique," an ideology celebrating the joys of domesticity.[4] As is well known, the feminine mystique flourished during the 1950s, when married women were in fact taking jobs in record numbers. The ideology seemed inappropriate for the times, and belated recognition of women's large-scale employment did not come until the feminist resurgence more than a decade later. Still, from the perspective of cultural materialism, the women's movement was ultimately a *result,* rather than a *cause* of women's massive entry into the labor force. Women did not take jobs because a feminist ideology "liberated" them to do so. As we will see in chapter 6, the reason why so many married women sought employment lies in such material factors as high rates of inflation and an increase in demand for female labor.

The advantages of cultural materialism—combined with an anthropological perspective—become clear when we contrast it with an ideological approach to women's roles. According to sociologist William Goode, changes in ideas altered the position of women in western society:

> I believe that the crucial crystallizing variable—i.e., the necessary but not sufficient cause of the betterment of western woman's position—was ideological: the gradual logical philosophical extension to women of originally Protestant notions about the rights and responsibilities of the individual undermined the traditional idea of "woman's proper place."[5]

This statement presents two problems. The "traditional idea of woman's proper place" refers to the common misconception that women in preindustrial societies do not work outside the home because cultural values deem such work inappropriate. Goode claims that this ideology changed in western society and a new value system emerged that permitted women to engage in work outside the home. Unfortunately, his facts are wrong. In many preindustrial societies women do work outside the household and do make an important contribution to subsistence. Goode assumes that women's traditional role is one of economic dependence and total confinement to the home sphere. In fact, female economic dependence and the very existence of a separate "feminine" domestic realm are relatively recent phenomena. In western society they are artifacts of industrialization; they date only from the nineteenth century and even then were based on class.

In addition to Goode's inaccurate information, there is also a serious flaw in his analysis. He fails to explain why and under what conditions Protestant values of individual rights and responsibilities were extended to women. He claims that this ideology spelled the end of traditional beliefs about women's proper place, but he does not explain under what *conditions* this momentous ideological change took place, why it occurred when and where it did, and what other changes made these new ideas appropriate.

One might raise similar questions about the revival of American feminism in the late 1960s. What caused it? Why did it occur when it did rather than ten or twenty years earlier? Common wisdom has it that the resurgence of feminism had essentially ideological roots, that the women's movement grew out of the civil rights movement of the 1960s. Women were sick and tired of being the "gofers" of the left and began to demand the same rights as men. This analysis overlooks the relatively sparse number of women active in the civil rights movement. It does nothing to explain why untold numbers of women were dissatisfied with the status quo and sought to change it. Others point to Betty Friedan's *The Feminine Mystique* as the first contemporary statement of female discontent and the founding document of the women's movement. To be sure, Friedan's book, first published in 1963, did strike a responsive chord and became a much discussed best-seller. But why the reaction to it? Why didn't Simone de Beauvoir's feminist tome *The Second Sex*, published in 1952 in the United States, also become an immediate best-seller?[6] Although de Beauvoir's book has been widely read in this country and elsewhere, its popularity postdates its publication by at least a decade. I conclude that when *The Second Sex* was first published it did not have a wide impact because conditions were not ripe for a feminist revival.

The suggestion that women were suddenly prompted to action by the civil rights movement or by a best-selling book ignores the conditions of millions of women's lives in the late 1950s and 1960s. More married women than ever before held jobs, but these jobs were usually low paying and dead-end. At the same time women continued to bear primary responsibility for child care and housework. Surely these conditions explain the roots of female discontent, discontent that led to the rebirth of feminism and the popularity of books that decried the contemporary version of women's "proper place."

Here we can see the value of a materialist conception of history. Seemingly indeterminant and inexplicable fluctuations in women's roles and their attendant ideologies become intelligible in light of their material causes. Cultural materialism provides no ready-made explanation for changes in any particular set of roles or in any particular system of beliefs. Instead, it analyzes the larger context in which these changes took place and then tries to answer the vital question: Why here and now?

◈ □ ○ △ □ ◈

Middle class American women as mothers, housewives, and workers are the focus of these pages. These roles and the prescriptions about them, although treated separately in this volume, are closely related. It is impossible, for example, to understand changes in the perception of the role of mother over the course of American history without also looking at women's work inside and outside the home. It is no mere coincidence that as the life-sustaining productive activities of middle class women dwindled, their maternal and housekeeping duties were thrown into sharp relief and became the subject of numerous prescriptive treatises.

Changes in roles and in their accompanying ideologies can only be explained within a larger material context. They cannot be understood apart from the productive and reproductive imperatives that prevailed at the time the changes occurred. For this reason I will intersperse a variety of data with my primary discussion of the roles of middle class women. At one time or another a number of material factors impinged on the definition of the roles of this class of American women, and I will focus on these factors in the pages to follow. Just which factors were important? They include such basic variables as household versus industrial production; a manufacturing versus a service oriented economy; the demand or lack of demand for middle class women's labor outside the home; the rate of inflation; the needs of business and industry for quality employees; and the changing costs and benefits of rearing the middle class children who would become those employees. This brief list will suffice; the actual explanation of how these and other material factors affected women's roles at different points in American history is the subject of this book.

I do not wish to imply that the infrastructural changes to be reviewed and their impact on the definition of the roles of middle class women are unique to American history. They are in fact part of the more widespread changes wrought by industrialization in the western world. So, for example, just as the shift from household to industrial production in the United States downgraded middle class women's domestic labor, a similar process took place in England (although somewhat earlier) as a consequence of industrialization there. The material changes described in these pages and their accompanying ideological shifts have close parallels in other western societies. My analysis, however, will be limited to the United States.

Before addressing substantive issues, I would like to make it clear what this book is and is not about. Following the warnings of historians Mary Beth Norton and Carol Ruth Berkin, I do not deal with the question of the relative status of middle class women at any given period in American history; I do not claim that middle class women were better or worse off during any particular era.[7] I certainly have my own opinions on the matter, but this book does not make such determinations. The assertion that women played a central role in the household economy of colonial days, for example, is not meant to suggest that women enjoyed equality with men as a result of their productive activities or that they had more power than mid-nineteenth-century housewives whose domestic production had been greatly curtailed. What I am concerned with is determining why women's roles changed and how these changes were reflected in contemporary perceptions of woman's nature and place.

To describe the ideological component of the roles of middle class women I have used what is termed "prescriptive history"—historical and contemporary books, manuals, and other popular writings that have advised women how to act, thus informing them what their roles are or ought to be. I reviewed all the most popular manuals published in any given period, including twentieth-century best-sellers or those known to have had large sales in the nineteenth century. In addition, I randomly selected other, apparently minor, prescriptive writings for each of the periods covered. I also surveyed articles from nineteenth-century ladies' magazines and twentieth-century mass circulation monthlies like the *Ladies' Home Journal* and *Good Housekeeping* in an attempt to recreate their assumptions about the proper roles for middle class women.

As a number of historians have pointed out, employing prescriptive writings in historical research is problematic.[8] It raises a number of unanswered, perhaps unanswerable, questions: Who bought these manuals and magazines? Were they actually read? And, if they were read, how seriously was their advice taken? Did such advice affect the way middle class women saw themselves? Did it influence their behavior?

As a social scientist I am well aware of the complex relationship between ideology and behavior, including the obvious limitations of prescriptive literature as a guide to such behavior. *At no point, therefore, am I suggesting that what the advice givers were saying, women were actually doing.* I am *not* analyzing how the advice given during different historical periods was translated into *actual* behavior by the women who lived during those periods: the influence of prescriptive writings on the lives of women is simply not the subject of this book. What use are such sources then? Historian Mary Beth Norton, for example, warns us about the "prescriptive pitfall" and argues that advice books are no more than male formulations of ideal female behavior.[9]

Prescriptive literature as a source for beliefs about American women is also suspect because of the strong class bias of the majority of this literature. Most child-care manuals and household guides were written by and intended for the white, urban middle class. The dictum "cleanliness is next to godliness," which appeared in so many late nineteenth-century housekeeping manuals, took a middle class standard of living for granted. And the directives of John B. Watson, the dean of American child-rearing experts in the 1920s, certainly assumed an affluent lifestyle; Watson insisted that every child have a room of its own.[10] These and other prescriptive writings were indeed addressed to the white middle class woman, and as such they do not and cannot provide us with a guide to contemporary views of poor, nonwhite, or immigrant women.

Some of the manuals also display a regional bias. During the nineteenth century, in particular, most domestic advisors were writers living in the older, more settled, eastern regions of the country. This bias is reflected in the housekeeping guides dating from the late 1800s; some took it for granted that all households had certain domestic equipment that was too costly or simply unavailable to poor or rural women.

Yet the middle class limitations of prescriptive data should not be exaggerated, for the ideals the injunctions contained may have filtered down to working class and immigrant groups. I agree with historian Carl Degler who argues that the "downward projection" of middle class values was likely "in a society like that of the United States, where class consciousness was weak, and widespread literacy permitted a large majority of women to inform themselves of the standards of the middle and upper classes." Not only were a majority of nineteenth-century Americans literate, but a majority belonged to the middle class. Degler estimates that if commercial farm families are included in that designation, up to 60 percent of the nineteenth-century American population was middle class. Then, too, we know that working class and immigrant women did read such "middle class" founts of advice as the early twentieth-century publications of the Children's Bureau.[11] It is still a moot question, of course, whether the dicta contained therein affected the behavior of these women, just as it is a moot question for their middle class counterparts.

Despite the limitations of prescriptive writings, such a source can tell us something about ideological trends during different periods of American history. For both the tone and content of books and articles dealing with motherhood, housekeeping, and women as workers *did* change over time. Why, for example, did a cult of motherhood emerge in the manuals after 1830? Why were late nineteenth-century housewives advised of the difficulty and high purpose of their domestic duties when such tasks were barely mentioned in the writings of an earlier era? Why, during the 1950s, were married woman told that it was all right to take a part-time job but not to pursue a full-time career? In other words, *how and why did the advice itself change over time?* If we use a cultural materialist model of society, these and other variations in the directives aimed at middle class American women are not free-floating and random; they are related to and shaped by the productive and reproductive conditions that prevailed at the time the advice was proffered.

Who were the advice givers and why did they consistently shore up the interests of American business and industry? Were they mere puppets who regularly did the bidding of certain elements in American society? Was there collusion between prescriptive writers and powerful elites whose interests lay in teaching women their proper place? I am not suggesting any conspiracy between women's advisors and groups that stood to benefit from the advice women were given. This implies a level of conscious and deliberate behavior that is unnecessary to my thesis that at most times in American history, there was a certain consistency, a mesh or fit, between the general dicta of the prescriptive writers and the basic economic and social requirements of society.

Some of the advice givers were best-selling authors of their day, while others filled the pages of the *Ladies' Home Journal, Good Housekeeping*, and other women's magazines. But the identity of these writers and their specific relationships to other elements in American society are not what is important to this analysis. What *is* important is that they wrote books and articles that were published and widely disseminated, books and articles expounding ideologies that helped perpetuate the current order by explaining and rationalizing the status quo and women's position in it. Moreover, the directives at any one time reveal a rather remarkable consensus which is difficult to attribute to chance. The mission of the prescriptive writers is clear. They provided ideologies about women's place in the scheme of things, a place that varied over time according to the exigencies of the material order.

A brief word about chronology. In terms of major productive changes and their effects on women's roles, the time span I call the nineteenth century did not really get under way until the 1830s. That decade was a watershed, and its significance is reflected in the arrangement of the chapters on the mother role and on housework. The same is true of the period I term the twentieth century. If we are interested in the transformation of the home by modern conveniences and concomitant changes in standards of good housekeeping, the twentieth century actually began after World War I. This too is reflected in the organization of the chapters on housework.

2 PUTTING MOTHERS ON THE PEDESTAL

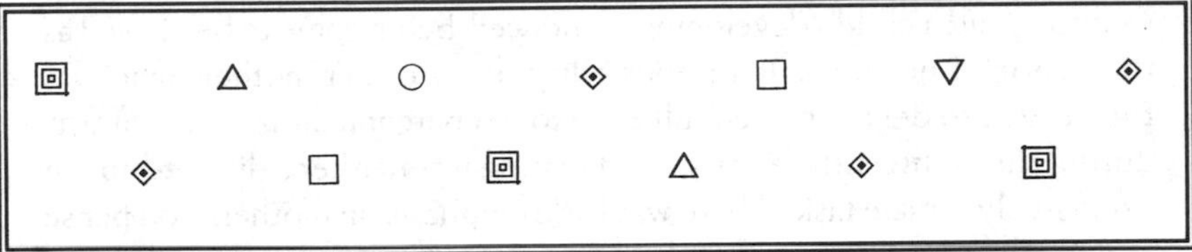

Motherhood as we know it today is a surprisingly new institution. It is also a unique one, the product of an affluent society. In most of human history and in most parts of the world even today, adult, able-bodied women have been, and still are, too valuable in their productive capacity to be spared for the exclusive care of children.

Jessie Bernard, *The Future of Motherhood,* 1974

Debates about the conflict between motherhood and work have lessened in intensity over the last decade as millions of middle class wives and mothers have taken jobs and as employment for these women has become the norm rather than the exception. But these developments have not met with unanimous approval. Just think of the demand by groups like the Moral Majority for a return to "traditional family values," code words for the presence of a full-time housewife-mother in the home. Nevertheless, biting denunciations of working mothers—so common during much of this century—are much less frequent today. Many women are pleased to be living in an era in which they are free to take a job or even pursue a career and in which their economic contribution to their families is recognized. They probably feel less uneasy about working because it is no longer an article of faith that their employment is harmful to their children. But what is often overlooked is that this is not the first time in American history when work and motherhood were thought compatible and when women's productive activities were seen as essential to their families' well-being.

Ideas about the "correct" maternal role have often changed over the last 250 years in the United States. Not until the nineteenth century, for example, did a child's development and well-being come to be viewed as the major, if not the sole responsibility of his or her mother, who was then urged to devote herself full-time to her parental duties. In contrast, during the eighteenth century child rearing was neither a discrete nor an exclusively female task. There was little emphasis on motherhood per se and both parents were simply advised to "raise up" their children together.

These and other changes in ideas about motherhood are not isolated cultural artifacts resulting from random ideological fashions. I will argue that these value changes were and are molded by changes in the nature of the family and the American economy. I intend to review the process whereby motherhood as a full-time career for middle class women first arose as women's role in the domestic economy diminished, "work" was removed from the household, the family became more isolated from the larger community, the need for educated and skilled children increased, and the birthrate declined. As a result of these developments, with minor variations, the exclusivity of the mother-child dyad and the incessant duties of motherhood emerged beginning in the 1830s as givens in American child-rearing manuals and other prescriptive writings aimed at the middle class.

One of the principal factors that have influenced the middle class mother's role and the ideology surrounding it is the decline of domestic production. During the colonial period when women were responsible for the manufacture and use of a wide variety of household products essential to daily living, women could not devote themselves full-time to motherhood. But in the early nineteenth century, as manufacturing left the home for the factory, middle class women found themselves "freed up" to spend more time on child care. And before long they were told that such full-time care was essential.

The daily presence or absence of men in the home also has shaped the American definition of motherhood. During colonial times when men, women, and children all worked together in or near the household, there were no firm distinctions in parental responsibilities. It was the duty of both parents to rear their children, and fathers were thought to be especially important to a proper religious education. But when a man's work began to take him away from the home for most of the day—an arrangement that began with the onset of industrialization nearly 200 years ago—child-rearing responsibilities fell heavily on the mother. And, once again, middle class mothers were told that this was in the nature of things.

Household size and its contacts with the outside world have also influenced the mother role. Prior to the nineteenth century, when most households were larger than the nuclear family, when they consisted of more people than just a married couple and their children, the presence of other adults who could take a hand in child care diluted maternal responsibility. Because the household was the site of both life and work, because there was a constant coming and going of people, the mother-child tie was but one of many relationships. As the country industrialized in the nineteenth century, however, the home and the place of work became separate. Women then remained as the only adults in the household and the mother-child relationship was thrown into sharp relief. Mothers took on all the burdens of child care, and their performance of these tasks became a major concern. Why? Because the middle class mother was advised that she and she alone had the weighty mission of transforming her children into the model citizens of the day.

Fertility rates also influence the mother role, but not always in the way one might expect. It seems logical that the more children a woman has, the more she will be defined by her maternal role, for the care and feeding of a large brood demand so much time. But this was not always the case. The emphasis on motherhood in the nineteenth century *increased* as fertility among the middle class *decreased*. One explanation of this anomaly lies in what has been called the "procreative imperative."[1]

Dummer Collection, Schlesinger Library, Radcliffe College

Woman With Two Children • *By the late nineteenth century, the mother-child unit was idealized. This photograph of a well-to-do mother and her children was taken in 1894.*

This refers to the promotion of cheap population growth by powerful elements in society which benefit from the rearing of "high quality" children. As industrialization continued, the need for skilled labor correspondingly increased. Thus, the reification of maternity during the nineteenth century reflects a dual attempt to stem the falling birthrate in the middle class and increase the quality of children through long-term mother care. The emphasis on maternity was also a way of solving what became known as "the woman question." Once a woman's productive skills were no longer needed, what was to occupy her time? The answer was summarized in a single word: *motherhood*.

This preoccupation with motherhood and the corollary assumption that an exclusive mother-child relationship is both natural and inevitable is by no means universal. Ethnographic evidence clearly points out the variability of child-care arrangements and the ideologies that justify them. One study of 186 societies from around the world, for example, found that in less than half—46 percent—mothers were the primary or exclusive caretakers of infants. In another 40 percent of the societies in the sample primary care of infants was the responsibility of others, usually siblings. An even more striking finding is that in less than 20 percent of the societies are mothers the primary or exclusive caretakers *after* infancy. The authors of this study conclude: "According to our ratings, in the majority of these societies mothers are not the principal caretakers or companions of young children."[2]

How are we to explain this conclusion which contradicts the deeply held modern American belief in the central role of the mother in child care? A number of factors are involved in the explanation, but one clue is that the living arrangement we take so much for granted—the married woman's residence in a nuclear family household made up exclusively of parents and children—is extremely rare cross-culturally. Such households are found in only 6.1 percent of the societies listed in the massive Human Relations Area Files, the largest systematic compilation of cross-cultural data in the world.[3] So in the majority of societies other kin present in the household relieve the mother of some of the burden of child care.

Another factor that influences the degree of maternal responsibility is the nature and location of women's productive activities. In societies with economies based on hunting and gathering or agriculture, young children typically are taken care of by an older sibling or by their mother or other female relative while these women are gathering or gardening. But in industrial societies where the work place and the household are separate, production and child care are incompatible. It is in these same societies—ones in which women's activities typically are limited to the domestic sphere—that we find the duties of parenting weighing most heavily on the mother.[4]

A study of mothers in six cultures points up the relative rarity of western industrial child-care patterns. In the American community represented in the study 92 percent of the mothers said that they usually or always took care of their babies and children by themselves. The other five societies displayed considerably less maternal responsibility for child care. In the words of the authors: "The mothers in the U.S. sample have a significantly heavier burden (or joy) of baby care than the mothers in any other society." They explain: "Living in nuclear families isolated from their relatives and with all their older children in school most of the day the [American] mother spends more time in charge of both babies and older children than any other group."[5]

These studies suggest that the preoccupation of American experts with the mother-child relationship almost certainly is a result of social and economic developments in the United States and western industrialized societies in general, societies that are characterized more than most others by exclusive mother-child care arrangements. What we have come to think of as inevitable and biologically necessary is in great measure a consequence of our society's particular social and economic system. We are certainly not unique in believing that our brand of mother-child relationship is natural and normal. People in every culture firmly believe that *their* child-rearing practices stem from nature itself.[6]

◈ □ ○ △ □ ◈

What sort of evidence is there that American perceptions of the mother role did in fact change with industrialization? Sermons, child-care manuals, magazine articles, and other forms of popular literature are rich sources for contemporary images of the mother role. The maternal role, however, cannot be understood apart from other facets of child rearing. The role prescribed for fathers during various periods in

American history certainly affected the role prescribed for mothers. Perceptions of the nature of children necessarily had an impact on definitions of proper mothering. And, finally, the varying child-care methods recommended by prescriptive writers certainly influenced the writers' views of the maternal role since it was mothers, for the most part, who were expected to carry out their recommendations. For these reasons the prescriptive literature on mothering must be seen within the context of general child-rearing advice.

I am well aware of the limits of using child-care manuals and other sources of advice to accomplish what I have set out to do. This literature records *prescriptive dicta, not actual practice,* and of course is subject to rationalizations and selective emphasis. Moreover, the findings of at least one study suggest that child-care advice seems to have the *least* effect on just those women most likely to be aware of it. One scholar has seriously questioned whether child-rearing manuals are evidence of either child-rearing values or child-rearing behavior. He claims that the manuals really tell us about "child rearing manual writing values."[7] Finally, American advice books and similar literature, aimed at a literate middle and upper middle class audience, reflect the class biases of that intended audience.

The use of prescriptive writings, however, still has an important place in a study of the changing perceptions of the middle class mother in the United States, for even though child-rearing advice may not have influenced behavior, what is unquestionably true is that *the nature of the advice itself changed over time* and that the depiction of the mother role varied in crucial ways over the course of American history. There was moreover a remarkable consensus among the advice givers of any given era as to what constituted the "correct" maternal role.

The central problem of these pages then is to determine the larger social and economic forces that influenced the advice being offered and the conditions under which advice changed. The emphasis on the mother-child dyad, which first appeared in the early nineteenth century, for example, would have been almost inconceivable one hundred years earlier; the conditions allowing women to devote themselves exclusively to child care simply did not exist during that earlier period. Prescriptive writings thus emerge as cultural documents describing ideology, which itself is a product of the social and economic conditions of the day.

The focus of this chapter is the advice proffered to middle class American women on their motherly duties from Colonial times to 1940. The most significant contrast in prescriptive maternal roles lies between the colonial era and the years that immediately followed, a contrast that does not appear again until the contemporary period. A discussion of the maternal role after World War II, including its dramatic redefinition by child-care experts over the last decade, appears in chapter 3.

Raise Up Your Children Together: The Colonial Period to 1785

Children in their first days, have greater benefit of good mothers. . . . But afterwards, when they come to riper years, good fathers are more behoveful of their forming in virtue and good manners.

John Robinson, Pastor and Founder, Plymouth Colony

A distinct maternal role would have been incompatible with the realities of life during colonial times. The mother-child relationship was enmeshed in the myriad daily tasks women performed for their families' survival. They kept house, tended gardens, raised poultry and cattle, churned milk into butter and cream, butchered livestock, tanned skins, pickled and preserved food, made candles, buttons, soap, beer, and cider, gathered and processed medicinal herbs, and spun and wove wool and cotton for family clothes. The wives of farmers, merchants, and artisans were kept busy with these duties and the wives of merchants and artisans often helped in their husbands' businesses as well. Child rearing therefore largely centered on teaching children the skills needed to keep the domestic economy going. Child rearing was not a *separate* task; it was something that simply took place within the daily round of activities. It is little wonder that in 1790 a New England mother could write that her two children "had grown out of the way" and are "very little troble [*sic*]" when the younger of the two was still nursing.[8]

The agrarian economy of the seventeenth and eighteenth centuries presented no clear-cut separation between the home and the world of work; the boundary between the preindustrial family and society was permeable. Male and female spheres were contiguous and often overlapped, and the demands of the domestic economy ensured that neither sex was excluded from productive labor. Fathers, moreover, took an active role in child rearing because they worked near the household. Craftsmen and tradesmen usually had their shops at home and farmers spent the long winter months there. The prescriptive literature of the day rarely or imprecisely distinguished between "female" or domestic themes and the "masculine" world of work. The few colonial domestic guides addressed both men and women under the assumption that they worked together in the household.[9]

Scholars now agree that the colonial family was not an extended one as was once thought; the best estimates are that at least 80 percent were nuclear (but not nuclear in the same way as the small isolated nuclear family of the industrial era). The colonial family was nuclear in the formal sense in that parents and children were at its core, but mothers and fathers usually were not the only adults living in the household. Some families took in maiden aunts, or perhaps an aged parent, others had apprentices or journeymen, while domestic servants were common in the households of the prosperous. Moreover, because the typical colonial couple had six to eight offspring, children ranging from infancy to adolescence were commonly found in the same household. Finally, the practice of "putting out" children and taking others in ensured that at least some children were not brought up exclusively by their parents. What is central to the discussion here is that during the colonial period children's relationships were not nearly as mother-centered as they later came to be in the smaller industrial variant of the nuclear family. Given the composition of the colonial American household, children must have received support from and been disciplined by a number of adults—their parents, apprentices or servants, older siblings, and perhaps other relatives as well.[10]

Children themselves were hardly recognized as a separate human category in the American colonies of the seventeenth and eighteenth centuries. "There was little sense that children might somehow be a special group with their own needs and interests and capacities," writes one historian. Virtually all of the child-rearing advice of the day emphasized that children were "meer Loans from God, which He may call for when He pleases." Parents were told to bring up their children as good Christians and discipline was emphasized, but no mention was made of developing the child's personality, intelligence, or individuality. Quite to the contrary, most sermons dwelt on the importance of breaking the child's "will."[11]

Some children were "put out" to work as early as six or seven years of age, and those who remained with their parents were expected to help with household chores. Girls as young as six could spin flax and boys helped in farming tasks or fetched wood. Childhood was at best a span of years lasting considerably less than a decade. Even had a family wanted a prolonged, leisurely childhood for its offspring, this was a luxury few could afford.[12]

Since infant mortality rates were high, parents expected to lose some of their children. Infant mortality in the seventeenth century, for example, ranged from 10 to 30 percent in different parts of the colonies; this high rate was acknowledged in the sermons of the day. Cotton Mather counseled women how to behave on the death of a child: "She does not roar like a Beast, and howl, I cannot bear it; but She rather says, I can take anything at the Hands of God."[13]

Although not a great deal is known about seventeenth- and eighteenth-century advice on child rearing and parental roles—the few manuals of the period were of English origin—we can glean some indication of parental duties in the American colonies from the sermons of the day. In a 1712 sermon entitled "The Well Ordered Family or, Relative Duties," Benjamin Wadsworth, pastor of the Church of Christ in Boston, distinguished mothers' responsibilities from fathers' when he urged the former to "suckle their children." But then he went on to say: "Having given these hints about Mothers, I may say of Parents (Comprehending both Father and Mother) they should provide for the outward supply and comfort of their Children. They should nourish and bring them up." In the lengthy discussion of religious instruction and the teaching of good manners and discipline that followed, all of Wadsworth's injunctions were addressed to "Parents." Another New England minister in speaking of parents moralized, "If God in his Providence hath bestowed on them Children . . . they have each of them a share in the government of them."[14]

Colonial clergymen were generally consistent in their sermons treating parental roles. Fathers were to supervise the secular and religious education of their children, teaching them to fear and respect God, but mothers also were advised of their responsibilities in this training. Both parents were admonished to set good examples for their children, and both were held responsible for their children's general well-being. Except for the greater authority bestowed on the father as head of the family, the prescribed roles for parents made no important distinctions on the basis of sex. Similarly, even in funeral sermons for women, there was little mention of motherhood as opposed to the more generalized concept of parenthood. In the few sermons specifically addressed to mothers, the duties laid out were the same as those addressed to both parents, and "none of these were distinctly maternal obligations."[15]

To be sure, women were thought to have special ties to their children during infancy, and infants were described as "hers" by both men and women. The realities of reproduction were certainly recognized, and here we find special advice to mothers. A number of clergy inveighed against the practice of wet nursing, which in fact was quite rare in the American colonies. In describing the duties of a righteous woman Cotton Mather admonished: "Her care for the Bodies of her Children shows itself in the nursing of them herself. . . . She is not a Dame that shall scorn to nourish in the World, the Children whom she has already nourished in her Womb." Wet nursing was condemned because it was thought contrary to God's will and dangerous to the physical health of the child, not because it was believed to interfere with the development of a bond between mother and child. Some ministers actually warned women against "excessive fondness" for their children.[16]

Once children reached the age of one or two, when their survival was more certain, all directives regarding child rearing were addressed to *both* parents. Fathers were expected to take a larger role once children reached an educable age. This was particularly true among the Puritans, who believed that the "masculine" qualities of religious understanding and self-discipline were essential in child rearing. One of the few distinctions made in the sermons of the day was in vocational training; this was the responsibility of the parent of the same sex as the child, although sometimes responsibility was removed from the family entirely. Children, particularly boys, often were sent out at age nine or ten to apprentice in other households while children from other families were taken in to serve as apprentices.[17]

A cult of motherhood did not exist because it would have been incongruous in this setting. Women were far too busy to devote long hours to purely maternal duties, and fathers, older siblings, and other adults were also on hand to see to children's needs and discipline. Moreover, because of high mortality rates, a woman was not likely to become obsessive about her children, some of whom would not survive to adulthood. It is not surprising that, as one scholar has remarked of the colonial period, " . . . motherhood was singularly unidealized, usually disregarded as a subject, and even at times actually denigrated." Although women bore and cared for very young children, this role received less emphasis in the prescriptive literature than nearly any other aspect of women's lives. Motherhood, when it was discussed at all, was merged with the parental, domestic, and religious obligations of both sexes.[18]

The Transition: 1785–1820

> *Much depends upon your maternal care in the first stage of life; it is a pleasing duty, to which you are honorably called, both by nature and the custom of all nations.*
>
> Hugh Smith, *Letters to Married Women on Nursing and the Management of Children*, 1796

The cult of motherhood is usually associated with the middle and late nineteenth century, but we can see its roots in the prescriptive literature of the very late eighteenth century and the first decades of the nineteenth century. During these years the earliest hints of a special and distinct maternal role began appearing in sermons, domestic guides, medical volumes and child-rearing manuals; for the first time writers began stressing the critical importance of maternal care in early childhood.

It is significant that these years also witnessed the beginnings of the industrial revolution. Markets slowly expanded, agricultural efficiency increased, transportation costs decreased—all developments that led to greater specialization in the economic division of labor. What is centrally important to my argument is that home industry, which typified the colonial period, began to wane. Gradually home manufacture for family use was replaced by standardized factory production for the wider market. The first industry that moved from the home to the factory was textile manufacture, one of women's traditional household tasks. As early as 1807 there were a dozen large textile mills in New England, and by 1810 farm families could buy cloth in village shops and from itinerant peddlers.[19]

The replacement of homespun by manufactured goods was nonetheless a gradual process. In 1810 Secretary of the Treasury Albert Gallatin estimated that "about two-thirds of the clothing, including . . . house and table linen used by the inhabitants of the United States, who do not reside in cities, is the product of family manufactures." In terms of monetary value this was about ten times the amount produced outside the home. Class membership and place of residence were primary factors in the reduction of home manufacture; more prosperous families, urban dwellers, and those living in the older settled areas of the East led the way in the substitution of store-bought goods for homemade ones.[20]

While women's role in the domestic economy gradually diminished, important changes also were taking place in the family. By the late eighteenth century the domestic sphere had begun to contract; there were fewer servants than there had been earlier, the practice of taking in apprentices and journeymen had all but ceased, and with the expansion of economic opportunities fathers were spending less time at home. The physical separation of the home and the place of work already was under way for artisans, merchants and professionals. But while fewer adults remained in the household, children were now living in it until they reached adolescence. With the demise of the "putting out" system, middle class children were no longer apprenticed to other families and by 1820 they generally lived at home until about the age of fifteen. The nuclear family itself became smaller as the birthrate declined, particularly in the more densely populated eastern regions of the country. A study of Gloucester, Massachusetts, found that women who married before 1740 had an average of 6.7 children while those who married after that date averaged 4.6 children. Similarly, by the late eighteenth century in Andover, Massachusetts, women typically had five or six children when their grandmothers had averaged seven or eight.[21]

Not only was the middle class household smaller in size but with the onset of industrialization it was no longer a wholly self-contained unit whose members were bound by common tasks. For the first time the place, scope, and pace of men's and women's work began to differ sharply. As a distinct division of labor gradually arose between the home and the world of work, the household's contacts with the outside decreased. By the first decades of the nineteenth century the term *home* had come to be synonymous with *place of retirement* or *retreat.*[22]

Ideologies about the nature of children also began to change. By 1800 the Calvinist belief in infant damnation had begun to give way to the Lockean doctrine of the tabula rasa, which stressed the lack of innate evil (or good), and the importance of experience in molding the child. In 1796 one physician wrote, " . . . that any children are born with vicious inclinations, I would not willingly believe." Children, at least middle class children, began to be seen as individuals. They were no longer viewed as "miniature adults" whose natural inclinations toward evil had to be broken; childhood was becoming a distinct period in the life cycle. The dictum that children were to be treated as individuals with special needs and potentials requiring special nurturing placed a new and heavy responsibility on parents; failure in child rearing could no longer "be blamed on native corruption," explains one historian.[23]

These altered views of children coincided with the decline of the birthrate in the late eighteenth and early nineteenth centuries. The decline in New England, for example, was greatest between 1810 and 1830, and, according to one scholar, during these years "the new sensibility towards children first became highly visible."[24] But the lower birthrate, implying fewer children per family and perhaps more attention paid to each child, only partially explains the fundamental change in thinking about children. Both the gradual redefinition of women's role and the redefinition of childhood were linked to larger societal changes affecting middle class life.

The prescriptive literature on child care in these years was in many ways transitional between the stark dicta of the colonial clergy and the effusive writings of the later nineteenth century advice givers. Prior to about 1830 such literature did not enjoy mass circulation but appeared in periodical articles, printed sermons, and occasional treatises. All of it came under the rubric "domestic education" and was written by ministers, physicians, and parents for a white middle and upper middle class audience. Most pertinent here was the transitional image of the role of the middle class mother. Motherhood in fact was being revamped. Duties that had once belonged to both mothers and fathers or to fathers alone were now becoming the near exclusive province of mothers. One historian of the period notes that "now fathers began to recede into the background in writings about the domestic education of children."

Treatises on the treatment of childhood diseases, diet, hygiene, and exercise for young children now addressed mothers alone. Some of the medical texts also offered advice on the psychological management of young children, stressing for the first time the importance of the mother's influence during the impressionable years.[25]

Arguments against wet nursing also took on a new cast. Whereas earlier commentators condemned the practice for its ill effects on a child's health, writers now added that wet nursing tainted the child's character. One of the earliest references to a special relationship between mother and child appears in this context. A 1798 tract printed in England (but read in America) urged women to nurse their children so as to avoid "the destruction, or at least the diminution of the sympathy between mother and child." Nursing was no longer simply a woman's religious duty but the key to her future happiness as well. "Those children who are neglected by their mothers during their infant years," wrote Dr. Hugh Smith in 1796, "forget all duty and affection towards them, when such mothers are in the decline of life." The same author exalted in the joys of breast feeding: "Tell me you who know the rapturous delight, how complete is the bliss of enfolding in your longing arms the dear, dear fruits of all your pains!"[26]

Jane West's *Letters to Young Ladies*, published in London in 1806 but widely read in America, is an interesting prescriptive volume that illustrates the transitional tone of much of the advice literature of the period. Like Puritan clergymen of earlier years, West warned her readers that "excessive affection is one of the most common faults of mothers" and suggested that "the instructor . . . who requires a mother to be the *constant* companion of her children, will render her such a wife as will drive most husbands from their firesides." Nor was it necessary for a mother to keep her children entirely out of the hands of servants since "she need not fear that their minds will be vitiated during the short intervals in which she entrusts them to the care of their attendants." There were few allusions to fathers and their child-rearing duties were never spelled out as they had been in the earlier literature. But while the advice is addressed to mothers, West never contended that every maternal mood and action indelibly marked the future character of a child.[27]

Another early guide is Dr. William Buchan's *Advice to Mothers*, published in Boston in 1809. The growing importance of the maternal role is obvious here. "The more I reflect on the situation of a mother, the more I am struck by the extent of her powers," wrote Dr. Buchan. Clearly not all mothers are equal: "By a mother I do not mean the woman who merely brings a child into the world, but her who faithfully discharges the duties of a parent—whose chief concern is the well-being of her infant." But mothers walked a narrow line between neglect and overindulgence. "The obvious paths of nature are alike foresaken by the woman who gives up the care of her infant to a hireling . . . who neglects her duties as a mother; and by her who carries these duties to excess; who makes an idol of her child."[28] This is the first mention of a theme that was to be heard over and over again in the prescriptive writings of the nineteenth and much of the twentieth centuries. Mothers must be ever on guard to do their job properly—always lurking in the background of the advice books were the pitiful figures of mothers who had failed, mothers who had not taken their duties seriously, or mothers who had performed them with excessive zeal.

One of the first child-rearing manuals published in the United States was *The Maternal Physician* (1811). Its author, an anonymous "American matron," discussed the treatment of childhood diseases and suggested ways of ensuring an infant's health and well-being, but she also foreshadowed the later nineteenth-century manuals in her overwrought celebration of the joys of motherhood: " . . . what can equal a mother's ecstasy when she catches the first emanation of mind in the . . . smile of her babe? Ten thousand raptures thrill her bosom before a tooth is formed." The author strongly favored breast feeding and decried the fashionable "tyranny" of putting a child out to wet nurse: "How dead to the finest feelings of our nature must that mother be, who can voluntarily banish her infant from her bosom." The manual deals only with the care of children from birth to age two; after this age, claimed the author, "children in general . . . grow more robust . . . and will increase in health and strength without any attention except the ordinary care conducive to cleanliness and exercise."[29] This statement reflected an attempt to reduce infant mortality, for during the first two years of life children were at greatest risk.

Emphasis on the mother role was not limited to advice manuals. Between 1800 and 1820 a new theme appeared in many New England sermons: mothers are more important than fathers in shaping "the tastes, sentiments, and habits of children." One New Hampshire minister proclaimed in 1806: "Weighty beyond expression is the charge devolved to the female parent. It is not within the province of human wisdom to calculate all the happy consequences resulting from the persevering assiduity of mothers." While sermons of the day did not deny all paternal responsibility, they made clear that raising children was a specialized domestic activity that was largely the province of mothers. As one scholar of the period notes, this "emphasis departed from (and undermined) the patriarchal family ideal in which the mother, while entrusted with the physical care of her children, left their religious, moral, and intellectual guidance to her husband."[30]

Although little is known about the actual child-rearing practices in the early nineteenth century, it is clear that the aim of the advice manuals and the sermons dealing with the topic was to increase the amount of time and attention mothers devoted to infants and small children. For the first time in American history the care of young children was viewed as a full-time task, as a distinct profession requiring special knowledge. What had once been done according to tradition now demanded proper study. Even arguments favoring women's education now came to be couched in terms of the woman's role as mother; women were to be educated because the formation of the future citizens of the republic lay in their hands.[31] It is ironic, indeed, but by no means coincidental, that as their sphere narrowed and became more isolated, middle class women were told that their sphere's importance to the future of the new nation was boundless.

Historian Ruth H. Bloch notes that economic factors exercised a "push-pull" effect on child-rearing responsibilities. As the domestic production of middle class mothers began to wane and their domestic work lost its commercial value, fathers began to spend more and more time working outside the home, as did other adults who had once resided in the household.[32] Women, left alone at home with their children, who were now living there until adolescence, began to assume almost complete responsibility for child care. The prescriptive literature, with its newly expanded definition of motherhood, was thus a response to these structural changes in society. In essence, as the female role in domestic production declined, the middle class woman was told to focus on reproduction.

Motherhood, a Fearful Responsibility: 1820–1870

The rush of the new country left the men no time to be fathers; they were away all day and children came to be left entirely in the care of their mothers.

Arthur W. Calhoun
A Social History of the Family,
Vol. 2, 1918

Mothers have as powerful an influence over the welfare of future generations, as all other earthly causes combined.

Reverend John S. C. Abbott, *The Mother at Home,* 1833

The concept of the mother role which prevailed from the late eighteenth century to about 1820 was, in the words of one historian, "a rare and subdued hint of the extravagant celebration of motherhood to come."[33] Beginning in the 1820s and gaining momentum in the 1830s and 1840s, a flood of manuals and periodical articles gave advice on the maternal role, exulted in the joys of motherhood, and told women that good mothering was not only the key to their own and their children's happiness but crucial to the nation's destiny as well.

The period between 1820 and 1860 was one of rapid industrialization; industrial production in fact doubled every decade. Although most Americans were still working in agriculture—79 percent at the start of the period and 65 percent forty years later—rather than in manufacturing, it was an increasingly commercialized agriculture that with every passing year produced more for the market than for home consumption. This was also a period when the U.S. population was becoming more urbanized. In 1820 only 7 percent of Americans lived in cities, but by 1860, 20 percent of Americans were urban residents.[34]

The most salient change occurring during these years was the eventual demise of the self-sufficient household. The growth of industry, technological advances, improvements in transportation, and the increasing specialization of agriculture made more goods available, and the household became more and more reliant on the market to meet its needs. In simple terms the period between 1820 and 1860 witnessed the substitution of store-bought goods for home-manufactured goods, and this development had a profound impact on women's work. Even as early as the 1820s women's domestic production had diminished in scope and variety to the extent that they were left with only a residue of their former household duties. In New England by 1830 home spinning and weaving were largely replaced by manufactured textiles, and by mid-century women's productive skills had become even more superfluous: butter, candles, soap, medicines, buttons, and cloth were widely available in stores. By 1860 women's contribution to household production continued to a significant extent only in remote frontier regions. The noted feminist and abolitionist Sarah Grimké remarked on the decline of home manufacture in 1838: "When all manufactures were domestic, then the domestic function might well consume all the time of a very able-bodied woman. But nowadays . . . when so much of woman's work is done by the butcher and the baker, by the tailor and the cook, and the gas maker . . . you see how much of woman's time is left for other functions."[35]

The removal of production from the home to the factory led to the breakdown of the once close relationship between the household and the business of society. For the first time "life," that is, the home, was divided from "work." Not only had the two spheres become separate, they were now seen as incompatible; the home was a retreat from the competitive world of commerce and industry, a place of warmth and respite where moral values prevailed. The business of the world no longer took place at home.

These economic and social developments were of course not unique to the United States. A similar series of events occurred in England in the seventeenth century. There, in the words of one scholar of the period, "the old familial economic partnership of husband and wife was being undermined. The wife was being driven from her productive role. The concept of the husband supporting his family was replacing mutuality in earning power . . . [the wife's] place might still be in the home, but her husband was no longer an integral part of it."[36]

The American household continued to shrink throughout the nineteenth century. By 1850 the ancillary household members had moved out—an unmarried sister might be teaching school in town and greater numbers of domestic servants were leaving the middle class household to take factory jobs. Philip Greven's study of census data from eleven states illustrates this point. In 1790 the average number of freepersons per household was 5.8; in 1850 it was 5.5; and by 1890 it had declined to 4.9.[37] Part of this decrease, however, resulted from a falling birthrate.

Ideas about the nature of children continued to evolve. The neutral tabula rasa of the first decades of the nineteenth century was supplanted by the idea of the "sweet angels of the Romantic era." After 1830 children were routinely depicted as beings of great purity and innocence. They were naturally close to God and their virtuous proclivities had only to be gently molded to ensure eternal salvation. Closely allied with this idealized image of the young was the conviction that *mothers and mothers alone* had the power to transform malleable infants into moral, productive adults. For this reason many warned against the dangers of hiring nurses, for even the best nurse was never an adequate substitute for the mother herself. Only a mother's care and influence, not that of fathers, older siblings, relatives or servants, could fulfill the special physical and spiritual needs of the growing child. Motherhood had not only become a careerlike responsibility but the responsibility had grown longer and longer in duration. By the mid-nineteenth century middle class children remained at home until well into adolescence, and throughout the century there was a tendency to prolong dependence. Children left home at a later and later age.[38]

Some scholars claim that the nineteenth century's concern with the child as an individual and with proper child-rearing methods was the result of a decline in infant mortality. Parents, they argue, became more certain that their children would grow to adulthood and so were willing to invest more time and energy in them. Historian Carl Degler faults this thesis, citing data that suggest that infant mortality did not decline. In fact, infant mortality might even have been higher than the official statistics indicate with the likelihood of a high mortality rate among unreported births. One could argue on this basis that at least part of the growing concern for the child was because infant mortality rates did remain so high. Catherine Beecher and other manual writers contended that proper child care could help prevent the deaths of infants and young children.[39]

Population growth from reproduction did in fact decline steadily as the birthrate fell throughout the nineteenth century. By 1850 the average white woman was bearing only half as many children as her grandmother had. Even more striking is the 50 percent decline in the completed fertility rate for the century as a whole; it fell from 7.04 children per white woman in 1800 to 3.56 in 1900. The question, of course, is why did women bear fewer children? In the words of anthropologist Marvin Harris, in an industrializing, urbanizing society children "tend to cost more and to be economically less valuable to their parents than children on farms."[40]

Children in agrarian societies cost relatively little to raise and they help out by doing a variety of tasks even when they are young. But in cities the expense of rearing children increases as does their period of dependency; most or all of the items a child needs must be purchased, and schooling is required before the child can become economically independent. In essence, urban children contribute less and cost more. Therefore, as the nineteenth century progressed, the shift in the costs and benefits of having children particularly affected the middle class, whose children required longer and longer periods of socialization before they could make it on their own outside the home. The rearing of "quality" children, children who enjoyed a long period of dependency while they were schooled to take their "rightful" position in society, was an ever more costly process. Is it any wonder then that the average middle class family had fewer and fewer children as the century progressed?

The immense outpouring of advice manuals and other prescriptive writings after 1830 cannot be adequately explained by continued high levels of infant mortality or even by the fact that women were having fewer children and simply had the time to make a greater investment in each one. Another factor in the advice-giving boom was the nation's slowly growing need for children who would be reared to become professionals or to take the business and management positions being created by the industrializing process. What better and cheaper way to accomplish this than by urging middle class women to devote many years and large quantities of their (unpaid) time and energy to nurturing the future captains of business and industry?

Another key to understanding the paeans to motherhood is the falling fertility rate of the middle class. But the relationship is by no means a simple one. It seems logical that if women had been taking these paeans seriously they would have had more rather than fewer children, and it is of course naive to assume that fertility decisions are made on the basis of advice books. I believe the link between the two is as follows: as fertility declined among the white middle class, there was growing alarm in certain quarters. Where were the future leaders in business and industry to come from? Who was going to manage the nation's burgeoning industries? At a time when the fertility of the nonwhite and the foreign-born was higher than that of native-born whites, the country's elite feared that the "backbone" of the nation was being diluted by "lesser types." The glorification of maternity which was directed at potential mothers of the "backbone," was an attempt, albeit an unsuccessful one, to encourage their reproductive activity.[41]

Scholars are not certain just how people in the nineteenth century controlled their fertility, but there is evidence that American women began practicing abortion more frequently after 1840. One historian estimates one abortion for every twenty-five or thirty live births during the first decades of the century, a proportion that rose to about one in every five or six live births during the 1850s and 1860s. Most contemporary physicians agreed that the primary motive for abortion was control of family size, and they cited as evidence the fact that by far the largest group practicing abortion was married women. It is significant that prior to the nineteenth century there were no laws prohibiting abortion during the first few months of pregnancy. The procedure was not illegal until "quickening," that is, until the first movements of the fetus are felt at about four months. The first laws banning abortion were passed between 1821 and 1841; during those two decades ten states and one territory specifically outlawed its practice. By the time of the Civil War nearly every state had laws prohibiting abortion at all stages of fetal development.[42]

I do not think that mere coincidence accounts for concern about the falling birthrate, laws banning abortion, and the publication of numerous child-care manuals and articles lauding the maternal role, all appearing at roughly the same time. The outpourings of the advice givers reflected the wider anxiety about middle class women's declining fertility and sought to counteract it by dwelling on the joys of motherhood for their white, middle class audience.

The contraction of women's productive activities in the now smaller and more isolated nuclear household provided the necessary setting for this expanding emphasis on the mother role. There was now a sizable, literate audience of homebound women who could be advised of the importance of motherhood and given suggestions of time-consuming methods for its proper discharge. In short, as the domestic sphere contracted and middle class women found their lives increasingly centered around their husbands and children, they were advised of the gravity of their redefined role. What higher calling was there than shaping the future leaders of the nation?

◈ □ ○ △ □ ◈

Maternal Ideals

> *Maternity! ecstatic sound! so twined round our heart, that it must cease to throb ere we forget it, it is our first love, it is part of our religion.*
>
> *The Ladies' Museum*, 1825

A number of recurrent themes in nineteenth-century child-rearing manuals and periodical articles were only weakly developed or were entirely absent from the prescriptive writings of an earlier era. Foremost among these are that child care is the exclusive province of women, that motherhood is their *primary* function, and that mothers, and mothers alone, are responsible for their children's character development and future success or failure. By the 1830s motherhood had been transformed into a mission so that "the entire burden of the child's well-being in this life and the next" was in its mother's hands.[43] These themes, moreover, were not limited to child-rearing manuals. Popular novels, poems, and biographies of famous men all stressed the important role of the mother in shaping her child's fate. Middle class women were told that they had it in their power to produce joy or misery, depending on how they performed their parental duties. These sentiments were echoed in a burgeoning literature on "female character" which claimed that women were innately nurturant, domestic, and selfless, all qualities that made them "naturals" at child rearing.

One of the most striking features of the child-rearing advice of the mid-nineteenth century is the disappearance of references to fathers. While some earlier tracts were addressed exclusively to mothers, most were written for "parents," and there was even an occasional "advice to fathers" manual. The shift from *parental* to *maternal* responsibility is evident in Philip Greven's collection of sermons, treatises, and other sources of advice on child rearing dating from 1628 to 1861.[44] The first eight excerpts, originally published between 1628 and 1814, are all addressed to "parents." It is not until John Abbott's 1833 essay "On the Mother's Role in Education" that the maternal role is highlighted and mothers are given the primary responsibility for child care.

Mothers were offered abundant advice on the feeding, dressing, washing, and general management of infants and young children. They were told how to deal with teething, toilet training, masturbation, and childhood diseases. But the mother's physical care of her children was a minor task compared to her job of socializing them. Women were advised that their every thought and gesture, no matter how seemingly inconsequential, carried a message to the child. Women were to be ever on their guard lest they impede their offspring's moral development.

Many writers stressed the sentimental benefits of an activity that received no material rewards. "How entire and perfect is the dominion over the unformed character of your infant. Write what you will, upon the printless tablet, with your wand of love," wrote Mrs. Sigourney in *Letters to Mothers* (1838). "Deathless is the influence of the faithful Mother over her innocent child," thundered Reverend Thayer. "Her impressions on the heart are like letters cut in brass and granite."[45]

Women's education is justified, some advice givers claimed, because of women's influence on the next generation. *Maternal* education, however, was what they really sought. In an 1845 tome, for example, Edward Mansfield cited three reasons for educating women: " . . . that they should as *mothers*, be the fit teachers of infant men. That they should be the fit teachers of American men. That they should be the fit teachers of Christian men."[46]

Motherhood, as depicted in the prescriptive writings of the mid-nineteenth century, was a full-time occupation demanding time-consuming unpaid labor. "It truly requires all the affection of even a fond mother to administer dutifully to the numerous wants of a young child," wrote William Dewees. Mrs. Sigourney agreed. She saw a mother as "a sentinel who should never sleep at her post," recommending that women get household help to perform manual tasks so that the mother "may be able to become the constant directress of her children." There is no question that mothering was work; infants should be fed on demand, and toilet training and "moral education" should begin at a few months of age. Cleanliness was stressed and clothes were to be washed often and changed as soon as they got dirty. Furthermore, the good mother would keep careful records of her children's behavior and development. The

Reverend Abbott told mothers to "study their duty," while Mrs. Sigourney urged women to "study night and day the science that promotes the welfare of our infant."[47]

Mothers, according to the advice givers, were perfectly suited to care for their children; no one else could do the job as well or, one might add, as cheaply. As far as a mother's duties permitted, she was to "take the entire care of her own child," advised the popular domestic writer, Lydia Maria Child. During the first "sacred" year, concurred Mrs. Sigourney, "trust not your treasure too much to the charge of hirelings. Have it under your superintendence night and day. The duty of your office admits of no substitute." But what of other family members? Are they of no help? Yes: " . . . brothers and sisters, the father, all perform their part, but the mother does the most," opined the author of a *Parents Magazine* article, who went on to issue a stern warning. Children whose mothers did not "take the entire care of them" faced real danger; a mother "cannot be long relieved without hazard or exchanged without loss."[48]

A corollary of the focus on mothers was the disappearance of fathers from the child-rearing manuals of the nineteenth century. Advice books assumed that children spent most of their time with their mothers, not their fathers, even though by law and custom final authority was patriarchal. Paternal responsibilities were rarely spelled out. For example, in answering the question "Is there nothing for fathers to do?" Reverend Abbott responded that there are many paternal duties "which will require time and care." But the only duties he actually stipulated for fathers were "to lead their families to God" and to teach their children to "honor" their mother. Although some advice givers saw fathers as the primary disciplinarians in the family, others urged mothers to punish their children's misbehavior before fathers returned home in the evening. Even daily prayers, once led by the father as head of the household, had now become the province of the mother.[49]

The occasional references to fathers in the prescriptive writings of the day either remarked on their sovereignty in the home or noted their real responsibilities outside of it. A father's duties, advised the *Ladies' Companion*, are "the acquisition of wealth, the advancement of his children in worldly honor—these are his self-imposed tasks." But some writers did lament the absence of fathers from the home. In an article entitled "Paternal Neglect" in an 1842 issue of *Parents Magazine*, Reverend Abbott claimed that the father's absence was "one of the abundant sources of domestic sorrow." "The father," he continued, "eager in the pursuit of business, toils early and late, and finds no time to fulfill . . . duties to his children." Nevertheless, Abbott's token statement on the importance of fatherhood is belied in his manual, *The Mother at Home,* where he insists that even children with "brutally intemperate" fathers can be reared properly through their mothers' struggle and sacrifice. In the final analysis maternal influence prevailed.[50]

By the mid-nineteenth century a gooey sentimentality had come to distinguish motherhood from fatherhood. A sample from a "ladies magazine" of the day reveals the tone: "Is there a feeling that activates the human heart so powerful as that of maternal affection? Who but women can feel the tender sensation so strong? The father, indeed, may press his lovely infant to his manly heart, but does it thrill with those feelings which irresistibly overcome the mother?"[51]

These patterns of ideological change are also apparent in an analysis of sixteenth- to nineteenth-century child-rearing responsibilities in England. English manuals of the sixteenth and seventeenth centuries told parents to "co-rear" their children: eighteenth-century manuals depicted mothers as the primary child rearers but expressed some anxiety about this; by the nineteenth century mothers were the primary rearers "without anxiety."[52]

In America by mid-century good mothering was not only essential to the well-being and future of the child but the lack of such exclusive care was considered a threat to the very moral fiber of the nation. "The destiny of a nation is shaped by its character," Reverend Beckwith proclaimed, "and that character . . . will ever be found to be molded chiefly by maternal hands." "When our land is filled with pious and patriotic mothers, then will it be filled with virtuous and patriotic men," agreed Reverend Abbott. But it is clear that women's contribution to the young republic was to be indirect. In the words of Daniel Webster: "It is by promulgation of sound morals in the community, and more especially by the training and instruction of the young that woman performs her part toward the preservation of a free government."[53]

As part of the effort to convince middle class women of their crucial role in the nation's destiny—a role wholly dependent on the diligent performance of their maternal duties—moral educators frequently cited the mothers of famous men. Just look at the glorious results of good mothering, women were told. George Washington's mother was a particular favorite. "The *mother* of Washington is entitled to the nation's gratitude," wrote Reverend Abbott. "She, in great measure formed the character of the hero and the statesman. We are indebted to God for the gift of Washington; but we are no less indebted to him for the gift of his inestimable mother." Women were urged to take their nurturing seriously, for they never knew what the future held. "The mother," according to the *Ladies' Magazine*, "may, in the unconscious child before her, behold some future Washington or Franklin." Yes, cautioned Mrs. Sigourney, a mother never knows but that "she may be appointed to rear some future statesman for her nation's helm."[54] One book of this genre, *Mothers of the Wise and Good*, went through four editions, while a host of magazine articles recounted the lives of famous men and their mothers' beneficial influence on them. The mother's influence, however, could take another turn. To put it colloquially, good mothers produced good boys and bad mothers produced bad boys. Abbott singled out Lord Byron's mother for castigation. She was "just the reverse of Lady Washington," he wrote. "It was the mother of Byron who laid the foundation for his preeminence in guilt . . . and it was the mother who fostered . . . those passions which made the son a curse to his fellow-men." The message was clear: a weak or negligent mother could create a moral monster to the detriment of all humanity.[55]

Many advice writers dwelt long and graphically on the general evils that sprang from poor mothering. An 1841 issue of *Parents Magazine* contained a case study of a convict, whose life of crime was analyzed in the following terms: "His mother, although hopefully pious, never prayed with him in private. . . . There was no maternal association in the place of their residence." Then a warning was issued: "Reader, are you a parent? . . . *Train up a child in the way he should go.*" Even such cataclysms as the French Revolution, with its "atheism, licentiousness, and intemperance," could be avoided by "seizing upon the infant mind and training it up under moral and religious influence," suggested another author in the same magazine. Mrs. Elizabeth Hall, writing in *The Mother's Assistant*, made the point succinctly: "Perhaps there is no proposition that is so hackneyed, and at the same time so little understood, as that women are the prime cause of all the good and evil in human actions. . . . Yes, mothers, in a certain sense the destiny of a redeemed world is put into your hands."[56] Mothers were given a strong message. They were the potential source of *both* evil and good in the world, so that they had best be mindful of the proper performance of their maternal duties.

Many authors pointed out that while women should not go out into the world, the mother role, because of its far-reaching influence, still gave women a lofty position in society. "Though she may not teach from the portico nor thunder from the forum . . . she may form and send forth the sages that shall govern and renovate the world," wrote Catherine Beecher, the popular domestic educator. "The patriotism of women," Mrs. Sigourney agreed, "is not to thunder in senates"—it is to be expressed in the "office of maternal teacher." A writer in *Ladies' Magazine* noted that a mother's influence is "unseen, unfelt," but through it "she is forming the future patriot, statesman, or enemy of his country; more than this she is sowing the seeds of virtue or vice which will fit him for Heaven or for eternal misery."[57]

The rewards of motherhood were extravagantly described by the advice givers. To wit: "My friends," wrote Mrs. Sigourney, "if in becoming a mother, you have reached the climax of your happiness, you have also taken a higher place on the scale of being." Since children have the power to change their mothers for the better and bring them joy, no matter how difficult the tasks of motherhood, a mother "would willingly have endured a thousand fold for such a payment." Children also could provide their mothers with eternal salvation. "Does not the little cherub in his way guide you to heaven, marking the pathway by the flowers he scatters as he goes?" queried Mrs. Child. There was no doubt that children were the key to feminine fulfillment. The love of children, proclaimed an editorial in *Godey's Ladies Book*, "is as necessary to a woman's perfect development, as the sunshine and the rain are to the health and beauty of the flowers." Not only was a woman's entire happiness dependent on her civilizing task, her very identity was derived from it. "A woman is nobody. A wife is everything . . . and a mother is, next to God, all powerful," trumpeted a writer in a Philadelphia newspaper at mid-century.[58]

This preoccupation with motherhood is baffling unless firmly set within its larger social and economic context. The demise of the self-contained household economy, the isolation of a much reduced living unit, the separation of the home from the work place, and the resultant segregation of daily life into male and female spheres were all elements in the stage setting in which this ideology emerged. These factors, rather than any strong domestic propensity in women, explain the overweening emphasis on the mother role. On this point I take issue with the historian Carl Degler, who writes that since only women bore and could feed children in the early years, it is not surprising that "the ideology of domesticity stressed that women's destiny was motherhood." But hadn't women always borne and nursed children? Why does this ideology appear in full strength only after 1820? In the words of another historian, Mary Ryan, why for the first time was "childhood socialization, and not merely the physical care of infants . . . subsumed under the category of motherhood?" Why, asks another student of the subject, if there had always been mothers, had motherhood just been invented? The answer lies in the structural changes occurring in nineteenth-century society, changes that led to the increased seclusion of women and children in the home, the decreasing burden of household manufacture, the need for "high quality" children, and the growing concern with the declining birthrate of the white middle class. These changes more than adequately explain why motherhood, as never before, "stood out as a discrete task."[59]

Conscious Motherhood: 1870–1900

Woman of this age has to learn that "to save man" is "to study man."
Emma Marwedel, *Conscious Motherhood,* 1887

Guides to child care came increasingly under professional scrutiny and control from the 1870s on. The late nineteenth century witnessed the beginnings of "scientific" child study, and a number of works on child development were widely read by the general public. The "scientizing" of child rearing was part of a general movement that viewed science as the key to solving social problems. The basic tenet of child study was that scientific child care could produce the type of adults essential to the nation's greatness; it would also reduce or eliminate criminality and vice of all kinds. The scientific study of children and child care eventually led to the founding of the National Congress of Mothers, the Child Study Association, and numerous informal child study clubs.[60]

The result was the "professionalization of motherhood." Women were no longer fit for motherhood simply because of their "maternal instincts" or "higher moral principles"; they were told to study the role, be trained for it. "Doctors and lawyers and clergymen fit themselves to have charge of human lives. Why should not mothers?" asked a writer in *The Cosmopolitan* magazine. He suggested that women study "the scientific principles affecting their life's work" so that "motherhood will come to be looked upon as truly a 'profession.' " Emma Marwedel urged women to make "science" their "ally" in the "practical and theoretical preparation" necessary for competent mothering. By the 1890s middle class women were being urged to "study" their children. "Few mothers at this time have undertaken anything like a systematic study of children," lamented a writer in the *Child Study Monthly*, "though they may have devoted the best years of their lives in training their own."[61]

As motherhood was being transformed into a profession for middle class women, it soon became clear who was going to tell these women how to prepare for it—the child study "experts," most of whom were trained in the new discipline of psychology. But mothers were not to be equal partners in this endeavor. They were told to make careful notes on their children's development and behavior, to provide the raw data for the "experts" who then devised the rules that mothers were to follow. These rules were actually detailed sets of instructions that varied according to the child's stage of development. "Prenatal education," advised Miss Marwedel, should begin "the instant a mother knows herself pregnant [since] science, the absolute power of the age, tells us by clearly proved facts that our children are not born as well as they should be."[62]

All this emphasis on the science of child rearing did not entirely supplant the sentimental characterizations of motherhood associated with earlier days. "Motherhood!" trilled Dr. Trall in *The Mother's Hygienic Handbook*. "There is no word, except God, of greater influence in human language." It is "the most powerful religious mission trusted to the hands of mankind," agreed Miss Marwedel. And the sugary cult of motherhood received a boost in the pages of the *Ladies' Home Journal* when it began publication in 1889. According to its first editor, Edward Bok, a mother was still the "fountainhead" of the home and her "civilizing force" was undiminished because "man in the outer world is her emissary, carrying out the ideas she early implants in his mind."[63]

The cult of motherhood served a new use during the final decades of the nineteenth century. It was used to argue against women's suffrage. Giving a woman the vote, proclaimed Senator George West in 1887, "would take her down from that pedestal where she is today, influencing as a mother the minds of her offspring." "Woman was created to be a wife and mother," declared Orestes Brownsun, "to manage a family, to take care of children and tend to their early training," not to participate in political life. But then women's maternal role was used by others as the reason why women should be given the vote. Suffragist Julia Ward Howe claimed that it was entirely appropriate that the "mother of the race, the guardian of its helpless infancy" be allowed to lend her purifying influence to the dissolute world of politics.[64]

Although arguments for and against women's suffrage were cloaked in terms of the maternal role, there was widespread agreement that the mother role was totally incompatible with paid employment. Married women, but most especially mothers, would upset the natural order of society and do untold damage to their offspring if they worked outside the home (see chapter 6). In fact, very few married women held jobs during the late nineteenth century. In 1890 only 3.3 percent of married women were in the labor force, and nearly without exception married women who did work came from the very poorest sectors of society.[65]

Contemporary social critics and prescriptive writers did not wholly agree on another issue: whether it was better to have few or many children. Nevertheless, denunciations of small families and of women who limited their fertility were more common during the last years of the century than they had been earlier. Catherine Beecher, for one, deplored the "worldliness which tempts men and women to avoid large families, often by sinful methods, thus making the ignorant masses the chief supply of the future ruling majorities." Here again class bias is evident in the worry that the "lesser elements" were outproducing their "superiors." Another writer of the day, a medical doctor, saw laziness as the evil underlying the failure to procreate in large numbers. He criticized women who because of the "trouble and pains of gestation and nursing" and the "temporary privation of social and fashionable enjoyment" come to the conclusion that "children are a nuisance." But another physician defended small families. "It is more important what kind of a child we raise than how many. It is better to produce one lion than twelve donkeys."[66] Despite this disagreement, demographic data are certain: the birthrate continued to decline. The following figures show the average number of children born to white women during the last decades of the nineteenth century.

1870	4.55 children/white woman
1880	4.24 children/white woman
1890	3.76 children/white woman
1900	3.56 children/white woman

SOURCE: Ansley J. Coale and Melvin Zelnik, *New Estimates of Fertility and Population in the United States* (Princeton, N.J., 1963), p. 36.

Fifty to seventy-five percent of this decline can be attributed to family limitation within marriage—the rest is a result of the relatively larger percentage of women who never married or who married at a later age.

But how were couples in the late nineteenth century limiting their fertility? Most contemporary observers agreed that between 1880 and 1900 the incidence of abortion declined among middle and upper middle class married women. By that time abortion had been outlawed in every state of the union, and after 1880 American courts began to deal more harshly with indicted abortionists. Scholars now believe that by the last decades of the century married middle class women were controlling fertility and the spacing of children through contraception rather than abortion, although abstinence and coitus interruptus were probably common as well. What is noteworthy here is that contraceptive devices had also been declared illegal. The federal Comstock Law, passed in 1873, prohibited the sending of "obscene" material through the U.S. mail, and the law specifically defined contraceptive devices as "obscene." Following the federal law a series of state statutes also sought to limit the availability of contraceptives. Twenty-four states banned the advertising, publication, or distribution of contraceptive information and another fourteen states made it illegal to inform anyone about birth control devices.[67]

The legal prohibition of abortion and contraception make sense within the context of the fears created by the birthrate's continued downward trend. The cry of "race suicide" was heard in some quarters as the conviction grew that immigrants and the poor would outproduce the native-born middle class. The banning of techniques to control fertility can also be seen as part of what has been termed the "procreative imperative," the promotion of population growth by influential elites that benefit from the rearing of "quality" children. The still young nation required a large labor force to continue its rapid industrialization and to fulfill the myriad labor demands of its booming white collar sector. Moreover, a growing population would ensure a larger market for the goods and services being produced in ever greater quantities by American business and industry.[68]

Why then, despite the obstacles to fertility control and the continued emphasis on the importance of the mother role, did middle class women have fewer and fewer children? While children were a decided asset in agrarian societies, large families became less economically advantageous for one segment of the population—the middle class—as industrialization and urbanization progressed. A journalist, writing at the turn of the century, neatly summarized the social and economic forces making for smaller families among the more affluent: "Children are an expensive luxury. They cost a lot to raise; they are late in getting to work, because of the long training they must have; and few parents get anything back from them. What I mean is that nowadays raising children is an outlay, financially speaking."[69]

It is ironic that as middle class women gained greater control over their fertility and produced fewer children, the maternal role as depicted in the prescriptive writings of the day demanded greater and greater commitment. Middle class women were now having only three or four children but they were being urged to spend even more time and energy on each one. The full flowering of "scientific" motherhood in the twentieth century meant that child-care experts provided women with a plethora of further advice on how to keep busy in the ever narrowing domestic sphere.

Mother No Longer Knows Best: 1900–1940

The sentimental view of motherliness as the ever holy, ever infallible power must be abandoned. Motherliness is as yet but a glorious stuff awaiting its shaping artist.
Ellen Key, *The Renaissance of Motherhood,* 1914

At the turn of the century, it is said, "America discovered the child as the leading figure in the family, if not in history itself."[70] But the concentration on the child and the concomitant focus on motherhood had roots deep in the nineteenth century. The ideology that full-time mothering was essential to the proper development of the child met with little or no dissent in the prescriptive writings of the years 1900 to 1940. Even during the depression when economic necessity forced more married women than ever before to take jobs, the experts' relentless insistence on the centrality of the mother role did not abate.

The position of the professional child-care expert, the advisor par excellence on correct child-rearing methods, became more firmly entrenched in the era before World War II. So important was the molding of the child that the task could not be left to mere mothers. The experts of the day described the raising of a child as "no longer a duty or a joy, but a 'scientific' vocation that required intelligence and training."[71]

Starting around 1920 the child-care literature raised a new and frightening spectre: the dangerous mother. While it had long been thought that improper mothering could inflict damage on the child, poor mothers were considered the exception rather than the rule. But under the hegemony of behaviorism, psychologists and educators assumed that most mothers, because of their ignorance of the principles of human development, were raising weak and warped offspring. The solution prescribed for this tragic situation was to rigorously follow the dicta of the experts of the day, a regimen that recommended a highly scheduled, almost military approach to child raising.

While motherhood after the turn of the century was still a woman's central occupation, it was no longer her only one. Many middle class women were joining clubs, including ones that sought social reform. But these activities were not divorced from women's primary role. The movements favoring child labor laws and improved working conditions were clothed in part in maternal garb; women were said to care about such matters because of their domestic "instincts." Women had become "social housekeepers," according to historian Mary Ryan. Nevertheless, few challenged the notion that child rearing was a woman's principal responsibility. The change was that now other activities could be added to child care.[72]

Working outside the home was still unthinkable for "respectable" married women. In 1910 a mere 5 percent of married white women took

O'Reilly Papers, Schlesinger Library, Radcliffe College

"Sacred Motherhood" • *Only middle and upper class families could hope to conform to the depiction of the mother role in the advice manuals. This biting drawing was distributed by the Chicago Women's Trade Union League in the late nineteenth century.*

on outside jobs. And while it was becoming more acceptable for a "girl" briefly to hold an "appropriate" job before marriage, only "spinsters" could have serious career ambitions. The working mother was particularly anathema, and some of the women active in the social reform movement inveighed against mothers who took jobs. Florence Kelley, an officer in the Consumer's League, an organization that promoted protective legislation, specifically opposed day nurseries and legislative items that would have made it easier for mothers to be employed. According to Kelley, working women had fewer children, neglected the ones they did have, and were responsible for high rates of infant mortality, all "intolerable social costs." "It needs tremendous power to do one's duty to a single child," wrote Ellen Key, author of the best-selling *The Century of the Child*. She argued that "the present consequences of women's work done outside the home must cause pessimism; such work must be stopped."[73]

Many contemporary social critics also decried higher education for women, correctly noting that women with college degrees were less likely to marry and, if they did marry, more likely to produce fewer children than other women. But attacks on higher education for women were only part of a larger concern—the continued decline in the birthrate. In 1900, when child-rearing experts were urging women to have at least four children, the majority of women stopped with four, more typically with three. During the first two decades of the century birth control was widely practiced by middle class couples, and by 1920 most native-born whites were having only two children.[74]

G. Stanley Hall, considered the founder of the child study movement, worried about the impact of the lower birthrate on women. Their "bodies and souls," he wrote, are "made for maternity," so that they can "never find true repose for either without it." Unless women's education focused on motherhood, women graduates were destined to be "parturition phobics." Moreover, small families were not only perilous to women but to children as well. "Being an only child is a disease in itself," Hall wrote, and "to some extent, offspring limited to a pair of children also tend to be feeble." Ellen Key sounded a similar alarm in her *Renaissance of Motherhood*. "Has our race ever been afflicted with a more dangerous disease than the one which at present rages among women: the sick yearning to be 'freed' from the most essential attribute of their sex?" And who was blamed for this sorry state of affairs? Not just the "worn out drudges" or the "lazy creatures of luxury" but also the "women strong of body and worthy of motherhood" who chose either celibacy or to bear only one child.[75]

The most vociferous and best known voice of the day condemning small families was that of President Theodore Roosevelt. In an address before the National Congress of Mothers he proclaimed that the man or woman who "deliberately forgoes" the blessings of children, "whether from viciousness, coldness, or self-indulgence . . . why such a creature merits contempt as hearty as any visited upon the soldier who runs away in battle." He cited with scorn the unnamed clergyman who said that except for the very rich, people should rear only two children to give them opportunities and "a taste of a few of the good things in life." "If the average family in which there are children," Roosevelt fumed, "contained but two children, the Nation as a whole would decrease in population so rapidly that in two or three generations it would very deservedly be on the point of extinction. A race that practiced such a doctrine, that is, a race that practiced race suicide, would thereby conclusively show that it was unfit to exist."[76]

Against the background of the heated debate concerning small families and the declining birthrate, dozens of child-care associations and child study groups were being set up. In 1912 some fifty major associations and numerous smaller ones were organized into the Federation of Child Study. Two years later the United States Congress passed a unanimous resolution—with no debate—establishing Mother's Day. The resolution read, in part:

> Whereas the service rendered the United States by the American mother is the greatest source of the country's strength and inspiration . . . Whereas the American mother is doing so much for the home, for moral spirits and religion, hence so much for good government and humanity . . . Therefore, be it resolved that the second Sunday in May will be celebrated as Mother's Day.[77]

Books and popular magazines continued to spew forth recommendations on proper mothering. A telling analysis of articles on child rearing in three mass circulation women's magazines for selected years between 1892 and 1959 uncovered a relationship between the number of articles published and the birthrate. At times of high birthrate, there were many articles, but "the nadir both for birthrate and articles on child rearing was the depression year of 1935."[78]

The advice offered during the first decades of the twentieth century was of two types. Prior to about 1915 women were urged to be moral and loving, perhaps even indulgent toward their children, although the experts continued to insist that training and study were necessary to do the job well. But by the early 1920s under the sway of behaviorism, women were warned against "smother love" and were told to stress discipline and regularity; the watchword became "independence training."

A best-selling manual at the turn of the century was L. Emmett Holt's *The Care and Feeding of Infants*. First published in 1896, it remained popular for twenty years and went through several editions. This straightforward little book discusses basic care in dispassionate terms. Not a single line is devoted to the psychology of the child or its emotional needs; nor is the maternal role even mentioned. G. Stanley Hall's *Youth: Its Education, Regimen, and Hygiene* (1904) is more typical of the general tenor of child-care guides of the day. Hall did not consider maternal affection enough to ensure a child's proper development. He argued that women must be specifically educated for motherhood in order to learn how to react to their children. With each stage the child passed through, the mother's study became more complex.[79]

Hall spent many pages in the volume ruing higher education for women, which made them "overdraw" their "reserves" and lose their "mammary functions" so that they could not nurse; this led to "abnormal or incomplete development" in their offspring. A highly educated women, said Hall, "has taken up and utilized in her own life all that was meant for her descendants." In the worst cases, such women became completely sterile and this "elimination of maternity," lamented Hall, "is one of the greatest calamities . . . of our age." Hall's solution to this unhappy state of affairs was to provide women with an education that "fits their natures," that is, to educate them "primarily and chiefly for motherhood." "We must never forget," he warned, that "motherhood is a very different thing from fatherhood"—he was adamant that the sexes be trained accordingly, urging that "coeducation must cease at the dawn of adolescence" so that "in its highest sense maternity might be the heart of all the higher training of young women."[80]

Similar notions about proper education for women filled the pages of the *Ladies' Home Journal.* In a 1900 issue an article written by an "American mother" criticized higher education for women on the grounds that nine out of ten women became housewives. "I know of no college for women in which nursing, cookery, or any of the practical arts which she will need after as a wife and mother can be learned." And what sort of education does the "American mother" call for? One that "recognizes the differences between the sexes and trains a girl thoroughly for her womanly work." The debate had not been put to rest a decade later when an article entitled "Is the American Girl Being Miseducated?" appeared in the same magazine. The answer to the question was a ringing affirmative: "If . . . education is to mean training then our college women's education today is a joke." What is needed is education for "our life's business"—courses in "domestic science, physical hygiene, home economics, and domestic architecture and decoration."[81]

While scientific motherhood was being prescribed by child-rearing experts of the day, the spiritual glorification of the maternal role—so typical of the previous century—was by no means lost. "As for the mother," intoned President Roosevelt in his address before the National Congress of Mothers, "her very name stands for loving unselfishness and self-abnegation and in any society fit to exist, it is fraught with associations which render it holy." "Not woman," wrote Ellen Key in 1909, "but the mother is the most precious possession of the nation." Nor had the gravity of the role been diminished in any way: "Into the woman's keeping is committed the destiny of the generations to come," Roosevelt told his audience.[82]

The persistent emphasis on motherhood should be seen as part of a continuing effort to answer "the woman question" first raised in the nineteenth century. What was to be the role and position of middle class women in a rapidly industrializing society now that their traditional productive skills were no longer needed? What were they to do all day to keep them occupied? The answer was still—as it had been at least since the 1830s—the child.

The child, no longer a productive member of society or a "miniature adult," had now become "a kind of evolutionary protoplasm, a means of control over society's not so distant future." Woman's job was thus to shape that future. Why then should she not be content? "A woman," editorialized the *Ladies Home Journal,* "will often envy a man his chance to go into the world and make laws. But, in comparison, what is the law-maker to the man-maker?" Ellen Key also told women to appreciate their noble calling: "Women in parliament and in journalism, their representation in the local and general government . . . science and literature, all this will produce small results until women realize that the transformation of society begins with the unborn child, and with the conditions of its coming into existence, its physical and psychical training."[83]

Not only was motherhood a lofty profession, it was also a time-consuming one. Women certainly had enough work to fill their hours if they followed the directives of the child-rearing experts. A woman, wrote Dorothy Canfield in 1914, must observe every action of her child at every age, for the mother held the key to the child's future character and potential. Canfield further advised mothers to reserve a half hour every night before bedtime for "meditation devoted to the cultivation of the scientific spirit as applied to our children." Shouldn't a mother be ashamed, she asked, "that a man in a greenhouse should devote more intelligent attention to a radish plant than she to her own children?" Ellen Key wrote that it was unnecessary to devote every waking hour to child care, but "our soul is to be filled by the child." Mothers were to think of their children constantly—while sitting at home, taking a walk, lying down. In order to do this mothers were advised to "limit their social activities" and remain "entirely free from working to earn a living during the most critical years of the child's training."[84]

Mothers were told to be in virtually constant attendance on their children, but what were fathers supposed to be doing? Most experts of the day equivocated on the subject of the father's role in child care. While some paid lip service to the importance of fathers in childhood education, none spelled out the male's duties. A writer in the *Ladies' Home Journal* stressed that "father's failures" are less serious than "mother's mistakes" because fathers are "out of the child's life so much of the time." Nevertheless, the advisor suggested that fathers "forget at times their worldly business" and remember that they are "guiding souls upon their upward and outward way." An editorial in a 1915 issue of the same magazine indicates the rather narrow duties prescribed for fathers of the era. The writer regrets that many men, when questioned about their children, reply "That's for my wife." But paternity clearly has limited parameters; a father becomes important only when the child reaches school age. Education takes place "outside the home" so that "it is within the father's scope of interest." At this point masculine influence is essential because "a child's education is too momentous a matter to be left up to even the wisest of mothers."[85]

Ellen Key, who recommended that all women should be required to take a course on housekeeping and child care "as a condition for the right to marry," worried far less about the training of men for their parental duties. Fathers are sometimes "endowed with a genius for education," but since they are the breadwinners and are not trained for fatherhood their "influence as a rule is insignificant." She called for a greater role for fathers as "educators" of their children, but only when the "care for the maintenance of the family does not press them down to the ground." And she cautioned that while men perform as well as or better than women in the world of work, "in the home . . . men cannot supplant the spirit and activities" of mothers. Nor can anyone else for that matter—"can the heart in an organism be replaced by a pumping engine, however ingenious?" she asked.[86]

Scheduling Takes Command

> *Won't you remember when you are tempted to pet your child that mother love is a dangerous instrument? An instrument which may inflict a never healing wound.*
>
> John B. Watson
>
> *Psychological Care of Infant and Child,* 1928

The major tenet of the child-rearing literature of the 1920s and 1930s was that mothers are dangerous, dangerous to the health and well-being of their children and ultimately to society at large. The double message that mothers had received since the nineteenth century—that they were the cause of all good and evil in the world—was no longer a balanced one. Now mothers were assumed guilty of damaging their children unless proven innocent. The cause, said the experts, is women's lack of expertise in "mothercraft." In the words of historian Sheila Rothman, the prescriptive writings of the period "reduced the competence of the mother to the point where she almost seemed a criminal figure, stunting and warping her child's development."[87]

The dominant figure in the "mothers are dangerous" school of child care was psychologist John B. Watson, the author of a widely read manual. No advice giver of the day was untouched by his theories. The best-selling child-care pamphlets published by the Children's Bureau, an agency of the U.S. government, incorporated his ideas and guaranteed them a large audience. Watson castigated irrational, emotional mother love for its devastating effects. Such love, he argued, led to weak, dependent children, to children with "crippled personalities" who would never make it in the tough competitive world of industrial capitalism. Rather than coddling children and overwhelming them with excessive affection, mothers should stress regularity, punctuality, discipline, and cleanliness, qualities that made them finely tuned to the needs of business and industry.

Doubting that women could successfully carry out his recommendations, Watson sarcastically dedicated his manual, *Psychological Care of Infant and Child*, "to the first mother who brings up a happy child." Although children could be reared more "scientifically" away from their parents, the home, he conceded, was here to stay. The task of the behaviorist then was to work with the raw material at hand, that is, to get the mother "to take a new view . . . of her responsibility for her experiment in child rearing." What Watson called for was "not more babies, but better brought up babies." No one could doubt that his dicta were directed at the middle class for he urged potential parents not to have children at all unless they could afford separate bedrooms for each child, a prerequisite for carrying out behaviorist doctrines.[88]

The core of Watson's view of maternity is found in his chapter "The Danger of Too Much Mother Love." "Invalidism," he warned, is in the making "in the majority of American homes." Children are being "over-coddled" because their mothers are "starved for love." "The fact . . . that we rarely see a happy child is proof," said Watson, "that women are failing in their mission. The solution? Mothers, advised Watson, should treat their children "as though they were young adults." "Never hug and kiss them," he warned, "never let them sit on your lap." If a mother simply could not resist showing some sign of affection toward her children, Watson suggested she "kiss them once on the forehead at bedtime, but shake hands with them in the morning."[89]

Watson wrote that he couldn't help wishing "that it were possible to rotate mothers occasionally" in order to avoid the development of excessive affection between mother and child. But since this couldn't be done, he recommended that children be left alone for part of the day so that "over-conditioning" would be given a chance to die down. Watson realized that his advice would not be easy for some mothers. "If your heart is too tender," he wrote, "and you must watch the child, make yourself a peephole so that you can see it without being seen, or use a periscope."[90]

Watson's warnings about the dangers of mother love were echoed by nearly every child-rearing expert of the day. The 1925 Children's Bureau pamphlet *Child Management* cautioned its readers that "the very love of the mother prevents her from successfully fulfilling the obligations of her parenthood." The mother who fails to train her child in independence because she gets satisfaction when "he clings to her so tenaciously" will later regret her actions. She may be making it "impossible for the boy or girl to stand alone in years to come." Five years later another Children's Bureau pamphlet delivered the same message in a simple-minded, condescending tone: "Do you want your child's love for yourself? A good mother is happy to see a child happy, no matter where he is. She is a bad mother if she is sorry when he is happy without her." And the readers of a 1927 issue of the *Ladies' Home Journal* were told of the unfortunate consequences of "smother love." "Never Too Young to Learn Responsibility" is the story of a boy who was "coddled" by his mother and "guarded zealously from everything without." During adolescence he was a "general favorite because no one suspected his underlying weaknesses." But it was not long before they were exposed. When he reached adulthood he failed miserably in his father's business since "he had never been assisted in developing the qualities to handle responsibility."[91]

Many women, wrote the authors of the 1928 manual *Parents and Children*, find it "astonishing . . . that mother love has been found by science to be inherently dangerous," but the authors did not doubt that it was. In a chapter called "The Dangerous Mother," they review the damning evidence. The growth in knowledge of personality development, they wrote, has led to "a clear understanding of the danger of parents, especially mothers." "From whatever quarter the scientist comes to the study of human behavior—psychology, sociology, education—he finds that the unwise behavior of the mother has had much to do with the wrong starting of the personality trend."[92]

Another tenet of the Watsonian school of child rearing was scheduling. Children were to be kept to a rigid schedule for feeding, sleeping, toilet training, and nearly all other activities; any deviation from routine was viewed as harmful and was only recommended when a child was sick. Independence training was the goal and everything else was secondary to its pursuit. The emphasis on regularity is a recurrent feature in all of the prescriptive literature of the period. In child care, wrote Mrs. Max West, author of the first edition of the Children's Bureau pamphlet *Infant Care* published in 1914, "perhaps the first and most essential habit is that of regularity. This begins at birth and applies to all the physical functions of the baby." And the 1929 edition of the pamphlet repeated these instructions: "Through training in regularity of feeding, sleeping, and elimination the tiny baby will receive his first lesson in character building."[93]

Infants were to be fed regularly every four hours. Every edition of *Infant Care* (1914, 1929, 1938) published during the Watsonian era stressed feeding on a rigid schedule. The 1930 Children's Bureau pamphlet *Are You Training Your Child to Be Happy?* gave mothers a "lesson" on how to feed their babies. It was Watson's principles in microcosm written on a second grade level:

> *Begin when he is born.*
> Feed him at exactly the same hours every day.
> Let him sleep after each feeding.
> Do not feed him just because he cries.
> Let him wait until the right time.
> If you make him wait, his stomach will begin to wait.
> His mind will learn that he will not get things by crying.

Mary McCarthy's novel *The Group*, set in the 1930s, contains a graphic depiction of a young mother trying to follow these principles:

> The sound of a baby's crying made itself heard in the silence. . . .
> "That's Stephen again," said Mrs. Hartshorn. "I recognize his voice. He yells louder than any other baby in the nursery."
> Mrs. Hartshorn looked at her watch. "Can't the nurse bring him in now," she wondered. "It's quarter to six."
> "The *schedule*, mother!" cried Priss. "The reason babies in your time had colic wasn't because they were breast-fed, but because they

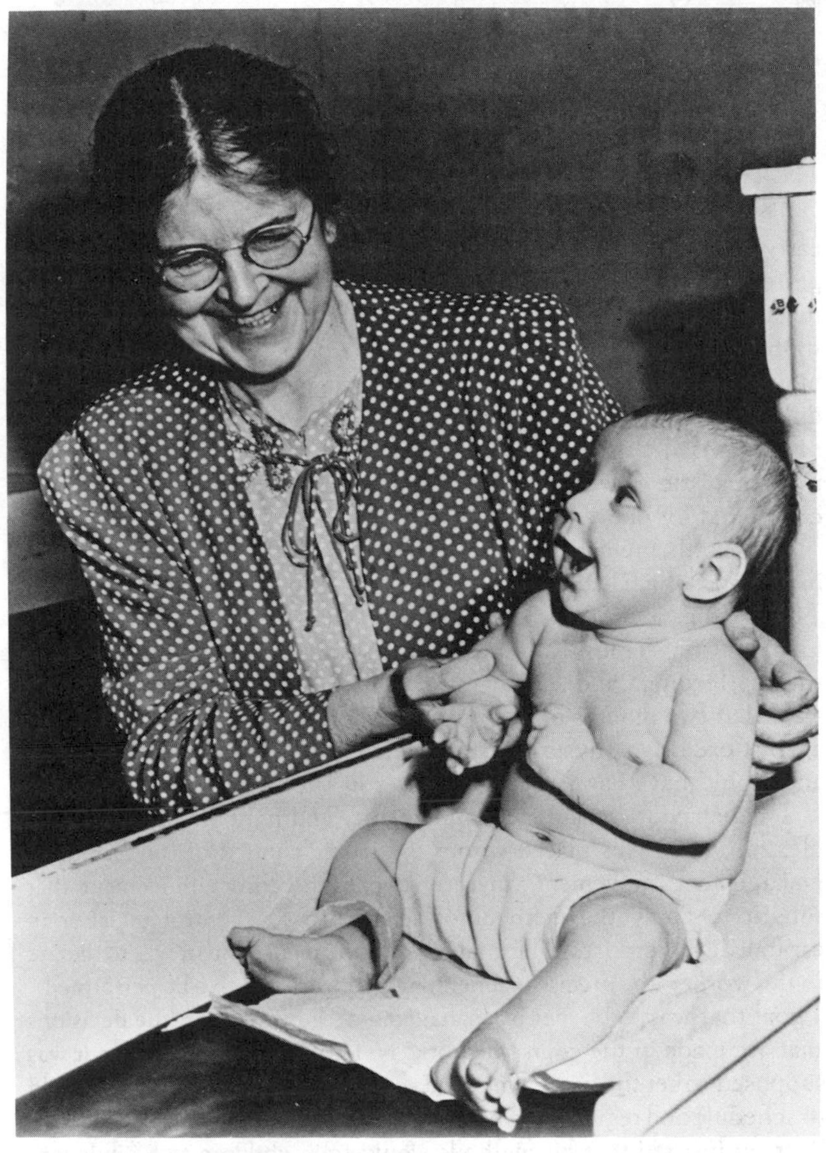

Eliot Papers, Schlesinger Library, Radcliffe College

Dr. Martha M. Eliot Weighing Baby • *Dr. Martha M. Eliot was Director of the Children's Bureau and author of one of the editions of the widely read pamphlet,* Infant Care.

were picked up at all sorts of irregular times and fed whenever they cried. The point is to have a schedule and to stick to it absolutely."[94]

Toilet training, according to Watson's scenario, was to begin very early and be pursued vigorously. The 1929 edition of *Infant Care* suggested that training could begin when the baby was one month old but must always be started by three months. "Almost any baby can be trained so that there are no soiled diapers to wash after he is six or eight months old," the author of the pamphlet suggested optimistically. The difficulty of training a baby that young must have dawned on the authors of the revised 1938 edition of the pamphlet, for they advised a slightly more realistic schedule: training was to begin at six months and be completed by one year.[95]

These rather remarkable developments in child care were also current in England which had its very own Watson in the person of Sir Frederick Truby King, author of the best-selling *Feeding and Care of Baby* (1913). Like Watson, Truby King urged English mothers to rigidly schedule eating, feeding, and elimination, recommending that the latter be started at two months of age. Also like Watson, Truby King cautioned against excessive physical contact which risked overstimulating babies and would have harmful consequences in later life.[96]

The behaviorist insistence on regularity and tight scheduling is perplexing unless it is placed within the larger context of the "scientific management" movement, an early twentieth-century movement that sought to apply the methods of science to the control of labor in capitalistic enterprises. The goal of scientific management was to dictate to the worker "the precise manner in which work [was] to be performed," a goal that was to be met by management's control over "the decisions that are made in the course of work."[97] Thus, just as management was supposed to set the pace, time, and scope of work, the mother was told to schedule and regulate the hours of feeding, sleeping, and elimination. Watson insisted that his methods would train children to be independent, but it is unclear how removal of control over activities—from baby to mother (or worker to manager)—instills autonomy and self-reliance. A more likely result of the industrial model of child care is the rearing of individuals who fit into a working world that not only demanded regularity and discipline but conformity to outside direction as well.

The recommendations of Watson and his followers should not be seen as totally new ideas in the history of American child-rearing advice. The dicta that children should be trained to "stand on their own two feet" and should not be coddled or kept dependent by excessive maternal affection were themes that appeared again and again in the prescriptive literature from the colonial period. The innovation of the behaviorists was not their advice per se; rather it was the welding of the time-worn dicta of the Protestant ethic to the findings of "science" in order to prove that what was good for capitalism was good for the child.

But if Watson's scientific principles were molding children to the requirements of industrial capitalism, they were doing so at the expense of their mothers' time and energy. Watson was unconcerned with the impact his advice had on a mother's workload since the behaviorists concluded that maternal convenience was scarcely worthy of attention when so much was at stake. Mother was to spend hours chauffeuring her children to music and dance lessons, sports events, and other activities meant to nurture independence; in her leisure time, she was expected to study the child-care manuals to find out just what it was she was doing wrong. Watson's methods, in fact, increased women's work. "The attempt to develop independence in infants," notes historian Mary Ryan, "was particularly productive of nervous exhaustion entailing as it did the pressure to toilet train an infant by three months; feed the child precisely on schedule; and endure the childish tantrums and long bouts of screeching that were deemed healthy."[98]

A number of Watson's followers tried to explain why "smother love" had suddenly loomed as such a problem. A speaker at the 1930 White House Conference on the Health and Protection of Children offered this explanation: "Freed by labor saving devices from many of the tasks which formerly kept her occupied, living in a small apartment, she has little to do except exercise close supervision over the children's affairs. As a result, the mother is likely to form such a close attachment to the child that he is robbed of his initiative and spontaneity." The authors of the manual *Parents and Children* agreed with this interpretation. Noting that the contemporary mother was giving her children better physical care than her mother gave her, the authors saw the reverse as true in terms of "her influence in the more subtle relationships." The root of the problem, they claimed, is that the modern mother has more leisure, which gives her "the opportunity to impress herself too much upon the child." In short, "her influence is excessive."[99]

One might think that with all the danger of overexposure to "Mom" the experts would have called for a much greater role for "Dad." In fact, some of them did so, but within clearly defined limits. "It may be natural and good for young children to be more with their mothers than their fathers, but it is certainly not wholesome for these children to be brought up almost exclusively in the fellowship of their mothers," according to one child-care manual. This is a good example of the way the paternal role was viewed during the 1920s and 1930s; a dose of father was seen as a good antidote for an overdose of mother, but there was never any doubt that the responsibility for child care still lay in maternal hands. The authors of *Parents and Children* recommended "a half hour a day of real companionship with the father" and suggested that a father occasionally take his children out to lunch or the theater. "Surely five or six afternoons *a year* spent in this fashion represent no serious drain either upon [his] time or [his] pocketbook." The authors of the 1938 edition of *Infant Care* also took a decidedly narrow view of the father role. "It would be wise," the pamphlet advised, "for the father to help with the care of the baby so that if the mother becomes ill or has to leave home for a period *he can meet this emergency until help can be provided.*"[100]

One obvious solution to the problem of excessive mothering was never recommended by the experts. None of them encouraged women "to leave the family setting and make a genuine commitment to a career or task outside the home. A hobby? Yes. Anything more serious or full-time? No." Watson himself is very clear on this. Writing in a 1927 issue of *The Nation* he deemed it acceptable for married women to pursue careers *so long as they did not have children*. "Having children," he wrote, "is almost an insuperable barrier to a career. The rearing of children and the running of a home for them is a profession second to none in its demands for technique."[101]

The distinction between *women's* working and *mothers'* working is an important one that was made throughout the 1920s and 1930s. Even those who advocated paid employment for married women drew the line at mothers. "Being there is the greatest contribution we mothers can make in the lives of our children," averred one supporter of vocational training for women. The general consensus was that mothers already had a profession. "Baby care" is described as an "art" by the author of the 1929 edition of *Infant Care*. "It is the most important task any woman ever undertakes and she should apply to this work the same diligence and sustained effort that she would give to the most exacting profession." In 1924 Vassar College established the School of Euthenics with the avowed aim of raising "motherhood to a profession worthy of [woman's] finest talents and greatest intellectual gifts." And the nineteenth-century notion that a woman's career was her children, particularly her sons, was still being touted. An article in a 1934 issue of *Pictorial Review* declared that "it is better to be the mother of a Michelangelo than a second rate 'lady painter'; the mother of a Shakespeare, a Dante, or Homer, than a 'very pleasing lady poet.' "[102]

A low rate of employment among middle class married women and a continuing decline in the birthrate were features of the setting in which Watsonian doctrines were being espoused. Few married women held jobs. In 1920, 7 percent were in the labor force and by 1930 that figure had increased to just under 12 percent. Most married women who worked clearly did so out of necessity. They were principally employed in the lowest paying and most menial occupations. During the depression many were forced to take whatever jobs they could find to make up for their husbands' lost wages. It was also during this period that the nation's birthrate reached its then all time low. Because of economic conditions, it plunged during the 1930s, making for an overall decline of 41 percent between 1900 and 1936.[103]

Although the popular advice givers and the child-rearing experts lambasted mothers who worked outside the home, the writers seemed little concerned with the fact that women were having fewer children. Watson, in particular, urged quality rather than quantity in child rearing, and it certainly is difficult to imagine a mother of many children sticking to the strict scheduling demanded by behaviorist dogma. Perhaps general economic conditions were simply too severe during the depression for even the most ardent pro-natalist to have seriously suggested that women's duty lay in giving birth to more mouths to feed.

Depending on the decade, mothers are told to consult the experts or follow their instincts; to show their feelings or disguise themselves in discretion; to allow the twig to bend or train it from the start.

Mother's Day editorial, *New York Times*, 10 May 1981

Three periods stand out in the changing image of the mother role in the prescriptive literature dating from colonial times to the years preceding World War II. During the colonial era the advice of the clergy—the major prescriptive voices of the day—minimized differences in parental roles and duties. Ministers assumed that child rearing was not a discrete task but something that took place amid the daily round of activities necessary to the ongoing domestic economy. Parents were told to "raise up" their children together, and other than the father's role in religious instruction and the mother's duty to nurse her infant, parenting was not a specialized function within the ken of one sex or the other. Nor was there any indication that a special tie existed between mother and child.

This image of generalized parenting began to change during the last years of the eighteenth century. As the country began to industialize, women's productive household activities started to wane and the home and the world of work gradually became differentiated. The spheres of the sexes began to diverge as "work" became something that only men did, while women were left in charge of a now reduced domestic realm, a realm consisting of themselves and their children. During these years the first glimmerings of a distinct maternal role began to appear in the prescriptive literature. The early writings were tentative, for the conditions under which the maternal role was thrown into relief came about gradually. Nevertheless, for the first time we find sermons and pamphlets dealing with the topic of child rearing addressed to "mothers" rather than to "parents," along with a few early discussions of the importance of maternal care to the growing child. The prescriptive writings of these years were in a real sense transitional. The stern colonial dicta of rearing righteous, God-fearing children, dicta directed at both parents, were now rarely heard, but the "extravagant celebration of motherhood" associated with the nineteenth century was still to come.

As industrialization continued apace, by the third decade of the nineteenth century a sizable audience of homebound middle class women emerged as the targets of a vast outpouring of advice to mothers.

These flowery paeans to motherhood contained strong directives. Mothers and mothers alone undertook the herculean job of molding their children into the model middle class adults of the age. Children required the full-time care and devotion of their mothers, care that could be provided by no one else. Mothers must perform this task with high purpose and great diligence, for one false move, one dereliction of duty, could mark the child for all eternity. But if the mother followed the dictates of the advice givers, motherhood would be the most important achievement of her life. No activity, therefore, could surpass in importance the activity of mothering.

The marked emphasis on the maternal role and the importance of mother-child ties propounded by the child-rearing experts of the first four decades of the present century was not *qualitatively* different from that which prevailed during much of the nineteenth century. *Styles* of child rearing had of course changed, "science" had become an instrument for instructing middle class mothers on how to carry out their maternal duties, and the principles of management had been applied to the sphere of child care for the first time. But the concentration on the mother as the child rearer par excellence, the insistence that no one else could take her place, and the assumption that women's most important, if not sole, task in life was the rearing of healthy, well-adjusted offspring had roots deep in the nineteenth century. It was not until profound changes occurred in the roles of middle class women in the decades following World War II that it behooved the child-care experts and popular advice givers alike to tardily, but momentously, redefine the mother role and the duties it entailed.

3 MOTHERS DESCEND

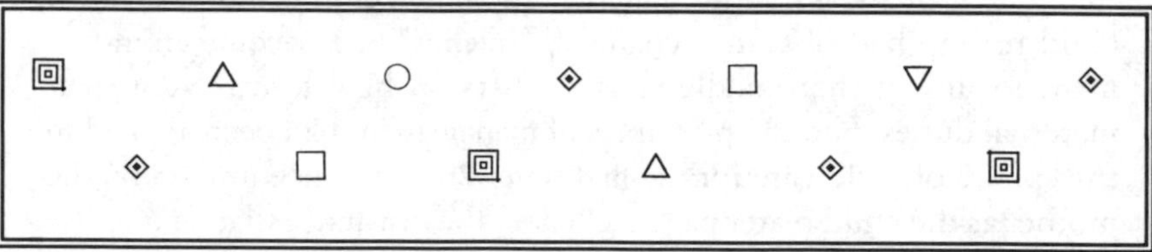

The idea of imprisoning each woman alone in a small, separate and self-contained dwelling is a modern invention, dependent upon an advanced technology.
Phillip Slater, *Pursuit of Loneliness,* 1976

Something new came over America in the years immediately before and after World War II. The rigid methods of child care recommended by Watson and the behaviorists were suddenly displaced by the ideals of the much lauded and much damned "permissive" school of child rearing. The goal of child care was no longer to stymie the natural inclinations of the infant but to give them free rein. Since spontaneity and self-expression were now thought important to the developing child, the child would now lead and the mother would follow.

Permissiveness was not only a doctrine that applied to child care, it also has been called "a national mood, a wind of change" that swept through all facets of American life.[1] It is now generally recognized that advice counseling permissive child care and self-scheduling was in tune with the postwar economy's dependence on ever rising levels of consumption. The old concerns of inculcating discipline and self-control—qualities demanded by a future-oriented work ethic—were replaced by an emphasis on individuality and a tendency toward self-indulgence, traits that harmonized with the consumption orientation of the late 1940s and the 1950s. Continued commercial prosperity was at least partly dependent on a strong gratification ethic. And what better way to instill the urge than by permissive training during the earliest years? It is no mere coincidence that the teachings of Dr. Benjamin Spock and other permissive ideologues appeared at a time of vast consumer output, a time when ever greater levels of demand required impulsive gratification.

Another element in postwar child-rearing advice was the psychoanalytic doctrines of Sigmund Freud. The concern with the Oedipal and Elektra complexes was an underlying theme in many of the prescriptive writings of the late 1940s and 1950s. While mothers were told to be accessible, loving, truly feminine figures, fathers were to serve as role models for their sons and chivalric heroes for their daughters. Lurking in the background of these dicta was the favorite bogeywoman of the era, the horrific "Mom." She came in two varieties. There was the masculine, aggressive Mom and the whining, mousy Mom who in either case dominated her children and refused to allow them their independence. Aside from letting children and infants follow their instincts, sex appropriate behavior on the part of both parents was the watchword of the child-care experts of the day.

But how did the middle class mother, the focus of our attention, fare in this climate of permissive self-expression? She still had primary, if not sole, responsibility for child care and housework. But there was a new element in her life: she was no longer confined to the home. Everyone knows that millions of wives and mothers held jobs during World War II, but what few people realize is that not all these women rushed back to their ivy-covered cottages once hostilities had ceased. The entire setting for this chapter in fact is one in which married middle class women, including mothers, at first gradually but then more rapidly began entering the labor force in greater numbers than ever before.

Postwar inflation, rising standards of consumption, and a boom in the number of jobs available in traditionally female occupations were the forces that led women from the home to the work place. Both push and pull factors were involved. During the 1950s and early 1960s married women took jobs, often part-time, to be able to buy the extras—a second car, a major appliance, a college education for their children—that were part of middle class consumption patterns. But beginning in the mid-1960s, the start of the great inflation surge, the income of married women became more and more crucial to the family budget—to help pay for food, clothing, the house mortgage, and other basic expenses. By the 1970s the two-income family in the United States was the norm, and with the exception of the families of highly paid business and professional men, two incomes had become essential for maintaining a middle class standard of living.

Women not only wanted and/or needed jobs, but another vital element in the surge of female employment was the availability of jobs for them—in record numbers. During the three decades after World War II women were hired for twenty-five million *new* jobs, and by the late 1970s two out of three new jobs were filled by women. These figures in turn reflect the phenomenal growth of the service and information sectors of the economy in the postwar period. As is all too obvious from today's unemployment figures, this growth has been at the expense of the manufacturing sector. By the early 1980s service and information jobs outnumbered manufacturing jobs by at least two to one.[2]

The types of jobs created over the last thirty years were just the ones traditionally held by women—single, childless women for the most part before the war, but women nonetheless. Now new secretarial, clerical, and retail jobs, jobs in nursing, elementary school teaching, and social work, all beckoned the middle class housewife. And she was certainly in demand. Not only could she be paid less than a man—some 40 cents on the dollar less—but she was also literate and often highly educated. She was an employer's dream come true. And because inflation was gnawing away at the family budget, she was available.

Another element in the social and economic background for permissive child rearing was the fertility rate after World War II. First, it rose sharply through the 1950s and then nosedived during the late 1960s and

1970s. In retrospect, the baby boom of the 1950s was a short-term reversal of the long-term decline in the fertility rate in the United States, a decline that dated from at least the early nineteenth century. But what about today? Common wisdom has it that women are having fewer children because they are in the labor force. While there is some relationship between employment and fertility, I do not believe that middle class women are having fewer children *only* because of their entry into the labor force. They are having fewer children for the same reason they are taking jobs: the high cost of maintaining a middle class standard of living. Raising a child in the United States today is an expensive undertaking. It is little wonder then that as the cost of living has gone up over the last two decades, the completed fertility rate for middle class women has declined.

◈ □ ○ △ □ ◈

Perusal of the child-care advice published during the 1940s and 1950s would never lead a reader to suspect that growing numbers of children did *not* have full-time mothers available to cater to their needs. The *methods* of child care had changed in the prescriptive writings of the period, but the ideal mother the writers described had not. Advice givers still spoke to the ever present mother who was to follow the (revised) dictates of the experts. An exclusive mother-child dyad was still deemed essential for the child's healthy development. And Mom was still to blame if anything went wrong.

The disjunction between the experts' vision of motherhood and the reality of women's lives grew as the 1950s turned into the 1960s. Rising inflation and new white collar jobs drew large numbers of middle class married women into the labor force. While in the 1950s a majority of working mothers had no children under age eighteen, by the 1960s more and more mothers of school age children held jobs. The turning point came in 1972 when for the first time more mothers of school age children were employed than were not. This trend continued in the 1970s: the mothers of younger and younger children flooded the job market. Today 60 percent of all women with children under eighteen are employed.[3]

The child-rearing experts' recognition of the new facts of life was slow in coming. In some of the child-care manuals of the 1960s we see a

Courtesy of Benjamin Spock, M.D.

Dr. Benjamin Spock • *Dr. Benjamin Spock's* Baby and Child Care *sold millions of copies and was the most influential child care manual during the post-World War II era. He is widely credited as the originator of "permissive" child rearing.*

dawning awareness that mother is not home all the time and that father has some responsibility for caring for his children. But not until the 1970s did both popular manual writers and child-care experts alike fully awaken to the fact of widespread maternal employment and the changing nature of child care that resulted. For the first time since the early nineteenth century, full-time mothering was no longer viewed as essential for a child's health, happiness, and proper development. The hoary dogma that an exclusive mother-child relationship was both natural and inevitable came under attack. Mothering was no longer the prerogative of females alone. Fathers, it was discovered, had the capacity to mother as well as mothers did if given the opportunity. Times indeed had changed, but the structural conditions of postwar American society rather than some sudden bolt of understanding on the part of the advice givers were ultimately responsible for this remarkable redefinition of the mother role.

◈ □ ○ △ □ ◈

Spock-marked Mothers and "Moms": 1940–1960

Let us, contemporary mothers, together regain that common sense which is yours, which has been yours before you allowed yourselves to be intimidated by the omniscient totalitarians of one denomination or another.

Leo Kanner, *In Defense of Mothers,* 1941

The mother . . . must subordinate her need for sleep, for recreation, for getting the housework done or for pursuing non-domestic interests at all times. Moreover, she is expected to do so with a sense of deep satisfaction and happiness.

Sibylle Escalona
"A Commentary upon Some Recent Changes in Child Rearing Practices," 1953

Tentative signs during the 1930s revealed that child-care experts had started to question the wisdom of behaviorist dogma. Were early independence training and restricted doses of maternal affection *really* what was best for children, they asked. "It's perfectly safe to love your children," proclaimed *Parent's Magazine*. The pendulum clearly had begun to swing away from the "let them cry" school of the Watsonian era to the cuddling, permissive, "wean them late" school of the Spockean age. The detached, mechanical mother was to be replaced by one displaying warmth and emotion. "Self-demand" became the motto of the movement, and by 1940 two-thirds of all the articles in the *Ladies' Home Journal*, *Woman's Home Companion*, and *Good Housekeeping* advised mothers to allow their babies to set their own feeding and sleeping schedules. "It is reasonable to feed a baby when he's hungry. It is unreasonable to make him wait," admonished a writer in a 1940 issue of *Good Housekeeping*.[4]

Babies still dominated their mothers' lives, only now it was the babies rather than the mothers who set the timetable. "Any . . . schedule must of necessity take into account the balance of all the infant's natural activities and the life routine must be carefully and gradually worked out with this in mind," wrote Dr. Margaret Ribble in her popular pre-Spock manual, *Rights of Infants*. Developmental psychologists Gessell and Ilg agreed with this advice: the baby, they claimed, helps his mother "work out an optimal and flexible schedule suited to his changing needs." "We have happier children," concurred *Good Housekeeping*, "since we have learned to adapt ourselves to the baby's body rhythms and natural inclinations." The new message of the experts was clear: "Babies . . . no longer need their mothers to limit them, to teach them discipline or to set a model that they could aspire to—instead, they need their mothers only to follow them around and meet their needs for stimulation, play, and affection."[5]

"Mothers," the experts said, "relax and trust yourselves." Women were told to stop beating their breasts in self-reproach and wailing "I know it's all my fault!" "*What* is all *whose* fault?" asked Dr. Leo Kanner in his 1941 volume *In Defense of Mothers*. He urged mothers not to listen to the so-called experts whose goal was "to put fear of their particular gods into their audiences." His advice, in contrast, was based on "common sense." So too was that of Dr. Spock. The first edition of his enormously popular child-care manual was entitled *The Common Sense Book of Baby and Child Care*. Dr. Spock, "the confidence man," told mothers to ignore all the conflicting theories and take the anxiety out of child care by following their own instincts. It was now all right to comfort their children without fear of spoiling them, so long as mother felt right about what she was doing.

But instincts could only go so far. "Though resourceful and self-reliant, a good mother is not self-sufficient," wrote Dr. Kanner. A wise mother consults often with her physician since she understands that "mother cannot always know best." Spock also gave mothers limited autonomy; he advised them to consult their pediatricians about even the most minor problems of child care. In addition, his instructions were often so specific and simple-minded as to make a mockery out of his dictum that mothers should follow their "instincts." Here, for example, are his instructions on preparing for the baby's bath:

> Before starting the bath, be sure you have everything you need close at hand. If you forget the towel, you'll have to go after it holding a dripping baby in your arms.
>
> Take your wristwatch off.
> An apron keeps your clothes drier.
> Have at hand:
> soap
> washcloth
> towel
> lotion or powder if you use either
> shirt, diaper, pins, nightie.[6]

The experts recommended self-confidence to the mother; they also recommended fun. Martha Wolfenstein calls this "fun morality." Child care was to be a game enjoyed by mother and baby alike. The 1942 edition of *Infant Care* suggested that mothers make play a part of all their baby's activities. As Wolfenstein notes, it was no longer "adequate for the mother to perform efficiently the necessary routines for her baby; she must also see that these are fun for both of them"[7]

But what did the permissive, self-scheduling ethic of the day mean for the caregiver herself? Now that the infant was to dictate its demands to its mother, her routine was to be determined by those requirements. As one student of child-care literature has pointed out: "Self-demand, especially when the baby is breastfed or when it is believed that close contact between the mother and the child at feeding time is important, means that all other activities must be adapted to the child's rhythm and makes it almost impossible to get away from home." Dr. Ribble, who recommended that infants be breastfed every three hours until they were three months old, warned that a mother must "function for her infant for many months because it is not until after the faculties of speech and locomotion have developed that he can cope with *any* separation from the mother without danger."[8] Writers also counseled the mother to strictly limit her outside activities during this period so as not to "miss" her child's saying a new word or tying its shoelaces for the first time. Giving the child plenty of freedom to explore the world necessarily entailed patience and labor in cleaning up the endless messes that resulted. All this, of course, meant that women could not work outside the home if they wanted to rear healthy offspring. The good mother of the Spockean era gave her children her undivided attention.

Spock was not alone in advising that only full-time mothering was sufficient for a child's proper development. The Briton, John Bowlby, best known for his studies of maternal deprivation in children, argued that an infant and child's experience of a "warm, intimate, and continuous relationship with his mother [is] essential for mental health." The lack of such an experience, in fact, is how Bowlby defined maternal deprivation. Moreover, Bowlby quite literally meant full-time care: "The provision of constant attention night and day, seven days a week and 365 days a year, is possible only for a woman who derives profound satisfaction" from seeing her child grow into adulthood.[9] Mothers now were not only supposed to be in constant attendance on their children, but also to derive "profound satisfaction" from these duties.

Not only good physical care was required. Spock and other writers superimposed "an emotional workday on the mother's physical workday." Mother must always be mindful of her own behavior so as to insure a propitious environment for her children's development. She must walk a fine line between too much and too little attention—although during the permissive era too much was better than too little. Sociologist Philip Slater has pointed out just how labor-intensive and all-consuming the maternal role was supposed to be during those years. He paraphrases Dr. Spock's advice to mothers: "You have the capacity to rear a masterpiece. Such an activity is the most important thing you can do and should therefore rightfully absorb all your time and energy."[10]

The ideal mother of the postwar decades was completely fulfilled by carrying out all the minute and often tedious tasks of child care, fulfillment that came naturally from her maternal instinct. "Womanly women," wrote Dr. Ribble, "will get unique mental stimulus . . . from contact with the first principles of life." Such a woman was alert to all the nuances of her children's behavior. To stimulate their intellectual growth she spent hours engaging in baby talk, playing games, and generally reducing herself to an infantile level. Moreover, she had few or no interests outside her home. In the words of one scholar: "The mother of Dr. Spock's manual is an apolitical person without any social involvements. . . . She exists largely to rear her young and has time off to pursue a few private activities."[11]

While Dr. Spock admitted that the demands of motherhood were sometimes trying, he advised mothers who got depressed to "go to a movie or to the beauty parlor, or to get yourself a new hat or dress." But employment was never a solution to maternal boredom or depression:

> . . . useful, well adjusted citizens are the most valuable possessions a country has, and good mother care during early childhood is the surest way to produce them. . . . If a mother realizes clearly how vital this kind of care is to a small child, it may make it easier for her to decide that the extra money she might earn, or the satisfaction she might receive from an outside job, is not so important after all.

This advice makes plain that the tenets of permissivism did not extend to mothers. The authors of a history of experts' advice to women have acidly commented that "by some curious asymmetry in the permissive ideology, everyone in the family lived for themselves, but [the mother] lived for *them*. This contradiction was supposedly resolved with the psychoanalytic notion that women *enjoyed* self-denial, that they were basically masochistic by nature."[12]

The idealized image of the mother-child unit of the Spockean school contended with a strong countercurrent in the popular literature of the same period. During the late 1940s and 1950s psychoanalysts and their popularizers discovered that the mother-child relationship was often pathological; its symptoms were problem children and problem adults. To be sure, this line of thinking was not entirely new. The "damned if you do and damned if you don't" message is found in the prescriptive writings as far back as the nineteenth century, but it reached new peaks of vitriol during the postwar years.

The frightening specters of "Momism," maternal overprotection, and maternal neurosis were first raised in Philip Wylie's best-seller, *Generation of Vipers*, published in 1942. "Megaloid momworship has got completely out of hand," he proclaimed. "Our land, subjectively mapped, would have more silver cords and apron strings crisscrossing it than railroads and telephone wires." Wylie seemed to open the floodgates to over a decade of stinging attacks on mothers. Dr. David Levy followed this lead and in 1943 published *Maternal Overprotection*. Based on a "sample" of twenty women and their children, Levy concluded that overprotective mothers were of two types: they were either (1) submissive or (2) domineering and produced children who were either (1) selfish, demanding, and undisciplined or (2) docile, goody-goodies. The conclusions of the study are a marvel of scientific obfuscation since Levy said he found no common behavior patterns in either the mothers or the children in his sample, the data on which his conclusions were based. Perhaps he didn't need to *prove* what he *knew* was there.[13]

Levy's study was followed three years later by another attack on mothers, this one by psychiatrist Edward Strecker, who wanted to account for the thousands of "casualties" he saw in the neuropsychiatric wards of the army and navy hospitals in which he worked during the war. Why, he asked, were so many men complaining of vague headaches and backaches, of "plain tiredness" and other symptoms that had no physical basis? His answer in a word, was immaturity. And its causes? Moms, of course, but specifically those women who derived "emotional satisfaction, simple repletion" from keeping their children "paddling about in a kind of psychological amniotic fluid rather than letting them swim away with the bold and decisive strokes of maturity from the emotional maternal womb." According to Strecker, mothers were responsible not only for their children's problems but for a variety of social ills. "The effects of Mom and her activities," Strecker wrote, "goes far beyond the single individual that she dominates in childhood. Her effect is cumulative and far reaching." Anthropologist Geoffrey Gorer has noted just how devastating Moms could be: "According to [Strecker], Mom, the clinging possessive mother, not only causes psychoneurosis, she is the main cause of every unpleasant phenomenon from schizophrenia, through lynching to National Socialism and Japanese Emperor Worship!"[14]

It is not clear what part of this vogue was simple psychological reductionism and what part was pure mother blame. Nevertheless, some of the child-rearing manuals of the day harped on similar themes. Dr. Kanner, who defended mothers from the advice of the "experts," still cautioned against the dangers of "smother love." It is, he wrote, "the most egotistically selfish thing on earth. It is a caricature of mother love. . . . Its aim is domination . . . and it forges chains. While some children miraculously survive the smothering, others are crushed by it." The authors of the 1944 manual *It's a Wise Parent* warned against excessive maternal attention: "We all know women," they wrote, "who fancy themselves as sacrificing everything for their children. They are impossible as parents or anything else."[15]

And so in the 1950s middle class women were still being admonished about the dire consequences of too little or too much mother love. Women who lost their temper at the antics of their toddlers or left them to cry were accused of rejecting the child and inflicting untold psychological damage. Women who at one time or another felt hostile or aggressive toward their children were not simply making them neurotic; they were destroying them.

Family sociologist E. E. LeMasters tried to analyze these widespread attacks on mothers. He claimed that the attacks were related to the emancipation of women that began during World War I and reached its zenith by World War II when "the American mother had become the bad guy in our family system." He explained the source of anger: "When any group of human beings in a society battles its way out of an inferior social position, hostility is always generated." He went on to suggest that it was quite possible "that American mothers achieved more equality than they wanted." What they had in mind was a "50—50 partnership" that "turned out to be closer to 70—30 or even 80—20, with the American father having all the fun with the children and the mother all of the headaches." LeMaster's analysis, however, implies that the mother's near total responsibility for her children was a recent phenomenon, which was not the case. I suggest that whatever problems might have arisen because of smother love were related to the hothouse isolation of the home in which American women and children found themselves confined during the first half of the twentieth century. As Barbara Ehrenreich and Deidre English have pointedly noted: "It did not enter the experts' minds to question the theory [locking mother and child together exclusively] or to be alarmed at the terrible solitude in which most women were attempting to raise their children; the theory was solid; the home was sacred; it was the women who had failed."[16]

The child-care manuals of the 1940s and 1950s disagreed on how much time and energy fathers should devote to their children, but the paternal role was invariably depicted as a mere shadow of the maternal one. Because the father is busy with his job and sees his infant so irregularly—and irregularity is disturbing to a young child—"it is often best if the father doesn't come into the child's routine until after the third month," Dr. Ribble recommended. Then he and other family members can briefly visit the baby in the morning and evening. After all, said Ribble, "one mother is really enough—provided she really mothers." Dr. Ribble described fathers as the "powers behind the mother's throne"; they lent her emotional support but did little in the way of actual child care. The author of the *Parent's Manual*, published in 1941, disagreed with this restricted notion of fatherhood: "Children need fathers as well as mothers and they need them from the earliest years." Although the mother has "the major responsibility for physical care and routine management," the father and child will get to know each other better if the father occasionally changes a diaper or supervises a meal—"even the youngest child, if given the chance, will develop a [special] feeling for his father." Then the author revealed the bogeyman behind her recommendations and issued a stern warning to parents: if all control of children falls to the mother, there is the danger that children will "grow up believing that women are born to be the world's real bosses; such a belief tends to breed passive men and aggressive women."[17]

Dr. Bowlby agreed with Dr. Ribble that fathers were shadowy figures behind the maternal throne. "In the young child's eyes father is second fiddle," Bowlby explained. Nevertheless, he termed fathers "useful" even during infancy. As breadwinners, they enabled their wives "to devote themselves unrestrictedly to the care of infant and toddler" and they also provided "love and companionship" to the mother so that she could maintain the "harmonious contented mood in which her infant thrives."[18]

While Dr. Spock addressed his *Baby and Child Care* to "loving parents," all of the advice is actually directed to mothers; only a handful of paragraphs in the 600-page volume are addressed to fathers. Moreover, it is clear that not too much help should be expected from men in daily child-care tasks. While it's "fine" for fathers "occasionally" to give a bottle or change diapers, "there are some fathers who get gooseflesh at the very idea of helping to care for a baby, and there's no good to be gained from trying to force them [since] most of them come around to enjoying their children later when they're more like real people." In one of the few passages meant for fathers, Dr. Spock instructed them on their role in inculcating sex-appropriate behavior. A daughter "gains confidence in herself as a girl and a woman from feeling his approval." But how can fathers accomplish this? "I'm thinking of the little things he can do, like complimenting her on her dress, or hairdo, or the cookies she's made." Dr. David Goodman offered similar advice. Children need fathers, Goodman wrote. Not only providers but "nice human fathers, cheerful and relaxed." Such fathers "do the things that only a man can do for their [children's] upbringing—like teaching little David how to bat a ball or giving Patricia a cavalier's attention when she's wearing a new frock with which she hopes to wow the boys."[19]

A facetious article in a 1954 issue of *Parent's Magazine* entitled "The Care and Feeding of Spock-marked Fathers" complained of the absence of fathers in Dr. Spock's famous manual and suggested that the doctor should have included a chapter on "the care of husbands." The author's point was that fathers were so excluded from Spock's idyllic mother-child unit that women should make it up to their husbands by applying Spock's advice on the rearing of older children. "The arrival of the baby," quipped the author, "should change a husband's life as little as possible, especially if he's been the only husband up to that time."[20]

During the 1950s some writers suggested that Dad should try to undo some of the damage inflicted by Mom. Fathers were said to be especially important as masculine role models for their sons. But the advice givers insisted that fathers engage in appropriate male behavior in order to serve this purpose; they certainly should not be seen doing the dishes, cooking, or pursuing other feminine activities. Fathers were also counseled that their other major parenting function was to keep Mom sexually satisfied so that she would not vent her frustrations on the kids. In the chapter "Live Your Gender!" Dr. Goodman wrote that "the American mother married to a business-bound husband lives her whole life in her children" with the result that she "smothers them with excessive care, affection, and protectiveness." Goodman's solution to this unhappy state of affairs: "If the American mother enjoyed the companionship of a romantic-minded husband, she might be more willing to let her children alone. . . . The truly feminine mother, fulfilled in her marriage to a truly masculine father, does not overprotect, dominate, or over-fondle her children."[21]

Late in the decade Margaret Mead expressed concern that men might be spending too much time fathering to the detriment of their careers. In her article "The Job of the Children's Mother's Husband" she noted that for the first time the male "elite . . . the statesmen, the financiers and entrepreneurs . . . are helping their servantless wives take care of little children." She had mixed feelings about such a turn of events:

> We have known for a long time that being a mother of several children was a full-time job and definitely interfered with a woman's career. Now it looks as if we are turning being a father into a full-time job too, with all a man's best energies going into the home, and too little left over for work outside.

Mead saw the increase in fathering as a postwar phenomenon and argued that the change was too recent to predict the effects. She specifically wondered what impact more fathering was going to have on the socialization of boys.[22]

If Mead saw a larger role for fathers during the permissive era, that novelty certainly was not evident in studies done by a number of contemporary scholars. The well-known 1957 study *Patterns of Child Rearing*, for example, sought "to secure reliable information about the varieties of experience that American children have had in their homes with their parents by the time they go to school." The authors interviewed 379 mothers but *not a single father*. A year later *The Changing American Parent* was published. These findings too were based on interviews exclusively with mothers, this time 582 women. Perhaps biases like these led British anthropologist Geoffrey Gorer to conclude in his study *The American People* that "in few societies is the role of the father more vestigial than in the United States."[23]

The prescriptive literature on the maternal role during the 1940s and 1950s appears to be at odds with its setting. It is not surprising that the continued emphasis on full-time motherhood coincided with a sharp increase in the birthrate following World War II, but at the same time, both during and after the war, married women entered the labor force in increasing numbers. How can we explain the apparent contradiction between the number of married women—including mothers—in the work place and the experts' relentless insistence that their only career was motherhood?

Between 1936 and 1940 the birthrate slowly began to revive from its depression era low. The momentum picked up during the war and culminated in the well-known "baby boom" of the postwar years. By 1960 the fertility rate of white women was almost as high as it had been at the end of the nineteenth century when women were averaging between three and four children each. The relationship between women's employment and their fertility rate is not fully understood, for although women in the labor force tend to have fewer children than those who are not, the correlation is by no means perfect. Witness events during World War II when large numbers of women took jobs but the birthrate continued to climb.[24]

Women's labor force participation zoomed by 32 percent during the war years. Most important for this discussion, 75 percent of the new war workers were married and one-third of them had children under fourteen years of age. Yet while various government agencies were urging women to participate in the war effort by taking jobs, the agencies emphasized the temporary status of women workers. One job manual for women workers during the war included this statement: "The mother stands at the heart of family life. She it is who will create the world after the war."[25]

During the 1950s, when a woman's desire for a career was seen as a disguised search for masculine identity, married middle class women continued to take jobs in large numbers. Between 1950 and 1960 more than four million married women entered the labor force, and many of these women were mothers as well as wives. In 1950, 22 percent of all women with children held jobs, and by the end of the decade the number of working mothers had increased by 400 percent over the 1940 figure.

The 1950s was a decade when many married women must have suffered from cognitive dissonance. While they were entering the labor force in record numbers, child-care experts and the popular media were lambasting working mothers and were extolling the "feminine mystique." A married woman only has two jobs, proclaimed Dr. Goodman, "one to care for her children, the other to keep a man happy." Agnes Meyer's comment in a 1955 *Ladies' Home Journal* article "Children in Trouble" is typical of the condemnation that greeted working mothers of the day: "I find that the upper income bracket child whose mother works because she wants more money, or because she considers it more 'stimulating,' often hates her with a frenzy that he doesn't understand because he feels that his mother prefers this thing called a job to him."[26]

This seeming anomaly between behavior and ideology may be partly explained by the age of women workers. During the 1950s the largest group of women entering the labor force were over forty-five years old. Most younger wives were still at home having three or four babies while their older counterparts were taking jobs. The child-care experts were recommending just this. Spock, for example, agreed that after a five- or six-year break when their children were small, mothers could return to work, as long as they were home when the children got home from school. But in an era when a woman typically had three or four children, this would mean a minimum of eight to ten years until the youngest child was in school. Only then could a mother feel free to take a part-time job without guilt.[27]

The experts' directives were clear and simple: women were to enter and withdraw from the job market in accordance with the family life cycle; part-time work was preferable to full-time employment; and under no circumstances should the demands of a career interfere with a woman's primary responsibility to her children. This advice conformed to the postwar economy's demand for particular types of female labor. Because of the growth of the service sector, large numbers of women were needed to work in offices, in retail stores, and in banks. These positions were often part-time or temporary, so they did not require the steady work commitment associated with pursuit of a career. In addition, one of the main features of these "female-typed" jobs was that they required little or no on-the-job training: women could take them and leave them at small cost to their employers (see chapter 6). The experts were saying, at least indirectly, that women should be content with the low-paying, low-status, part-time and temporary jobs available to them, for such employment did not conflict with "good mothering."

The Modern Mother's Dilemma, a popular 25-cent public affairs pamphlet of the mid-1950s, is an excellent illustration of the neat mesh between the experts' advice and the types of jobs for which middle class women were in demand during this period. The authors of the pamphlet explain that the dilemma was that women "have begun to wonder whether marriage and motherhood are all consuming." Yet mothers are guilt-ridden "if they long to get out of the house once in a while and work with other adults"—they are made to feel that they are "unconsciously rejecting their children." While the authors' bias is evident in the statement "it is ludicrous even to compare the rewards one gets from work or hobbies with the deep and rich rewards, the ever-new delight one's children give!" they nevertheless concede that the "either-or choice between family and career is unrealistic because it is unwholesome for a child to have his mother constantly and completely wrapped up in . . . his every move and reaction." Thus, both for her children's and her husband's sake, the pamphlet urges the modern mother to "develop more than the housewifely and maternal side of her nature."[28]

The pamphlet explains that the dilemma itself stems from the early age at which women complete raising a family. As a result, the authors continue, "today's older mothers and young grandmothers find themselves out of a job." A woman's life "typically falls into several distinct phases" and the situation of the mother with young children is very different from that of the forty-five-year-old woman whose children are grown.[29]

In order to prepare a mother for the day she will be out of a job, the authors advise the mother of small children to keep her hand in any field of interest she may have had before marriage by reading, going to concerts, subscribing to technical journals, or sewing her children's clothes. The authors also give examples of some of the strategies used by women to keep abreast of their particular field of interest. One woman who wanted to teach when her children were grown went to school one night a week while her children were still toddlers to earn credits for a teaching certificate. When her youngsters were in school from nine to three, she took a full load of courses toward her degree. A woman who had been a librarian before marriage served as a volunteer for the school library two days a week and eventually began writing children's books "in her spare time." "Part-time work is the ideal solution" for women with school age children, the authors of the pamphlet noted. They suggested jobs such as file clerk, receptionist, bookkeeper, typist, doctor's aide, and lab technician—all low-paying female ghettos—as fields in which part-time employment might be secured.[30]

These recommendations for dealing with the "mother's dilemma" were reinforced by the authors' depiction of the paternal role. "Fathers get to know children earlier these days since they lend a helping hand," and families benefit by becoming closer as a result of the father's greater participation. But then a stern caveat was issued: "Let it not be forgotten that Father is still the breadwinner" even when the wife works, because "his is the chief and continuous responsibility." While father can mind the children while mother cooks dinner, "the thing for Mother to bear in mind is that her husband can't be asked to take over too much. It is more than unfair to expect him to do half the housework as well as carry the load of a full-time job; it prevents him from doing his best work and keeps him from enjoying his home as he should."[31]

As more and more married women took jobs, the experts approved their actions under certain circumstances. Women could work part-time or after their children were grown, but their wage-earning activities were to fit in with and never take precedence over their primary responsibilities as mothers. By the 1960s, however, the reality of many women's lives had begun to challenge such advice.

Time for a Change: The 1960s

> *Life in America is made up of a tissue of fictions that do not accord with reality, and the omnipresent "Mommie" is one of them that could be very well dispensed with.*
>
> Alicia Patterson
> Address to the Radcliffe Alumnae Association, 1961

The experts' advice and their vision of the mother role began a transition in the 1960s. That decade paralleled the period at the turn of the nineteenth century when prescriptive writers began redrawing the image of motherhood as a result of industrialization. The increasing rate of maternal employment in the sixties eventually led to a recasting of the roles of middle class women, including their responsibilities to their children. But the decade itself was characterized by a disjunction between what most of the experts were saying and what growing numbers of middle class women were doing. This contradiction between ideology and reality—the leitmotif of the era—was not resolved until the 1970s when feminists and experts alike called for a reappraisal of all the old shibboleths about motherhood.

I call the 1960s transitional because of the mixed nature of advice in prescriptive writings. On the one hand, Dr. Spock cited the need for full-time mother care (the dictum appeared unchanged in the revised 1968 edition of *Baby and Child Care*). Writers also continued to express concern about the "toxic effect" of mother love. But on the other hand, a number of experts began noting the problems created for women themselves by the exclusive mother-child dyad. Researchers also began to accumulate evidence showing that maternal employment did not have the deleterious effects on children that were once supposed.

If Dr. Spock was tardy in changing his views on the incompatibility of motherhood and jobs, other experts did try to come to terms with maternal employment. "The children of women who are doing interesting work of their own during the day will often find more sensible and sympathetic mothers," psychiatrist Bruno Bettelheim wrote in a 1962 issue of *Harper's Magazine*. Focusing on the "problems of growing up female," Bettelheim suggested that "the mother who urges her girl toward intellectual achievement while staying at home herself poses a contradiction which probably is not lost on the girl."[32]

An interesting work of the era is Edith De Rham's *The Love Fraud*. De Rham made the revolutionary suggestion that the solution to the "parasitic relationship" between mothers and their children just might be maternal employment:

> If we may assume that the average adult will normally prefer to spend the majority of his or her time in the company of other adults, we may further deduce that the psychological interdependence of mother and child threatens to change the mother's personality in at least two ways: at best she will become childlike herself; at worst she will be transformed into the despised and voracious MOM.

Courtesy of Michael Kappy, M.D.

Mother Breastfeeding Child • *By the late 1960s, some child care experts no longer insisted that an exclusive mother-child relationship was essential to children's well-being.*

In order to avoid the emergence of this dangerous character, the author also called for a greater role for fathers in child care. "Without a doubt," she wrote, "a totally balanced, heterosexual approach to parenthood is vastly superior to the matriarchal system imposed *force majeure* on children today."[33]

While De Rham suggested jobs as cures for "Moms," psychoanalyst René Spitz continued the hallowed tradition of blaming mothers for a variety of psychosocial disorders. In his 1965 work *The First Year of Life*, he set about identifying the "psycho-toxic diseases of infancy." It was no surprise to anyone schooled in mother blame that Spitz found every mental and physical problem of childhood to have roots in a maternal disorder. Such a physiologically common disturbance as colic, for example, was said to be caused by the mother's "primary anxious over-permissiveness."[34]

Other writers of the decade began focusing on the paternal role. The 1963 edition of the popular government pamphlet *Infant Care* suggested that "wise mothers" let fathers share in the routines of baby care from the beginning. While "some fathers take over certain aspects of care regularly . . . others are more comfortable helping with household chores, thereby freeing the mother from these. But, whichever suits, the father is part of the picture." These phrases are absent from the earlier editions of the pamphlet. Dr. Ribble's revised 1965 edition of *Rights of Infants* eliminated the passages suggesting that fathers should not have regular contact with their infants until they were three months old. "That her husband is capable and interested in assuming his father role *from the start in this joint venture* assures a more successful outcome." But the old bugaboo of "smother love" was still heard. The reason why father's participation in child care "contributes immeasurably to the child's well-being is because it lessens considerably the chance of an exaggerated mother attachment." Even more significant is the change in the following sentence about a baby's needs. The 1943 edition read: " . . . his deepest need by far is the understanding care of one consistent individual—his mother." The 1965 edition was changed to "his deepest need is the understanding and consistent care of his parents." The pediatrician Haim Ginott represented the traditional approach. In 1965 he was still warning parents that fathers should not become too involved in diapering and feeding their babies because "there is the danger that the baby may end up with two mothers."[35] Ginott, notwithstanding, a subtle change in the nature and scope of the father role had taken place, a change that foreshadowed the decade to come.

A low-key but steady accumulation of psychological research in the early and mid-sixties began to question the widely held assumption that working mothers inevitably damaged their children. In a comprehensive study entitled *The Working Mother in America*, published in 1963, the authors concluded that maternal employment per se was neither an index of maternal deprivation nor the profound influence on children's development that had once been supposed. The study even suggested that maternal employment just might have a positive effect; the children of working mothers were found to be more independent than those of women who did not hold jobs.[36]

Some advice givers of the day seem to have been of two minds about working mothers. "Today many women are as deeply and successfully in business and professional duties as are men," Dr. Ribble wrote in the revised edition of her book. "Yet both can be adequate parents if they put thought, understanding and planning to work." These lines are absent from the 1943 edition. But in the following paragraph of the 1965 edition of her manual she once again made a clear distinction between the two parental roles:

> Perhaps with our new psychological insights into the dynamics of a child's mental growth, the meaning of motherhood and fatherhood may assume its rightful dignity, interest, and joy, and *the temporary withdrawal from a career for a woman* in order to create and nurture a new life may not be regarded as demeaning or as an unwanted . . . sacrifice.

Others were phrasing the issue differently: "If . . . one is to be plagued by the question 'Are working women good mothers?' one cannot help wondering in addition, 'Are working men good fathers?' "[37]

The entire notion that an exclusive mother-child relationship is essential for a child's proper development soon came under challenge. In a 1962 article Margaret Mead wrote that John Bowlby's influential work on the ill effects of maternal deprivation "was based on a mixed and unexamined set of premises." She was referring to Bowlby's insistence that there is a "biologically given need for continuity" in the mother-child relationship, that this relationship "cannot be safely distributed among several figures," and that "all interruptions in it are necessarily harmful . . . emotionally damaging, if not completely lethal." Mead pointed out the ethnocentrism implicit in Bowlby's assumptions: "Actually, such an exclusive and continuous relationship is only possible under highly artificial urban conditions, which combine the production of food outside the home with the practice of contraception." Bruno Bettelheim seemed to agree with Mead's cross-cultural perspective when he suggested that one way of resolving the conflict between women's employment and child care was to adopt "the system found in some other societies where women work—that is, entrusting part of infant care to older children or . . . relatives" or making arrangements for entrusting young children "to the care of well-qualified professional people, at least for part of the time."[38]

By the mid-1960s there were tentative suggestions that motherhood was not the only glory in a woman's life and that it was ludicrous, given economic realities, to continue to insist that the maternal role be all consuming. Probably the strongest statement came with the 1963 publication of Betty Friedan's *The Feminine Mystique.* Friedan wrote that a woman "must think of herself as a human being first." She must "make a life plan in terms of her own abilities, a commitment of her own to society, with which her commitments as wife and mother can be integrated." In 1965 sociologist Alice Rossi called for a new view of motherhood as an "important highlight but not as the exclusive basis for a sense of self-fulfillment and purpose in life."[39] To be sure, women in the nascent feminist movement were most often the first to propose a revamped mother role, but it was not long before motherhood also began to be depicted in a new light in the writings of both the popular and professional child-care experts.

Fathers Are Parents Too: The 1970s

> *I always assumed that the parent taking the greater share of young children . . . would be the mother, whether or not she wanted an outside career. . . . Now I realize that the father's responsibility is as great as the mother's.*
>
> Benjamin Spock
> *Baby and Child Care,* 1976 rev. ed.

> *There is nothing to indicate any biological need for an exclusive primary bond; nothing to suggest that mothering cannot be shared by several people.*
>
> Rudolph Schaffer, *Mothering,* 1977

"Do babies need mothers?" Harvard psychologist Rudolph Schaffer asked in the last chapter of his book on mothering. "Yes," he replied, "if it means that they need to be involved in a love relationship and that a limited range of familiar people should provide consistent care throughout the years of childhood. No—if it means that the mother must be the one who gave birth, that no other person can take her place. No again—if we take mothering to involve an exclusive relationship that must encapsulate the child's total social and emotional life."[40]

Statements like these became common during the 1970s as experts began questioning the assumptions that were the basis for much of the earlier advice on the mother role. Where were the data, they asked, that showed the mother to be biologically the most capable person for socializing infants and young children? Where was the evidence that infants seek out and bond only with their mothers rather than their fathers or other familiar persons? "Is the capacity to feel 'maternal' emotions and behave in a 'motherly' way restricted to females?" they queried. And finally, is an exclusive mother-infant arrangement beneficial for either woman or child?[41]

"Mother," insisted Schaffer, "*can be any person of either sex.*" A child becomes attached to the individual who is sensitive, responsive, and emotionally involved. It is these qualities of personality, not kinship or sex per se, that are important in developing bonds. Moreover, the authors of a volume on child development noted that evidence from a number of studies suggested that "fathers can develop the kinds of strong bonds with infants traditionally reserved for mothers," showing that " 'the mothering instinct' is not embedded in the bodies and souls of females alone." Newborns show no consistent preference for one parent or the other. It is the person who holds, feeds, and stimulates the baby "to whom initial attachments are made." Citing this data, Schaffer claimed that there is "no reason why the mothering role should not be filled as competently by males as by females." The father's relative lack of involvement in child care, he concluded, "is a cultural rather than a biological phenomenon."[42]

Criticism of the earlier work on mother-child attachment increased as a result of these findings. Writers suggested, for example, that the studies of René Spitz and John Bowlby were not based on "normal" separation of infants from their parents but on children institutionalized in hospitals and orphanages, "children who often suffered from inadequate environmental and human stimulation" and from poor and inconsistent care. One critic of Spitz and Bowlby accused them of being "dangerously unscientific" in extrapolating data based on institutionalized infants to "the much more common situation in which infants leave their homes for part of the day, are cared for by other responsible individuals, and are returned again to their homes."[43]

Bowlby's assertion that a child is initially unable to form attachments to more than one person—"his ever present mother"—also was called into question. "An infant is not confined to just one bond," Schaffer wrote. "Once he has reached the stage of forming specific attachments, he is capable of maintaining a number at the same time." Harvard psychologist Jerome Kagan agreed: The notion that a child can form only a single attachment is "like saying a person can only love one other person. And that's nonsense." Studies have shown that infants can have multiple attachments that include older siblings, grandparents, and especially fathers. Nor does attachment to several people imply less depth of feeling: "Love, even in babies, has no limits," Schaffer noted. In response, Bowlby himself now claims that his theories of mother-child attachment have been misinterpreted. In a 1974 letter to the *London Times* he wrote that "the tie to be taken into account" in deciding child placement "is always the tie to the *mother figure*, something entirely distinct from the now discredited blood tie."[44]

In *The Reproduction of Mothering* Nancy Chodorow pointed out the confusion between "the necessity of exclusive mother-infant arrangements with the scientific evidence showing the need for high quality *continuity* in child care by a person or a few people." Today, most experts agree that what is important to the development of infants and children is consistent, sensitive care by an adult or adults in an environment of love, affection, and stimulation. This is certainly a far cry from the traditional dogma that it was the mother alone who could provide such care.[45]

Mother blame was also muted during the 1970s. Recent studies have taken mothers off the hook on which they have long been impaled, a hook that held them responsible for a wide variety of ills in their children ranging from schizophrenia to autism and hyperactivity. "Mothers simply do not deserve all the blame—or all the credit—for what their children become," two child development experts insisted in a 1978 volume. The mother was no longer to be seen as "standing alone, bestriding her children like some giant psychological colossus." Where mother blame was still heard, it was usually linked to structural conditions, that is, to the hothouse isolation of the exclusive mother-child relationship rather than to any general failing of mothers themselves. It is the "height of vanity to assume that an unformed child could tolerate such massive inputs of one person's personality," wrote sociologist Philip Slater, continuing:

> In most societies the impact of the mother's character defects is diluted by the presence of many other nurturing agents. In middle class America the mother . . . tends to be the exclusive daytime adult contact of the child. . . . This means that every maternal quirk, every maternal hangup and every maternal deprivation is experienced by the child as heavily amplified noise from which there is no escape.[46]

The reversal of views on the mother role was most dramatic on the question of maternal employment. Nearly in unison, social scientists and authors of child-care manuals alike began to advise mothers that taking a job did not have the detrimental effect on children that it was once believed to have—so long as high quality substitute care was available. After a thorough review of the literature on the impact of maternal employment, social psychologist Helen Bee concluded that "when the mother is satisfied by her role and adequate alternative care is arranged, the separation of the mother from her child that accompanies maternal employment has no demonstrable negative effect." The authors of a child development book concurred, noting that "if a mother is happy in what she is doing, then it does not really matter—from the standpoint of how well she brings up her children—whether she chooses to be a homemaker or a worker outside." But what about infants and very young children? Doesn't the child's age when the mother leaves the home to work make a difference? "*Probably not*," replied these same authors, "assuming there is adequate and stable substitute care." Harvard pediatrician Mary Howell agreed that "substitute care while mothers are at work need not be harmful to infants, if given by loving and attentive adults."[47]

Writers now suggest that there may even be some positive effects of maternal employment. Some studies have found that children of working mothers are more self-reliant and less anxious than those whose mothers are home all the time. Moreover, the only long-term effect seems to be that by college age the children of employed women have less stereotyped views of sex roles than those of women who have not held jobs. When the children of working mothers do have development problems, "they seem to be associated more with family instability or inadequate care [when the mother is gone] than with working per se."[48]

Nothing is more symbolic of the experts' changed attitude on maternal employment than Dr. Spock's 1976 deletion of his discussion "The Working Mother," which had appeared in all earlier editions of *Baby and Child Care* in the section "Special Problems." An entirely new chapter, "The Family Is Changing," included sections on how outside work might improve parents, on both parents' rights to outside careers, and on qualities to look for in a parent substitute. Moreover, Spock was very forceful in his new-found feminism. "Parents who know they need a career or a certain kind of work for fulfillment," he wrote, "should not simply give it up for their children." He suggested that such parents "work out some kind of compromise between their two jobs and the needs of their children, usually with the help of other caregivers."[49]

Books and regular magazine columns on working mothers proliferated during the 1970s. Many sought to reassure women that maternal employment was all right. "Good workers are good mothers and vice versa," the author of the 1972 volume *The Working Mother* wrote, for "the very qualities which make good workers are those which make good mothers." A popular pamphlet published by the Child Study Association in 1975, *The Mother Who Works Outside the Home*, told working mothers that "guilt doesn't have to go with the territory. Working mothers have to remember that they are people themselves, with legitimate needs, and that when these needs are met, they function better as wives and mothers." Letty Cottin Pogrebin advised readers in a 1974 *Ladies' Home Journal* article that her interviews with children of working mothers revealed that children did not resent their mother's jobs and did not feel envious of kids with mothers at home.[50]

The new ideas on mothers who work cannot be discussed apart from the new ideas on the effects of day care on infants and young children. Studies conducted during the 1970s found no differences in mother-child attachment between infants reared at home exclusively by their mothers and those who spent time in child-care centers. Some former critics of day care withdrew their opposition to it. Harvard professor

Jerome Kagan, head of a five-year study of the effects of day care on children, noted that he once wrote two articles on its purported evils. "Now I run a day-care center," he said in an interview, "and I changed my mind. All of us have strong prejudices that are religious in intensity but not always based on *fact*." Pediatrician T. Berry Brazelton no longer sees day care as "taking the child away from the family, but as a way of helping the family through choices, of keeping the family together, and keeping the mother caring about the child." Finally, as Nancy Chodorow has pointed out, child care with a few adults caring for a few children—as in good day-care centers—has a longer historical and cross-cultural tradition than the exclusive mother-child arrangement.[51]

Changing views of the mother role and of the effects of day care were accompanied during the 1970s by a surge in research on the father role. This new interest in fatherhood is found in both scholarly studies and in popular child-rearing literature. My survey of the *Cumulative Book Index* for the years 1950–1979 clearly indicates this trend. During the 1950s ten books were published on the subject of fathering and fatherhood; during the 1960s eighteen books, and from 1970 through 1979 fifty books. Just how few studies had been done on fathers and young children prior to 1970 can be gauged from the remarks of Milton Kotelchuck, a doctoral candidate at Harvard who did the first laboratory observations of father-child interactions. So little research had been done on the topic, he said, that it took him but "a half hour to review all the literature"—and he read "the full articles, not the abstracts!" Similarly, in a survey of 444 papers on family research published between 1963 and 1968, only eleven contained data on fathers and husbands.[52]

Prior to the early seventies not only was there a dearth of research on the paternal role but what little research there was usually dealt with father absence and the resulting lack of a male role model in the home. "Most of what we know about the impact of fathers," wrote social psychologist Helen Bee in 1974, "comes from studies of *absent* fathers." And studies of such fathers certainly "do not tell us much about the positive effects of fathers' presence." Moreover, father absence was defined in a limited way. It meant the lack of a father because of death, divorce, or abandonment, but it did not apply to fathers who were away all day and who worked overtime and on weekends. Even when researchers attempted to measure the impact of fathers on child development, they often assumed it "normal for men *not* to interact with their children."[53]

This limited view of the father's role and influence has been supplanted over the last decade by growing interest in father-child interactions and research on the impact of fathers on their children's development. An added benefit of this research has been the revision of some long held notions about the mother role. One of the first such studies was Milton Kotelchuck's on the nature of a father's ties to his children. In an attempt to disprove the theory that "the attachment between mothers and infants was unique or biologically built in," he set up a laboratory experiment to measure the reactions of young children to the presence of strangers. Why this approach? Because, Kotelchuck said, "the work done on attachment between children and mothers always ranges mothers against strangers. Then, of course, the attachment between child and parent is clearly unique." "But what about *other* familiar persons?" he wanted to know. "What about fathers?" Kotelchuck found that "infants respond similarly to mothers and fathers," that is, "they will protest the departure of either parent, but not the departure of a stranger." They clearly missed their fathers as well as their mothers when they left the room. Kotelchuck summarized the significance of his findings: "It becomes clearer and clearer that when another familiar person like the father is introduced into a setting, the presumed uniqueness of the mother-child relationship seems to disappear. . . . it becomes obvious that fathers are indeed important to their infants."[54]

Not only do babies need and miss their fathers, but fathers need and miss their babies if they are allowed to have physical contact with them soon after birth. In a study of "engrossment," that is, "a feeling of preoccupation, absorption, and interest in their newborn," fathers who were permitted such contact did become engrossed in their infants. The authors of the study believe all fathers have the "basic, innate potential" for the development of this phenomenon that "may have important ramifications in the subsequent . . . mental health of the child." Practices that inhibit this early contact, however, may lead to "paternal deprivation" since potential engrossment may fail to occur.[55]

One study of primate behavior suggested that "perhaps fathers, when given the chance, could be just as successful as mothers are at raising healthy infants." In this study, reported in a 1974 issue of *Psychology*

Today, the researchers took a one-month-old rhesus monkey away from its mother and gave it to a male "surrogate mother" named Mellow. They described what followed: "The attachment between the two became so strong that when we separated them for two days, at the end of seven months, Mellow raged and bit himself so severely that he cut several major blood vessels in his leg." The baby rhesus in turn regressed in behavior and gave many distress signals. The two were then brought back together and the baby monkey has shown "entirely normal physical and social development." The researchers comment on their experiment:

> Our research has uncovered a substantial potential for nurturant parental care in as relatively inflexible a creature as the male rhesus monkey. . . . If [such monkeys], characterized as indifferent or even hostile to infants in the wild, can become intimately attached to them in the laboratory, what might this augur for man? The biological basis for assigning social roles comes into question.[56]

As a result of these and other similar findings the experts have begun to acknowledge the importance of the father role. "The father's involvement—or lack of it—does seem to make a difference," the authors of *A Child's Journey* wrote. "There is convincing evidence," they continued, "that the father's inadequacy or absence can erode the child's emotional well-being and that his wholesome, committed presence can help promote the mental health of his children." The authors of *Responsible Parenthood* also stressed that the father's mere presence "is not enough in itself to answer a child's paternal needs and that the earlier in the child's life the father's involvement begins, the better"—starting with his attendance at birth. Moreover, paternal influence does not seem to be very different from maternal influence in promoting children's well-being. After an extensive review of the literature on the subject, Marshall Hamilton concluded that many personality and social characteristics "are strongly influenced by particular behavior pattens of the parents with the relationship influenced relatively little by the sex of . . . the parents. . . . The father's influence seems to be more or less identical with that of the mother." Mother is thus not always to blame for her children's psychological problems. These "appear to be influenced at least as much by the father's behavior in those studies where investigators have made the effort to study the father's influence."[57]

Many of the authors of the popular child-rearing manuals of the 1970s appeared to agree with the idea that "from a child's point of view, it matters little what sex the mother is." The dean of American child-care experts, Dr. Benjamin Spock, not only changed his views on working mothers but did a complete about-face in terms of parental responsibilities in the revised 1976 edition of *Baby and Child Care.* He was guilty, he has written of the earlier editions of his book, of "harboring an underlying sexism" when he assumed that "women will always play the major role in child care." The central tenet of the revised edition changed dramatically: the mother-child dyad was transformed into a triad to include the father. Infants and young children, said Spock, require "a sensitive, enthusiastic kind of care if they are to become warm hearted, creative people," but this care can come just as well from "loving fathers" as from "loving mothers."[58]

The 1976 edition of the manual contains an entirely new section called "The Father as Parent" in which Spock noted with approval that men have begun to participate in "all aspects of home and child care and there is no reason why fathers shouldn't be able to do these jobs as well as mothers and contribute equally to the children's security and development." But, he cautioned, "the benefit is lost if this work is done as a favor to their wives, since that implies that it's really not their work." The male excuse that he "is not used to the idea of participating in baby care and will wait until the child is more like a human being" will no longer wash with Dr. Spock: "Valuable time is lost that way," he claims. Spock concluded his admonitions to fathers by writing that "it will be a great day when fathers consider the care of their children to be as important to them as their jobs and careers."[59]

Well-known Harvard pediatrician T. Berry Brazelton also lauded the growing involvement of fathers in child care. "No development in our society," he wrote in a 1981 issue of *Redbook,* "has been better news than the trend toward father's participating more equally in nurturing the family." Fathers can be as adept as mothers in caring for their children, the experts now claimed. "I see nothing that a mother does (except breast feeding) that a father cannot do," Dr. Burton L. White wrote in his 1975 volume *The First Three Years of Life.* Parenting is learned, said the experts, and is therefore not the prerogative of either sex. "*Both* mothers and fathers . . . must be prepared for their child-rearing functions," emphasized one commentator on the family. "One significant feature of parenthood is that *neither* parent has much previous training for the work," argued Virginia Held. Another writer stated baldly that it is wrong to assume that "the mother will know what to do."[60]

The authors of the 1975 book *The Mother Person* decried the "anti-assistance behavior" practiced by some fathers when it comes to child care. Such fathers either "spontaneously, instinctively, unconsciously, and unfailingly assign all child care to the woman, or they simply refuse to see what needs doing." Letty Cottin Pogrebin, in a 1980 issue of *Ladies' Home Journal*, advised women not to put up with this kind of behavior. "Feeding, cleaning, and dressing a child are not acts of love. They're functions you perform lovingly—and either parent can do them." Women should not feel guilty about "wanting to share the work of child care," she went on, "because that's what it is: WORK—repetitive, tedious, often lonely and exhausting."[61]

While some writers were expanding the paternal role, others were resoundingly rejecting old definitions of the maternal one. A new genre of popular literature on the mother role began to appear during the 1970s as a number of women admitted the frustrations, boredom, and just plain resentment that often accompanied mothering. "We've been taught," wrote the authors of *The Mother Person*, "that mothering is sublime to any complete female, and that's a false lesson to be immediately unlearned." Motherhood is presented as "easy, fun and vastly fulfilling" by the popular media, and this has "created a pervasive myth that victimizes every mother," agreed Shirley Radl in *Mother's Day Is Over*. "Mother represents a life that never was and a world that never will be, i. e., *unconditional* affirmation of the child's life and needs. . . . It is a beautiful dream, a poetic fantasy, but it is doomed to failure because women *are* human beings," averred Angela Barron McBride in *The Growth and Development of Mothers*.[62]

The authors of these works detailed the mixture of ambivalence and guilt that pervaded their lives because of the "motherhood mystique." "I would die for him," Jane Lazarre said of her son in *The Mother Knot*, " . . . but he has destroyed my life and I only live to find a way of getting it back again." While propounding the joys of motherhood, "the community in no way prepared us for a routine which would be thankless, endless, dull, and nerve wracking," the authors of *The Mother Person* noted bitterly. For many women "the scale of motherhood does not really balance out. The rewards are not great enough to offset the difficulties

Courtesy of Michael Kappy, M.D.

Father Feeding Child • *Fathers entered the pages of the child rearing manuals of the 1970s and were told that they too had an important role to play in child care.*

and plain unpleasantness of so much of the job," concurred Shirley Radl. It should come as no surprise that all of these authors call for the equal participation of fathers in child care, well-run day-care centers, and an end to society's view of the child as "some greenhouse plant, being pinched and shaped and trimmed by the hands of a single gardener."[63]

It is not mere coincidence that "one-child alternative" and anti-natalist tracts began appearing during the seventies. "Necessity . . . is the mother of the single child," Didi Moore explained in *The New York Times Magazine*. As more and more married women took jobs, they had their first child later and later, making it more likely that their first child would be an *only* child. And, of course, with inflation, the cost of rearing children had risen steadily over the decade. It is little wonder that research on only-children boomed. Between 1978 and 1981 the Center for Population Research of the National Institute of Child Health and Human Development funded eleven separate studies of only-children at a cost of two million dollars. And the results? Being an only-child is neither "a disease in itself," as G. Stanley Hall claimed in 1904, nor do only children appear to be disadvantaged in any way when compared to their counterparts with siblings. In fact, wrote Maya Pines in an article in *Psychology Today*, "only-children come out looking a little better than others their age with regard to intelligence, achievement, and relations with adults. They are, on the average, no more maladjusted or self-centered than other children." Clearly, the myth of the only-child as a problem child was becoming obsolete as social and economic pressures for small families increased.[64]

Two people are an efficient unit that can cope with life better than the usual child-centered family, Alvin Toffler announced in his 1970 best-seller *Future Shock*. Betty Rollin agreed. In "Motherhood: Who Needs It?", first published in *Look Magazine* in 1970 and reprinted several times, she wrote that it is not a question of whether children are sweet and marvelous to rear or not; rather the question is whether one wants to pay the price for it. Rollin concluded that it is "more dangerous and ridiculous" to assume that all women are equipped for motherhood than to assume that "everyone with vocal chords should seek a career in the opera." Sociologist Jeanne Binstock predicted that in years to come "we may be quite surprised to discover that no more women will choose to be mothers than men choose to be engineers." These statements were followed by a spate of popular books espousing similar antinatalist views. And in 1973, with the founding of the National Organization of Non-Parents, for some the radical deemphasis on the mother role had become complete.[65]

I want to stress that not all social scientists and authors of child-care manuals writing during the 1970s discarded traditional ideologies on the sensitive issues of child rearing, motherhood, and fatherhood. Given the revolutionary nature of the research findings and the advice being offered, some dissent from majority opinion should come as no surprise. John Bowlby certainly did not back down on his view that the single, ever present mother is necessary to a child's development. In a 1980 interview in *Ladies Home Journal* he was still insisting that "looking after a baby or toddler is a 24 hour a day, 7 days a week job," making him "skeptical whether a working mother, unless she is Superwoman, can successfully combine her parenting role with a job outside the home." When asked about women who can't afford to stay home with their children and who must work, he acknowledged that while inflation is a problem, "it's a question of what you put first—your standard of living or the health and happiness of your children." "But what about fathers?" the interviewer persisted. "Does it matter what parent cares for the kids?" There is not enough evidence to know if it makes a difference, Bowlby replied, "whether mother or father stays home."[66]

Similar views were expressed by University of Michigan professor Selma Fraiberg in her 1977 book *Every Child's Birthright*. After a long review of "the disease of nonattachment" in institutionalized children who have been deprived of all mothering, she jumped to the conclusion, citing little data, that this is also the fate of children placed in day-care centers. "The minimum guarantee for the evolution of the human bond is prolonged intimacy with a nurturing person." This used to come automatically with breast feeding, said Fraiberg, but with bottle feeding "the insurance must be provided by the mother herself." But the mother's sole responsibility does not end in infancy, according to Fraiberg, since it is only after the age of three and sometimes later that "most children can tolerate separation from the mother for a half day." Moreover, it is not until the age of six that children normally "can manage" a full day's separation with good "mother substitutes" after school hours.[67]

No child should be "asked to accept long partings from his Mother during his first year," opined Erna Wright, author of the 1973 manual *Common Sense in Child Rearing*. "If you have to work for pressing economic reasons," she continued, "and by pressing, I mean you can't meet the food bill by Wednesday—that's different." Because mothers in this manual have sole responsibility for their children, mothers' desires are always secondary. "You are not a bad mother just because you want a career," she soothed, "but you are if you allow your ambition to damage your child psychologically." Therefore, if your child "resists" a baby-sitter, says Wright, "I'm afraid you'll just have to resign your job." The 1980 edition of *Infant Care* sought to instill similar fears in its (female) readers. Although there are photographs of both fathers and mothers caring for babies throughout the pamphlet, one of the few specific references to mothers, rather than to parents, is in this passage: "Every mother should carefully consider whether the money and satisfaction she gets from returning to work is worth the cost to her and her family. Good child care is always expensive, and poor child care causes a great deal of trouble and worry for the mother and can be dangerous to the baby."[68]

Part of the backlash against the redefined mother role is apparent in some writers' insistence that day-care centers, no matter how good, can never meet the nurturing standards of the isolated family unit. "I firmly believe," Wright wrote, "the ideal is still a home with a loving amateur mother and father in it and not a substitute-dominated nursery, however well run it might be." This same line was used by Richard Nixon when he vetoed a federal day-care bill in the early 1970s. His veto message explained that such care would "diminish both parental authority and parental involvement with children, particularly in the early decisive years when social attitudes and conscience and religious and moral principles are first inculcated."[69]

A different line of attack came from psychoanalyst Elaine Heffner. Some women, she scolded, have come to completely deny "all that has been learned about the meaning of a *primary* loving relationship in the development of the uniquely human qualities we have long cherished." She found this particularly alarming because "whether it grows out of internal need or external reality, for the most part child care is still the mother's responsibility." Feminists are singled out for condemnation: they tell women, she claimed, that "in order to be whole they must sacrifice the impulse to mother." They have given mothers permission "to abandon responsibility to children in favor of personal fulfillment."[70]

Some writers refused to abandon traditional thinking about the father role. "Your husband's role is just not as important as yours," Erna Wright wrote in the 1973 child care manual *Common Sense in Child Rearing*. "No father is ever so emotionally and biologically involved with his children as a mother; he cannot be." Wright maintained that women should not assume that their husbands will help them a great deal, for "the degree to which fathers are willing to assist in the practical upbringing of a child . . . is variable." While some men "take naturally" to feeding, bathing, and diapering, "a father doesn't love his child any less . . . if he just can't bring himself to help out in this way." Concurring with prefeminist Dr. Spock, Wright advised that there is no use "bullying" the husband to participate in child care because he will become "resentful and resistant." All a woman can do is "persuade gently—and appreciate however little or much he does."[71]

Some women's magazines also resisted a redefined role for fathers. Journalist Vivian Gornick reported that she wanted to do an article on Kotelchuck's work on the importance of father-child ties for *Family Circle Magazine*. But the magazine's editor initially refused her suggestion and replied, "You mean you want me to tell our readers that everything we've been telling them all these years isn't true?" When the article was finally published in the magazine, it was heavily edited so that Kotelchuck's findings were considerably diluted and their significance appeared murky at best. Similarly, James Levine, author of *Who Will Raise the Children?*—a book on "househusbands," single and adoptive fathers, and fathers who share equally in child care—submitted a portion of the book as a popular article to a women's magazine. The editor promptly rejected it and explained that "the argument that men make as good mothers as women wouldn't make a big hit with our readers."[72]

Not everyone agrees that there has been a decided change in the depiction of the mother role by the experts themselves. In a 1971 article on the influence of feminism on child development books, Zelda S. Klapper concluded that "not one author questions the availability of any evidence that the biological mother is . . . crucial in early development." Klapper also stated that the books she had reviewed agree with the traditional position that an exclusive mother-child relationship is necessary for proper development to take place.[73] I suggest that Klapper's survey, which was based on books published in the late 1960s through 1971, was premature. The impact of new ideas on motherhood stemming from the feminist movement and from large-scale maternal employment could hardly have appeared in print by that concluding date.

Han's Sebald's 1976 volume *Momism: The Silent Disease of America* is a curious blend of old and new thinking on the mother role. It is essentially a new analysis of an old "problem"—Mom—but it is also an attack on many of the traditional ideas on mothering. The star of the book is "the type of mother who is expert on character assassination." It is she who is to blame for drug and mental problems, sexual dysfunctions, totalitarian beliefs, and suicide in her offspring. Sebald's attacks on "Moms" were as vitriolic as any heard in the 1940s and 1950s, but his suggested causes and cures for Momism were far different, embodying as they did the thinking of the 1970s. Sebald called for "freely chosen motherhood" as one cure: "What is badly needed is full awakening to the fact that motherhood is just one alternative among a number of different life-styles." Since "unbalanced child raising" in which the father takes little or no part also makes for the growth of Moms, Sebald recommended active paternal involvement in child care. His final solution to the "momistic trend" was maternal employment and child-care centers. The time has passed, he noted, when experts believed that "children require 24-hour-a-day care by their biological mothers to have normal development." In fact, it is "not at all certain whether such extensive care is good for the child." Now jobs for mothers and well-staffed child-care centers were being touted as solutions to the old bugaboo, "smother love."[74]

Although some dissent appeared, the 1970s were generally the scene of the most pervasive and far-reaching updating of the mother role in the United States since the early nineteenth century. Just what were the social and economic factors responsible for this momentous ideological change? Some would undoubtedly argue that the rise and proliferation of a feminist ideology in the late 1960s and 1970s led child-care experts such as Dr. Spock to change their attitudes and recant their earlier advice, but this explanation skirts the issue of *why* feminism arose when it did. A more useful approach is to view the women's movement and feminist ideology, including the new thinking on parenthood, as *outgrowths* of larger social and economic forces that had their roots in the 1950s, the decade during which married middle class women were for the first time entering the labor force in large numbers. As more and more women with children took jobs, the experts continued to insist that motherhood was a full-time occupation and the only career a woman should want or need. This gap between ideology and reality must have grown during the 1960s when the labor force participation rates of women continued to spiral upward. In 1950 just over 18 percent of women with children under eighteen years old held jobs; by 1960 that figure had climbed to nearly 28 percent; and by 1970 it was close to 40 percent. It was not mere chance that the publication of Betty Friedan's *The Feminine Mystique* in 1963 caused so much comment and became a best-seller. One could certainly argue that "the problem with no name" which she identified in the book was in part caused by the enormous incongruity between the experts' dicta on motherhood and the reality of women's daily lives.[75]

Anthropologists have long realized that there is often a time lag between changes in a society's social and economic structures and in its ideologies. The anachronistic child-rearing literature of the 1950s and most of the 1960s, a time when large numbers of mothers would not or could not devote themselves exclusively to their children's care, is a good example of such a disjunction. The inherent contradiction between the ideology of full-time motherhood and the economic fact of women's large-scale employment was simply too great. The rise of feminist ideology and the experts' dramatic reversals on child care were delayed responses to basic changes in American society. Foremost among these changes was the employment of married women, particularly those with young children.

The discussion of why middle class wives and mothers took jobs in record numbers during the 1960s and 1970s is the subject of chapter 6. Here I merely wish to note the results. The year 1972 marked a turning point; for the first time more mothers of school age children were employed than were not. Another crossroads was reached in 1979 when over half (51.9 percent) of all mothers with children under eighteen were in the labor force. Today the figure is nearly 60 percent. The most salient statistic for our purposes was that reflecting the astounding increase in the number of mothers with children *under six* entering the job market. We must look back three decades in order to put these figures into perspective. In 1950, 12 percent of women with pre-school age children were employed; in 1960 this figure had risen to 19 percent; in

1970, to 30 percent; and by 1979, to 43 percent. In sum, the number of employed women with young children had increased by 250 percent over a thirty-year period![76]

The backdrop of this remarkable change in maternal employment was a falling birthrate. The birthrate declined rapidly between 1960 and 1980, and during the late 1970s it reached the lowest rate ever recorded in the United States. A 1971 Census Bureau survey of young women found that for the first time in American history the ideal family size was fewer than three children. A 1978 study of married women aged 18 to 24 noted that they expected to average 2.2 children each, but in the same year the average completed family size was 1.8, so that women were actually having fewer children than they had planned. This is a notable change from the years 1955 to 1959 when a woman of child-bearing age could expect to have 3.7 children and the years 1965 to 1969 when the average was 2.6 children per woman.[77]

This dramatic decline in family size is partly a result of the greatly increased costs of raising children. A Department of Agriculture study estimated that rearing a child born in 1960 to the age of eighteen cost a family of moderate means $34,300. But the same child born in 1979—assuming a 10 percent rate of inflation—would cost $165,300 from birth to age eighteen. If we add to this figure the mother's lost earnings if she stays home for five years to care for the child and such middle class amenities as music lessons and summer camp, the cost rises to an astronomical $250,000, a sum which does not include any expenditure for higher education! A 1973 Presidential Commission on Population Growth estimate of per capita income in the year 2000 provides another perspective. The study concluded that if the average American woman had two rather than three children, per capita income would be 15 percent higher. Given these figures, it is little wonder that the one-child and no-child options have become more acceptable.[78]

What is the relationship between these two profound changes in American society? Is the growing rate of maternal employment leading women to have fewer children so that there will be little or no break in their earning capacity? Or does the existence of smaller families make women more likely to seek employment? Economists and demographers cannot agree whether women's employment or lower fertility rates has causal priority. Both factors are obviously involved in the average family's attempt to cope with the high cost of living. Inflation has driven up the cost of rearing children, and inflation has also put a premium on a second family income, an income derived from the labor of wives and mothers.

It is within this setting that the child-care experts have been changing their tune. In a society in which fully half of all mothers are employed—mothers who are having fewer and fewer children and whose income has become essential for maintaining a middle class standard of living—it would be ridiculous for the experts to continue to insist on the necessity of an exclusive mother-child relationship. This is also the setting for the experts' sudden discovery that the average child has *two* parents. The growing awareness of the importance of fathering and the new research on father-child ties comes at a time when full-time mothering is no longer the norm. Advice givers and social scientists alike have abandoned their focus on the isolated mother-child dyad and have replaced it with a call for quality and continuity in child care, care that can be provided by a limited number of loving and concerned adults, male and female, in the home or outside of it.

◈ □ ○ △ □ ◈

Child-Care Advice, Social Science, and the National Setting

> *The culture commands that the mother is more important to the child than the father and the social scientists will be damned if they discover otherwise.*
>
> Vivian Gornick
> "Here's News: Fathers Mother as Much as Mothers," 1975

> *Science had once attacked entrenched authority, but the new scientific expert became an authority himself. His business was not to seek out what is true, but to pronounce what is appropriate.*
>
> Barbara Ehrenreich and Deidre English
> *For Her Own Good,* 1978

Changing ideas about child care are not simple ideological fashions that vary randomly through time. Nor are these ideas based on timeless truths of a moral or scientific variety. Attitudes about the maternal role are ultimately grounded in and shaped by the larger societal conditions under which they arise. While the authors of child-care manuals and other prescriptive writings may seem to be merely describing the roles that mothers and fathers play in child rearing, they are in fact attempting to sustain these roles by providing ideologies or "scientific" theories that prove that the particular child-rearing pattern of the day is part of the natural order of things.

Early in the twentieth century amateur advice givers were joined by experts from the social sciences in pronouncing on what was right and appropriate in mothering and child care. But however much we may emphasize the word *science* when referring to social science, it is clear that its theories do not arise in some sterile vacuum wholly divorced from external social and economic conditions. The creation and acceptance of social science theory and research depends on time and place. I can provide a good example. In 1963 two Scottish psychologists conducted an experiment on sixty infants and came up with findings similar to those Milton Kotelchuck later reported on the strong ties between babies and their fathers. According to Kotelchuck, the Scottish study received almost no recognition. At best, it was treated as a casual observation. Why was this so? Because, in the words of Vivian Gornick, "observations made before their time are rarely treated as discoveries, instead they are treated as curiosities, perhaps aberrations, footnotes to a text that remains obdurately welded to the presumptions of the culture."[79] In contrast, Kotelchuck's work on father-child ties a decade later was not ignored, although his findings were watered down for publication in a mass circulation magazine. During the 1970s he as well as other researchers began to reveal the importance of the father-child relationship, a time when the recognition of such a relationship synchronized with the deemphasis of the mother-child dyad which had been brought about by conditions of widespread maternal employment.

A broad historical and cross-cultural perspective of the mother role highlights the degree to which social scientists and other advice givers are bound by time and space. The long emphasis in the United States on the need for an exclusive mother-child arrangement is a good example. There simply is no evidence that the lack of such an intense one-on-one relationship inevitably leads to neurosis or other more dire consequences. If such a relationship were in fact essential, we would have to conclude that prior to the nineteenth century and in many cultures past and present its absence produced damaged children and damaged adults. We would have to believe that mothers throughout the ages have failed their offspring and that only within the last 150 years in the United States and other western industrialized societies have the psychological needs of children been met.

The near exclusive assignment of parenting to women was and, to the extent that it still exists, remains a condition of our particular society. It is not found in all human societies; nor did it exist in our own early history. If children only make strong attachments to their mothers it is because mothers have been the primary or exclusive caregivers in middle class American homes for the last century and a half, not because of the intrinsic nature of attachment or because of an innate need in the child. Social scientists' emphasis on an exclusive mother-child relationship must then be seen as an attempt to justify a local and temporary cultural pattern by citing eternal biological "facts." Margaret Mead recognized this justification more than twenty years ago, and it is worth quoting her at some length:

> At present, the specific biological situation of the continuing relationship of the child to its biological mother and its need for care by human beings are being hopelessly confused in the growing insistence that child and biological mother . . . must never be separated, that all separation, even for a few days, is inevitably damaging and that if long enough, it does irreversible damage.
>
> This . . . is a new and subtle form of anti-feminism in which men—under the guise of exalting the importance of maternity—are tying women more tightly to their children than has been thought necessary since the invention of bottle feeding and baby carriages.[80]

The experts' insistence that mothering is a full-time job is another aspect of their advice that can be questioned from an historical and cross-cultural perspective. *Child rearing is not a full-time job unless it is made so by the advice of the experts themselves.* Throughout most of history and in most societies women have been busy with a variety of tasks, and child rearing was of necessity a part-time activity. Sociologist Philip Slater has noted that "the idea of devoting the better part of one's day to child care seldom occurred to anyone because few women had the time for it before."[81] But with the gradual demise of domestic production and the decrease in household size and its growing isolation, it was not long before the advice givers were suggesting just that. If middle class women were perplexed as to how to fill endless hours in the care of children or questioned whether such timeless devotion was necessary, they merely had to turn to the pages of the advice books to be reassured that no amount of time and effort was too great an expenditure in the pursuit of their noble and monumental calling.

The authors of advice books and other prescriptive writings are clearly buffeted by the social and economic conditions of their times. This does not mean, however, that there is always a perfect fit between the prescriptive dicta propounded in a given period and the material conditions of that period. Because these dicta are gradual responses to changing social and economic structures, a time lag may separate what the advice givers are advising and what societal conditions are demanding. When such a disjunction between ideology and behavior occurs, it will not be too long before an intense revision of ideology takes place. This is exactly what happened in the prescriptive writings of the 1970s. During the two preceding decades middle class wives and mothers went to work in great numbers, but the child-care experts of the 1950s and 1960s gave little or no recognition to this fact. They continued to insist that it was at the peril of their children's health and happiness that mothers devoted anything less than full-time care to their offspring—advice that was simply incompatible with the growing incidence of maternal employment. At some point the conflict between what the advisors were *saying* and what women were *doing* became too great. The "disciplinary matrix" of the child care dicta was, in the words of Elizabeth Janeway, no longer "coping efficiently with everyday events in the world of reality."[82] Enter the experts of the 1970s. We were mistaken, they cried, and while some completely reversed their earlier stance on the importance of full-time mothering and the sanctity of the mother-child dyad, others attacked the theories and advice of their earlier counterparts as old-fashioned, misleading, or just plain wrong. During no period in American history has the revision of prescriptive mandates been more profound than during the 1970s. The times demanded a change, and as in the past, women's advisors responded to these demands by an appropriate updating of the image of the maternal role and the duties it entails.

We have now passed the point in history when a full-time mother role is possible, even if desired, for a majority of women in the United States. But what of the future? Will the experts once again change their views and return to a traditional exaltation of the mother-child unit? Will they once again insist that women devote themselves exclusively to mothering? If my analysis is correct, the answer must be that it depends on future social and economic conditions in American society. We may devoutly hope that the thinking and events of recent years—the changes in women's roles, the realization that fathers are parents too, and the recognition that what children really need is the warm, loving attention of a few consistent caregivers—have permanently revamped the maternal role. But unless we are soothsayers able to predict the future course of the American economy, we cannot say with any certainty just how motherhood will be defined in years to come.

4 GOOD HOUSEKEEPING

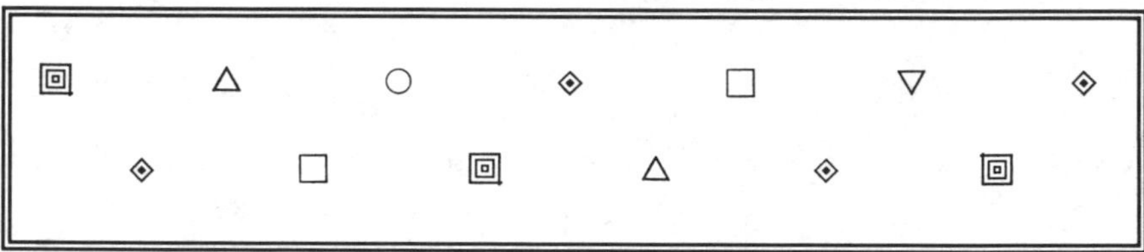

Woman should stand behind man as the comrade of his soul, not the servant of his body.

Charlotte Perkins Gilman, *Women and Economics,* 1898

It is sometimes said that American women have taken jobs because housework no longer ties them to the home. Middle class women in the United States, afterall, are blessed with a wider array of time-saving and labor-saving devices than any other women in history. The ingenuity of American industry seems to have freed women from the drudgery of traditional housework and given them both the time and the energy needed to work outside the home. With a many-cycled clothes washer, a multi-gadgeted Cuisinart, and a high-suction vacuum cleaner, the modern woman might easily whirl through household tasks with the efficiency of television's white tornado. The only problem with this conventional wisdom is that it is not true.[1]

In fact, at least a twenty-year delay separated the spread of labor-saving devices in the United States and the massive entry of married middle class women into the labor force.[2] If the time women saved using these devices was crucial to their taking jobs, why did they wait more than two decades to leave the home? The conventional wisdom also assumes that housework in the industrial age, benefiting from all that modern technology has to offer, is far less time-consuming than it was in the past when women not only cleaned and cooked but also manufactured a good portion of the articles used in the home.

Unquestionably, the nature of housework in this country has been transformed over the last three hundred years as the family, once a unit of both production and consumption, became a unit of consumption alone. The preindustrial housewife produced goods primarily for household use, and she sold or traded the surplus products of her labor, which gave her some degree of economic independence. Her work was far more diverse and central to the survival of her family than are the tasks performed by contemporary housewives. She was responsible for spinning and weaving the material used for family clothing and linens; she transformed all sorts of foodstuffs from their raw state into edible form; she manufactured candles, soap, buttons, home remedies, and a myriad of other items, to say nothing of the time she spent gardening and tending the family livestock. Laboring under this workload, the preindustrial housewife spent relatively little time on the tasks we consider central to housework today: cleaning, cooking meals, and doing the family wash. The lofty standards of cleanliness which have prevailed in twentieth-century America are of relatively recent origin; colonial era housewives spent their time doing far more essential tasks than getting their floors "cleaner than clean" or their husbands' shirts "whiter than white."

Because men, women, and children worked side by side in and around the household before the Industrial Revolution, there was little distinction between "work" and "life." Women were not forced to choose between work and domesticity as alternative careers. Moreover, work in general was task-oriented rather than time-oriented. Work continued until the task was completed regardless of the time involved. The working day was longer or shorter according to the chore being performed.[3]

All these arrangements were to change with industrialization. Much of women's traditional work—making clothes, manufacturing, canning—moved out of the home. But their other tasks remained: child care, meal preparation, household maintenance. With the demise of domestic production, women not only became more economically dependent because they no longer produced goods for trade or sale but their work became less tangible. While it must have been easy for family members to appreciate the work of the wife-mother who was responsible for making the very clothes that they wore, the value of housework in the industrial age is more difficult to measure because it is less visible, less concrete.

Housework in the industrial era does retain one similarity to preindustrial work in general. For the modern housewife, unlike the time-oriented, nine-to-five wage earner of the modern age, is still task-oriented. Her workday is organized around the tasks she performs. She works longer or shorter hours depending on whether she is doing the laundry that day or preparing a meal for guests. Because her workday is not bound by the eight-hour schedule of the paid employee, the common plaint arises that "a woman's work is never done."

How, with industrialization, did "real" work come to be something that was done outside the home, and how did it affect women's work in the home? How were the changes associated with industrialization reflected in the domestic manuals and other sources of advice intended for the homebound woman? These are questions this chapter investigates. The demise of household production, the employment of single working class women in factories, the resulting servant shortage, and the eventual transformation of the home by utilities and other modern conveniences were all factors in the conversion of the married middle class woman into the archetypical housewife.

As industrialization progressed in the United States, the type of domestic work done by middle class women, on the one hand, and by poorer rural and working class women, on the other hand, diverged in important ways. The domestic activities of working class and rural women were affected later and to a lesser degree by the industrializing economy. Household production, for example, continued, at least to some extent, until the late nineteenth century in working class and rural homes, while middle class women, particularly those living in towns and cities, had long abandoned domestic manufacture. What came to be termed the "servant problem" in the mid-nineteenth century was eminently a problem of middle class women; working class and rural women had rarely had the luxury of a paid servant to help them with their domestic chores. Finally, utilities and other household conveniences had begun to transform middle-class homes by 1900, but such modern amenities did not become common in working class households until about 1930 and in rural areas until after World War II.

All of these changes were reflected in the transformation of the family itself. Its primary function was altered as the result of the shift from a preindustrial to an industrial system of production. From a unit that had produced food and other goods needed to sustain daily life, the family became the principal unit for socializing and educating children who would become the workers and managers essential to the industrializing economy. The family had become a unit whose productive activities were limited to housework and child rearing.[4]

Working class housewives were producing and rearing future workers—their children—and materially and psychologically maintaining current workers—their husbands. The middle class housewife's domestic labor had a parallel function, for she was producing and rearing the children who would become the white collar workers of business and industry. The domestic labor of middle and working class women can be viewed in this way if it is borne in mind that one of the peculiar features of women's household labor is that it does not determine class affiliation. The class to which a woman belongs is not a function of her *own* work; it is defined by the class of her husband and the class of the future workers whom she produces and rears. Middle class women, like working class women, were producing and socializing a segment of the next generation. As I suggested in chapter 2, middle class women were rearing the long dependent "quality children" who would eventually take their "rightful" place in the middle and upper levels of the nation's industrial enterprises. Maintaining a home, planning meals, and seeing to it that the physical, emotional, and educational needs of their offspring were met was vital to the grooming process. Middle class women were also creating a haven to which their husbands could escape and renew themselves before returning to the stressful world of early industrial capitalism.

The important role of middle class housewives in the new industrializing economy was not lost on the authors of home and family care manuals who took great pains to inform women of the loftiness of their domestic duties. By the mid-nineteenth century women's domestic advisors were glorifying the home sphere and telling women all the reasons why they should remain in it. As the household production of middle class women dwindled, a virtual flood of works followed, proclaiming housewifery a profession second to none. Next to motherhood, housewifery was woman's highest calling; her dedicated performance of domestic tasks was essential not only to the health and well-being of her family but to the nation as a whole.

The timing of the first appearance of these works is also significant because it raised questions about the nature of housework and the function of the housewife, concerns that could only arise in an industrialized society. Sociologist Ann Oakley has noted that, "other people in different cultures may live in families, but they do not necessarily have housewives." In preindustrial societies there is no distinction between "life" and "work"; work is not something done outside of and separate from the home. All adults, in fact, work. Anthropologists studying such societies have referred to this as the embeddedness of the domestic unit.[5]

It is also well to remember that cooking and cleaning have not always and everywhere been done by women; it is only our own cultural biases that equate domestic labor with the adult female role. As Margaret Mead noted, the concept of "domestic work" is a cultural category that is by no means universal. In traditional societies tasks such as caring for young children, carrying water, and cooking sometimes are done by children or old people of either sex, and in colonial societies domestic work was often done by native men. It is for these reasons that anthropologists deny that females are universally domestic. In the words of anthropologist George Peter Murdock, "While a number of occupations are universally masculine, *none* is everywhere feminine."[6]

Colonial Housekeeping

Pennsylvania newspaper advertisement for a housekeeper (1780): *". . . cleanly, industrious, perfectly qualified to direct & manage the female concerns of country business as raising small stock, dairying, marketing, combing, carding, spinning, knitting, sewing, pickling, preserving, etc."*

Housework was a central part of family economy during the early years of settlement and in frontier regions into the nineteenth century. It was as necessary for sheer survival and as central to daily subsistence as any work performed by men. It was, moreover, done in a social setting. Relatives and friends usually lived within walking distance of one another and a housewife's older children or perhaps an unmarried sister helped her in the daily round of activities. The colonial housewife performed her work in the midst of life, and in this sense, housework did not exist as a separate activity. Women were not isolated from the workaday world—they were part of it.

Prior to American independence, various British policies made it difficult for colonists to import the goods they needed. Other policies inhibited the development of a shop or factory system. Home manufacture was far more important in the northern colonies and in frontier areas than in the southern colonies because southern colonists could exchange tobacco and other staples for imported goods. But home manufacture was not limited to the north; witness the statement of a visitor to North Carolina in 1714: "The women are the most Industrious Sex in that place, and by their good Housewifery, make a good deal of Cloath of their own cotton, Wool and Flax; some of them keeping their families (though large) very decently apparel'd. . . ."[7]

Once the British parliament began taxing manufactured goods, colonial legislation was passed to encourage home manufacture of wool, linen, and cotton cloth. The wearing of homespun in fact became a mark of distinction and a symbol of defiance of British policies. During the American Revolution home manufacture increased because of the drastic reduction of imports from England; people from Maine to Georgia had to manufacture nearly all of life's necessities themselves. After independence there was a brief resumption of imports, but they dropped off and household manufacture was again revived. It was to remain central to the life of the new nation until the 1830s when the spread of the factory system made ready-made goods more widely available.[8]

The colonial woman's work consisted of tasks involved in the manufacture of household goods, tasks that left the household with the onset of industrialization, and tasks seen as central to housework in the modern era—cooking, laundry, and general household maintenance. There was certainly some local variation in the domestic activities of colonial women based on their place of residence and their social class. The general rule was that the more rural and isolated the household, the heavier the woman's workload. Nonetheless, the basic tasks of town women were similar to those of their rural counterparts, although the former were more likely to buy meat, butter, and cheese and were somewhat less likely to manufacture their own cloth. Even in wealthy households with many servants the "lady of the house" and her daughters helped with the daily chores, and the wives of planters in the south devoted their time to the administration of the activities of house slaves and to helping prepare meals for their families and frequent guests. Unlike women in the northern colonies and on the frontier, wealthy southern women usually did not spin or weave cloth or produce household goods since these items could be purchased with the proceeds from the sale of tobacco. With this exception, "home-made was an adjective that might be applied to nearly every article in the house." The degree of self-sufficiency of many households can be gauged from a farmer who wrote in 1787 that his total annual expenditure was $10, for "salt, nails, and the like. Nothing to eat, drink, or wear was bought as my farm provided all."[9]

Certainly the most important part of the colonial woman's work was producing cloth. This was a time-consuming task, for more than a dozen steps were involved before the product was complete. All spinning was done by women and every household had at least one spinner. Weaving, however, was sometimes done by itinerant artisans who wove cloth for a living.[10] Once the cloth was finished it had to be sewn into household linens and family clothing. All stockings and mittens were knitted at home, and in their spare time women did fancy handiwork: they netted fringes for curtains, embroidered coverlets and petticoats, and undertook a variety of other needlework projects.

Women were also responsible for manufacturing many household goods. They made candles and soap and collected herbs and plants and brewed them into home remedies. They made brooms and buttons, and they spent hours preserving fruits and vegetables, brewing beer and cider, and smoking, pickling, and salting meat, game, and fish.

Cooking the family's meals was particularly laborious. Although meals were simple, usually consisting of a single course with little variety, bread had to be baked, cows milked, butter churned, eggs collected, and vegetable gardens tended. Cooking was done on an open hearth and iron pots, which could weigh up to 40 pounds, had to be constantly stirred. Perhaps because so much time was spent in the actual production of food, little time was left over for preparing elaborate dishes or for meal cleanup. The items used at meals were simple and easy to clean. Plates of pewter were wiped off and wooden tankards rinsed. "There was little to make extra and difficult work—no glass to wash with anxious care, no elaborate silver to clean—only a few pieces of pewter to polish occasionally."[11]

Given the burdens of home production, women were left with little time for the jobs that today are labeled housework. Although preindustrial homes were simple, colonial standards of cleanliness would undoubtedly horrify any twentieth-century housewife. Travelers in the colonies were often shocked by the dirtiness of rural American households. As one historian of the period has written: "It seems clear either that cleanliness was not highly valued or that farm wives, fully occupied with other tasks, simply had no time to worry about sweeping floors, airing bedding, or putting things away." Clothes were not changed very often and when they became dirty they were allowed to accumulate and were washed once a month or in some households once every three months. Houses were not cleaned daily or even weekly but *annually*.[12]

Colonial women had little need for advice givers to tell them how to fill their time or to inform them of the importance of their chores. Since women produced a large proportion of the articles used in the home, their days were filled with activities that made the very survival of their families possible. No one ever seems to have questioned the value of their work. I have been unable to find any directives dating from preindustrial days which singled out women's activities for special mention. There seems to have been a complete lack of consciousness about any special or unique domestic role for women.

The Elevation of Housewifery: 1830–1870

> *. . . I am fully confident that if there be a profession or occupation, which is in its nature, truly dignified, & to which philosophy & philosophic instruction are more necessary or more applicable than to almost any other, it is that of housekeeping.*
>
> William A. Alcott
>
> *The Young Housekeeper: or, Thoughts on Food and Cookery*, 1838

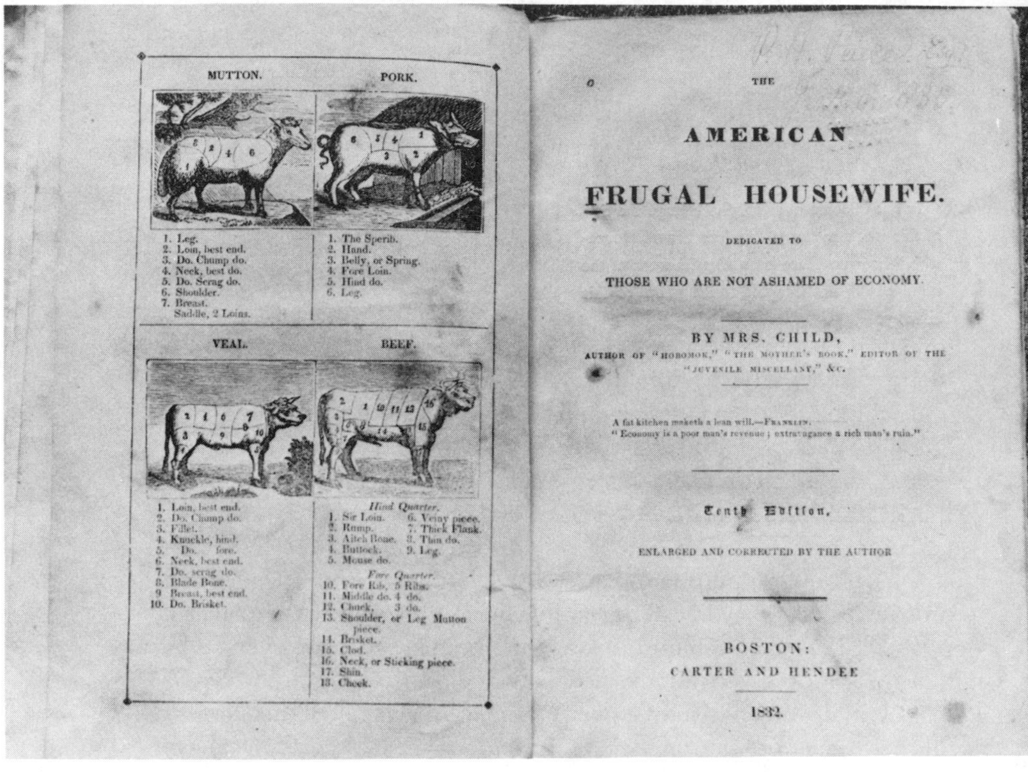

MUTTON. PORK.

1. Leg.
2. Loin, best end.
3. Do. Chump do.
4. Neck, best do.
5. Do. Scrag do.
6. Shoulder.
7. Breast.
Saddle, 2 Loins.

1. The Sperib.
2. Hand.
3. Belly, or Spring.
4. Fore Loin.
5. Hind do.
6. Leg.

VEAL. BEEF.

1. Loin, best end.
2. Do. Chump do.
3. Fillet.
4. Knuckle, hind.
5. Do. fore.
6. Neck, best end.
7. Do. scrag do.
8. Blade Bone.
9. Breast, best end.
10. Do. Brisket.

Hind Quarter.
1. Sir Loin.
2. Rump.
3. Aitch Bone.
4. Buttock.
5. Mouse do.
6. Veiny piece.
7. Thick Flank.
8. Thin do.
9. Leg.

Fore Quarter.
10. Fore Rib, 5 Ribs.
11. Middle do. 4 do.
12. Chuck, 3 do.
13. Shoulder, or Leg Mutton piece.
14. Brisket.
15. Clod.
16. Neck, or Sticking piece.
17. Shin.
18. Cheek.

THE

AMERICAN

FRUGAL HOUSEWIFE.

DEDICATED TO

THOSE WHO ARE NOT ASHAMED OF ECONOMY.

BY MRS. CHILD,

AUTHOR OF "HOBOMOK," "THE MOTHER'S BOOK," EDITOR OF THE "JUVENILE MISCELLANY," &c.

A fat kitchen maketh a lean will.—Franklin.
"Economy is a poor man's revenue; extravagance a rich man's ruin."

Tenth Edition,

ENLARGED AND CORRECTED BY THE AUTHOR

BOSTON:
CARTER AND HENDEE
1832.

Schlesinger Library, Radcliffe College

The American Frugal Housewife • *During the 1830s, for the first time, housekeeping manuals advised women of their specialized domestic role. The American Frugal Housewife by Lydia Maria Child was one of the earliest domestic manuals published in this country.*

Housekeeping during the early years of the nineteenth century differed little from housework during the colonial period. Between 1790 and 1810 family manufacture enabled the new nation to become independent of foreign imports, particularly in the manufacture of textiles for clothing and household use. Embargoes on the importation of foreign goods, along with the westward movement of population, kept people dependent on homemade products. Even as late as 1820 it was estimated that some two-thirds of the textiles manufactured in the United States were homespun.[13]

The transfer of production from the household to the factory occurred in stages at different times in various parts of the country. The family stage of manufacture was followed by an "itinerant stage" during which families hired someone to do part of the manufacturing process or sent semifinished products to outside business establishments for completion. Dyeing mills, for example, would ready wool cloth for sewing, and linen could be given out for bleaching. During the final stages of industrialization, production was completely transferred first to small and later to large factories. The timing of these stages followed a general rule: the longer a community had been settled, the earlier and more complete its transfer to factory production.[14]

The first tasks to leave the home were usually those requiring the most specialized skills. Spinning, for example, was done at home long after weaving had been turned over to the village weaver; factory-made men's clothing was available long before women's clothing.[15] As factory production increased, more and more tasks left the home. Weaving, spinning, tailoring, sewing, butchering, baking, candle and soap making, poultry and garden keeping were all eventually taken over by commercial establishments. But it was not until the end of the nineteenth century or even in the early years of the twentieth century that all of these activities left the home for the factory.

The activity that most profoundly affected women's domestic work during the preindustrial era was the manufacture of cloth for clothing and household use. This time-consuming and never-ending chore was an absolutely essential one. The removal of cloth manufacture from the home to the factory therefore had a major impact on how women spent their day. The first factory that performed all the processes to transform raw cotton into finished cloth was established in New England in 1813. By 1830 spinning and weaving were done in factories in most of the older sections of the country. At the same time itinerant peddlers began to sell all sorts of goods that had once been made at home—pins, scissors, needles, combs, buttons, and cotton goods among others. As a result, according to one historian of the epoch, by 1830 the factory system was sufficiently widespread in New England, the Middle Atlantic states, and parts of the West "to relieve the housewives of a great deal of the strenuous labor which their foremothers had been obliged to perform."[16]

In area after area, as soon as manufactured goods could be purchased, households abandoned their own system of production. Between 1840 and 1860 homemade goods had been almost entirely displaced by manufactured ones, even in the more isolated regions of the country. Better inland transportation, the spread of factories, an increase in trade between regions, a rise in price for farm products, and a decline in price for factory-made goods all sounded the death knell of the old family system of production.[17]

The decade of the 1830s marked a turning point in good housekeeping in the older settled regions of the country. And it was not long before changes in the housekeeper's tasks were reflected in household manuals and other prescriptive writings. The differences in tone and direction of the new advice givers of the day are highlighted by a comparison with some of their predecessors.

Household guides of the eighteenth and early nineteenth centuries were simple, straightforward lists of "receipts" (recipes) and directions for making a wide variety of household products. Most of these manuals were addressed to men and women; the authors took it for granted that *both* sexes worked together in and around the home. Typical of this genre is H. I. Harwell's *The Domestic Manual* (1816). "The following receipts," Harwell wrote, "are offered to the Public, in the full belief, that among them, every person will find something of advantage to himself" and that even to "the man of wealth and leisure, they will at least afford a series of interesting experiments."[18] The manual appears to be addressed to men since Harwell uses masculine pronouns when he gives advice on such diverse topics as destroying moths, brewing a "fine cordial" of Holland gin, removing stains from cloth, obtaining oil from flowers, preserving meat and fruit, repairing gun barrels, making furniture wax, wine, and ink, and an ointment for getting rid of freckles.

Another early household guide was John Aikin's *The Arts of Life*, first published in 1803. It consists of a series of letters addressed to "my dear boy" and provides information on food, agriculture, manufacturing, and architecture. Aikin's manual advises his readers on the "arts of life" because he considers it "unworthy of a man . . . to rely upon the exertions of others."[19] What follows is a set of instructions for preparing various foodstuffs, raising crops, and manufacturing flax, hemp, cotton, and wool cloth.

Harwell's and Aikin's matter-of-fact household hints contrast with the prescriptive writings that began appearing in 1830. Lydia Maria Child's *The American Frugal Housewife,* first published in that year, was a precursor of things to come. This manual, despite its title, is addressed to "every member of the family," and while it offers numerous household hints it is more than a simple list of "receipts." Child's aim is to teach frugality in both time and money; "live within one's means," she directs her readers. But more relevant to the subject at hand is her call for a specialized "home education" for young ladies. Child rues the fact that schools do not teach girls "feminine employments" or "domestic habits."[20]

A number of themes appear for the first time in the household manuals of the 1830s and 1840s which are remarkably similar to those found in the motherhood manuals of the era. Like motherhood, housework was elaborated and exalted and women were advised that their responsibilities were far more awesome than the mere physical maintenance of their families. Women no longer simply cooked meals and cleaned house, they promoted the "Health, Comfort, and Prosperity" of their husbands and children.[21]

Women were told that they were "naturally domestic" by the advice givers of the day, who sought to enlighten them on the tasks and duties of their special sphere. "If a woman does not know how the various work of a house should be done," Eliza Farrar wrote in 1836, "she might as well know nothing, for that is her express vocation." "For a woman to be domestic is so consonant with every feeling of her heart, & so true to her nature," agreed Mrs. Graves in an 1843 volume, "that when she is not so it must be the result of a training which has counteracted the designs of Providence." Now the home was woman's province, the world of work was man's, a distinction that would have been inconceivable a few decades earlier. In the words of one manual writer:

> A neat and well conducted house, with fires and lights always as they should be; and a table where the food is inviting . . . are comforts that are not lightly prized by any married man; and it is but just that he who perhaps labours hard in his business or profession to procure the means of obtaining them, should not be disappointed in their application, particularly when the deficiencies are caused by the mismanagement of the woman who should consider it her special care to render his home agreeable to him.[22]

Yet despite the supposed natural domesticity of women, they were to be trained for their life's work. "Is it not as much a matter of public concern," queried Catherine Beecher in her popular manual *A Treaty on Domestic Economy*, that a woman be "properly qualified for her duties, as that ministers, lawyers and physicians, should be prepared for theirs?" Reverend William Alcott wholeheartedly agreed with these sentiments. "The theory and practice of housewifery is indispensable to a correct female education," he wrote in 1838. Just as with motherhood, arguments favoring women's schooling were couched in terms of improving their stewardship of the home. "Why," asked the advice givers, "should not that science and art, which a woman is to practice her whole life, be studied and recited?" "Domestic education," as Miss Beecher called it, should be taught in female seminaries "on an equal or superior ground to Chemistry, Philosophy, and Mathematics."[23]

The author of an article in an 1839 issue of *Godey's Lady's Book* argued that female education should not be limited to just the "domestic arts" because the sciences could also be useful in the household. "Take chemistry for example; what an advantage it must be for the lady who superintends the roasting of a leg of mutton to have a thorough knowledge of the nature and action of free caloric!" Study geometry? Of course, since, through some acquaintance with it "a lady may be able to cut out a garment more skillfully than one who is ignorant of that science."[24]

All of the advice givers insisted that domestic duties were not incompatible with "mental improvement" or "intellectual enjoyment." Doing housework is not only good for one's physical health, Mrs. L. G. Abele assured her readers in an 1853 manual, but its practice also "does not impede . . . the attainment of a high degree of mental culture." By following the housekeeping hints suggested in the manuals, women could produce "the best effect with the least expense of time and labor," thus freeing themselves for higher "intellectual, benevolent, and religious" pursuits that were to be carried out *within* the home.[25]

Women were constantly entreated not to underestimate the dignity and importance of their domestic labors. Housekeeping is no less a science than geography and mathematics, proclaimed Reverend Alcott. Mrs. Lydia Sigourney had no doubt that it was truly challenging work: "The science of housekeeping affords exercise for the judgement and energy, ready recollection, and patient self-possession, that are the characteristics of a superior mind." Miss Beecher urged that young girls be taught to respect their future profession. "Every woman should imbibe, from early youth, the impression, that she is training for the discharge of the most important, the most difficult, and the most sacred and interesting duties that can possibly employ the highest intellect."[26]

The message paramount in all of this literature was that a woman did not merely minister to the physical needs of her family, she was also "the enlightened instructor and guide of wakening minds, her husband's counsellor, and the guardian and purifier of the morals of her household." Her job was a weighty one indeed; its influence more far-reaching than that of the minister: "He may watch, and labor, and pray for the soul; but the housekeeper can do more than all this. She presides over, and moulds, and shapes. She forms the 'house' the soul 'lives in'; and, in this way, almost entirely directs the notions and tendancies of the soul itself." A child's early environment, the quality of its food and drink, and the general atmosphere of the household were to be carefully monitored. The housewife "has more to do than to attend pots and kettles," wrote Reverend Alcott. "She has the temporal, and, to some extent, the eternal well-being of those around her at her disposal."[27]

Even though a woman's sphere was limited to the home, her influence reached far beyond it; her duties were proclaimed as weighty and as difficult as those of any man of the world. "No statesman, at the lead of a nation's affairs," wrote Miss Beecher, "had more frequent calls for wisdom, firmness, tact, discrimination, prudence, and versatility of talent" than a woman who systematically performs her household duties. For Reverend Alcott, no "mission, foreign or domestic, has higher claims . . . than the mission of the housekeeper" because her duties demand "a degree of self-government and self-sacrifice, which is seldom if ever required of him who goes to India or the Sandwich Islands."[28]

The other side of the advice givers' reification of the housewife's role was their condemnation of the "false shame" that some women felt about keeping house. Reverend Alcott found it "astonishing" that housekeeping was thought "disreputable" and those who attend to it with their own hands "vulgar." "Nothing," he insisted, "can be more directly at variance with the truth." Beecher also criticized the "aristocratic feeling" that domestic labor is "degrading." The real objects of "contempt" should be the "ladies" who spend their days in "idleness and folly," not the good woman "whose time and thoughts are wholly occupied in the manual labors of her nursery and her kitchen, and who knows nothing beyond them."[29]

Housekeeping, like mothering, was pictured in the manuals of the era as a double-edged sword. When the work was done well, a felicitous outcome was virtually assured, but woe to the woman who failed to take her domestic chores seriously! All manner of evil could be traced to the "impure atmosphere of filthy apartments" and the eating of "oily, indigestible, or poisonous food." Does not the housekeeper, who is "director and guide of some half dozen children" realize that "her every error—in eating, drinking, conversing—is educating them? Does she not know that she . . . is treading at every moment on the verge of destruction, physical and moral?" demanded Reverend Alcott.[30]

Many of society's problems were traced to the lax housekeeper. Children who have "first been prisoners in the domestic circle," children "whose appetites have become perverted by exciting food and drink," are the very ones who eventually wind up as "state prisoners." The lack of "domestic virtues" in women led to homes filled with "discontent, irritability of temper, and estrangement of affection." Indeed, in Europe, wrote one author, it was just these "irregularities of domestic life" that caused "almost all the disturbances of society."[31]

Housekeeping, like mothering, was far too important to entrust to anyone else. In fact, from the advice givers' point of view, the two tasks were inextricably linked. Good housekeeping meant good mothering. Since housework was a "science," wrote one of women's domestic advisors, it was about time that "wise and discreet mothers" took it into their own hands, instead of leaving it to "those who have no interest in it." This was one of the reasons that young girls should be taught housekeeping from an early age "instead of teaching them the fatal error that it is servants . . . who should do these things."[32]

An ethnic bias was apparent in these pronouncements, for the "dangers of foreign influence in the home" had become a code phrase for reaction against Irish women who were rapidly replacing native-born women as the primary pool of domestic workers. The decline in the number of servants, in general, as more and more single working class women took better paying factory jobs, was the backdrop for the entire discussion of the "servant problem," a topic that received considerable attention in all of the manuals of the period. Their authors, however, did not agree on what to do about the servant problem. While some took the presence of servants for granted, others felt that a woman who needed servants should "not consider it a privilege, but a misfortune." At least one advice giver, Eliza Leslie, saw the housewife's role as supervisory and managerial. She suggested that a well-run household required that "the mistress or her representative visit the kitchen at least once a day" to check on the servants' work. The servant problem, she wrote, may actually stem from "the deterioriation of mistresses in the knowledge and practice of all that is necessary to a well-ordered household." Here too, as with motherhood, George Washington's female relatives were cited as paragons of domestic virtue. Mrs. George Washington, Mrs. Leslie noted approvingly, accompanied her manservant daily to a Philadelphia market to select food for her household.[33]

Mrs. Graves seemed to be of two minds about the need for servants. While she argued that servants are never a "substitute for the vigilant superintendence of the mistress of the family," a woman might employ them in order to devote more time to her children. And, she added prophetically, it will only be when there are "better mechanical contrivances" in the household that the need for servants will finally cease. Reverend Alcott, however, left no doubt as to where he stood on the issue. He would prefer that "every mother could perform all the duties of her family" without the help of servants. Miss Beecher saw the servant shortage as a blessing in disguise because it forced the daughters of a household to become proficient in all manner of domestic tasks.[34]

Not only were women to devote their time to the care and sustenance of their families but should they have a moment to spare, some of the advice givers offered the sort of time-filling, make-work suggestions that came to characterize the prescriptive writings of a later era. Reverend Alcott urged housewives to keep a detailed daily journal of their activities, including their "successes and failures in cooking and other duties." Mrs. Abele also advised women to keep careful records and to write down "any new and valuable mode or remedy you have learned from others."[35]

Of course, no advice giver told women to spend their every waking moment on the *physical* care of their families. After all, women had to have time for their role as moral stewards of the home. Catherine Beecher, in fact, decried the elaboration of some domestic duties: "The furnishing a needless variety of food, the conveniences of dwellings, and the adornments of dress, often take a larger portion of time than is given to any other object." The objects she refers to are "benevolence, religious devotion, and intellectual improvement."[36] But the obvious point is that she never saw the time saved from simplifying housework as a means of allowing women to engage in paid activities *outside* the home.

The ideology implicit in all of this advice reflected a radical change from the relatively fluid sexual division of labor that had characterized preindustrial America to the sharp dichotomy between men's and women's spheres that arose as the "important" work of society left the home. Many of the prescriptive writers were dealing with housework not as an isolated problem but as a direct link to the whole question of the status of middle class women or what was then called "the female question." In the case of Catherine Beecher and some of her contemporaries, elevating the status of housework, a quintessential part of women's new domain, was the answer to feminism. Beecher herself opposed female suffrage and saw a scientized and professionalized domestic sphere as the key to raising women's status and power in the home. Feminists who sought to draw women away from "their allotted sphere," who urged the violation of "that Gospel injunction that women should be keepers of the home," would be undercut, said Mrs. Graves, if only women realized the importance and nobility of their sacred calling.[37]

Housework and the "Female Question": 1870–1900

> *In the shadows of domesticity . . . women performed myriad social and economic services which neither the husbands' wages nor the employers' capital were able or willing to provide.*
>
> Mary P. Ryan
> "Femininity and Capitalism in Antebellum America," 1979

The technological innovations that occurred in the final third of the nineteenth century began to revolutionize the domestic tasks of middle class housewives. While a variety of appliances and commodities that were potential labor savers first appeared during these decades, the invention of these devices must be distinguished from their actual

North Bennet Street Industrial School Papers, Schlesinger Library, Radcliffe College

Woman Spinning • *Until factory made cloth became available, women's most time consuming domestic activity was spinning and weaving to produce cloth for family clothes and household linens.*

diffusion into the home, as historian Susan Strasser points out. Most household labor savers existed before 1900, but many were found only in the homes of wealthy urban families prior to that date. Indoor plumbing, electricity, and gas were still considered luxuries in the late nineteenth century.[38]

This disclaimer in mind, it was still true that by the late 1800s housework *had* been simplified for most women as a result of the greater availability of new products and new services. Certainly the time and labor involved in clothing a family had diminished as the manufacture of cloth was transferred from household to factory. By 1860 almost no women still spun and wove fabric, and the invention of the sewing machine in 1846—an invention that spread more rapidly than any other labor-saving device—also simplified this once onerous chore. Although women's and children's clothing generally was still sewn at home and only the wealthy employed seamstresses and tailors, men's apparel was often store-bought after the Civil War.[39]

The greater availability and variety of foodstuffs affected food preparation. Better transportation and refrigeration meant that fruits and vegetables could be purchased during a greater portion of the year, and meat prices declined as meat became easier to market. City dwellers could now purchase dairy products, and by the 1880s women living in urban areas could buy nearly all of the things that twenty-five years earlier they had "put up" themselves.[40]

While prepared food was available by the closing decades of the nineteenth century, it was still considered a luxury. Store-bought bread was the only item commonly used by all urban classes. In rural areas most food was still grown and prepared at home, and even the food bought in cities was sold in bulk and had to be processed at home. Meat was often butchered in the kitchen and ham and bacon had to be cooked and sliced; coffee beans were ground and roasted, and sugar, which came in lump form, had to be pounded. Nevertheless, by the end of the century stores were stocked with a variety of new products—canned soups, preserves, spices, and condiments—that must have saved the middle class housewife time and energy when she prepared her family's meals.[41]

Cooking was also made easier as the open fireplace gave way to the cast-iron stove. While a lot of labor was still needed to haul wood or coal and light the fire, stoves were more efficient than fireplaces and simplified meal preparation to some extent. Many small labor savers—apple corers, eggbeaters, slicers and parers of various kinds—also came on the market in the late nineteenth century.[42]

New sources of water, light, and energy also lightened household chores. Perhaps no task was more altered than the family laundry. During much of the nineteenth century washing clothes involved chopping wood to heat the water that was drawn by hand. Each article of clothing and household linen was then individually scrubbed, rinsed in clean water, hung to dry, and ironed. Laundry day was so named because doing the family wash did take an entire day. Two innovations helped alleviate this drudgery. Manual washing machines with wringers were gradually becoming more common and by 1900 commercial laundries were being used to some extent by all urban classes.[43]

Running water certainly made life simpler for those who had it. Plumbing was fairly common in large urban areas by the close of the century and it made housework easier by eliminating the need to haul water for the laundry, the dishes, and the cooking. Then too the greater availability of gas and electricity for light and heat cut down on the laborious chores of hauling wood and cleaning the soot and grime created by coal- and wood-burning stoves.[44]

Although most of these innovations were only found in more prosperous city households, this was the very audience that writers of prescriptive manuals sought to educate. By the late nineteenth century housework had been made simpler for the urban middle class housewife, who also was likely to have a servant to assist her in her chores. The role of the working class housewife, on the contrary, was quite different. With less money to spend, she substituted her physical labor for middle class purchasing power. She kept her family clothed and fed during times of unemployment and other financial setbacks. Poorer women, even in cities, sometimes raised their own livestock, kept gardens, and manufactured soap and other items that their wealthier counterparts had long become accustomed to purchasing. Under the burden of these tasks, working class wives certainly did not need anyone to advise them how to spend their days; nor were they likely to have the time or money to buy and peruse advice manuals.

The middle class housewife now confronted a new challenge, for a novel and fearsome element was added to her list of domestic chores. She was to be the family's guardian against that newly discovered scourge of humanity, the household germ. During the 1880s scientists realized that disease was not caused by "bad air" but by material agents that could be eradicated. The germ theory of disease set off a hysteria about the spread of disease through contagion. Never had the dictum "cleanliness is next to godliness" been more soberly considered. The horrors of poor housekeeping were much discussed by the prescriptive writers of the day. "Moths and dust and rust invade the most *secret* recesses" of the home, warned Helen Campell. The housewife was to stand sentinel against this menace. Simple cleaning was not enough; her task now was to ferret out germs, to clean all the nooks and crannies where the silent enemy lay in wait, ready for attack. Women who were dilatory housekeepers, women who did not take these dicta seriously, only had themselves to blame if their children or husbands fell ill.[45]

As servants became scarcer, writers began to depict them as sources of contagion; the woman who wanted to ensure her family's health and well-being had best do without them. "Breakage and general disaster attend the progress of Bridget and Chloe," warned Miss Campell. Catherine Beecher and her sister Harriet Beecher Stowe, writing in *The American Woman's Home*, a revised edition of Beecher's earlier manual, agreed with this assessment: "Every mistress of a family knows that her cares increase with every additional servant."[46]

It was no mere coincidence that as housekeeping tasks were simplified because of improved technology, women were urged on to newer, ever higher, standards of cleanliness. While the new mechanical devices and the spread of utilities made housework less burdensome, the advice givers multiplied their advice so that women's work was no less time-consuming. Take indoor plumbing, for example. Before its advent, families used measures to conserve water in order to lighten the domestic load. People changed clothes and household linens less often, they bathed less frequently, and dish and bath water were reused. But as historian Strasser notes, "More water meant more washing."[47]

Just as science had discovered germs, so science began to transform the entire management of the home. Beecher and Stowe assured their readers that their new volume contained "the latest results of science" as it pertained to housekeeping. The goal of womens' domestic advisors had become nothing less than the professionalization of the housewife's role. Scientific nutrition and hygiene were the watchwords of the day. Women's work, said their counselors, will achieve dignity only when it has the same status as men's work. Beecher and Stowe articulated this aim when they wrote that their manual sought to "render each department of women's true profession as much desired and respected as are the most honored professions of men." In order to truly professionalize housework, said the writers, women must be trained for it, just as men are trained for their life's work. While businessmen go through some form of apprenticeship, for most women "housekeeping is a combination of accidental forces from whose working it is hoped breakfasts and dinners will be evolved at regular periods."[48]

The new household technology was the key to upgrading and professionalizing housework for many in domestic science circles. Two historians of the late nineteenth century note that "domestic machines appealed to the domestic science movement more as grantors of status than as practical aids in housework." The home was often described as a "machine" or as a "laboratory" in which women were the chief technicians. An 1881 manual advised a woman to "regard her kitchen as a laboratory in which careful manipulations will produce exact results."[49]

However fanciful and contrived these suggestions may seem, they were earnest attempts to deal with what was perceived as the growing "female question." Now that the middle class housewife had lost nearly all of her productive functions, what was she to do all day? With fewer and fewer things to make, what was to be her purpose in life? In the words of one contemporary commentator: "Once, the household industries gave to the staying-home woman a fair share of the labor, but today there are few and the 'homemaker' suffers under enforced idleness, ungratified longing, and non-productive time killing."[50]

One potential solution to the "female question"—outside employment—was never considered by the advice givers. The very thought of the middle class married woman's taking a job was anathema to the writers because employment was believed incompatible with mothering and homemaking. Nothing must be allowed to interfere with woman's crucial role as producer and socializer of such an important segment of the next generation. Not only did middle class women bear and groom the "high quality" children on which U.S. business and industry would eventually depend but they also provided a variety of free services to their husbands, the present generation of white collar and professional employees. After industrialization men of all classes became dependent on wages and salaries, which in many cases were not sufficient to pay for all the services required to feed, clothe, and house their families. There is no question that the wage and salary structure of industrial capitalism was—and still is—dependent on the child care, cooking, and cleaning done gratis by housewives. If their services had to be remunerated, male wages and salaries would have had to be higher or alternatively employers would have had to provide free or low-cost restaurants, commercial laundries, and other facilities. In addition, because the commodities bought with male income were not in final, consumable form, the domestic labor of the housewife was an essential ingredient in the productive process. The point is that women's household labor provided hidden benefits to American business and industry.[51]

I am not suggesting that a conspiracy was afoot among the authors of the prescriptive manuals of the day, but there is no doubt that their pronouncements meshed neatly with the requirements of the new domestic order wrought by industrialization. The advice givers sent a potent message to the now dependent middle class housewife, a woman no longer engaged in the productive work of life, a woman whose primary role was rearing and creating a proper environment for her children. The cult of homemaking was now firmly wedded to the cult of motherhood to form a powerful ideology meant to ensure that married middle class women did not question their "proper place."

Housework Made Easy? 1900–1920

At the same time that technological developments made it possible for women to spend less time at housework, cultural values demanded that they spend more time perfecting the household arts.

Gordon, Buhle, and Schrom, "Women in American Society: An Historical Contribution," 1971

To be happy in your work you must idealize it. Cultivate the power of seeing the poetical, the beautiful, and the scientific side of housekeeping.

Ladies' Home Journal, 1905

The period 1900–1920 set the stage for the transformation of the role of the middle class housewife, a transformation that was not complete until the 1920s. During the early years of this century a variety of household goods came on the market for the first time, and the housewife's new role was to manage their consumption. The conventional wisdom about the impact of technological innovations on housework also made its first appearance in that era: the new labor-saving devices were said to have revolutionized the work of the American homemaker. The very phrase "labor-saving devices" indicates the drift of the orthodoxy that averred that the marvels of technological know-how practically did away with laborious, time-consuming domestic chores. Is this true? Did the time spent on housework decrease notably with the spread of household conveniences? Or is it the case that while the nature of women's domestic chores changed as a result of the new technology, the time spent on them did not?[52]

A look at the components of housework in the industrial era and the economic and technological backdrop that shaped domestic tasks contributes to the answers to these questions. The core of housework in twentieth-century America is the buying of goods and their preparation for family use. Some have compared the household to a factory; the housewife purchases raw materials on the market and through her labor changes them into a form that her family can use. In the words of one home economist: "The tasks that remain in the home can less and less be described as making goods; the better descriptive term is making goods available at the time and in the place and combinations desired."[53]

Managing consumption is a central feature of housework in the modern era. Consumption involves work, it takes time, and the higher the standard of consumption, the more work and time it takes. "Beyond a certain point," writes economist John Kenneth Galbraith, "the possession and consumption of goods becomes burdensome unless the tasks associated therewith can be delegated."[54] Gourmet meals require someone to cook them, large houses need someone to maintain and manage them, and large wardrobes need someone to keep them clean and in good repair.

The importance of the housewife's role as administrator of consumption can not be overstated, for if her services had to be remunerated household consumption would necessarily be limited. Imagine what it would cost to hire someone to "select, transport, prepare, repair, maintain, clean, service, store, protect and otherwise perform the tasks that are associated with the consumption of goods."[55] Without the free services of the housewife the expansion of household consumption critical to the growth of the American economy in this century would have been severely curtailed.

A majority of Americans live in nuclear families consisting of a married couple and their children. These living arrangements have affected the nature of housework and the amount of consumption that takes place in the home. The nuclear family is eminently repetitious both in the work required for its maintenance and in the goods it uses to meet its daily needs. A housewife typically services the needs of only one other adult and a few children. She cooks, cleans, and does laundry for a handful of people—and every other housewife is doing likewise in her home. For this reason the small nuclear family is an ideal consumption unit; each family buys consumer products for its own use. Think of how much smaller the market for refrigerators, stoves, washers, dryers, and other appliances would be if households were larger and there were far fewer of them. In the words of Margaret Mead: "Where one large pot of coffee once served a household of ten or twelve, there are three or four small pots to be made and watched and washed and polished."[56]

By 1900 households numbering twelve people were definitely the exception in most areas of the country. Housewives found themselves performing their domestic tasks for fewer and fewer people in ever greater isolation. Families were having fewer children and the practice of taking in boarders or lodgers declined sharply as the century wore on. In 1900 an average of 4.8 people lived in the typical American home; by 1930 that number had dropped to 4.1. Parents and children were the core of family life to the exclusion of all others.[57]

The new domestic technology of the early twentieth century was clearly designed for this small, individualized, home-centered culture. The innovations were never meant to remove housework from the home. Improvements in appliances for cooking and refrigeration were to be used to prepare meals at home. The clothes washer was intended for household use and, in the long run, it probably increased housework because as this appliance became cheaper and more widely available, fewer families sent clothes and linens out to commercial establishments for laundering.

Economist Heidi Hartmann has suggested that during the first decades of the century American business and industry found it more profitable to produce products than to produce services. More money could be made from manufacturing refrigerators and washing machines than from operating restaurants and commercial laundries. As a result, certain services returned to the home, like doing laundry, while others were never commercialized, like preparing meals, because they could not be as profitably provided as durable goods. It is certainly true that commodity production shifted toward consumer durables during the early years of the century. Production greatly expanded and decreased costs resulting from mass production brought many consumer products—such as cars, prepared foods, ready-made clothes, and household appliances—within the range of the average family. Consumer expenditure on durables nearly doubled between 1900 and 1930, and it is clear that during those decades "the industrially fabricated content of the home was defined and demarcated, more and more, by the external priorities of capitalism."[58]

Just what sorts of products for the home were becoming available at the time? Washing machines began to replace washboards around 1900, although these early machines were not fully automatic and the housewife had to fill and drain them. Ice boxes also appeared in more and more homes after 1900, as did vacuum cleaners and electric irons. Also after that date, most men's clothing was store-bought, although working class women still made their own and their children's clothing at home.[59]

The spread of many household appliances was dependent on the presence of power sources. Few turn-of-the-century homes were wired for electricity, but the growth of public utilities by 1920 permitted the electrification of nearly half of all urban and rural nonfarm households. Electric power was important as a source of light and as a source of energy. It meant that housewives no longer had to clean and fill oil lamps daily and that they could use the myriad small appliances then coming on the market. After World War I, for example, the old flatirons that had to be heated repeatedly were quickly replaced by electric irons.[60]

Gas for heating and cooking also had become the norm in urban households by 1920. After 1918 the *Ladies' Home Journal* no longer carried ads for coal- or wood-burning stoves, and a Bureau of Labor Statistics study of twelve cities found that 86 percent of the households surveyed had gas or electric lighting by that date. Modern power sources were of course far slower in reaching rural areas, and even by the late 1920s cooking with kerosene or wood and coal and kerosene lighting were still the norms in farm households.[61]

Indoor plumbing was invented long before it was widely available in homes because its use depended on construction of sewer lines and waterworks. Still, as early as 1900 most people in towns and cities had access to public water. Indoor plumbing and hot water spread rapidly during the second decade of the century as evidenced by the absence of magazine references after 1918 to heating water on the stove for laundry or bathing.[62]

The spread of utilities had a much greater impact on housework than labor-saving devices. Electricity, gas, indoor plumbing, central heating, and hot water virtually eliminated the most laborious chores that had faced the preindustrial housekeeper. The new methods of cooking and heating were cleaner and easier; they did not involve hauling wood or coal or scouring away the heavy grease and grime created by wood- and coal-burning stoves. With running water, particularly hot water, the housewife no longer had to fetch and boil water for home use. The convenience of these developments was duly noted by an observer who wrote in 1916 that "any woman—at least any woman who lives within reach of gas and electricity—can banish most of the ordinary cares of housework." But as economist Heidi Hartmann is careful to point out, while the spread of utilities changed the way that work was done in the home, "the work itself was *not* taken out of the house."[63] Housework still required a full-time homemaker.

Two factors, place of residence and social class, exercised some early influence on the transformation of housework by technological innovations and thus affected the labor involved in housekeeping. Although farm households benefited from the new technology less and later than did urban ones, more and more Americans were moving to urban areas during the first decades of the twentieth century. In 1900 nearly 40 percent of the population lived in cities; by 1920 over half of the population was urban.[64] But even in rural areas much of the new domestic technology was widely available by the 1930s and 1940s. Differences in rural and urban methods of good housekeeping, while profound during the first decades of the century, virtually disappeared by mid-century as electric lines crisscrossed the countryside and consumer goods were marketed nationally.

Social class also initially influenced women's domestic labor. But here too, while working class families could not afford the new household conveniences when they first came on the market, lower prices resulting from mass production soon led to their dispersal across class lines. By the 1920s working class women were able to buy at least some of the labor savers that their middle class counterparts already took for granted. As a result, status differences between housewives were reduced. According to sociologist Theodore Caplow, housewifery had become "an occupational culture of remarkable uniformity in which not only the technics but the values [were] effectively standardized. This identity of métier transcends class lines and regional boundaries."[65]

The decline in the number of household servants during the first decades of the century also meant that the experiences of middle and working class housewives became more alike. As time went on, the middle class housewife was almost as rarely assisted by servants in her household chores as the working class wife had always been. In 1909 only one family in fifteen employed any servants at all and a mere 8 percent had live-in help. The number of servants continued to decline as immigrant women abandoned domestic work for better paying factory jobs. Despite the overall increase in population, the number of those employed in domestic occupations decreased by 49 percent between 1870 and 1920.[66]

Middle class women were told that the "servant problem" was a blessing in disguise. "The happiest women of my acquaintance," wrote one home economist in 1901, "are the ones independent of servants." Why? Because children learn household tasks and it is from servantless homes that "our best men and women of today have come." Articles with titles like "How I Plan a Week's Work without a Servant" began appearing in women's magazines. Their readers were also reminded that servants were sources of physical and moral contagion.[67] Middle class housewives were being retrained to make do without domestic help, all the while being told how lucky they were that technology had finally liberated them from dependence on this alien element within the home.

Yet despite labor-saving devices, fewer servants meant more rather than less work for the average middle class housewife. For the first time, working alone in her insular sphere, domestic chores fell to her; no other adults were available to help out. Where laundry had been sent out to commercial establishments or had been done by a laundress hired for that purpose, a washing machine in the home meant that the housewife was responsible for doing all of the family laundry. As historian Ruth Schwartz Cowan points out, the appliances themselves seemed to have changed the very tasks they were invented to facilitate. In her words: "If the washing machine made household laundry simpler, it may also have made it more demanding by raising standards of cleanliness; at the turn of the century very few farmers expected to have a clean suit of underwear every day."[68]

Nothing inherent in the new household appliances actually made the chores associated with them more time-consuming. What promoted the greater expenditure of time was rising standards of good housekeeping which were vehemently espoused in both the popular media and in the expanding home economics movement. In the words of one home economist: "Conventional standards as to what is 'nice' have continually demanded cleaner linen, more table service, more carefully ironed garments."[69]

A never ending source of work was the continuing war on germs, "those pesky bacteria whose magnified portraits stared out from the pages of *House Beautiful* like the faces of the Wanted on a post office bulletin board." An article in a 1905 issue of the *Ladies' Home Journal* cautioned women about germ-carrying dust: "We should be very careful as to how we sweep and dust a room. Once the dust is set in motion there is no knowing where some of the spores contained in it will lodge." Helen Campbell, a home economist, wrote that women's "one great task" was "to keep the world clean." Ellen Swallow Richards, one of the founders of the home economics movement, was even more vehement on this point. "Cleanness, the state of being clean," she wrote in 1914, is "a sanitary necessity of the Twentieth Century whatever it may cost." Clearly the annual spring cleaning of preindustrial days would no longer do. Cleanliness was to be a daily pursuit.[70]

A higher standard of cleanliness was only one of the new elements of housework that made demands on a woman's time. Cooking now involved a thorough knowledge of nutrition, particularly in feeding young children. Bottles had to be carefully sterilized, formulas mixed and heated, and balanced meals planned and prepared. Shopping also took time, both because of the careful selection of purchases and the time spent traveling to and from stores. "The housewife is the buying agent for the home," proclaimed a 1915 *Ladies' Home Journal* article, and she "must take time to spend wisely." She should not distrust the domestic

Frederick Papers, Schlesinger Library, Radcliffe College

Maid Mopping the Floor • *As domestic help became scarce towards the end of the nineteenth century, the authors of household manuals advised against employing servants.*

devices coming on the market but should judge each one on its merits to "let the inventions of men save her time and labor and steps."[71]

Housekeeping tasks may have changed in nature and in relative importance as a result of the revolution in domestic technology, but this clearly did not free the housewife from her domain. The marketing of many labor-saving devices both assumed and assured that much of women's traditional work remained firmly ensconced in the home. Just as lightening the workload was not the aim of the capitalist use of machinery, it was also not the goal of the manufacturers of household conveniences.[72]

A small group of dissenters deplored these developments. The famed late nineteenth-century feminist Charlotte Perkins Gilman challenged the basic sexual division of labor, arguing that housework was not a fair exchange for a woman's support from her husband's earnings; if it were, low-income housewives would get the most support since they worked the hardest at domestic chores. Gilman argued that preparing healthy, nutritious meals was a science and should be in the hands of experts. She called for communal kitchens staffed by trained cooks. Housecleaning would be more efficient if it were centralized and done with mechanical aids and "scientific skill." Why, Gilman asked, should there be a "tyranny of bric-à-brac" in which the labor of a woman's life was "to wait upon these things, and keep them clean?"[73]

Thorstein Veblen also saw through the rhetoric of those who championed the new domestic developments as the deliverance of women. Much of the housewife's domestic work was nothing more than "ceremonial cleanliness" involving "wasted effort" in an attempt to maintain the family's social status. "The lady of the house," Veblen wrote scornfully, is really "the chief menial of the household."[74]

These lone voices found little support, and proponents of "the home fried doughnut school of moral philosophy" won the day.[75] Take housework out of the home, they cried? What will that do to children's physical and moral development? What will that do to the home, the one quiet refuge to which the family breadwinner can safely retire after a hard day's work? No, they insisted, no one can replace the solicitous ministrations of the wife-mother as she selflessly devotes her days to the care and feeding of her family.

The time was ripe for the flowering of the home economics movement. While the new domestic technology was eating away at many traditional housekeeping functions, the "science" of home economics supplied an ideology that breathed new life into the faltering sphere of domestic labor and bolstered its importance. Its canons also set out the new standards of good housekeeping which, along with make-work activities, ensured that whatever time the housewife saved using her new mechanical contrivances would be more than taken up in meeting the needs of her home and her family.

The roots of the home economics (or domestic science) movement can be traced to nineteenth-century household manuals such as those by Catherine Beecher. Still, it was not until the founding of the Home Economics Association in 1909 and the proliferation of home economics courses in schools and colleges in the first decades of this century that the movement really got under way. Home economics was defined as "the study of the economic, sanitary, and aesthetic aspect of food, clothing and shelter" by the Home Economics Association, which successfully lobbied to have the new discipline made part of the regular school curriculum. Some thirty-five states set up home economics courses in the public schools, and in 1917 the Smith-Hughes Act provided a federal subsidy for courses in the subject to train "girls and women for useful employment as housedaughters and homemakers engaged in the occupations and management of the home."[76]

Books on how to teach the "domestic arts" at various grade levels and home economics textbooks suitable for elementary, high school, and college students began to flood the market. The home economists viewed their subject as the essence of a good female education. The study of home economics for women, wrote the author of a teacher training manual, "is so vital an expression of her nature that any curriculum that does not include training for the home sphere ignores the very center about which her life revolves."[77] The table of contents of this manual lists such topics as physics and chemistry, the chemistry of foods and dietetics, cooking and serving meals, bacteriology and biology, laundering, economics and sociology—rather an odd mix of subjects! More revealing are the author's suggested lesson plans. One gives instructions for teaching seventh-grade girls the art of sewing an apron.

The aims of this lesson, writes the author, are not merely to cut and sew an apron but "to emphasize the importance of cleanliness and economy." Teachers are told to ask their pupils such challenging questions as "Why are aprons worn? Are all aprons alike? In what condition should cooking aprons always be?"[78]

The effort to elevate housework into something more than drudge labor is evident in one home economics text written for elementary school children. In a lesson on "dirt and dust," the authors ask their young readers: "Have you ever thought of cleaning as artistic work? Nothing can be beautiful unless it is clean, and you are adding to the beauty in your house as well as its healthfulness in all the sweeping and dusting and washing that are so necessary."[79]

The study of home economics was used to justify higher education for women, the argument being that it made them better wives and mothers. The time-worn suggestion that homemaking was as much a career as law and medicine was also resurrected, and there were professionals willing and able to teach it. The author of the 1919 text *Housewifery*, for example, is identified as an "Instructor in Housewifery and Laundering at Teacher's College, Columbia University."[80]

A good dose of home economics was proposed as the antidote to the problem of "late marriage" among educated women. Quoting a 1911 teacher's guide: "The author believes college women would marry earlier in life if their interests were enlisted in the study of problems directly connected with homemaking; there can be nothing more interesting for the average normal woman. Women's study of proper food, proper clothing and shelter . . . benefits humanity more than years of study of Greek and Latin classics." But what of the woman who devoted her time to traditional academic subjects? Writers cited the "truly pitiable" case of "a girl of fine mind, a graduate of one of the Eastern colleges for women" who although "perfectly prepared in mathematics" was so totally ignorant of household affairs that she did not even know how to sew a shirtwaist and the only thing she could cook was fudge![81]

The champions of home economcs saw the discipline as an application of chemistry, physics, and biology to the mundane world of housekeeping. For Ellen Swallow Richards, the widely acknowledged founder of the movement and the holder of a graduate degree in chemistry from the Massachusetts Institute of Technology, scientizing housework transformed it into a creative and crucial sphere. The seriousness with which the early home economists crusaded for their cause can be noted from the Proceedings of the Second Lake Placid Conference on Home Economics. "Home and social economics have so vital a connection with every branch of education," declared one participant, "that, in a way, we must carry the whole burden at once, though we feel like Atlas with a world on our backs. Let us remember that we are of one attacking party. All along the line we must storm the defenses and plant our standards."[82]

Some proponents of home economics were less severe and depicted housekeeping as a wonderful blend of science and art. An editorial in a 1905 issue of the *Ladies' Home Journal* was of this genre: In preparing meals, "if you will use your imagination you can bring up pictures of many lands," its author rhapsodized, while at the same time "you have studies in the chemistry and physics of cookery." Women were advised that in washing dishes "the silver, glass, and china should appeal to your aesthetic taste."[83]

Whatever their tone, the home economists urged women to question both their standards and their efficiency in the home. But the goal of the movement was most emphatically *not* to give women more leisure or to allow them to seek paid employment; rather, it was to promote the exchange of certain housewifely duties for other ones. For example, a participant in the Third Lake Placid Conference censured women who "wasted time" preparing elaborate dishes that would be consumed in fifteen minutes: "If the time given by many women to fancy cooking were given to studying food values and the money spent in buying better cooking utensils, much would be gained." Efficiency in housework was also intended to "free" women to spend more time helping their husbands with their careers and their children with their homework; it would also allow them to do more charitable work. Critics even worried that with all the new domestic contrivances the modern housewife would become "dangerously idle," in the words of a 1911 editorial in the *Ladies' Home Journal*. The same editorial criticized women who complained that they were "tied down" with housework and child care, moralizing that "what a certain type of woman needs today more than anything else is some task that would 'tie her down.' Our whole social fabric would be better for it."[84]

A new component of the home economics movement—the scientific management approach to good housekeeping—began to flourish during the second decade of this century. The home was to be a professionally managed factory and the housewife was to follow the same sort of principles that Frederick Taylor had developed for industry. Scientific management was to the realm of housekeeping what John Watson's behaviorist dicta (also influenced by Taylorism) were to the realm of mothering. Efficiency and scheduling were central to both. Women were told to analyze how they spent their time, to make lists of their tasks, and to estimate the time required to complete them most efficiently. Women were to stick to a strict schedule and not give more time to a chore than it required. This, claimed the scientific managers, would eliminate the need for servants and would make housework challenging. Where the old housekeeping meant drudgery, "the new housekeeping takes drudgery out of the home," reported a 1915 article in the *Ladies' Home Journal*. Moreover, as the housewife follows the dictates of science, her job is "lifted up into a profession."[85]

"Homemaking," proclaimed Christine Frederick, will become an "object of keen mental interest" once the housewife adopts "an efficiency attitude of mind." Her book *The New Housekeeping*, which was serialized in the *Ladies' Home Journal* in 1912, was the bible of the home efficiency movement. Frederick addressed herself to the "refined, educated" middle class woman because housekeeping for the very wealthy and for the very poor was not seen as a problem. After all, said Frederick, the wealthy have servants to attend to such work, and for the poor housekeeping is "less complex" because "society demands no standard from them."[86] In the introduction to her volume Frederick tells how she became interested in applying scientific methods to the household. "I won't have you men do all the great and noble things!" she told her husband. "I'm going to find out how these [efficiency] experts conduct their investigations . . . and then apply it to *my* factory, *my* business, *my* home." If the home is a business, then the housewife is its executive director and her household appliances are the tools of her trade. Industrialization, far from taking away women's occupation, Frederick soothed, has put the modern housewife "into even a more responsible position, that of spender and buyer—she has become purchasing agent of the home and of society."[87]

The language of business pervaded the scientific management approach to housework. Women were told that because their home appliances were an "investment" they ought to be concerned with their "return on investment" and on their "depreciation." The analogy between the home and the business world is also evident in some of the titles published between 1910 and 1920: *Increasing Home Efficiency, The Home and Its Management, The Efficient Kitchen,* and *The Business of the Household.* In 1913 the National Society for the Promotion of Industrial Education described housekeeping as "a big, vital progressive enterprise, requiring as much skill in the administration of its affairs as a manufacturing plant or a business undertaking."[88]

One of the keys to scientizing the domestic sphere and making it more businesslike was the efficient use of time. But the efficient use of time first required work, that is, time-motion studies. "Motion study," wrote Frederick, "means close analysis of work, whether it is peeling potatoes, making bread, or dusting a room." The object was to analyze each task "so that we may learn to do it in a way that is most pleasant and least fatiguing." The housewife will be delighted to find that where it took her 45 minutes to wash 80 dishes, with more efficient methods it will take her only 30 minutes. Frederick urged women to analyze the height and arrangement of their domestic equipment and to cut down on needless motions when doing a particular chore.[89]

Because the housewife's home was her "business," writers urged her to keep painstaking records of household affairs. She should not only record household accounts, medical records, and addresses but "toilet and laundry hints, baby hygiene, entertainment suggestions, jokes and quotations" plus create a general inventory of all household items. In addition, she should maintain a pantry record, a preserve record, a linen record, and a library record (according to the subject of the book). It was also a good idea to label all drawers in the house indicating the condition of their contents.[90]

Just as efficiency and scheduling in child care would give women free time to peruse the manuals containing the latest dicta of the behaviorists, so too, by following scientific methods of housekeeping, women would have more time to study the principles on which their housework was based. It should be clear at this point that in reality the new "efficient" methods of housekeeping were not really efficient at all. They actually meant more work, rather than less work, because they added a series of new, time-consuming activities to women's traditional domestic tasks.

How can we explain the remarkably convergent efforts to scientize housework and child care during the first decades of the twentieth century? Like the behaviorists' demand for regularity and discipline in child rearing, the stress on efficiency in housework can only be understood within the context of industrial capitalism. Scientific management principles pervaded economic and social ethics; attempts were made to use it to control labor in business and industry and to vigorously mold children into a compliant and self-disciplined future labor force. The work of the home could not be left untouched in this milieu; it could not continue to be done in a lax and disorganized manner. If children were to be reared under strict behaviorist principles, the home itself must be systematized and regulated. After all, what better example could a child have than a mother diligently following a strict and efficient routine as she prepared dinner, cleaned house, and did the laundry?

Given the commitment that was necessary for a true science of housekeeping, "there is a very strong case against the presence of the permanent worker in the home," Frederick wrote in 1919. Not only were "good tools not always to be trusted in the hands of servants" but it was only in "the servantless household" that the "*exact standards*" could be followed.[91]

Employment for married women was completely out of the question for much the same reason. "Our greatest enemy," Frederick proclaimed in 1914, "is the woman with the career." Why? Because when she does housework "she feels she is weighted down." The woman with an "unnatural craving" for a career was denigrated. "It is just as stimulating to bake a sponge cake on a six minute schedule as it is to monotonously address envelopes for three hours in a downtown office." The antidote to such unnatural cravings was, of course, scientific housekeeping, because "the science of homemaking and of motherhood, if followed out on an efficient plan, can be the most glorious career open to any woman."[92]

Despite myriad suggestions about how to do housework, the home economists and the scientific managers assiduously avoided discussing certain aspects of the domestic realm. The traditional sexual division of labor was never questioned. Nor were the social and economic issues surrounding women's unpaid domestic labor ever raised. All of the problematic features of being a full-time housewife in the industrial era were simply ignored.

Good housekeeping in the United States in the twentieth century is fraught with contradictions and ambiguities. Housewives find themselves in something akin to a preindustrial setting, one in which a woman's home and work place are not separate. Yet housewives live in a world in which this unity is no longer the norm. Several problems arise from this arrangement. Housewives can never get away from their work; it is always with them because there is always something to be done. At the same time, domestic chores, because they are done at home and are not remunerated, are not recognized as work by law and custom.

The housewife, working alone in her own home, lacks an audience. No one is there to judge or appreciate what she is doing. She is neither systematically rewarded nor criticized for her performance because there is no public consensus as to what a housewife should do and when and how she should do it. There are no organizations that set standards of excellence and sanction those who do not live up to them. The housewife has no means of measuring her performance against those who do the same work, no real way of assuring herself that she is doing a good job.

Housework also lacks a concrete measure of value. It is neither legally nor economically considered work. A housewife's services are not counted in the gross national product and the federal social security system does not recognize them as such. Since earning money is the main way that the worth of an activity is measured, unpaid labor, no matter how strenuous and time-consuming, is less valued socially than paid labor.

The absence of required tasks and the formlessness of the housewife's day also can be problematic features of housework. A woman can decide to vacuum the rugs and wash the kitchen floor and bake a cake—or she can decide not to do any of these things. The point is that she does not have to do any of them. She can put them off for tomorrow or next week. Housework consists of many different tasks requiring different levels of skill and concentration. A woman may switch tasks all day long, going from one to another and then back again. She may be endlessly interrupted by a crying child, a ringing telephone, or a pot boiling over so that she does not finish the tasks she had set out for herself.

A housewife's work may also lack a sense of completion because the same chores must be done over and over again, day in and day out. Beds must be made, tables and bric-à-brac dusted, and dishes washed. Yet the products of the housewife's labor soon disappear; beds are slept in and must be remade, dust resettles on surfaces and must be wiped away, and meals create a new sinkful of dirty dishes.

The objection can be raised that domestic chores have always been repetitive and without a sense of closure. Still, in the preindustrial era the seasonal organization of life must have given women some feeling of specific accomplishment. The fall canning and the spring housecleaning were major undertakings that stayed done for a whole year. In the modern period, however, there is no set seasonal routine, no grand enterprise that, when completed, does not have to be taken up again for a considerable period of time.

Not only is the twentieth-century housewife's work impermanent, it is not noticed because it is intangible. The gourmet meal that she labors over for hours is consumed in fifteen or twenty minutes, and no one is likely to remark on her newly vacuumed carpet. Almost the only time a woman's domestic activities are noticed is when they are *not* done. A pile of dirty laundry or an unmade bed make an impact on the senses that a sparkling clean kitchen or a dust-free living room cannot. What concrete accomplishments can the modern housewife point to then? Unlike the preindustrial housewife, who could show off the garments she had sewn or the rows of canned fruits and vegetables she had preserved, the work of the contemporary homemaker is much more difficult to appreciate because it makes no permanent visible change in the home.

Housework is also held in low esteem because it is said to involve only unskilled manual labor. In fact, a wide range of knowledge is demanded of housewives. While it is true that the bare necessities of housework—cleaning and cooking simple meals—involve minimal skill, other tasks, such as gourmet cooking, home decoration, and sewing clothes may assume a high level of proficiency. Moreover, the basic skills needed for homemaking are nearly uniform for the entire adult female population. Sociologist Theodore Caplow noted that "the same job requirements are imposed on morons and on women of superior intelligence."[93]

There is one other aspect of housewifery in the industrial era that the home economists and scientific managers did their upmost to conceal: good housekeeping in twentieth-century America is simply not a full-time job. Given the ubiquitous domestic conveniences of the average American household, and excluding child care, housework is really part-time work. The real essentials of housework—cooking, cleaning, and doing the laundry—can be done in a few hours a day. Only when women's advisors demand lofty standards of cleanliness, elaborate meal preparation, and domestic make-work activities of various kinds is homemaking transformed into a full-time occupation.

The final question, of course, is just what purpose was served in obscuring the problematic nature of contemporary housework and keeping women contented and fully occupied in the home? During the early decades of the century American business and industry became ever more dependent on the production and mass distribution of consumer goods. As this occurred, family life and its consumption patterns became critical to the continued expansion of the economy. But since buying, using, and maintaining consumer items takes time and effort, someone had to take charge of these activities for the family. What better and more appropriate role for the middle class housewife, who had lost many of her traditional domestic functions?

The home economists and scientific managers came up with an ingenious rationale for keeping women—the overseers of consumption—ensconced in the home. By elaborating housework, the prescriptive writers provided women with endless but "essential" suggestions of how to fill their time. By equating the home with a business and elevating the housewife to a managerial position within it, they sought to convince well-educated middle class women of the professional nature of their unpaid labor. And by advising women of the need for high domestic standards, standards that only the full-time housewife could hope to maintain, they sought to disabuse women of any thought of paid employment. Finally, if a woman was bored or discontented with her domestic lot, she was told that she only had herself to blame. A woman's problems, Frederick insisted, stemmed from "her own lack of personal efficiency," not circumstances, fate, or other people. Certainly no writer blamed the nature of housework in the industrial era. The final irony was that if the modern housewife, surrounded by her labor-saving devices, took the pronouncements of these writers seriously, she probably found herself busier than ever before.[94]

5 HOUSE BEAUTIFUL

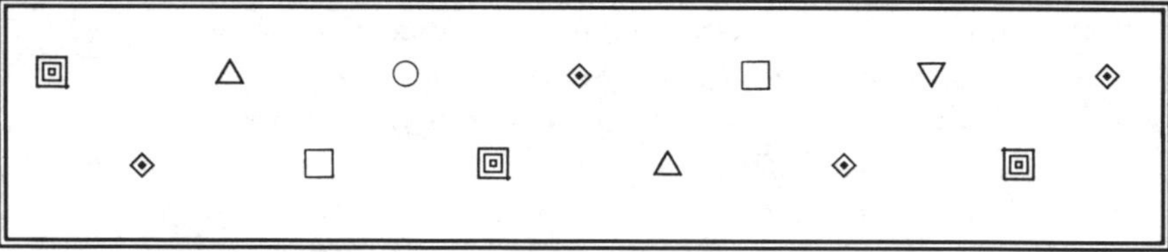

No laborer in the world is expected to work for room, board and love—except the housewife.

Letty Cottin Pogrebin, "Rethinking Housework," 1978

The 1920s were a watershed in good housekeeping in the United States. The currents present during the first two decades of this century—the spread of utilities and labor-saving devices, the decline in the number of household servants, and the training of women as administrators of consumption—crystallized during the 1920s and set the tone of housework for years to come. And an important new ingredient was added to the domestic stew during the decade: mass advertising. The advertising-laden pages of the women's magazines of the twenties are testimony to the degree to which buying had superseded producing. "In earlier days," notes historian Ruth Schwartz Cowan, "the young housewife had to be taught to make things well; in the 1920s she had to be taught to buy things well."[1] Business and advertising made a powerful team in extolling the joys of the "new freedom" to be found in purchasing the mass-produced goods then coming on the market.

Housewives, the major purchasing agents of the home, were now vitally important to American business and industry. A larger volume of sales was made possible in part by the full-time housewife's focus on consumption. Economist Staffan Burenstam Linder has noted the time and energy demanded by ever greater rates of consumption. "As the volume of consumption increases," he wrote, "requirements for the care and maintenance of these goods also tends to increase. We get bigger houses to clean, bigger gardens to look after, a car to wash . . . and a television to repair."[2]

The popular media ignored the time and work involved in consumption, and from the 1920s the American middle class housewife was widely depicted as a "lady of leisure" whose myriad labor-saving devices left her little to do all day. While a woman's duties had certainly changed, higher standards of cleanliness, an elaboration of housekeeping tasks, and rising social expectations in the requirements of proper family care all ensured that the full-time housewife spent a great deal of time seeing that her family was well clothed, well fed, and well housed. Despite the plethora of modern household conveniences, there is little evidence that housework was less time-consuming and less demanding than it had been before American business and industry entered and transformed the home.

The image of "house beautiful" which prevailed from the 1920s through the 1950s did not begin to crack until the late 1960s or 1970s. Then, with more than half of all married women in the labor force, the lofty and elaborate standards of good housekeeping that had been espoused by women's domestic advisors for decades were trampled under the burden of the double day. Women held two jobs—one at work and one at home—and no longer needed advice on how to stay busy. Times indeed had changed; homemaking, for the first time since industrialization, was no longer a full-time career for the majority of married middle class women.

Selling Mrs. Consumer: 1920s—1930s

. . . the home woman as purchasing agent is essential to present well-being and social progress.

Benjamin Andrews, "The Home Woman as Buyer and Controller of Consumption," 1929

Why is it never said that the really crucial function, the really important role that women serve as housewives, is to buy more things for the house.

Betty Friedan, *The Feminine Mystique,* 1974

The role of the housewife in the 1920s was that of consumer par excellence. Housewives had indeed become the major purchasing agents of the nation. By 1929 women bought 80 percent of the products used by their families, and business and advertisers saw them as the best channels for getting products into the home. The pages of women's magazines were filled with tips on "wise shopping" and with articles on how to use the latest domestic appliances properly. One home economist cited "the grave responsibility of the homemaker as purchaser." Christine Frederick wrote in 1929, "Mrs. Consumer has billions to spend—the greatest surplus money value ever given to women in all history" and "she is having a gorgeous time spending it." Neither Frederick nor the women's magazines were the least bit reticent in their efforts to persuade women to purchase the newly available household conveniences. An editorial in the *Ladies' Home Journal* had extravagant praise for woman as consumer:

> For the first time in the world's history it is possible for a nation's women in general to have . . . homes and the means of furnishing them in keeping with their instinctive longings. The women of America are to be congratulated, not only on the opportunity but because of the manner they are responding to it. When the record is written this may stand as their greatest contribution.[3]

What was the background for this focus on consumption? Following World War I factories devoted to the war industry rapidly converted to the production of consumer goods, and because of their relatively stable markets and large marketing potential the consumer goods industries were the first sector of the economy to become dominated by large-scale enterprises. By the 1920s two-thirds of national income was being spent on consumer items: staples, canned and prepared food, clothing, furniture, household appliances, and automobiles, among others. Moreover, between 1909 and 1927 there was a 500 percent increase in expenditures for household appliances and a 250 percent increase in expenditures for ready-made clothing.[4]

Buying on credit also expanded the horizons of the consumer and enabled manufacturers to sell far more household products than would otherwise have been possible. The installment payment plan was introduced in the 1920s and it made possible the purchase of expensive home appliances that a family would use for many years. By 1925, 90 percent of all washing machines, sewing machines, and refrigerators were sold on credit as were 85 percent of all vacuum cleaners and 70 percent of all kitchen ranges.[5]

The massive entry of commercial products into the home left no area of housework unaffected. Of course, the prerequisite for such conveniences was the spread of public utilities. By 1925 just under 70 percent of all urban and nonfarm rural households in the United States had electricity. After World War I, coal- and wood-burning stoves rapidly gave way to gas and oil stoves. A 1925 survey of Ohio households found that 90 percent had gas ranges, and by 1930 cooking with coal and wood had completely died out in urban areas. Gas, oil, and electric heat were far preferable to the grease- and grime-producing coal-burning furnace. Indoor plumbing also became common during the 1920s, and it was just after the war that bathroom fixtures were mass-produced for the first time.[6]

As mass production and credit buying became prevalent the prices of household appliances decreased and more and more families could afford to own them. Electric refrigerators, for example, cost a whopping $900 when they first came on the market in 1916, but by 1929 the price had fallen to $180. As a result, refrigerator sales increased by 276 percent during the decade, although the icebox was still the norm until well into the 1930s.[7]

Washing machine sales also boomed as their price fell from the mid-1920s. Although electric washers made doing laundry easier, the machines still had to be monitored because they did not go through the washing cycles automatically and lacked a spin-dry cycle. The housewife had to stand by her washer to start it and stop it at the right time, to add soap flakes—which were first marketed about 1920—and to put the

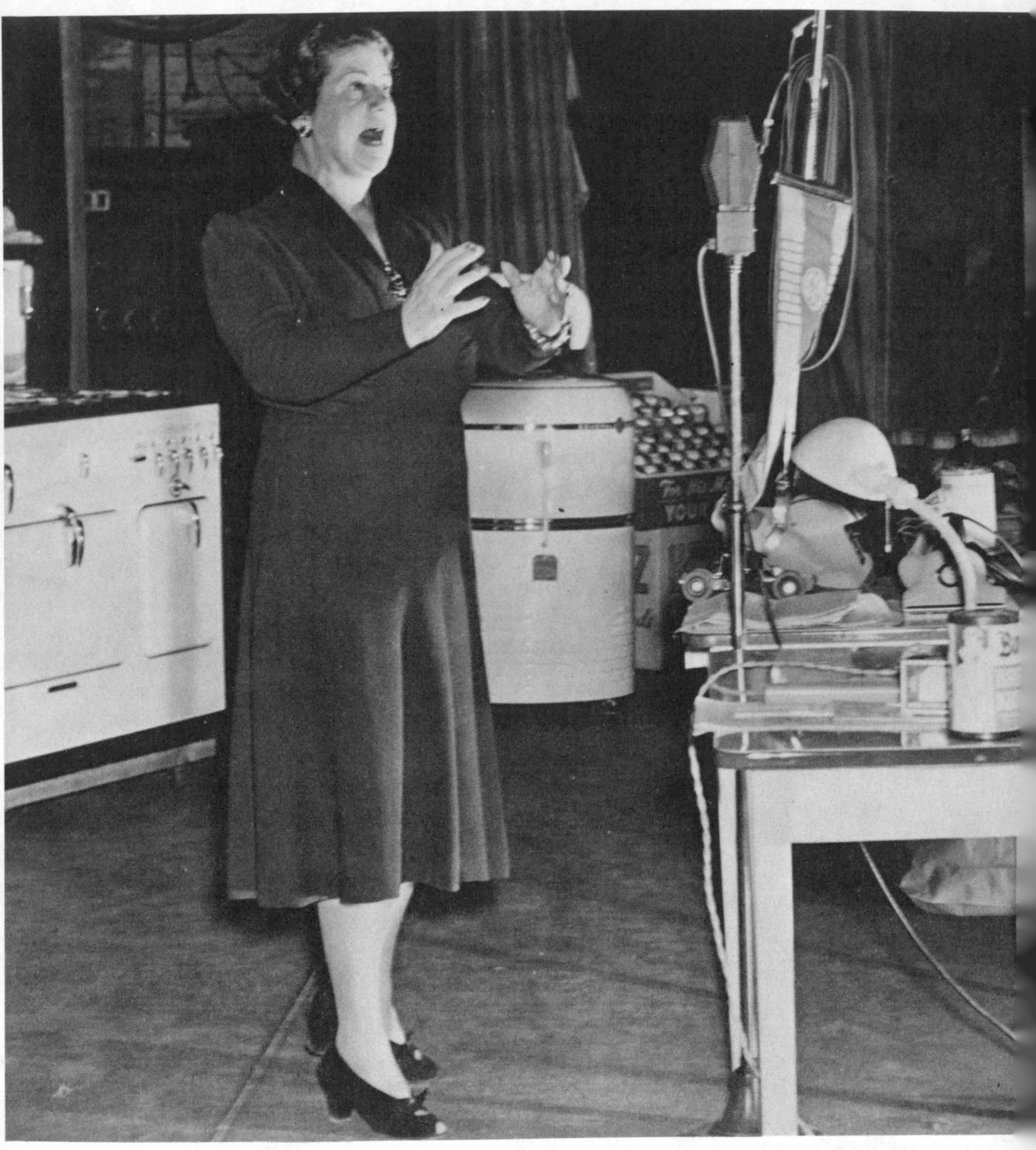

Frederick Papers, Schlesinger Library, Radcliffe College

Christine Frederick • *Christine Frederick was a leader of the "household engineering" movement of the 1920s. Here she is in 1950 advising her audience on the use of the latest household appliances.*

clothes through the wringer by hand. Fully automatic washing machines were not available until the 1940s.[8]

The new kitchen appliances and the many new food products on the market simplified meal preparation. By the end of World War I, the variety of canned goods available was nearly as great as it is today; soup, vegetables, fruit, meat, and beans all could be bought in cans. Boxes of crackers, cold cereals, and mixes of various kinds lined grocers shelves. By the 1920s housewives were far more likely to buy bread than to bake it at home.[9]

Family clothing was also more often store-bought than homemade by the 1920s. In their 1929 study of "Middletown" (Muncie, Indiana), sociologists Robert and Helen Lynd found that 80 percent of working class wives and 90 percent of "business class" wives did not sew their own or their children's clothes but bought them in stores.[10]

Domestic servants in the 1920s were even less common than they had been during the first two decades of the century. Better work opportunities and higher wages in other sectors meant that only relatively wealthy families could afford to hire help. By 1920 a live-in servant was paid an average of $25 per week plus room and board, while her counterpart in 1890 had received an average of $4 a week in wages. The Lynds reported that business class wives had half the number of servants that their mothers had had three decades earlier, and they were far more likely to employ a woman who "came-in" once or twice a week than to have full-time live-in help.[11]

These statistics were mirrored in the women's magazines of the 1920s. In 1918 issues of the *Ladies' Home Journal* many ads depicted servants, but a decade later it was the scrupulously groomed housewife herself who was running the vacuum cleaner or doing the laundry. In Ruth Schwartz Cowan's words: "The ideal housewife of the 1920s and 1930s did not have servants; or to put it another way, the servants she had were electrical, not human."[12]

The manufacturers of household appliances and their advertising agencies were quick to appreciate the phenomenon of the servantless home and use it to sell their products. A 1928 ad for Hotpoint advised a woman to economize by buying a new gas range and getting rid of her maid. An editorial in a 1929 issue of *Ladies' Home Journal* suggested the following trade-off: "The price of a maid for a year, invested in modern household equipment, will run a house so completely and easily that perhaps the maid will never be wanted." And in her 1929 book *Selling Mrs. Consumer,* Christine Frederick made no bones about the connection between consumer sales and the lack of servants: "When the wife herself was forced to take up servants' tasks, then she became eager for tools and mechanisms which would save her own hands, her own muscles, her personal time or conserve her appearance."[13]

Economist John Kenneth Galbraith has called this transformation of women into a "crypto-servant class" an economic accomplishment of the first order. The demise of domestic servants, said Galbraith, along with higher levels of consumption, "created an urgent need for labor to administer or otherwise manage consumption." Hence the "servant-wife," the full-time housewife who chose products and saw to their upkeep. This is a major economic accomplishment, according to Galbraith, because the housewife's work permitted consumption to expand more or less indefinitely, an expansion essential to the continued growth of American capitalism. In the words of Stuart Ewen, author of *Captains of Consciousness,* an account of the growth of the advertising industry in the 1920s: "The transcendence of traditional consumer markets and buying habits required people to buy, not to satisfy their own fundamental needs, but rather to satisfy the real historic needs of capitalist productive machinery."[14]

The transformation of women into servant substitutes, however, presented certain problems. Domestic servants had always had low status; they did the dirty work of the household and were paid low wages. Could the middle class housewife retain her status and at the same time clean toilets and scour pots and pans? Jane Davison has written that "social considerations demanded that a woman's collar seem to be white, though she obviously knew that, out of sight, its lining had a bluish tinge."[15]

Women's domestic advisors, backed by the consumer and advertising industries, came up with an ingenious solution to this dilemma, a solution Galbraith has termed the "convenient social virtue." The convenient social virtue is a value judgment that cleverly finds merit in behavior that serves an important function for the more powerful segments of society. Such behavior is praised and it receives social approval instead of being remunerated. In the case at hand, the convenient social virtue reduced the costs of consumption by substituting social praise for pay.[16]

In order to sever the housewife's identification with the domestic servant and to commend her for her work, the women's magazines of the 1920s waxed long and eloquent on the differences in emotional quality between the loving wife and mother and the "uneducated" (read: black or immigrant) maid.[17] Housewives did not simply cook for their families, they made them wholesome, nutritious meals that built strong minds and strong bodies; women did not merely scrub floors, they routed germs that might attack their children; they did not just sew curtains or reupholster furniture, they created an attractive environment in which their families would thrive. Could such loving care and attention to detail be expected of hired servants? Of course not. The cultural message was clear and the woman who ignored it was made to feel guilty: no maid could ever perform housework with the same degree of emotional attachment as the woman of the house could.

The attempt to sever the housewife's potential identification with the role of domestic servant was done by ignoring the manual labor involved in housework and stressing its managerial content. In the words of a *Ladies' Home Journal* editorial, the modern homemaker "has a many-sided job calling for all the skill and training of a big business executive." Few businessmen, and only those in executive positions, agreed the author of an article in the same journal, "have an equal opportunity with the housekeeper for the exercise of dignified executive work." Housekeeping, she concluded, "is a Real Job, a business." Some advertisements contained the same message; for instance, a 1924 ad: "Through her dealings as business manager of the home, the modern woman brings sound commercial sense to bear on her judgement of a Ford closed car."[18]

The core of the housewife's managerial role was of course her position as purchasing agent of the home. "Organized training for successful spending" seemed to be the chief preoccupation of the women's magazines published in the 1920s. Some two-thirds of all advertising was directed at the "home woman." Thrift was out, consumerism was in; buying things was equated with the "good life." An editorial in the *Ladies' Home Journal* proclaimed that "the American home was never a more satisfying place than it is today. Science and invention have outfitted it with a great range of conveniences and comforts." The "old antique worshiping standard," as Christine Frederick called it, became abhorrent as the magazine writers emphasized modernity and sneered at traditional methods of housekeeping. "Home has caught up with Industry in this mechanical age," women were told; "it is no longer on a handwork basis—it was out of fashion and bound to suffer as long as it remained so."[19]

The women's magazines of the 1920s also promoted buying through product-testing services, mail-order shopping, pamphlets, and promotional schemes of various kinds, all in the guise of "educating the consumer." In fact, the concern with buying and spending so pervaded the magazines that the distinction between ads and articles is blurred, so fervently did both extol the benefits of consumer goods. The author of a 1927 *Ladies' Home Journal* piece entitled "Why Housework Is Not Drudgery" boasts that she owns all the latest appliances—a clothes washer, electric iron, even a dishwasher, which was very rare in those days—and explains why she bought them: ". . . because we like order and cleanliness we have invested in every practical labor saver within our reach in order to get the work out of the way quickly."[20]

Some of the advertising copy in the women's magazines semantically turned consumption into production, thus assuring women that they had not lost their economic function. Buying was "a productive act" because it could "multiply manyfold the satisfactions from a given income." Through wise buying women could save money or make it go farther; in so doing they were creating something of value by giving their families a higher standard of living. Other ads suggested that "buying" was more creative than "making": buying gave women the freedom to choose from the vast array of consumer goods coming on the market.[21]

Another tactic used to sell household goods to women was to raise the specters of fear, embarrassment, and guilt. Ruth Schwartz Cowan described the unfortunate woman who was "embarrassed if her friends arrived to find that her sink was clogged, guilty if her children went to school in soiled clothes, guilty if she didn't eradicate all the germs behind the bathroom sink . . . guilty if her daughter was not popular with the crowd (her mother having failed to keep her dresses properly ironed)." Just as mothers could permanently damage their children by not taking the advice of the child-rearing experts seriously, so too they risked their offspring's health and happiness if they failed to use certain products. In a 1925 ad for Grapenuts cereal, an unidentified "famous scientist" told women: "Tell me what your children eat and I will show you what kind of men and women they will be!" A 1926 ad for Lysol warned women that even "doorknobs threaten children . . . with disease."[22]

The concrete benefits of using the new products were loudly proclaimed. Women would become better mothers because they would have more time to spend with their children. Robert and Helen Lynd cite the following ad for an electric company:

> This is the test of a successful mother—she puts first things first. She does not give to sweeping the time that belongs to her children . . . the wise woman delegates to electricity all that electricity can do. She cannot delegate the one task most important. Human lives are in her keeping; their future is molded by her hands and heart.

So too the new products made for younger, more glamorous wives. Here is a 1929 ad in the *Saturday Evening Post*:

> I was the woman whose husband gave her each Christmas some pretty trinket. The woman whose youth was skipping away from her too fast. The woman whose cleaning burdens were too heavy. . . . In one short year I have discovered that youth need not go swiftly—that cleaning duties need not be burdensome. For last Christmas my husband gave me a *Hoover*.[23]

The seduction of this line of reasoning is remarkable: If women bought these products, advertisers and their allies in the media said, they would become better wives and mothers because they would spend less time on housework and more time with their families. Two messages came across loud and clear: women's place was still in the home and time saved was certainly not meant to be spent in outside employment.

The impossibility of having a "house beautiful" *and* a job was a popular theme of the day. "The home will suffer a kind of domestic suicide" if the housewife becomes a regular wage earner, warned a home economist. Why should women want jobs anyway when homemaking was such a creative endeavor? "Offices rarely reflect the personality of those working in them," women were told, "but homes—have you seen one of those new purple and pink bathrooms?" "Part-time wives are the scourge of present-day domesticity," a critic of "pin money slaves" informed her audience. If fewer women took jobs, there would be "fewer grimy curtains hung askew by careless helpers from Harlem."[24]

Why this insistence that a woman could not hope to be an adequate homemaker if she took a job? The influx of immigrants from Europe from the mid-nineteenth century had provided an adequate supply of male labor to fill the jobs available. Prevailing social values expected married men to work to support themselves and their families while their wives tended to them and produced and reared their successors. This arrangement was satisfactory to powerful segments of American society. Women's unpaid domestic labor groomed future workers and managers for business and industry at little or less cost than if their services had to be remunerated, and it also ensured a growing market for consumer goods. Not only were married women unneeded in the labor force, but who would rear the next generation if they were to take jobs? And what would happen to the birthrate if married women left home?

At the same time many working men, backed by their unions, strongly opposed the entry of married women into the labor force. What would happen to male wages if there were an influx of married women into the job market? How would the working man ever be able to support his family if forced to compete with a vast new supply of cheap labor? So from the nineteenth century, women's domestic advisors busied themselves expounding all the reasons why marriage and motherhood were simply incompatible with paid employment.

The editorials, articles, and advertisements in women's magazines seemed to be doing for homemaking in the 1920s what Dr. Spock did for child rearing two decades later: encouraging immediate gratification. Just as discipline and self-control were later repudiated for raising children, so too frugality and saving for a rainy day were now frowned on in housekeeping. Women were encouraged to spend, to buy the latest model, the newest product. Christine Frederick wrote approvingly of the housewife who "does not hesitate to throw out of her house much that is still useful, even half-new, in order to make room for the newest 'best.' "[25] This ideology promoted even greater consumption because each new possession required special equipment to care for it or special products to use with it. If a woman bought a rug, she would certainly need an electric vacuum; if she got a washing machine, she would need soap flakes; and if she purchased an electric iron, she would also require an ironing board.

As part of the promotion of products, manufacturers encouraged the idea of the "industrialized home" in which the same work techniques used in industry would be adapted to the household. Frederick advised advertisers that "they must educate, train, and *transfer a worker from a hand and craft technique over into a tool technique.*" Just as scientific principles were used to manage labor in capitalist enterprises, so too they were to guide the housewife in her daily round of activities. The routines of the factory operative were the new model for the woman working in the home.[26]

"Household engineering" was the 1920s rubric for scientific management of the domestic sphere. "Are you a household engineer?" asked a writer in *Ladies' Home Journal*. "Have you learned that there are ways of taking at least some of the drudgery out of the old, familiar household routine?" she queried her readers. Probably the most widely read manual

Frederick Papers, Schlesinger Library, Radcliffe College

Store Window • *From the 1920s on, a wide variety of household goods came on the market. Women's magazines informed their readers how to decorate their homes and improve their lifestyles by buying the new products.*

containing advice of this genre was Lillian Gilbreth's 1928 *The Homemaker and Her Job*. Gilbreth, an industrial psychologist and coauthor with her husband of *Cheaper by the Dozen*, argued that drudgery in housework was simply the result of "wasted energy." And her solution: a detailed study of housework including surveys, calendars, records, and measurements of the time and motion involved in each housekeeping activity. Efficiency was the goal, efficiency that would lead to "the largest number of happiness minutes for the largest number of people."[27]

Here are some of Gilbreth's specific suggestions. A "process chart" should be constructed for each activity to find "the one best way to do the work." The "string and pin method" is one way of making such a chart. Here, an observer follows a worker around with a ball of string and measures the distance the worker travels in completing a task. A plan of the work place is drawn up, with pins indicating the points where the worker has changed direction. Then the lengths of string are measured to scale and are wound around the pins, showing the path the worker covered.[28]

The pin-and-string method can be used for a time-motion study of after-meal cleanup. A child with a string follows mother while she clears the table and stacks the dishes. The child makes a sketch of the dining room and kitchen and plots mother's path on it. As mother changes her method of doing the dishes, a string of a different color will be used to mark her path—a different color string shows her improvement. Once this part of the study is complete, the best way of doing a chore is determined and changes in the work place or equipment may be made to increase efficiency. The "one best way" is written down on an instruction sheet and posted so that everyone doing the task will perform it in the same way. "No one who has not made such a pin plan," Gilbreth headily wrote, "can know how interesting the process is," and if all household tasks were analyzed in this way even "the simplest kinds of work, those classed as 'unskilled labor,' may be made skilled."[29] Gilbreth never questioned the large investment of time necessary to find the "one best way" of doing a task, nor did she raise the possibility that finding the "one best way" might actually take more time than the amount of time saved by using the new method.

It was probably the rare housewife who actually followed the time-consuming suggestions of Gilbreth and her cohorts, but the elaboration of homemaking in the women's magazines and the household manuals of the era was meant to ensure that all housewives put in a full day's work. Robert and Helen Lynd noted in their study of "Middletown" that while the physical labor of housework was less than it had been a generation earlier, "rising standards in other respects use up saved time." This is also evident in the response of a writer in *Ladies' Home Journal* to her husband's claim that contemporary housewives live in a "veritable utopia of leisure" compared to their grandmothers:

> Because we housewives of today have the tools to reach it, we dig every day after dust that grandmother left to a spring cataclysm. If few of us have nine children for a weekly bath, we have two or three for a daily immersion. If our consciences don't prick over vacant pie shelves or empty cookie jars, they do over meals in which a vitamin may be omitted or a calorie lacking.[30]

Other contemporary observers agreed that good housekeeping meant ever higher standards for the home woman. "Our progressive standards of what is necessary and what is 'nice,' " a home economist wrote in 1923, "are constantly adding work to the housewife's task." He saw this trend as a mark of "social progress" because its results were better hygiene and diet, more clothing and household equipment, and more "personal oversight of the child by the parents."[31]

These new standards could increase the housewife's work load significantly. An easy task like making a bed could become labor intensive if the new standard required that the mattress be turned twice a week and the linen stripped from the bed and aired every day. New standards of cleanliness meant that the housewife did not just do a desultory dusting of the obvious surfaces but dusted the legs of chairs, books, lampshades, and knicknacks. If she followed the advice of one manual for "new brides," she dusted *everything every day*. This manual also advised that she move all the furniture once a week and vacuum on and under rugs, books, curtains, and window shades. Other weekly activities included cleaning and rearranging cupboards, cleaning the refrigerator, polishing the silver, waxing the floors, dusting doors, windowsills, and dustboards, and cleaning out the closets. The annual spring cleaning was transformed into a monumental undertaking in which the housewife was told to carry out the bedsprings to be "aired and brushed" along with all the mattresses and rugs in the house. Walls and ceilings, including those in the closet, were to be scrubbed down. Drawers were to be emptied out and washed, as were the inside of chests and cabinets. Faced with these herculean tasks, should a woman doubt the joys of spring cleaning, she had only to remember that it produced a house "with such a hushed and dewy, newborn expression that you want to walk [through it on] tiptoe."[32]

Some might still argue that the new labor-saving devices saved the housewife time despite these higher standards. But most of the devices were devoted to a single task and simply replaced older equipment: the electric vacuum replaced the broom and the gas range replaced the fire stove. The core of housekeeping remained firmly entrenched in the home; while a machine might do the work more efficiently, the catch was that someone still had to be there to operate the device and satisfy the higher standards the experts dictated.

One housekeeping task, doing the laundry, probably became *more* time-consuming with the advent of the new household technology. A 1907–1908 survey found that 88 percent of middle income families hired laundresses or sent at least some of their clothes and linen to commercial establishments for laundering. But by the 1920s, 60 percent of this income group was using home washers, and by the 1930s, only 15 percent of them sent any clothes or linens to commercial establishments. The Lynds pointed out that as washing machines and electric irons became more common in "Middletown," commercial laundries were used less:

> The heavy investment of the individual family in an electric washing machine costing $60 to $200 tends to perpetuate a questionable institutional set up—whereby many individual homes repeat common tasks day after day in isolated units—by forcing back into the individual home a process that was following belatedly the trend in industry towards centralized operation.[33]

So while the new electric washer certainly made the physical process of washing clothes less arduous, it did not result in time saved for the average housewife, who now found herself doing all of the family laundry. No matter how inexpensive the services, commercial laundries could not compete with the free labor provided by the housewife.

There is also evidence that the new labor-saving devices did not relieve the boredom of household chores. A 1931 study of 306 middle income housewives found that they considered doing the laundry and cleaning the most fatiguing parts of their day. Yet all of these women owned electric vacuums, irons, and washing machines, the very devices that were thought to make housework easier.[34]

Clearly the higher standards of cleanliness and nutrition and the new household devices did *not* mean that housewives spent fewer hours doing housework. A number of time budget studies dating from the 1920s and 1930s verify this assertion. One study found that middle class housewives averaged 51 hours a week doing housework, with little variation between urban and rural women; another showed that contrary to popular belief the new household technology hardly saved any time at all. The latter study compared two groups of farm wives; one group had neither electricity nor indoor plumbing, the other group had both. The women with modern conveniences devoted less time to cooking, washing, and cleaning and more time to sewing, ironing, and child care than the women without them. But the most relevant finding of the study was that the women who had electricity and indoor plumbing reduced their housework time by only one hour and ten minutes per week—a mere 2 percent of the total average time spent weekly on housework. No wonder a home economist writing in the 1930s concluded that "in most families the introduction of better equipment does not at present seem likely to reduce greatly the total working day."[35]

These studies also challenged the much heralded claim that the housewife was now primarily a manager and consumer rather than a manual laborer. Research showed that the bulk of the housewife's day was still being spent on routine housework—meal preparation and cleanup, housecleaning, laundering, and mending—with only an average of two and a half hours a week devoted to "purchasing, planning, and supervising." The housewife then, in the words of one contemporary student of the family, was "still predominantly a housekeeper, rather than a household manager."[36]

The Great Depression of the 1930s, however, did produce an exception, for housewives became entrepreneurs of sorts in allocating scarce resources under trying economic conditions. Never was it truer that women were the "shock absorbers" of the economy, "the people primarily responsible for adjusting the family to the cyclical problems of capitalism." The long-term trend toward the greater use of manufactured products in the home was temporarily reversed. As men lost their jobs and family income shrank, women's unpaid household production took on renewed importance. Housewives struggled to maintain their families' standard of living by substituting their own labor for the goods and services that in better days they had purchased.[37]

One tactic the depression era housewife used was to cut down on the amount of food and clothing bought by the family. A resurgence of home canning took place during the 1930s; more canning jars were sold in 1931 than at any time during the preceding decade. There was a concomitant drop in the sale of canned goods in stores.* Women once again began making clothes at home, although many had to attend night classes to learn how to sew. Housewives also contributed to family income by doing laundry for other people, making baked goods for sale, and taking in boarders. The women's magazines of the thirties did their part for the cause of family economy. They stressed thrift and advised women how to stretch their dollars. One suggestion was that women shop in person rather than over the phone so that they could ferret out the best bargains. A do-it-yourself craze pervaded the magazines as they instructed women how to paint old furniture, reupholster sofas and chairs, and sew curtains. As Ruth Schwartz Cowan points out, during the depression "cash wasn't available, but time was—women's time."[38]

Good housekeeping during the 1920s and 1930s was something of a paradox. Despite the deluge of labor-saving devices, a plethora of new household products, and the spread of power sources, homemaking remained a full-time job. Certainly it could have been otherwise. The new technologies could have been rationalized on a large scale. Commercial laundries, widely used during the first two decades of this century, could have increased in number. Commercial cleaning services, employing all the latest mechanical equipment, could have been started. Communal kitchens, with commercial scale ranges and refrigerators to prepare meals, might have been opened. None of these things happened. In fact, as we have seen, the new technologies were used in a very different way; they were designed for and sold to the small, individualized nuclear family unit.

*It was not only during the Great Depression that women substituted their own labor for store-bought products in order to make family income go farther, but also in 1971, in Great Britain, a time of high unemployment, sales of convenience foods fell by 5 percent.

Why this preference for the small scale and private? Was there something inherently repugnant about commercial companies invading the sanctity of the domestic realm? Was it because an early version of the "feminine mystique" arose which ensured that the tasks of feeding and caring for the family would remain firmly in feminine hands? While it is true that a feminine mystique did emerge during those decades, did this ideology *cause* housework to stay in the home despite the new technology? I think not.[39]

If we analyze the housewife's role in the larger setting of a burgeoning consumer economy, the new technology's failure to rationalize housework and to liberate women from its demands becomes more intelligible. The housewife had a key role to play and in Stuart Ewen's words "the agencies of consumption made the wife a part of a corporately defined productive and distributive process."[40] The housewife was in charge of administering consumption and this was precisely the position in which business and industry wanted her. Without millions of such administrators in home after home, buying, using, and maintaining all the new products and appliances, the expanding consumer economy would have expanded a great deal less. In addition, the small nuclear family was an eminently saleable unit; enormous numbers of domestic appliances could be sold to individual households. Perhaps this is the real reason why the very idea of large-scale or commercial housekeeping was so contrary to American values.

All the rhetoric about educating housewives for their new role as "purchasing agents of the home" must also be seen in this context. Did business and industry *really* want women to become careful and informed buyers of their products? This is very unlikely. Two students of the subject write that "in an economy dependent on the multiplication of family 'needs' nothing could be more dangerous than a knowledgeable 'scientific' consumer." Christine Frederick, the primary advocate of advertisers in the 1920s, told manufacturers not to bother explaining to Mrs. Consumer how an appliance works because women are not "mechanically minded." In fact, Frederick's depiction of the "general character" of Mrs. Consumer—she is "predominately emotional" and "proceeds more along the lines of instinct than upon theory or reason"—makes one suspect that businessmen and advertisers never really sought an informed female clientele for their products. The truth is probably closer to the blunt remarks of one observer of the American scene in

1922: "American business loves the housewife for the same reason it loves China—that is, for her economic backwardness."[41]

Busy Work and Make-work: The 1950s and 1960s

Since World War II, as never before, the business of American housewives has been busyness.

Jane Davison, *The Fall of a Doll's House,* 1980

The years following World War II were marked by the continued spread of utilities and household appliances and a concomitant standardization of the ingredients that went into making the "house beautiful." The electrification of rural areas following the war and the national marketing of household products produced one standard for all American housewives to follow. Whether they lived in large urban areas, small towns, or remote farms no longer mattered. Housewives everywhere received the same prescriptive messages.

Not only was the new technology available to more families but there was a lot more of it. By the 1950s the average home contained seven times as much capital equipment as it had in the 1920s, and older appliances had given way to newer, purportedly more efficient models. By the 1950s the wringer washing machine had been replaced by the fully automatic washer, and in the 1960s the automatic dryer and wash-and-wear fabrics supposedly conquered the last vestiges of laundry-day woe. Dishwashers became ubiquitous as did small appliances like electric toasters, blenders, and juicers. Convenience foods crowded supermarket shelves in greater profusion than ever before, and frozen foods, including that quintessential invention of the 1950s, the "TV dinner," vied for space in store freezers.[42]

Housework during the era of the feminine mystique continued its elaboration, an elaboration that made certain that women spent no less time doing housework than they had thirty years earlier. A seemingly endless array of make-work activities were proposed by women's domestic advisors who, joined by business and advertisers, tried to resolve some of the more problematic aspects of housework in the industrial age. A variety of suggestions, for example, aimed to make housework more visible by producing tangible objects for the home. Women's magazines were filled with directions for crocheting doilies, knitting afghans, and making needlepoint throw pillows. Products such as cake mixes were intentionally left incomplete so that by adding an egg or a cup of milk to the mix the housewife would have a sense of being part of the productive process. One ad for an efficiency kitchen noted the housewife's sense of isolation as she worked alone in her home. Cooking need not be a laborious duty, read the copy. "It's the isolation that hurts; why must this be done in solitary confinement?"[43]

Playing to some of the difficulties inherent in modern housewifery also was used to promote sales of products for the home. Manufacturers were told that they must maintain a "neat balance" between stressing the labor-saving qualities of their appliances and claiming that the latest model vacuum cleaner or clothes washer would save so much time that the housewife would feel "lazy, or uneasy or bored" and would be reluctant to buy it. Convincing the housewife she needed a variety of specialized products for similar chores would not only increase sales, it would upgrade and professionalize her low status. A report done in the mid-1940s on the preferences of homemakers had this to say: "When [the housewife] uses one product for washing clothes, a second for washing dishes, a third for walls, a fourth for floors, a fifth for venetian blinds, etc., rather than all-purpose cleaner, she feels less like an unskilled laborer, more like an engineer, an expert." The same report also pointed out another irksome feature of contemporary housework: the feeling that it is never finished. And the solution? Deep cleaning. Advertising that stressed deep cleaning "holds out the sense of completion," wrote the marketing experts. If the housewife could be convinced that a particular cleanser got at the deep down, hidden dirt, this would alleviate one of the most frustrating aspects of her job.[44]

Many of these directives actually made for more work. In fact, housework in the 1950s and 1960s is remarkable for just how much time it did take. The time budget studies done in the 1960s finally laid to rest the old argument that modern technology reduced the demands of housework; not a single study found that the time spent on housework had declined over the four previous decades despite the enormous increase and improvement in household equipment. Housewives reported almost the same amount of time for housework as they had twenty, thirty, and forty years earlier. In fact, the total number of hours devoted to housework had actually *increased* somewhat over the forty-year period.[45]

Despite differences in sampling and reporting techniques, the conclusions of the time budget studies were consistent. Most of them asked housewives to keep a record of how they spent their time in five- to fifteen-minute intervals over a day, a week, or a month. Here are some of their findings. In the mid 1960s full-time homemakers averaged about eight hours a day or fifty-six hours a week doing housework compared to the average fifty-two hour work week of their counterparts in the 1920s. Some housekeeping tasks had become less time-consuming over the four decades while others took more time. Food preparation and meal cleanup declined thirty minutes a day between the 1920s and 1960s, but this was balanced by a more than thirty-minute increase in the time devoted to shopping and record keeping. Housewives in the 1960s, in fact, spent an inordinate amount of time—one full working day a week—shopping and traveling to and from stores. They also gave more time to general home care—an average of twelve hours a week—than housewives in the 1920s, who spent about nine and a half hours a week at it. Perhaps the most striking statistic to come out of the time budget studies is the amount of time women spent doing laundry: it increased from about five and a half to six and a half hours per week over this period, an incredible figure given the presence of a washer and dryer in most homes. The laundry data, however, does mesh with the general finding that there was no relationship between the number of appliances in the home and the time spent on housework.*[46]

We know how much time housewives devoted to domestic tasks, but how does this compare with employed women's housework time? In 1966 women with full-time jobs spent an average of 26 hours a week doing housework, slightly less than half the time spent by full-time housewives. In fact, if we add the time spent on the job to that doing housework, the total work week of employed women was only an hour and a half longer than that of full-time homemakers. Why did women

*It is not only in the United States that the use of labor-saving devices has not been translated into real time savings. A time-use survey of twelve countries also found that the acquisition of labor-saving devices may actually result in an increase in working hours (see Szalai, *The Use of Time*).

with jobs spend so much less time on housework? Employed women were no more likely to have servants or to receive help from family members than their jobless counterparts, nor did they have more labor-saving appliances in their homes.[47] There is also no evidence that employed women had abandoned American standards of order and cleanliness and lived in homes that were more slovenly than those of full-time homemakers.

A domestic variant of Parkinson's Law helps explain why housewives spent so many hours at these chores. Sociologist C. Northcote Parkinson explains that "work expands so as to fill the time available for completion."[48] This is how it worked in the home. The full-time housewife of the 1950s and 1960s found herself in the following quandary: her role demanded that she devote her days to domestic activities that were simply not sufficient to fill her time. But the lack of real work did not necessarily result in leisure because whatever work there was to be done, following Parkinson's law, increased in complexity and importance in direct proportion to the time available for doing it. The job of good housekeeping was enlarged, housework tasks were elaborated in order to take up more time, and the full-time housewife found herself without a moment to spare.

Betty Friedan comments on the busyness of the suburban housewives she interviewed in the late 1950s for *The Feminine Mystique*: "They were so *busy*—busy shopping, chauffering, using their dishwashers and dryers and electric mixers, busy gardening, waxing, polishing." Friedan also reports that some of these women were amazed to find that once they took a job or found a serious interest outside the home they could do in one hour the chores that had taken them six hours to complete when they were home all day.[49] In other words, without more challenging work to be done, they had transformed housework into an all-encompassing activity.

Doing the laundry is a good example of the way in which a domestic task can assume monumental proportions. Clothes and linens can be sorted by color and material and washed separately using different washing cycles and different laundry products. In this way many small loads of wash are done rather than one large load. Then there are the items that are too delicate for the machine and must be washed by hand. Sheets and towels can be hung on the line to dry so that they smell fresher and get whiter than if they were dried by machine. The more

Massachusetts Society for Social Health Collection, Schlesinger Library, Radcliffe College

Women With Children in Supermarket • *By the 1950s, the supermarket, with its wide array of food products, had replaced the small family owned grocery store.*

things that "need" washing, the more time it takes to load, unload, fold, iron, and put them away. Washing clothes after a single wearing and laundering sheets twice a week are sure-fire ways of increasing the workload. Then, if there is any time left over, the housewife can always iron the sheets and underwear.

The ways of increasing the hours given to housework are innumerable. The number of dirty dishes to be washed can expand to the capacity of the dishwasher (maternal or mechanical) to clean them. Cooking can become a major chore, despite convenience foods, if different menus are prepared for different family members and homemade baby food is substituted for the commercial variety. A homemaker can spend a full day making spaghetti and meat sauce, using a pasta maker, a meat grinder, and a Cuisinart. "Eat off the floor" standards of cleanliness can take hours to maintain, particularly when there are children and pets in the home.

The mass media and advertisers facilitated the operation of a domestic Parkinson's Law by proposing a wide array of superfluous make-work activities to fill the housewife's time. A good example is the column "Hints from Heloise" by Heloise Cruse, which was syndicated in 512 newspapers around the country.[50] Heloise was ostensibly offering hints to save "you, the housewife and homemaker" time and money, but not more than a handful of her suggestions can be justified in these terms. For example, her method of making mailing labels—by buying gummed wrapping tape and writing one's name and address over and over again the length of the tape—ignores the existence of such labels at a very low cost. Her suggestion for making Christmas wrapping by sewing pieces of fabric together and decorating them with sequins, beads, and rickrack eliminates the need for the store-bought variety. One hint gives an elaborate method for preparing homemade dog food, while another offers a detailed recipe for making finger paints. The woman who could not afford new wallpaper was told that she could create a springlike atmosphere in her bathroom by carefully cutting out leaves of ivy from a piece of plastic material and then pasting them individually on her medicine cabinet to form a trellis leading into a pot of real ivy near the sink. These hints are difficult to justify on the basis of the money they save unless the time spent by the person doing them has no value.

The unimportance of the housewife's time is also evident in Heloise's make-work cleaning tips. Silver polish does wonders for shining curtain rods, she informed her readers. Kitchen cabinets can be emptied, scoured, and lined with layer upon layer of waxed paper and silver foil. Bedsprings can be hauled out of the house and hosed down. When one reader wrote to Heloise telling her of her "disgust, shame, and embarrassment" when guests saw the discolored grouting in her bathroom, Heloise supplied a nifty solution for bleaching it. There were some limits to the amount of cleaning that was absolutely essential. For example, Heloise advised that it was not necessary to clean under the bed *every day*. "Girls," she told her readers, "remember that never yet has my husband or a guest lifted up the bedspread to see if I had dusted under the bed."

According to Heloise, all sorts of things can be transformed into other things with a little time and effort. Plastic bleach bottles can be made into birdhouses, "cleaning blouses" can be sewn from old towels, bathroom curtains can be created from plastic tablecloths, and a mop can be made from dish rags. Plastic flowers will "bloom again" with a touch of fingernail polish. Old throw pillows can be made like new again by stuffing them with lint from the clothes dryer and covering them with a shower cap or hairdo protector. Finally, Heloise offers an ingenious suggestion for making a planter out of a dish drainer by hanging it backward on the wall and entwining it with artificial flowers.

What is evident in many of these hints is that they not only make work but get highly visible results and give an aura of creativity to otherwise humdrum domestic tasks. One of the problems of housework in the modern era is its lack of "conspicuous contribution"; that is, housework is difficult to appreciate because it leaves no permanent, noticeable change in the home.[51] But Heloise's "creative" hints have one important advantage over most household chores: they are eminently visible. A dish drainer entwined with artificial flowers hanging on the wall would certainly be difficult to miss!

The comments of one of the British housewives interviewed for a study done by sociologist Ann Oakley indicates the importance of making one's work noticed. "You dust the same thing every day and it's never appreciated," she told Oakley, "whereas if you're decorating something . . . there's something always gained out of it." Oakley suggests that many of her informants liked seeing clothes drying on the line for much the same reason: "Perfect cleanliness is the commercial ideal, but the clothes must be *seen* to be clean. Public visibility is achieved when the clothes hang out in the garden."[52]

The do-it-yourself movement that boomed in the 1950s probably had its roots in this desire for visibility. A 1955 article in *McCalls* entitled "Do It Yourself Takes Over" reported that 75 percent of the readers surveyed did their own house painting and 60 percent did their own wallpapering. One woman interviewed for the article is quoted as saying: "You do it yourself to save money of course. But there's something else too. Maybe it's creative therapy for the world we live in."[53]

Advertisers have long played to the housewife's need for recognition of her work. One television commercial shows a woman's husband and children commenting for the first time on the softness of her laundry after she had switched to Downy Fabric Softener. "They notice the difference," she sighs contentedly. In an ad for Folger's coffee an obviously delighted woman is surprised when her husband remarks on the deliciousness of her coffee. An apron-clad housewife in a Clorox commercial says, "If I can tell, anybody can," and the copy for Soft Puf Tissues reads: "That's the value my family notices." Still another ad makes this need for recognition explicit: a woman explains that she has switched to a particular brand of cleanser only because its effectiveness has been noticed by her husband, who never commented on her housework before.

Heloise's hints and similar advice tried to deal with another problematic feature of modern housework: the housewife's resentment of allegations that she did nothing all day. Oakley found that the housewives she interviewed often expressed this resentment. Heloise's suggestions not only lead to conspicuous changes in the home's decor but they prove that the housewife really *is* working. The common wisdom that housework is not real work might be laid to rest if the housewife could point to the bathroom she had just finished wallpapering or the new curtains she had sewn herself. These activities would prove that she was not only fully occupied but that her work was indispensable. As Margaret Mead wrote in 1955, the modern housewife is plagued with "the fear that even though she never has any time, she is not perhaps doing a full-time job." Given this fear, the time it takes to do a task may become more important than actually accomplishing the task one set out to do.[54]

The application of Parkinson's Law to the home makes for two types of activities. Some are clearly superfluous, time-consuming projects like the ones suggested by Heloise. But others—sewing children's clothes, painting the kitchen, reupholstering furniture—certainly can be classified as real, even necessary work. And of course if the tasks are done with the unpaid labor of the housewife, they also save the family money. Ultimately, both sorts of activities help to fill the housewife's day and transform housekeeping into a full-time occupation.

Marketing studies advised manufacturers of household products and their advertising agencies of the homemaker's worry that her job was not really full-time. A book on working class housewives told advertisers that such women "need to be busy keeping house—both because they need to feel they are doing something worthwhile and because they have few psychic resources for occupying themselves." The labor-saving aspects of household products should not be overemphasized, cautioned the writers, because "advertising which places too great emphasis on easing the housewife's burden runs the risk of being reacted to negatively because it seems to detract from her personal importance." Manufacturers were warned that appliances that did everything for the housewife would not sell. One study claimed that an appliance that only required pushing a button would stymie the housewife's desire for participation. When asked what she thought about a particular cleaning apparatus, one housewife was reported to have said: "As for some magical push-button cleaning system, well, what would happen to my exercise, my feeling of accomplishment, and what would I do with my mornings?"[55]

Setting high standards and sticking to a routine was another tactic housewives could use to make their chores seem more like real work. Following a set of rules allowed the housewife to structure her work in a way that is taken for granted by salaried employees. Oakley noted that all the housewives she studied were able to specify their standards and the routines they followed for doing housework. "The spelling out of rules to be followed," she wrote, "places housework in the same category as other work—there are things that simply *have* to be done." But high standards and following a routine also mean more work. Oakley found that while there was no correlation between the number of hours housewives worked and the number of children or appliances they had, there *was* a correlation between their standards and routines and the number of hours they spent at household tasks.[56]

Caring for the plethora of modern appliances owned by the typical American middle class family of the 1950s and 1960s also accounted for some of the time given to household chores. The actual structure of appliances manufactured for the home contributed to the work involved in caring for them. With more crevices and movable parts than their commercial counterparts, they were more difficult to clean and more likely to break down. Appliances used in commercial establishments, on the contrary, were designed to minimize care and repair. And repair, of course, means waiting for the repairman to arrive. Anyone who has waited for hours to have a phone installed or a dishwasher fixed will appreciate the time required for the upkeep of such a "labor-saving" device. While the promise to show up "sometime between 9 and 5" is undoubtedly convenient for the phone company and Sears, it indicates the general devaluation of the housewife's time and work. In the words of sociologist Philip Slater:

> Housewives are expected to operate without schedules. Repairmen . . . deliverymen, and so on, have been successful in refusing to constrict their own convenience by making scheduled appointments with housewives, who are expected to wait at home until the workman arrives. Nothing could convey more powerfully the low esteem in which the housewife is held than this disregard of daily scheduling needs. The lowest flunky in the masculine occupational hierarchy is given temporal superiority over every non-working woman.[57]

Modern household technology thus continued to be a mixed blessing for women. Not only did its upkeep and repair contribute to the long hours spent doing housework but deciding on just which toaster or refrigerator to buy or which brand of soapflakes worked best in the washing machine also took time. Even using "convenience foods" could be time-consuming. Someone had to drive to the supermarket to select them, wait in the checkout line, drive home, unload the car, and then prepare them. The very presence of these conveniences and devices in the home also created an incentive to work. It would simply not do to have a cake mix stay in the cupboard or the blender sit idle on the counter or the new vacuum cleaner lie unused in the utility room.

There was some public acknowledgment that the latest contrivances were never really meant to save the housewife's time. For example, a 1961 *New York Times* article on the future uses of home computers suggested that they would "free" the housewife for creative activities such as allowing her to "spend half her day preparing an exotic meal at which many foods would be tasted and consumed over a three hour period." One marketing report admitted that the presence of certain labor savers in the home did not really save labor at all. The vacuum cleaner had made "housekeeping more difficult than it used to be," according to the report, since women who own vacuum cleaners "felt compelled to do cleaning that wasn't really necessary."[58]

It seems unfair to blame the housewives of the era for the amount of time they devoted to housework or for the dissatisfaction many felt in doing it. And yet this is just what happened. It was the housewife's fault if she spent all day doing housework and did not have any leisure; she was inefficient and disorganized, said the critics of the day, blaming the victim. Was she unhappy being *only* a housewife? This too was her fault. There is nothing "inherently disagreeable" about housework, said women's critics, and the "disproportionate odium" that has been heaped on it is a result of "the repeated verbal fouling of their own nests by . . . disordered female theorists and the disorganization of the feelings of women in general." "Moral flabbiness" and "feminine neurosis" were the terms used to dismiss those women who were not satisfied with their domestic lot. Sociologist Mirra Komarovsky wrote in the 1950s that "the tendency to attribute the housewife's discontent to personal deficiency is widespread."[59] But with little else to occupy her time, with a social ethic requiring that she remain at home, and with a small-scale, individualized household technology designed to keep her there, is it any wonder that the housewife tried to keep busy doing work that was devalued, frustrating, and repetitive, work that was by its very nature unfulfilling?

Housework versus Paid Work; or What's Happened in the Feminist Era

> *To bake one's own bread in this day and age makes about as much sense as taking a covered wagon to California.*
>
> Edith De Rham, *The Love Fraud*, 1965

Good housekeeping in the age of feminism has been a mixed blessing for women. Married women have entered the labor force in record numbers and time budget studies done in the 1970s indicate that for the first time in fifty years the average number of hours spent doing housework has declined. Make-work domestic tips meant to enlarge the job of the homemaker now appear less frequently in women's magazines and household manuals; most contemporary household hints really seem meant to *save* time. But in one crucial way good housekeeping has not changed a great deal from decades past. Women, whether they have jobs or not, are still the primary caretakers of the home. Study after study has documented the phenomenon of the "double day" for working women. Despite full-time jobs and salaries that make a substantial contribution to family income, the sexual division of labor in the home remains basically unchanged. Most working women have two jobs: a paid one outside the home and an unpaid one at home.

One of the most intriguing findings of recent time budget studies is that the average number of hours spent on housework has declined not only for employed women but for full-time housewives as well. One survey compared time devoted to housework in 1965 and 1975. The full-time housewives questioned in 1975 reported that they spent an average of forty-four hours a week at household tasks, down from fifty hours a week in 1965, or a 17 percent decline over the decade. In 1965 employed women reported that they spent an average of twenty-six hours weekly on home care, but by 1975 that figure had fallen to twenty-one hours a week. A smaller survey of working women done in 1976 found that they averaged even fewer hours—17.4—per week doing housework.[60]

If women in the 1970s were spending less time on housework than they were a decade earlier, where were they getting help? From other family members partially, but only to a slight extent. The comparative survey mentioned above reported that men increased the time they spent on home care from nine hours a week in 1965 to ten hours a week in 1975, a difference of less than eight minutes a day. Whereas women had done 80 percent of the housework in 1965, by 1975 they were still doing 75 percent of it. All recent time budget studies in fact have found that women, employed or not, still contribute between 70 and 75 percent of the total time spent on housework; their husbands and children divide the remaining 25 to 30 percent about evenly between them. The upper limit in the number of hours men spend on household tasks is about 20 percent of that spent by their wives, regardless of whether their wives are employed or the age and number of children at home. The only time when men take over domestic chores is when their wives are simply unavailable, that is, when they are at work. In the words of two sociologists, in such cases, husbands provide "a reserve source of labor in times of particular need."[61]

Other evidence suggests that husbands of employed women give little extra help around the house. One study found that two-thirds of the men with working wives did few or no after-dinner chores. Studies also show that employed women spend more time doing housework on weekends than their husbands and that a man's leisure time is not diminished by having a working wife. It has even been proposed that the small amount of housework that men do perform may not compensate for the extra amount of housework their mere presence creates. Lending support to this trenchant hypothesis is the finding that single women with children spend considerably less time on housework than do married women with children, probably because part of married women's time is devoted to "husband care."[62]

Studies agree that while employment reduces the number of hours women devote to housework, these hours are not made up by men, the majority of whom still consider housework to be "women's work." Advertising agencies have recently become interested in men's views of housework because they want to know if commercials for laundry detergent should be aired along with those for beer during televised football games. One marketing report had this to say on the subject: "Today's man wants his woman to work at two jobs—one outside the home and one inside the home." Most men "are not willing to lift the traditional household responsibilities from their wives." They would rather buy labor-saving devices for them than help with the housework themselves. This study reported that more than 75 percent of the 200 men interviewed said that their wives had primary responsibility for cooking and 78 percent agreed that cleaning the bathroom was woman's work. Another marketing study found men to be more "fair minded" on the question of housework. Eighty-eight percent of the nearly 500 men sampled agreed that a man should at least "help out" if his wife is employed.[63]

Clearly, women today spend less time on housework, but this is not usually the result of a more equitable division of labor in the home. How then can we explain the fewer hours that women put in at household tasks? It is certainly true that household appliances are more ubiquitous than ever. In 1975, 70 percent of all American homes had washing machines, 58 percent had clothes dryers, 38 percent had dishwashers, and 5 percent had microwave ovens—a figure that undoubtedly has increased considerably since then. Nevertheless, there still is no systematic trend for women who own more appliances to spend less time on housework than women with fewer appliances. The microwave oven, in fact, is the *only* appliance that seems to make any real difference in terms of time; microwaves were found to save an average of ten minutes a day in meal preparation.[64]

Another possible explanation for the decline in hours devoted to housework is lowered housekeeping standards. The data on this is uncertain, but one study found that the largest decrease in time spent was in the area of general home care: cleaning, doing laundry, and washing dishes. There were also slight declines in the time spent shopping, record keeping, and doing home repairs. Cooking was the only housekeeping activity that showed any increase at all in the time devoted to it, albeit a very small increase, about four minutes a day.[65] Since studies indicate that cooking is the homemaking activity that women enjoy most and cleaning the one they like least, the time budget data may be reflecting these preferences.

If time spent in general home care has declined, does this translate into less immaculate houses and less than spotless clothing? Possibly. It may be that contemporary women, as the author of the above study suggests, "find a less tidy household more tolerable" now than they did ten years ago.[66] But there is another possibility as well: the demise of Parkinson's Law, at least for working women. Employed full-time or part-time outside the home, women may have become more efficient when working in the home. Because their jobs occupy so much of their time, there is no reason to elaborate domestic tasks in order to keep busy all day. Quite to the contrary; given the double day for most working women, their dilemma is finding enough time to do essential housekeeping chores.

Spending less time on housework, however, does not necessarily mean lower standards. If we agree that housekeeping under industrial conditions is really part-time work—unless it is made otherwise—it may well be that women today are maintaining roughly the same housekeeping standards as full-time homemakers did ten, twenty, and thirty years ago but maintaining them by working more efficiently over a shorter period of time. The problem is that housekeeping standards are elusive and difficult to measure. Is simplifying housework, for example, synonymous with lowering standards? Does the woman who prepares a simple but well-balanced meal of baked chicken and vegetables have lower standards than the one who spends hours in the kitchen concocting a Beef Wellington and a strawberry soufflé for dessert? Is the woman who changes the sheets once every two weeks rather than once or twice a week really shirking her domestic responsibilities?

A combination of factors probably accounts for the decrease in hours devoted to housework today. Contemporary standards of good housekeeping may be somewhat lower and simpler than their previous levels, and women also may be more efficient in using their domestic time. It could even be argued that the basic ingredients of good housekeeping in years past—an "eat off the floor" standard of cleanliness and an elaboration of domestic tasks—were in themselves inefficient. They were inefficient because they were unnecessary; such norms surely far exceed what is required for good hygiene and general family well-being.

How have women's traditional domestic advisors, the authors of articles on housekeeping tips and household manuals, dealt with these changes? For the full-time homemaker is no longer the norm and the majority of married women today have jobs. Probably the most typical response is the one found in the 1970 manual *The Working Mother's Guide to Her Home, Her Family, and Herself* by Alice Skelsey. "Whether you have been a compulsive housekeeper or the casual sort," Skelsey tells her readers, "once you add a job to your life you have to be an *efficient* housekeeper." The chapters devoted to housework emphasize cutting down on domestic tasks because "the only necessities are food, clothing and shelter." Beyond these basics and doing "laundry once in a while," Skelsey adds, cleaning should be based on personal standards, for "there isn't any law that says you have to change your sheets once a week." She advises women to give up activities that take up more time than is available, like baking bread and sewing children's clothes.[67]

Another contemporary manual advises women to pare down the "list of everything that has to be done in the house. . . . The house will not collapse if the wastebaskets are not emptied every day and the health department won't come after you if your breakfast dishes don't get washed until dinnertime." Suggestions for saving time and simplifying housework include marketing only once a week, using convenience foods, cooking one-dish meals, eating out as much as one's budget allows, and buying only wash-and-wear clothes.[68]

Other recent manuals consist of straightforward hints, a type of prescriptive writing very reminiscent of the "lists of receipts" popular in the eighteenth and early nineteenth centuries. The best-seller *Mary Ellen's Best of Helpful Hints* is of this genre. It provides a series of tips for cleaning various items in the home, doing laundry, sewing, gardening, and home repairs—hints which all seem meant to save time or simplify domestic chores. This and other contemporary manuals lack the overwrought descriptions of housewifely duties which characterized so much of this literature in the past.[69]

The traditional domestic sexual division of labor is taken for granted in some contemporary manuals but questioned in others. Skelsey estimates that it should take a woman between fifteen and twenty hours a week to do housekeeping chores, but since her book is written for married women who already *have* jobs, one might well ask about their husbands' contribution to keeping the home fires burning. At best, men "help out" on occasion. Skelsey advises a woman to consider her husband's preferences when asking him for help: "Does he like to cook? Does he detest kitchen work? Sleep late on Saturday? Enjoy a big breakfast on Sunday?" A woman should ask her husband to do only the things he enjoys, and then only when it is convenient for him. "If you use your head in asking your husband for help," she tells her readers, "it is highly unlikely that you will strip him of his manhood."[70]

Not all manuals take a double day for working women for granted. The author of a volume published in 1975, for example, insists that "housework is not 'women's work.' It is the responsibility of all who live in the home." Nor is it enough for men to simply "help out" occasionally: "Whatever the man of the house does should be seen as his contribution towards the living arrangements of the entire family—and not as help that he gives to you with your job of running the home." Similarly, most contemporary household manuals are no longer dedicated to "you the wife and mother" as they were in decades past. A 1981 volume of household hints, written by Heloise II, the daughter of the late Heloise Cruse, is addressed to "homemakers" rather than "housewives." Why? Because, she writes, "lots of us are men," bachelors, as well as "house husbands who've changed things around. While their wives work, a lot of them are discovering what us gals instinctively knew—there's something very satisfying about raising kids, keeping a home, cooking, cleaning, and nipping about in search of a bargain." But working women are not necessarily "excused from KP." "Mostly we're not because . . . in some way or other almost everyone is a homemaker." The cartoon illustrations in *Mary Ellen's Best of Helpful Hints* also indicate that housekeeping is no longer an exclusively female job; men are shown cutting onions, flipping eggs in a skillet, peeling potatoes, and looking ruefully at a shrunken sweater just retrieved from the clothes washer.[71]

Even contemporary manuals specifically intended for full-time housewives have changed. The author of *Women at Home* begins by telling her readers that "every woman at home needs to realize that she is not a wife to the house. Rather she is a person with individual interests. . . . A woman faced with guiding a new generation—with her heart and mind, not with her broom." Hire a servant? Fine, "if a woman doesn't care for housework and if housework can be planned for in the family budget, why shouldn't she hire someone to help her with it? No one does everything well." Quite a change from more than a century of advice about the wisdom of employing domestic servants![72]

Of course, not everything has changed in the world of prescriptive writing. There is the anachronistic "total woman" phenomenon to be considered. Marabel Morgan's best-seller *The Total Woman* actually does not have much to say about housework because most of her advice tells women how to please, accommodate, and obey their husbands. Nevertheless, there is no question of rearranging the traditional division of labor in the home. For Morgan housework is exclusively women's work. Her few housekeeping hints are meant to keep hubby happy. For example, she says it is a good idea to cook dinner and set the table for the evening meal right after breakfast in order to avoid the "4:30 syndrome" and have enough time to take a bubble bath before the man of the house gets home. Morgan also tells women that they should immediately attend to their husbands' requests: "When your husband asks you to do something, he expects it to be done without reminding you. The next time he delegates a job to you, write it down. Give it top priority on your list."[73]

Anachronistic or not, the runaway success of Morgan's book requires explanation. The book is directed at full-time homemakers, women who grew up during the 1950s and early 1960s when the housewife's role was largely unquestioned. But for more than fifteen years now these women have been exposed to the ideology of the women's movement which strikes at the heart of their long inculcation about women's "proper place." Many contemporary housewives are caught in a bind because, in the words of psychologist Rae André, "their transition to the new way of thinking is difficult, or may even be impossible if they are already caught up in the cycle of economic and psychological dependency encouraged—even demanded—by the woman-as-housewife dogma."[74] Morgan's appeal becomes intelligible within this context; her readers very much *want* to believe her when she tells them that their role as helpmates to their husbands is a completely satisfying one.

Yet despite the sales of her book, Morgan can transform fewer and fewer adult females into "total women." After all, the 60 percent of married women who are in the labor force in this country cannot dawdle in a bubble bath at 4:30 in the afternoon or greet their husbands at the door at 5:00 dressed in pink baby-doll pajamas and white boots, as Morgan suggests. It is also well to remember that *Mary Ellen's Best of Helpful Hints,* with its straightforward, no-nonsense approach to housekeeping, also is a best-seller. I expect more manuals of this genre in the future. If present employment trends continue, even more married women will have jobs and they will certainly need all the advice they can get on how to deal with the "normalization of the double day."[75]

As we approach the mid-1980s good housekeeping still presents problems for most women. While the traditional norm against mothers working has become obsolete, the social convention that sees housework as "women's work" is still very much with us. The findings of a marketing report that sought out men's attitudes toward housework may explain this holdover. "The major disadvantage that the typical husband perceives in having a working wife," the report noted, "is the effect not upon the children but upon himself: a husband has to spend more time on household chores that he does not like."[76] Because there is apparently much that is unpleasant in doing unpaid domestic labor, men have thus far been successful in continuing to label it "women's work." But perhaps the day is not far off when the distinction between being responsible for housework and merely "helping out," that is, giving the wife "a hand" doing the dishes or shopping for groceries, will no longer lie at the core of the domestic division of labor. The day may come when men and women will share on a more equitable basis the necessary work of the home.

When Is Work Not Work?

Housework today is done mostly by one sex and is socialized primarily into one sex, yet both psychologically and economically it supports both sexes.

Rae André, *Homemakers: The Forgotten Workers,* 1981

Since the onset of industrialization in the United States, the most salient feature of housework has remained unchanged: housework is not considered work. Even today, with the spread of feminism and the massive entry of women into the labor force, when women do chores at home they are not considered to be "working." Economists lend support to this idea by treating only those activities that contribute to the gross national product as work. Yet it is estimated that the unpaid domestic services of women equal about 25 percent of the GNP.[77] Social scientists argue that housework does not *produce* anything of monetary value. Housewives may bake bread or sew clothes, but these products are for family use, not for sale on the market.

Since World War II the American economy has shifted from an emphasis on the production of goods to the production of services, and housework certainly produces services for the family. Aren't these domestic services important to the economy? Apparently not, if one looks at how they are treated by various federal policies and government agencies. The services of the housewife are covered by neither social security nor unemployment insurance. For example, in computing social security payments the years spent doing unpaid household labor are not counted. Courts ignore or deemphasize the contributions of the housewife when deciding on alimony. Housework, unlike other types of work, is treated as nonwork; the housewife receives no benefits and no protection.

This "trivialization of domestic work" flies in the face of fact. Housework can be a full-time job; its hours are often no shorter than those of paid work. Housework involves not only time but labor. Cooking the family's meals, cleaning house, and washing clothes is indisputably work. When these services are paid for, no one denies that they are work. And without the free labor of the housewife and the double day of the employed woman, families could not live as well or as cheaply. One study estimates that about half of a family's disposable income comes from the unpaid work of family members, mostly the wife and mother.[78] But housework continues to be trivialized because to do otherwise would be costly. If women did not provide free domestic services, employers either would have to pay far higher wages so that employees could buy these services or business and industry would have to invest vast sums of money to underwrite inexpensive cafeterias, day-care centers, and laundries. If men, women, and children had to provide these services for themselves as individuals, many hours now devoted to jobs, schooling, and leisure would have to be redirected into domestic labor. The care and feeding of the present and future labor force and the maintenance of its standard of living is the true function of housework, a function that given its importance to the economy comes very cheaply.

Housework also involves the administration of consumption. Without the time and effort that millions of American women put into selecting, using, and caring for the myriad conveniences and devices on the market today, consumption would be greatly reduced. Perhaps this is the real reason why no major reorganization of housework has occurred over the last century. Each individualized nuclear family continues to be responsible for satisfying its daily needs for food, shelter, and child care, and women continue to bear the primary burden of meeting these needs. Still, with the increasing necessity of two-family incomes, a necessity that has propelled millions of married women into the job market, the time may soon come when millions of American husbands will wonder, as they make their way down the aisles of the supermarkets of the nation, "What shall I make for dinner tonight?"

6 WHEN IS A WOMAN'S PLACE IN THE HOME?

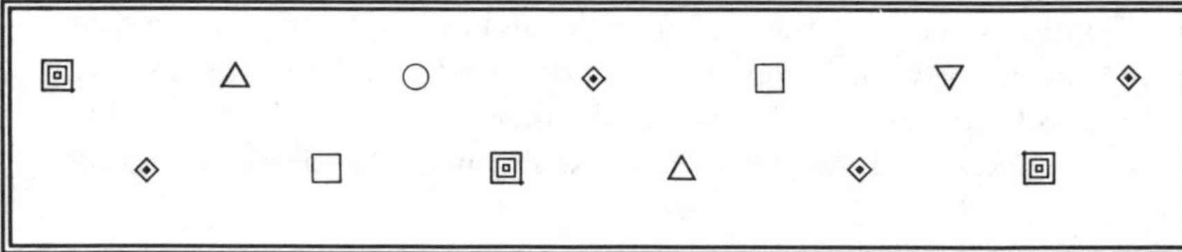

The doctrine that women belong in the home never carries more conviction than when it is allied with "proof" that women's activities outside the home are detrimental to the health and welfare of their families, and to the country as a whole.

Ann Oakley, *Women's Work,* 1976

Working women have received a lot of attention in the literature in recent years. As the number of women in the labor force soared past the 50 percent mark for the first time in American history, the media have pondered why women take jobs and the effect of working women on home and family. But women have entered and withdrawn from the job market at other times in the past, so the phenomenon of women working outside the home is not entirely new. This chapter will analyze the reasons for the changing rates of employment among middle class women and assess the attitudes toward women and work accompanying these changes. My aim is to specify the conditions under which the time-worn dictum "A woman's place is in the home" is either vehemently asserted or denied.

There are well-defined causes for the shifts in attitude toward working women. Probably the most important cause is the demand for female labor. A strong link, for example, exists between women's work during wartime and an ideology that views such work as acceptable, even patriotic, and not in conflict with a woman's domestic role. This ideology reflects sharp increases in the female labor force made necessary by the scarcity of male labor during periods of national and international conflict.

The demand for female labor also leads to higher employment rates for women. Economist Valerie Oppenheimer has shown that there are separate markets for male and female labor and that the rise in demand for women workers derives from the rise in demand for workers in typically female occupations such as clerical work and certain jobs in the professional and service categories. [1] In fact, an enormous increase in the jobs available in the "female" sector of the labor market over the last thirty years is one of the reasons why women's employment rate has grown so dramatically.

When standards of consumption are rising, women are also induced to take jobs because a second family income becomes essential for buying the consumer goods associated with a middle class life-style. At such times women's employment is met with grudging approval since such work becomes an extension, not a contradiction, of their domestic role. A woman works to buy "extras" for her family and is seen as contributing to its well-being.

High inflation also motivates middle class women to seek employment because their earnings become indispensable to maintaining their families' standard of living. Under inflationary conditions women work not merely to buy extras but to help pay for such basics as food, home mortgages, and health care. As a result, the ideology that postulates an insurmountable conflict between women's employment and their families' welfare fades and demands for equal pay for equal work take on new vigor.

What about the other side of the coin? What conditions make for a low rate of female employment among the middle class and a concomitant attitude decrying women's work outside the home? Contrary to popular wisdom, large-scale unemployment does not necessarily mean low work rates for women. The economic situation in 1982–1983 certainly disputes any connection between the two; the highest level of unemployment in three decades coexists with a record number of women holding jobs. It is true, however, that during certain times of economic crisis, such as the 1930s, women workers were condemned for taking jobs away from male breadwinners. Yet ironically, despite virulent attacks on working women during the Great Depression, the size of the female labor force actually grew during those years as women, out of sheer economic necessity, sought to replace lost male wages.

Female participation in the labor force seems to be lowest during what might be termed "neutral" periods when there is neither high unemployment, high inflation, nor a substantial demand for female labor. The 1920s was such a period; despite women's much heralded political and sexual emancipation, their employment rate remained low. In fact, the proportion of women working increased by only one percent over the preceding decade.[2]

While I do not wish to depict women as puppets buffeted by the irresistible forces of the American economy, evidence suggests that the size of the female labor force is directly affected by the scarcity of male labor during wartime, rising patterns of consumption, high inflation, and labor demand in "female" occupations. The data also suggest that attitudes about the propriety of employing certain classes of women—wives and mothers, the middle class and middle-aged—adjust to rather than cause changing work rates for these groups. Although at times attitudes have lagged behind the reality of large-scale female employment, as in the persistence of the feminine mystique in the 1950s and early 1960s, I contend that attitudes have never *initiated* changes in the rate at which women take jobs. Those who see attitudes as the primary determinants of women's employment obscure the causal processes that enhance or inhibit changes in female labor force participation. They fail to ask the vital question "Under what conditions do these changes occur?" But if we agree that attitudes are the result rather than the cause of women's changing rates of employment, then the reasons for these changes must be sought elsewhere.

◈ □ ○ △ □ ◈

A few general comments about women and work will preface my discussion of women in the labor force in the United States and contemporary attitudes toward their work. First, the contention that women have been "liberated" to work outside the home only within the last two decades is erroneous. This argument rests on the false assumption that there always has been a sharp distinction between the home and the place of work. In fact, this distinction is a relatively recent one and does not predate the industrial era. In economies based on agriculture and domestic production the problem of reconciling "home" and "work" did not arise because men, women, and children all lived and worked in the same place. The pronouncement "a woman's place is in the home" only developed *after* the home and place of work had become separate.

Second, women have always worked; the only difference is the type of work they performed. What sociologist Jessie Bernard calls the "institutionalization of motherhood," the concept that child rearing and housework are full-time activities, when viewed historically is a fairly recent phenomenon.[3] During a significant portion of American history the labor of able-bodied women was too valuable to devote to full-time child care.

Third, a broad cross-cultural and evolutionary perspective reveals the relative infrequency and recency of excluding women from productive activities. In the majority of hunter-gatherer and horticultural societies, which were the modes of adaptation for most of human history, women are very much involved in production. Some anthropologists argue that the provider/male and domestic/female division of labor first appeared in agricultural societies.[4] But even in agrarian societies, such as colonial North America, women were engaged in production, and the later preoccupation with the "appropriateness" of women working simply did not arise.

Finally, with few exceptions, only relatively affluent sectors of society can afford the luxury of full-time housewife-mothers. The ideology of women's economic dependence is therefore both a class-linked and a geographically limited phenomenon that first took hold among the middle and upper classes living in the eastern and southern regions of the United States. Sociologist Robert Smuts argues that "a family had to have the means to support its women in sheltered idleness before it could come to believe that this was their natural state."[5]

Clearly, such an ideology was grossly incompatible with the harsh demands made on pioneer women who helped settle the Great Plains and far western frontiers. Nor was economic dependence of women feasible for the majority of black families, given the economic realities of their lives. Black women have always worked in far larger proportions than their white counterparts. Ultimately, during much of American history the doctrine that a woman's place is in the home could be translated into practice by only a limited portion of the population.

◈ □ ○ △ □ ◈

Home Industry and Mill Industry: The Colonial Period and the Early Nineteenth Century

Prior to the nineteenth century most men and women worked together on the land and in the home, with a good deal of overlap in the type of work each sex performed. Labor power was particularly precious during the early years of settlement and rigid divisions of roles simply could not develop. An historian of the period has noted that "where a new world was being made women could not stick to the kitchen, let alone the boudoir."[6]

This is not to imply that men and women were engaged in identical activities. The usual sexual division of labor had men doing most of the agricultural tasks while women were in charge of home industry. The latter was extremely time-consuming prior to the American Revolution because housekeeping involved the manufacture of a large proportion of the articles used in the home.

Home manufacture was the key to a woman's outside income, for many of the items she produced at home were for sale or trade. This was particularly true of textile goods; women made lace, sewed, spun, and wove articles for sale. By the second half of the eighteenth century yarn and cloth were in great demand, and women produced these items at home, working under a commission system. Although it is not known how many women engaged in these activities or what they earned, it is clear that spinning and weaving were the most important occupations for women prior to the establishment of the factory system.[7]

Aside from home manufacture, other occupations that engaged significant numbers of women during the colonial era included shopkeeping, the keeping of taverns and "ordinaries" (inns), midwifery, nursing, teaching, domestic service, trading, and printing. Figures are scarce, but we know that a large number of women who engaged in these occupations were widows. Then too, because tradesmen, shopkeepers, and artisans typically worked out of their homes, it was assumed that married women would help their husbands in these enterprises. In the South, women who ran plantations in their husbands' absence were not uncommon, and a study of tort cases during the colonial period has shown that women had intimate knowledge of their husbands' businesses.[8]

While no hard data exists for how many women were employed in these activities, there is evidence that in the eighteenth century the numbers of women were larger, relative to the size of the labor force, than they were in the nineteenth century. For example, there were more businesswomen and female shopkeepers during the colonial period than there were in the 1830s. Various explanations have been offered, including huge increases in demand for goods in the late eighteenth century, when skilled labor was in short supply, or the lack of consistent cultural restrictions on women which might have barred them from certain nondomestic activities.[9] But the question remains: Why were such cultural restrictions ill defined in the late eighteenth century and strengthened some decades later?

Women's central role in the household economy of the colonial period was widely acknowledged. The Boston pastor Benjamin Wadsworth wrote of the division of labor: "The husband should endeavor that his wife should have food and raiment suitable to her. . . . The wife also in her place should do what she can that the man has a comfortable support." To Cotton Mather a virtuous woman was one who "seeks Wooll and Flax, and Works willingly with her hands." In short, "industry" was praised in both sexes, although by tradition men were seen as the principal "providers." Nonetheless, in the nearly self-contained household economy based on the interdependence of the sexes the ideology of the woman's "secondary" economic role was not emphasized. It was not until the advent of commercial farming, wage earning, and extradomestic manufacture that women's economic role, in the words of one historian, "appeared singular, their dependency prominent."[10]

When textile mills first opened in New England in the early nineteenth century many of the jobs created, especially spinning and weaving, were thought particularly suited to women. For these were the same tasks that women had carried out within the confines of the home and that were traditionally regarded as women's work. The early factories, then, did not open up new occupations for women, they simply transferred the place of employment. Girls and unmarried women made up a large percentage of the operatives of the new textile mills: as early as 1827, 90 percent of the cotton mill employees in Lowell, Massachusetts, were females, and by 1832 women outnumbered men by 110 percent in the cotton industry as a whole.[11]

Predominance of women in the early mills was also a result of a shortage of male labor. During this period men could easily become freeholders, and the opportunities for success were far greater in agriculture than in factory work. Until the 1840s the relatively low wages and status of factory employment offered few incentives to men; cheap land farther west and skilled jobs at higher pay in New England were far more attractive. The exodus of men from the latter region to farms in New York State and the Great Lake territory further promoted the employment of women and children in the New England mills.

The establishment of manufacturing is difficult in agrarian societies with low worker productivity, such as existed in the United States at that time, because most available labor is devoted to the production of food and other necessary agricultural products. Contemporaries feared that employing men in factories would lead to the neglect of agriculture, where the nation's economic interest was thought to lie. It was widely believed that manufacturing enterprises must not be established at the expense of the land. Years earlier, for example, George Washington wrote to General Lafayette that he would not allow the introduction of manufactured goods to prejudice agriculture. And he added prophetically: "I conceive much might be done in the way of women, children and others without taking one really necessary hand from tilling the earth."[12] Thus, so long as land was inexpensive and agriculture profitable, it was perhaps inevitable that the problems caused by the scarcity and high cost of male labor would be resolved by employing women.

Moreover, mill work was attractive to women because it paid higher wages than domestic service. Yet mill owners held down costs by paying women lower wages than they would have had to pay men. The reduced cost of labor in fact allowed American mills to compete successfully with the British textile industry.[13]

Because much of the new work involved traditionally "female" skills, some supported women's employment by arguing that it was simply an extension of the work that women had always done. Contemporary moralists also gave approval for women's factory employment by warning that women who did not take factory jobs "were doomed to idleness and its inseparable attendants, vice and guilt." Some mill owners even claimed that one of the main reasons for establishing the textile industry was to provide work for "respectable women to save them from poverty and idleness." Statesmen also vigorously endorsed women's factory work. Alexander Hamilton hailed it on the grounds that it permitted the development of manufacturing without taking men away from the fields. Again and again writers pointed out that communities gained by the establishment of mills in which women's labor could be used, that the employment of poor women and children would lessen the burden on society, and that the nation as a whole would benefit by making "women a source of wealth rather than an encumbrance."[14]

From Factory to Home: The Nineteenth Century

Industrial employment for women, at least unmarried women, proved acceptable as long as male labor remained scarce. During the first half of the nineteenth century women worked in more than a hundred different industrial occupations, although the total number of women employed as well as the number in each industry is unknown because industrial jobs were not delineated in any of the censuses prior to 1850.

During the period 1820–1840 women were concentrated in hand trades in which much of the work was done at home, in shops, or in small factories that had little or no machinery. Some of these manufacturing enterprises, for example, the textile and men's clothing industries, were areas in which technological advances had relatively little impact on productivity. Such industries did, however, require large numbers of workers, making labor costs a high proportion of total costs. The low wages offered by employers in their efforts to keep labor costs down were too meager to attract male operatives who had more remunerative positions open to them elsewhere. Women, on the contrary, had fewer alternatives for paid employment and so were willing to work for the low wages offered.

The women who went into factory employment were by and large from the poorer classes of society, and they were overwhelmingly single. The developing ideology of the distinct feminine domestic "sphere" thus focused on the married, middle class housewife; working class women were simply ignored.

By the 1840s women and children no longer provided a sufficient supply of unskilled labor to meet the growing demands of industry. The need for unskilled labor led to the first great wave of immigration from Europe. Many employers sought out immigrants from Ireland, Germany, and French Canada because they were willing to work for even lower wages than native-born American women. In the textile mills in Lowell, Massachusetts, for example, only 7 percent of the labor force was foreign-born in 1845, but by 1852 more than half of the workers were immigrants. Many female immigrants replaced American-born women in factories, but since immigration from Europe and Canada was predominantly male, the percentage of men in factories increased sharply in the 1850s. This, in turn, contributed to the overall decline in women's employment during the decade. The decline continued for the remainder of the century; between 1850 and 1900 the proportion of women in the industrial labor force dropped from 23 to 19 percent.[15]

A look at the cotton industry, a field in which women were heavily concentrated, helps to delineate the factors affecting women's employment in the nineteenth century. Women and children accounted for 87 percent of cotton mill operatives between 1810 and 1820 when the industry was in its infancy. As the century progressed, however, the proportion of men working in the mills steadily increased while the percentage of women declined. In 1850 women made up 64 percent of the cotton industry's labor force and in 1900, 49 percent.[16]

How then do we explain the replacement of women in an industry that from its inception had been heavily dominated by females? Elizabeth Abbott cites two factors that led to the decline of women's employment in the cotton mills. As the mills became increasingly mechanized, heavier machinery requiring work at increased speed and strength favored the employment of male operatives. The second factor was the change in the available labor supply. As immigration from Europe continued, the number of men willing to work at low wages in mill employment increased. At the same time the number of educated women seeking such employment decreased as higher status, white collar jobs—in teaching, offices, and shops—became more abundant. Abbott believes that the change in the male labor supply was the more decisive factor of the two. She contends that if male labor had remained scarce, mill machinery would have been modified for use by female operatives.[17] By 1900 a majority of the cotton industry's labor force consisted of men of foreign parentage, a group that scarcely existed to compete with the female labor pool during the first quarter of the nineteenth century when the mills were being established.

The Civil War was a turning point for women in the textile industry. The shutdown of mills during the war led women to seek other work, and when the mills reopened following the war, female operatives were largely displaced by male immigrants. Women also began working in metal and munitions factories during the Civil War, but after the crisis was over they were dismissed from jobs in heavy industry because, it was said, they were "too physically delicate" for such work. Also at this time barriers to hiring women for skilled factory positions solidified; most craft unions placed strong restrictions on women's membership from the late 1850s. Union leaders argued that the employment of women lowered wages and took jobs away from "male breadwinners." Since craft unions accounted for the majority of union membership during the last half of the nineteenth century, these barriers effectively kept women from union participation. At least some of the support for protective legislation aimed at women and children had the disguised goal of limiting their competition with men for factory jobs.[18]

Loud and often well-known voices decried women's factory employment from the mid-nineteenth century. Theodore Roosevelt claimed that the physical delicacy of women made them ill equipped for such work, and he feared the effects on the "race and the nation": "If the women do not recognize that the greatest thing for any woman is to be a good wife and mother, why, that nation has cause to be alarmed about its future." Others expressed similar views. In 1875 the head of the Massachusetts Bureau of Labor Statistics declared: "Married women ought not to be tolerated in the mills at all . . . for it is an evil that is sapping the life of our operative population, and must sooner or later be regulated, or, more properly, stopped." Finally, in 1897 the head of the Boston Central Labor Union opposed women's factory employment as "an insidious assault upon the home; it is the knife of the assassin aimed at the family circle . . . it excludes the woman from nature's dearest impulse . . . stripping them of the modest demeanor that lends a charm to their kind." These statements are odd, for very few *married* women were employed in mills or anywhere else outside the home. Throughout the nineteenth century the female labor force was overwhelmingly young and single.[19]

The doctrine of separate spheres, which relegated women to the home and men to the world of work, served nineteenth-century business interests in a number of ways. The middle class ideal of feminine domesticity was one to which thousands of poor, immigrant, and black working women were told to aspire. Thus many of these women viewed their jobs as temporary, as a brief interlude in their lives before they could achieve their true calling as wives and mothers. Workers without strong commitments to long-term employment were less likely to protest exploitative working conditions and low wages. Moreover, the doctrine of separate spheres allowed a woman's income to be seen as merely supplemental, a notion that was used to justify the nineteenth-century practice of paying women from one-third to one-half the prevailing wage paid to men. In addition, a docile, transient labor force is difficult to unionize. Feeling their life's work to be in the home, women had fewer incentives than men to fight for better working conditions. Finally, the cult of domesticity stigmatized men with working wives—a powerful incentive for men who were the sole support of their families. Long hours, perhaps under difficult conditions, were the price many men had to pay if they were to retain the respect conferred on those with dependent wives.[20]

The barriers to hiring women for skilled factory jobs created a pool of educated women who sought work elsewhere. As the nineteenth century progressed more and more professional and white collar positions, particularly in teaching, nursing, and sales, became available. Native-born, middle class women flocked to them as an alternative to factory employment. But during part of the century teaching was the *only* profession open to women, and school boards enthusiastically hired women because they could be paid half or even a third of the salaries men received. With meager funds to attract men as teachers, school boards waged active campaigns to recruit females whose dispositions, it was said, were uniquely suited to teaching the young. Teaching, particularly in the elementary grades, was quickly labeled "women's work."

The Civil War increased the demand for women teachers in both north and south because of the war's reduction of the male labor supply. By the end of the war there were more women than men teaching in the public schools. As public education continued to grow rapidly during the last decades of the century and as men turned away from teaching toward more lucrative positions in business and skilled trades, primary and secondary schools became female ghettoes. By 1870 two-thirds of all teachers were women, and by 1890 the figure had risen to more than three-quarters.[21]

Nursing, too, once a predominantly male profession, saw a large increase in women during the Civil War. Here again the low wages and relatively low status of nurses, who were classified as "domestic workers" until late in the century, failed to attract men to the profession. Two economists have analyzed the conditions under which both nursing and teaching came to be viewed as occupations suitable for women:

> Opportunities for women remained good in teaching and nursing because the employers of teachers and nurses were not willing or able to compete in labor markets for the services of men. Neither governments nor private charities could command resources sufficient to compete with farms, factories, and shops for the purchase of the labor of men. But well-educated women were available in large numbers for such work because they remained blocked from other occupations that could have used their abilities.[22]

Another occupation "feminized" during the latter part of the nineteenth century was librarianship. In 1878 two-thirds of all library workers were female; by 1910 women held nearly 80 percent of all library positions.[23] Here too the reasons for the predominance of women in the field were economic. Libraries, which were growing in size and number during the period, required educated but low-paid workers. Since public libraries were supported by tax money and private donations, they were expected to keep their labor costs down and to spend most of their income on books. Given the limited opportunities available to them, educated women willing to work for low wages quickly staffed these proliferating public institutions.

Office work was another white collar field that absorbed a substantial number of women during the second part of the nineteenth century. Women first entered offices during the Civil War when there was a dearth of potential male employees, and the invention of the typewriter in 1873 set the stage for the large-scale employment of women in business and commercial offices. Nonunionized and willing to perform skilled office work for lower wages than men, women gradually came to predominate in clerical and secretarial positions.

Women began to be hired for retail sales in the 1880s. The work called for at least a moderate education since literacy in English and knowledge of arithmetic were prerequisites for such jobs. Middle class women once again provided employers with a cheap pool of skilled labor, which made them particularly "appropriate" for such work. The Victorian image of women as "consumer specialists" conveniently meshed with the belief that women were adept at sales work, an idea not unrelated to the low cost of hiring them.

Late nineteenth-century attitudes toward the employment of women varied according to the woman's status. Unmarried women, it was argued, could be employed in certain "suitable" occupations, ones that did not tax their fragile constitutions or in any way threaten their femininity. Married women, in contrast, were not to work except in the most dire economic emergencies. The "cult of domesticity" gave married women primary responsibility for the care of home and children, a responsibility that could not be met if the woman took paid employment. A study of the factors involved in the employment of married women in Essex County, Massachusetts, in 1880, for example, found that the *only* condition that made a woman's work both necessary and socially acceptable was her husband's permanent or temporary inability to earn normal wages.[24]

Various arguments were presented against women's employment. Sociologist Robert Smuts cites six premises used in different combinations by late nineteenth-century moralists and opinion makers in their condemnation of women's work outside the home. Perhaps the most powerful of these was the belief that the female body was delicate and easily impaired by unfeminine activities. In *Sex in Industry* Azel Ames, a physician, claimed that women's employment was not only a threat to their proper menstruation but to their fertility, health, and sanity as well. In 1900 Edward Bok, the editor of *Ladies' Home Journal*, cited similar objections to employing women:

> It . . . is a plain, simple fact that women have shown themselves naturally incompetent to fill a great many of the business positions which they have sought to occupy. . . . The fact is that not one woman in a hundred can stand the physical strain of the keen pace which competition has forced upon every line of business today.[25]

Others opposed women's employment on the grounds that women were intellectually and temperamentally unsuited for paid work. Women, it was said, had certain innate mental and emotional qualities that were essential to their roles in society as wives and mothers; industrial and professional employment could impair these feminine qualities and cause mental instability. Perhaps equally widespread were moral arguments against women in the labor force. Women were supposed by nature, to be pure, modest, and lacking in passion, but these traits, like other feminine characteristics, were believed vulnerable and easily tainted. In order to preserve these qualities, women were to be kept away from tempting and compromising situations such as the unsupervised association with men at work. At all costs they were to be isolated from situations in which their sexual interest might be aroused.

Yet another argument against female employment involved the fear that such employment would overturn the "natural" order of society and the male's preeminent position within it. Related to this notion was the unquestioned assumption that working women took jobs away from men and deprived them of their livelihood. Such fears were voiced most loudly during years of economic uncertainty. Smuts wrote that "every depression brought a resurgence of the complaint that working women were stealing jobs that belonged to men."[26]

The historical evidence suggests that women did not in fact take work away from men, for they were hired for different jobs and so were not in direct competition with men. The employment of women and children, however, may have lowered the wage scale in certain industries. Since a significant percentage of mill workers were women and children and wages in the textile industry were lower than in any other, the "pernicious" economic effects of employing women and children were often cited with reference to that industry.

A final line of argument was directed at male relatives of employed women. Stated simply, female employment reflected badly on them. Men who "permitted" their wives, daughters, or sisters to work were either unable to support them, powerless to control them, or unconcerned with protecting them from the dangers of the outside world. Particularly among the middle class, the working wife or daughter was indicative of a man's weakness; he was expected to demonstrate his success by keeping them idle.

These rather convoluted ideas about women and work were by no means limited to the United States. A remarkably similar ideology also evolved in England during the mid-nineteenth century. British sociologist Ann Oakley cites the four principal arguments used by the ideologues of the day:

> Female employment was condemned on moral grounds, on grounds of damage to physical health, on grounds of neglect of home and family, and, lastly, simply on the grounds that it contravened the 'natural' division of labour between the sexes.[27]

These attitudes were reflections of the actual number of women holding outside employment during the late nineteenth century. Although American women did work in factories, offices, schools, and shops, these women were clearly exceptions to the rule. The majority of women, particularly married women, made home and family their full-time careers. Between 1870 and 1900 the proportion of working women in the female population varied between 14 and 21 percent, and by 1900 less than 4 percent of married white women were employed. Even in factories, the largest source of employment aside from domestic service, an 1887 Bureau of Labor study found that only 4 percent of the female operatives were married. Similarly, only one in 25 female school teachers was married, partly because many school districts banned the hiring of married women.[28]

In the late nineteenth century black women and immigrant women were the only married women who worked outside the home in significant numbers. In the 1890 census 25 percent of black married women, most of whom resided in the South, were reported to hold outside jobs. In Lowell and Fall River, Massachusetts, about 20 percent of foreign-born and first-generation married women were employed in the textile mills. That economic necessity was the primary factor leading married women to seek employment is illustrated by the fact that in 1890 more widows than wives were employed outside the home.[29]

The great majority of employed women in the final decades of the nineteenth century were either black, foreign-born, or young and single whites. Moreover, for the latter, work was temporary; almost all white women with jobs gave them up when they married. Even among married women without young children to rear or much else to do, very few worked; "once a girl assumed the full status of womanhood, she automatically stayed home."[30]

The Factory and the Office: The Early Twentieth Century

Victorian condemnation of working women was somewhat muted during the first two decades of the twentieth century as more women entered the job market in response to the increased demand for unskilled and semiskilled labor in the nation's burgeoning industries. In addition, despite increases in real wages after 1897, men's wages in many cases still remained too low to meet family needs. As a result, between 1900 and 1919 the female labor force grew by 50 percent.[31] Much of this increase can be traced to the influx of European immigrant women who were somewhat more likely to be employed than their native-born counterparts. Even though the relative proportion of women in factories declined between the Civil War and the early twentieth century, their absolute numbers grew rather rapidly as a result of labor demand and family necessity.

The 1905 census indicated that women in industrial employment were still heavily concentrated in a few fields—textiles, clothing trades, cigar making, printing, boot and shoe making—all industries requiring heavy inputs of unskilled and semiskilled labor. Employers willingly hired female operatives, particularly those of foreign birth, because an inexpensive labor supply was essential for new industries trying to make a profit. Poor, unskilled immigrants provided such a supply since the very survival of immigrant families often depended on all of their members being employed. The 1915 *Report on the Condition of Women and Children Wage Earners in the United States* recognized the link between the employment of women and the payment of low wages: "Almost everywhere women predominate in the unskilled work, probably because they could be secured for this at wages which would not attract men."[32]

While employers welcomed cheap immigrant labor, male or female, many contemporary social reformers and labor leaders viewed such labor with alarm. Immigrants, it was said, lowered wages and living standards, made it difficult to improve working conditions, and hindered the unionization of factory operatives. Citing these problems, some politicians intensified their efforts to restrict immigration, arguing that foreign laborers had an unfair advantage over native American workers in the competition for jobs. Working women also became the targets of those who feared the social consequences of a cheap labor supply. "Now that there is some fear lest profuse immigration give us an oversupply of labor, and that there may not be work enough for the men, it is the public moralist again who finds that women's proper place is at home," Elizabeth Abbott wrote in 1910. Nor had the moral argument against the employment of women entirely been laid to rest. The Chicago Vice Commission claimed in a 1911 report that women's employment, their entry into politics, the decay of the family, and rising rates of prostitution were all interrelated.[33]

Aside from factory employment, the majority of women working in 1910 were in domestic service, farm work, and a few professions. Professional women continued to be heavily concentrated in teaching and nursing; 76 percent of all female professionals were in one of those two fields. The number of women in sales and office positions doubled from the preceding decade. Particularly noteworthy is that as early as 1910 office work already had become a "female ghetto"; women held 83 percent of all typing and stenographic positions in that year. During the early part of the twentieth century a rapid expansion of business offices led employers to draw on the pool of educated female workers to fill clerical needs. These offices contrasted with those of the nineteenth century in which "some of the clerks were, in effect, apprenticing managers," as Margery Davies points out. "The expanded office structure, on the contrary, brought with it a rapid growth of low-level dead-end jobs."[34]

The age and marital profile of the typical female worker had changed somewhat since the turn of the century. Although three-fifths of the female labor force in 1910 was young and single, the remainder consisted of married, widowed, and divorced women, most of whom worked out of economic necessity. A 1910 U.S. Bureau of Labor study demolished the myth that women were working only for "pin money" by demonstrating the dependence of many families on the wages earned by their female members.[35]

Although the first years of the twentieth century were rather uneventful in terms of women's employment rates and opportunities, the picture changed dramatically with the outbreak of World War I. The demand for labor during the war opened many new jobs to women, and the customary and legal restrictions against employing them fell rapidly in business and industry. Large numbers of women were employed in munitions plants, as streetcar conductors, elevator operators, theater ushers, furnace stokers, and in some sales and clerical positions once held exclusively by men. The number of women employed in steel and iron foundries trebled during the war, and women doctors were employed by the U.S. Public Health Service for the first time. Still, as historian William Chafe points out, the war did not result in a large net increase in the number of women employed. Only about 5 percent of those who took jobs during wartime were entering the labor market for the first time. The majority of women working during the war simply transferred from lower paying jobs into higher paying ones that had been vacated by men.[36]

While the sight of women welding and laying railroad tracks was probably deeply disturbing to some, by the second year of the war women's entry into formerly masculine occupations had gained widespread acceptance. Even that bastion of domesticity, the *Ladies' Home Journal*, published laudatory articles on women in factory work. (Yet Edward Bok, the editor of the *Ladies' Home Journal*, came out firmly against women's suffrage following the war.)

Despite the changed employment picture for women during the war, the unstated assumption was that women would be called on to abandon their "masculine" jobs once hostilities ceased. And so they were. With the return of the troops, many women were dismissed from the positions they held during the wartime emergency. In Detroit women streetcar conductors were fired en masse; in New York twenty women judges lost

Table 6.1

Census Data on Women in the United States Labor Force

1900–1980

Year	1900	1910*	1920	1930	1940	1950	1960	1970	1980
Percentage of women 14 and over in labor force	20.4	25.2	23.3	24.3	25.4	29.0	34.5	45.0	51.4
Percentage change over previous decade		+23.5	− 7.5	+ 4.3	+ 4.5	+14.2	+19.0	+30.4	+14.2

SOURCE: Oppenheimer, *The Female Labor Force in the United States;* United States Department of Labor, *Perspectives on Working Women: A Databook* (Washington, D.C., 1980).

*There is no doubt that the 1910 census overestimated the number of women in the labor force because census takers received special instructions not to overlook women and to report them as gainfully occupied even if they were unpaid family workers. It is assumed therefore that the percentage increase between 1900 and 1910 was as gradual as it was in the decades prior to 1940 (Joseph Adna Hill, *Women in Gainful Occupations 1870 to 1920* [Westport, Conn., 1978; orig. published, 1929], chapter 3).

Table 6.2

Women as a Percentage of All Workers in the United States Labor Force

Year	1890	1900	1920	1930	1940	1945	1947	1950	1960	1970	1974	1976	1980
Percentage of all workers	17	18	20	22	25	36	28	29	33	38	39	40.7	42.5

SOURCE: United States Department of Labor, *Handbook on Women Workers* (Washington, D.C., 1975); "Women Entering Job Market at 'Extraordinary Pace,' " *New York Times*, 12 September, 1976; United States Department of Labor, *Perspectives on Working Women: A Databook* (Washington, D.C., 1980).

their positions once the armistice was signed; and by 1919 a Women's Bureau study noted that women were prohibited from taking 60 percent of all civil service examinations by reason of their sex. Appeals were made to women's "higher instincts" to induce them to give up their wartime jobs. The head of the Central Federated Labor Union of New York insisted in 1919 that "the same patriotism which induced women to enter industry during the war should induce them to vacate their positions after the war."[37]

Perhaps because of the war's brief duration, but more likely because women's labor was no longer in demand, women's wartime employment produced no large permanent increase in the number of working women. By 1920 there were only 800,000 more women in the labor force than there had been in 1910, a small figure in comparison with the overall increase in the size of the labor force and the general population. Only a handful of new positions—elevator operators and theater ushers—remained open to women after the war. The employment picture for women in 1919 clearly fell far short of the high expectations of feminists, who had hoped that the break with tradition in women's wartime employment and the intervening suffrage movement would result in a permanent change in women's employment status.

Sexual Emancipation and the Feminine Mystique: The 1920s

The widely heralded emancipation of women in the 1920s was an emancipation with clearly defined boundaries. It certainly did not include the freedom to pursue a career. The "feminine mystique," not yet named and exposed, was alive and well during the decade of the flapper. A look at employment figures for the period confirms this point. Between 1920 and 1930 the proportion of women in the labor force increased by only 1 percent, and the majority still retired from work once they married. The common view that women were economically emancipated during the twenties is based on growth in the female labor force of about two million between 1920 and 1930. This growth, however, largely reflected a general population increase rather than any profound change in women's economic activities.[38]

Nor did the type of jobs women held change very much. Women in industry still had the least skilled jobs that offered low wages and few possibilities for advancement; only a small minority of women belonged to labor unions. The only interest labor leaders showed in organizing women workers came in 1923 after the Supreme Court struck down minimum wage laws for women—the American Federation of Labor feared that nonunion women would undercut men in competition for factory jobs.

Only the employment of certain classes of women met with general approval. In 1923, for example, the Secretary of Labor condemned the employment of mothers in industry, stating that it would lead to disaster for the U.S. economy. The Women's Bureau, which had been established to protect the rights of women workers, took a similar stance regarding the employment of married women. Wives that work, the Bureau proclaimed, were a threat to the health and happiness of their families. A questionnaire given to 314 men early in the decade revealed that 65 percent agreed with the statement that "The married woman should devote her time to the home"; while another 31 percent agreed that married women could work outside the home only if they did not have young children.[39]

These attitudes often prompted bans on hiring married women. Even in such "feminine" fields as teaching, most school boards would not hire wives, and about half of the boards required teachers to quit when they married. In a similar vein, a 1928 *New York Times* article reported that when the Long Island Railroad was forced to reduce its work force because of economic exigencies, married women with employed husbands were the first to be let go.[40]

The types of white collar and professional positions that women held during the 1920s had also changed little since the turn of the century. The overwhelming majority of female professionals were still teachers and nurses, and the majority of women in the business world still held secretarial, clerical, and sales positions. In fact, the most important change in women's occupations between 1910 and 1920 was the advance in office positions from the fifth to the third most important source of employment for women. In the fields of medicine and dentistry women actually lost ground. At the turn of the century there had been some 11,000 female dentists and physicians, but by 1920 there were fewer than 10,000.[41]

Despite studies showing that about 90 percent of the women who held jobs during the decade did so to help support their families and that one in four was her family's principal wage earner, employers and opinion makers persisted in using the "pin money" argument to deride female employment. As historian William Chafe notes, this was a particularly vicious notion because employers who had convinced themselves that women worked only to buy frills felt less guilty when they paid women less than men.[42]

The 1920s consensus then was that women's place was in the home. While the single woman might work at a "suitable" job for a while, she was expected to retire after marriage to devote herself to home and family. A Department of Labor report on a meeting focusing on women in industry reflects this consensus: "Practically every speaker . . . recognized that women's interest in industry was at best only temporary, a stop-gap between whatever girlhood lay behind her and marriage."[43]

A married woman in the twenties just might pursue a career as long as she remained childless. But the 1923 headline "Woman President of Bank Does Housework in Her Own Home" makes it clear that such women were still primarily identified by their domestic role.[44] Combining career, marriage, *and* motherhood was simply unthinkable.

The women's magazines of the period glorified the domestic sphere, insisting that it was rewarding and creative. They carried a number of articles by prominent women who urged readers to find true fulfillment in the home. In an anonymous 1923 article entitled "I Wish I Had Married and Found Life," written according to the editors of *Good Housekeeping* by a woman of great fame, the author mentioned her highly successful career, but then added poignantly: "I count my gains small beside my losses. I have no mate, no child, no home—only substitutes for them." A 1927 article in the *Ladies' Home Journal* attacked the "career woman," insisting that a good marriage was a woman's best career if she wanted to be "deeply, fundamentally, wholly feminine." In the following year an editorial in *McCalls Magazine* announced that the American woman could only "arrive at her true eminence" as a wife and mother.[45] Although these widely read magazines did not initiate antagonism toward the employment of married women, they certainly reflected the fact that few married women held jobs, and they reinforced and rationalized women's exclusion from the labor force. The unspoken assumption characterizing the ideal American woman as a full-time mother and housewife was that she had a husband who could financially support her in these roles. Poor women, black women, and women who of necessity held factory jobs were simply ignored.

In many ways the decade of the 1920s was paradoxical for women. It was the first decade of women's suffrage, but women did not form the powerful voting block that feminists had expected and disappointingly few gained political office. It was the era of the emancipated flapper with her bobbed hair and scandalously short skirts who smoked in public and demanded the same rights to sexual self-expression that men enjoyed. But basic sex roles remained unchanged, and the career woman was

Records of the Women's Bureau, National Archives

Row of Telephone Operators • *The sexual segregation of the labor force is not new. This photograph of telephone operators was taken in 1927.*

disdained and despised because she challenged the traditional view that women's ultimate fulfillment lay in home and children.

Working Wives as "Thieving Parasites": The Depression Years

The onset of the Great Depression in the 1930s dashed the last hopes of feminists for equal participation in the job market. This may seem contradictory since the number of women holding jobs actually increased by some half million during the decade and married women were employed in larger numbers than ever before. But what the figures really show is that women took jobs out of desperate economic need during a time of high male unemployment. The figures do not reflect the social disapproval and virulent condemnation of working married women that was heard throughout the 1930s or the myriad formal and informal restrictions against hiring these women.

Under conditions of widespread unemployment, the prevailing attitude was that women should give up whatever career ambitions they had and stay home, thus leaving much needed jobs for men who, it was assumed, were the chief breadwinners of their families. One Chicago civic group declared that married women workers "are holding jobs that rightfully belong to the God-intended providers of the household," while a congresswoman concurred that "women's place is not out in the business world competing with men who have families to support."[46]

What these opinion makers ignored was that most married women did not work for "pocket money" or as a sign of emancipation; they worked because their incomes were necessary for their families' survival. Many women took whatever jobs they could find to replace the wages of unemployed husbands or to supplement their husbands' meager earnings. The fact is that during the depression years over one-half of all American families earned less than $1,200 annually. That the poorest sectors of the population supplied the bulk of the female labor force confirms that such employment arose out of necessity. In 1930 black and immigrant women accounted for 57 percent of all women workers. Given large-scale unemployment and the hostility toward hiring women, it is not surprising that married women were heavily concentrated in menial jobs that paid low wages—36 percent were employed in domestic and personal services and another 20 percent worked in canning and clothing factories.[47]

Women's employment situation during the 1930s is an anomaly. Despite the loud hue and cry against women taking jobs, the percentage of women working in 1940 was actually 25 percent higher than it had been in 1930, and the rates for working married women increased from 12 to 15 percent during the decade. Sociologist Ruth Milkman explains this contradiction by citing the highly sex-segregated nature of the labor market in which "female" occupations—clerical, trade, and service jobs—declined less and later than predominantly male occupations in manufacturing. At the same time, because of high male unemployment, women who had been full-time housewives were driven by necessity to find whatever jobs they could. Thus Milkman notes that "it was not possible for ideological forces to successfully push women out of the labor market. Such behavior was in direct opposition to [women's] material interests."[48]

Even a 3 percent increase of married women in the labor force during the depression is startling given the numerous bars against hiring them. The American Federation of Labor urged that hiring policies discriminate outright against married women whose husbands were employed. By 1939, 84 percent of all U.S. insurance companies had banned the hiring of married women, and similar restrictions were in force in 43 percent of the public utility companies, 29 percent of the manufacturing concerns, 23 percent of the small private businesses, and 13 percent of the department stores. Under the guise of antinepotism rules, the federal government also discriminated against married women by legislating that two married people could not both hold government jobs; although "people" referred equally to men and women, 80 percent of those fired were wives. On the state level, bills restricting the employment of married women were introduced in 26 state legislatures, and one New York assemblyman introduced a bill to heavily tax the personal income of married women, stating that his goal was to drive them out of the labor force. Although such legislation was passed only in Louisiana, the major reason for its failure was not lack of public support but the fear that it would be declared unconstitutional. Finally, barriers against married women in the teaching profession were even more widespread during the 1930s than in the preceding decade. A National Education Association survey of 1,500 school districts in 1930–1931 found that

77 percent refused to hire wives and 61 percent required women who married to resign from their teaching posts.[49]

The women's magazines of the era also did their part in heaping scorn on women who sought jobs, to say nothing of careers. Rose Wilder Lane told readers of the *Ladies' Home Journal* in 1936 that "your career is to make a good marriage," and in 1939 in the same journal Dorothy Thompson applauded a talented woman writer who had given up her career to devote herself full-time to her husband. The conflict between marriage, motherhood, and career was a popular theme in the fiction of the *Saturday Evening Post* of the period, and while single heroines were sometimes allowed careers, they inevitably abandoned them after marriage.[50]

The prospects for career women grew worse as the decade progressed. The proportion of women in the professions fell from 14.2 percent in 1930 to 12.3 percent in 1940, and the percentage of women earning doctorates declined relative to men. This loss of ground is evident in higher education. At the start of the decade women held 32 percent of the faculty positions in the nation's colleges and universities, but by the close of the decade their proportion had fallen to 26 percent.[51]

Another reflection of discrimination against women in the labor market during the thirties is their increasing rate of joblessness. In 1931 the percentage of women who were unemployed was slightly lower than that of men, but by 1938 women's jobless rate of 22 percent was 50 percent higher than men's. Milkman suggests that this high rate of unemployment stems primarily from increased competition among women for "female-typed" jobs. Black women fared even worse; a 1933 Department of Labor study found more than half of all black women out of work.[52]

Given the long hostility toward women's employment in the United States, women workers became convenient scapegoats for the many Americans unable to undersand the complex economic conditions that had brought about the depression. "Pin-money workers," that is, working women with employed husbands, were scathingly denounced as "thieving parasites" and "menaces to society." A 1937 public opinion poll showed that 82 percent of those sampled disapproved of working wives, and two years later 67 percent of those questioned about a bill prohibiting the employment of married women in business and industry said they approved of such legislation.[53] The provisions contained in the

1935 Social Security Act also powerfully conveyed the prevailing attitude toward women's employment. A basic assumption of this legislation was (and is) that men are the sole family breadwinners and that women receive social security benefits only as wives, not as workers in their own right. In short, although animosity toward women in the labor force was hardly an invention of the depression years, it did reach new virulence as more and more people were thrown out of work and bread lines became a common sight.

From Rosie the Riveter to the "Lost Sex": The 1940s

The female employment picture in 1940 is instructive because that year formed a baseline after which dramatic changes occurred in women's labor force activities. The overwhelming majority of women in 1940 still retired from work when they married; only 15 percent of married women and only 9 percent of those with children under fourteen held jobs. By the beginning of the forties, notes sociologist Robert Smuts, "the general case against women's employment had become a specific case against the employment of wives and mothers." Nonetheless, the proportion of wives working had doubled since the turn of the century. But the employment of married women was still closely linked to the economic status of their husbands—most wives who worked had to. In 1940 only 5 percent of the women whose husbands earned more than $3,000 annually were in the labor force; however, this figure rose to 24 percent for those with husbands earning less than $400 per year.[54]

In 1940 then the typical female worker was young and single, not unlike her counterpart in 1900. She also held the same types of jobs that women had held in the past. Although in 1940, far more women were working in secretarial and clerical jobs and far fewer in agriculture and domestic service, women were still greatly underrepresented in managerial positions and in the professions; in the latter category they were still principally confined to teaching and nursing. In industry, too, the picture had changed little; most women worked at low-paying jobs in plants producing consumer goods.

The cult of domesticity was being hailed in 1940 just as it had been a decade earlier. A 1940 issue of the *Ladies' Home Journal* carried an article by the well-known journalist Dorothy Thompson, who cautioned women not to follow in her professional footsteps, adding, "I have an increasing respect for those women who stick to their knitting." Moreover, 1940, the final year of the depression, marked the high point of discrimination against married women in employment. In that year a mere 13 percent of the nation's school districts were willing to hire married women, and bills restricting their employment were introduced in twenty-five state houses.[55]

The attack on Pearl Harbor changed all this. With wide public approval, World War II brought six and a half million additional women into the labor force. The reasons for this massive increase in women's employment and the abrupt change in social attitudes are not difficult to understand. At a time when the demand for workers in war-related industries rose sharply, there was a simultaneous contraction in the male labor supply. This imbalance between supply and demand pushed wages up significantly during a period when family income fell as millions of men were drafted. Women, the largest untapped labor reserve in the country, rushed in to fill the breach, hoping to recoup lost family wages by taking lucrative jobs in industry available to them for the first time.

The outbreak of the war not only ended serious opposition to working women but marked the start of a massive campaign by business and government to get women to take jobs. Public approval for this radical change was encouraged by the mass media, which depicted Rosie the Riveter as nothing short of a national heroine. Newspapers, magazines, and radio programs praised women who took jobs, extolled their contributions to the war effort, questioned the patriotism of those who refused to work, and gave a glamorous cast to work in munitions plants and other war-related industries. Once again the *Ladies' Home Journal* demonstrated its ability to shift its image of women in accordance with the nation's fortunes by featuring a female combat pilot on its cover!

The Office of War Information's Womanpower Campaign suggested that women who failed to take jobs should be made to feel responsible for prolonging the war. If a woman worried what her friends and neighbors would think if she took a job in industry, the OWI suggested that she be told that,

> eventually the neighbors are going to think it very strange if you are not working. They'll be working too. In fact, any strong, able-bodied woman who is not completely occupied with a job and

a home—is going to be considered a "slacker" just as much as the man who avoids the draft.[56]

Government agencies, from the War Department and the War Manpower Commission to the Selective Service Commission, urged employers to make use of the vast untapped reserves of "womanpower." One agency advised employers to recruit women for war work by telling them that it is "pleasant, and as easy as running a sewing machine or a vacuum cleaner."[57]

Initially this campaign was directed at single women, but as the war progressed and more workers were needed, employers threw out the old

National Archives

Women War Workers • *During World War II millions of wives and mothers took jobs for the first time, many in formerly "male" occupations. Here women take a lunch break at the Vega Aircraft Plant in Burbank, California (1943).*

rules restricting married women in business and industry and turned to them to fill vacancies. As part of this campaign the Office of War Information asked married women, "Are you being old-fashioned and getting by just being a 'good wife and mother'?" Almost all of the later government propaganda was aimed at housewives. None of it was directed at women who were employed prior to the war, that is, to poor women and black women who have been called "the other Rosies."[58]

These efforts met with obvious success since fully 75 percent of all women newly recruited for war work were married. And so an unintended consequence of the war was a major change in the makeup of the female labor force. In contrast to her predecessor, the typical working woman during the war was a middle-aged wife who was likely to be a mother as well. In fact, one-third of the new women war workers had children under 14 years of age. By the cessation of hostilities in 1945 close to half of all women workers were married and a majority were over 35.[59]

Another effect of the tremendous demand for workers during the war was a transformation in the types of jobs for which women were hired. Women worked as stevedores, blacksmiths, lumberjacks, and crane operators. They serviced airplanes, read blueprints, repaired roads, and worked in foundries. Those not directly employed in war industries worked in agriculture, drove taxis and buses, became stock analysts, bank officers, and chemists. By far the largest increase of women—460 percent by the end of the war—was in defense plants. Their numbers increased by over 100 percent in manufacturing, and the rolls of female employees in the federal government grew by two million during the war years.[60]

Given the huge demand for workers and the media campaign which made war work and patriotism synonymous, it is little wonder that public attitudes toward employing women, particularly married women, changed dramatically during the war. Whereas in 1937 working wives met with overwhelming disapproval in opinion polls, only five years later 60 percent of those sampled agreed that married women should take jobs in war industries; another 24 percent approved of married women working under certain conditions.[61]

The enormous impact of World War II on women's entry into the work force can be gauged from the proportion of women employed, which jumped from 25 to 36 percent between 1940 and 1945—a greater increase than in the preceding forty years! In terms of raw figures, an additional 6.5 million women took jobs during the war, an increase of 57 percent. Even more striking is the change in married women's labor force participation; during the war the proportion of wives working increased by 50 percent. For the first time in American history married women made up a majority of the female labor force.

These gains, unlike those made during World War I, were not immediately wiped out. A survey of women war workers in 1945 indicated that 61 percent intended to remain in the job market. Contrary to expectations, only 600,000 women voluntarily retired from the labor force with the cessation of hostilities, and by 1947 women had started reentering the labor force in sufficient numbers to begin making up for their job losses in the immediate postwar period. Not until the mid-1950s, however, did the women's labor force participation rate again reach peak war levels.[62]

Strong opposition to women's continued employment developed among those who feared a severe postwar wave of unemployment and recession, fears which never materialized. Many doubted that there were enough jobs for both women and returning veterans, and a number of companies reimposed prewar restrictions on hiring wives. Under the Selective Service Act veterans were given priority over war workers for jobs, and when factories were converted to peacetime production many women were fired, especially those who had worked in heavy industry. As a result, 60 percent of all wartime employees thrown out of work in the first months after V-E Day were females, and by November 1946 two million women had been dismissed from their wartime jobs. In addition to reimposing bans on hiring married women, many employers changed age requirements and fired women over 45; men, however, could remain on their jobs until age 65. The outcome of these discriminatory regulations was that women's layoff rate was 75 percent higher than men's.[63]

The mass media and public figures also participated in the effort to get women out of the work force and back to their traditional roles as wives and mothers. Many criticized women's employment, citing the increased incidence of juvenile delinquency during the war and blaming it on maternal neglect. Magazines and newspapers were full of stories about the sad fate of "latch key" children and other domestic woes caused by working wives. One Florida senator urged "wives and mothers to get back in the kitchen" to make room in the job market for returning veterans. Soon after V-E Day the company newspaper of a Portland, Oregon, shipyard (28 percent of whose employees were women at the height of the war) carried the article "The Kitchen—Women's Big Post-War Goal." The author asserted that women wanted to "put aside the welder's torch" and their "unfeminine" work clothes and return to domesticity in a "vine-covered cottage." Even before the war had ended, the *Saturday Evening Post* carried an article by a woman printer and labor veteran who advised the "ladies to give up their beachhead in man's industrial world when the war is over." She also compared her career unfavorably with that of the housewife-mother: "I know plenty of women who have gotten more out of life just by being feminine and taking a short cut to Shangri La by way of the alter."[64]

The diatribes against working women reached their peak with the publication of *Modern Woman: The Lost Sex* by Ferdinand Lundberg and Marynia Farnham in 1947. The book blamed virtually all of society's ills on women who had left the home to take jobs. The "independent woman" who sought a career was a "contradiction in terms" since women are by nature psychologically and biologically dependent on men. The formula for women's true happiness, the authors claimed, was acceptance of their innately passive nature, which could only be fulfilled by raising children and ensconcing themselves in domesticity. Women's employment, according to Lundberg and Farnham, was really a disguised search for masculine identity, a search that was wholly neurotic because it divorced women from their true selves.[65]

The surprise is that despite all the public pressure to retire to the home, many women stayed in the work force. But it is clear why they did so. The postwar period was a time of high inflation, and for many families two incomes had become essential for maintaining a middle class standard of living. Between 1945 and 1947, for example, meat prices rose by 122 percent. Rising consumer demand could only be satisfied through a second income that brought the new car or home or household appliances within reach of the average American family. At the same time, women profited from a labor shortage caused by the lack of young people entering the job market as a result of the low birth rate that prevailed during the 1930s. Women, including wives and mothers, went to work in increasing numbers as the demand for labor grew and as inflation and consumerism put a premium on additional income.[66]

A woman's job was grudgingly approved in the late 1940s as long as its goal was to give her family a better life. Wives who took jobs only to assist their families conformed to the traditional view of women as "helpmates." But career women with personal ambition or wives who took jobs to "fulfill themselves" met with overwhelming hostility. The priority of the domestic role was emphasized even in the lives of well-known and talented women. A 1949 *Ladies' Home Journal* article on Edna St. Vincent Millay showed her cooking a meal. Betty Friedan claims that the women's magazines of the day would only accept articles about women who were not really housewives if they were made to *sound like housewives*.[67]

Many Careers But Only One Vocation: The Domestic Fifties

The 1950s was another decade in which ideology and practice were contradictory. The "feminine mystique" and domesticity flourished at the same time as women entered the labor force in increasing numbers. While women's magazines were extolling the joys of togetherness, more and more wives and mothers were leaving home to take jobs. Although the campaign affirming the delights of home and family was aimed at mother-housewives, this was precisely the group seeking employment. The trend was so pronounced that by the end of the decade the "typical" woman worker was a middle-aged, middle class wife and mother.

Some statistics shed light on the changing composition of the female labor force during the fifties. Between 1950 and 1960 over four million married women took jobs, accounting for 60 percent of all new workers, male and female. In 1950, 24 percent of all married women and 22 percent of all women with children were employed. This meant that by the end of the decade the proportion of wives with jobs was double the 1940 figure and the number of working mothers had increased by 400 percent! The female labor force had also aged considerably; by the late 1950s the median age of employed women was 41. Finally, the class affiliation of women workers had also changed since 1940. In that year married women holding jobs were mainly from the working class, but by the end of the 1950s the working wife was just as likely to be well educated and middle class.[68]

The 1950s marked the emergence of a clear pattern in women's employment history. After finishing school, most women worked until marriage or the birth of their first child. They then retired from the labor force only to return when their youngest child had entered school. By 1956 nearly half of all mothers with school age children were employed at least part of the year. Women's labor force participation was clearly not smothered by the feminine mystique, although the new entrants in the job market were more likely to be older women with school age or grown children.

The attitudes toward the employment of women during the 1950s are neatly summarized in a 1957 National Manpower Council report: "Americans have not generally disapproved of women participating in paid employment," the report noted, but have always had "severe reservations about married women with small children working outside the home." The report went on to cite public opinion polls indicating that "Americans overwhelmingly disapprove of having the mother of young children go to work when her husband can support her." The report concluded that "both men and women take it for granted that the male is the family breadwinner and that he has the superior claim to available work, particularly over the woman who does not have to support herself."[69] These attitudes meshed nicely with the changing needs of the American economy for a particular type of labor.

Two factors seem to have favored increasing employment of married middle class women: (1) the increased demand for women workers because of the growth of those segments of the job market which largely employed females, and (2) the increased need for a second family income in order to purchase the consumer goods requisite for a middle class life-style.

Economist Valerie Oppenheimer has shown that as a result of sex segregation in the job market a separate demand for female labor developed. Oppenheimer noted the following features as characteristic of "female-typed" occupations: jobs that pay low wages and require some skill but little or no on-the-job training and jobs that require skills that women learn as part of the female role. Once a job is labeled "female" it tends to remain that way as long as there is no labor shortage or radical change in the nature of the job.[70]

Secretarial work (including clerks, typists, and stenographers), nursing, teaching, and certain types of retail sales are all "female" occupations by virtue of the predominance of women workers—more than 70 percent in these professions. Since the end of World War II the rise in demand for workers in these fields has been enormous; during the decade of the 1950s alone the size of their labor force increased by 48 percent. This growth was part of the dramatic shift in the nation's occupational structure from primarily manual and blue collar labor before World War II to service and white collar work in the postwar period.[71]

The rapid expansion of the service sector following the war has been attributed to the absence of unionization that took place in the industrial and manufacturing sector. Employers in the private sector found it more profitable to expand the production of services than the production of goods because of the relatively low cost of white and pink collar labor. Over half of the jobs in the service sector—56 percent to be exact—offer wages in the low-level range of the labor market and only 17 percent in the upper level. This contrasts with goods-producing jobs; 33 percent of these are in the low-level wage range and 26 percent are in the upper-level wage range.[72]

Most of the women entering the labor market in the 1950s took jobs in sex-segregated service occupations. Half were employed in areas in which 70 percent of the workers were female, and almost 60 percent were in fields in which the majority of workers were women.[73] Obviously, one of the reasons so many women took jobs in the 1950s is that there were so many new jobs open to them. Not only were more jobs available but they were jobs that employers had traditionally hired females to perform and that women were accustomed to doing.

Oppenheimer also explains why so many older married women took jobs: "Employers have often turned to married women and older women not so much because they have independently discovered the worth of such women but because they cannot get enough young single women." Since 1940 there has been a decline in the proportion of young single women in the U.S. population. This shift in age and marital status is a result of (1) a decline in the age at marriage and in the number of women never marrying, (2) the general aging of the population, and (3) the increase of women's average years of schooling, which keeps them out of the job market until a later age than in the past.[74] Thus, just as the demand for female workers was on the rise, the pool of young unmarried women, the traditional source of female labor, was contracting. Employers not surprisingly turned to older, married women to fill the breach, and these women, responding in part to opportunities never before available on such a scale, entered the job market in record numbers.

Employers' attitudes toward hiring middle-aged wives changed rather rapidly once the pool of young unmarried females proved too small to meet labor needs. The transformation in attitude is particularly evident in primary and secondary education, which experienced a dramatic teacher shortage because of the postwar baby boom. In 1950, 82 percent of the school districts in the U.S. hired wives as teachers, and by 1956, 97 percent did so, thus, effectively ending the old restrictions on employing married women.[75]

The second reason so many women sought employment during the 1950s was the growing need for two incomes in order to buy the vast array of consumer goods that had become synonymous with a middle class life-style. But not all wives went to work to buy "extras." Many families in the fifties were in the middle income range *only* because of the wife's additional wage contribution. In 1956, 70 percent of the families with $7,000 to $10,000 annual incomes had a second worker, principally the wife, in the labor force. Employment for these women, according to historian Peter Filene, "was neither outlet nor end. It was the means to raise their family's standard of living toward middle class abundance." That women's rate of entry into the labor force neither declined during the relatively severe recession of 1957–1958 nor revived the old notion that married women were "stealing" jobs from male breadwinners indicates the degree to which women's earnings were accepted as a normal and necessary part of family support. In short, the expansion of women's employment role during the 1950s reflected both the greater demand for their labor and the increased need for their earnings in a consumption-oriented economy.[76]

Holding a job, however, was very different from pursuing a career during the 1950s. Working women received at least grudging approval since they were contributing to their families' welfare and providing such "extras" as a second car or a college education for their children. The career woman, in contrast, had no place in this social ethic. She was depicted as an unhappy, frustrated individual who secretly longed for the security of home and family. This stereotype was rife in the women's magazines of the decade. Betty Friedan did a content analysis of the fiction in such publications and concluded: "The new feminine morality story is the exorcising of the forbidden career dream." And this "exorcism" seems to have been successful. A poll conducted among college women in the 1950s indicated that only 20 to 25 percent of them planned to turn their work experience into a career.[77]

The views of the Freudian psychoanalyst Helene Deutsch were popular during the period. According to Deutsch, a normal woman represses her masculine instincts that seek self-realization and identifies with the outside world through her husband and children. This repression, of course, meant that a career was out of the question. Deutsch adopted polar views: "a woman was either a well-adjusted homemaker or a feminist neurotic." In a similar vein a psychologist writing in a 1958 issue of the *Ladies' Home Journal* deplored higher education's ill effects on the female psyche:

> When a girl goes to college and cultivates her mind, this may stimulate, even inflate, her masculine side, and she can become avidly intellectual with a strong power drive, and then it is easy to become a doctor or lawyer who is hardly feminine at all.[78]

Combining home and career was out of the question. A woman might work to supply her family with "things," but her true fulfillment came from her domestic role: "Whether they work at outside jobs or not, today's young mothers find their greatest satisfaction in home, husband, and family," proclaimed the *Ladies' Home Journal*. In a 1950 article in the *Atlantic Monthly*, Agnes Meyer declared that while women have "many careers, they have only one vocation—motherhood." She then lambasted women who work but "do not have to," blaming them for a host of society's ills, from teenage crime to sexual immorality. The author of a 1956 article in *Life* magazine even questioned the sanity of such women, noting pointedly: "In New York City the 'career woman' can be seen in fullest bloom, and it is not irrelevant that New York City has the greatest concentration of psychiatrists." The author went on to claim that a woman with ambition is afflicted with a form of mental illness and is responsible for alcoholism in her husband and homosexuality in her children.[79]

Even anthropologists succumbed to the prevailing attitude that dichotomized the home-and-family and the career. Ashley Montagu, writing in the *Saturday Review* in 1958, left no doubt as to his position on the issue: "Being a good wife, a good mother, in short, a good homemaker is the most important of all occupations in the world. . . . I put it down as an axiom that no woman with a husband and small children can hold a full-time job and be a good homemaker at one and the same time." Montagu agreed with other opinion makers of the era, who argued that the colleges were not training women for their primary roles as wives and mothers:

> . . . our schools and colleges encourage women to go into the world to compete with men as if they were men. . . . The effect of such misguided education is that women are encouraged to develop aspirations which were designed exclusively to meet the needs of men . . . they are not told what it means to be a woman or what a woman's role should be in the home and in the community.[80]

The disparity between women's work and the attitudes it invoked in the 1950s is in a number of ways not as startling as it first appears. Partly in response to the demand for their labor, more women were holding jobs than ever before. At the same time approval of women's employment was clearly conditional. They might take jobs to pay for the extras needed to maintain a middle class standard of living, but they must not seek employment, particularly a career, because they felt it necessary for their own well-being. This attitude in a real sense coincided neatly with the labor requirements of the United States economy during the period. Large numbers of women were needed to work as secretaries, in retail sales, and in other sex-segregated occupations. These jobs were defined as temporary or part-time, conveniently taking advantage of the available labor supply and keeping it cheap and nonunionized. In short, the nature of the jobs themselves did not require the steady work commitment usually associated with pursuing a career.

Women, moreover, could take these jobs intermittently in accordance with the family life cycle—before marriage or after the children were in school—at small loss to their employers. As Oppenheimer notes, one of the main characteristics of "female-typed" jobs is that they require little or no on-the-job training. Women traditionally have not been hired for work that requires on-the-job training because, said their employers, women are "poor investments" who cannot be counted on to remain at work. This is not to imply that the occupations in which women are concentrated require no skills but that the skills have been acquired by the woman on her own before taking the job. This is certainly true of secretaries, teachers, nurses, and librarians.[81]

The employment of women in the United States did more than just meet the labor demands of business and industry—it also made an ever increasing level of consumption possible. A 1956 study showed that families with working wives tended to be more in debt than those in which women were not employed outside the home. Furthermore, these debts most often were for cars, refrigerators, and other household appliances, indicating that women were working to pay for *specific* items, which, in turn, helps explain why many of them worked on a part-time basis. Women, then, were not simply "administrators of consumption,"

Courtesy of Michael Kappy, M.D.

Office Workers • *Today more than 80 percent of all office workers are women and their annual average income is $11,000.*

as economist John Kenneth Galbraith termed housewives; they were producers of the wages that allowed greater consumption as well.[82]

The Other Family Breadwinner: 1960 to the Present

The changing trends in women's employment that started after World War II and continued through the 1950s gained momentum in the sixties and seventies. Recent changes, however, have been more quantitative than qualitative. Today working women have similar profiles to those who began entering the labor force in the postwar era: they are mothers, wives, the middle class, and the middle aged. Only now there are far more of them. Statistics are conclusive.

In 1960 women comprised 33 percent of the national labor force; today they account for 43 percent. In 1960, 35 percent of all adult women held jobs; by 1982, 52 percent of the female population was gainfully employed. In 1960, 30 percent of married women were in the labor force; that figure had risen to 51 percent by 1982. The most striking increase in female labor force participation has been among mothers. In 1960, 39 percent of women with school age children were employed; today the figure is 66 percent. The statistics are even more remarkable for women with children under six. In 1960 only 19 percent of them held jobs; today, *half* of them do.[83]

One aspect of the female employment picture that has not changed much is the type of jobs for which women are hired. During the 1960s and 1970s women remained heavily concentrated in traditionally female occupations. In fact by 1982 nearly 84 percent of all working women were employed in service industries. The "sex segregation" of the job market actually *increased* during the period. In 1960, 30 percent of all working women held clerical jobs, but by 1979, 35 percent of women workers were in similar positions. As recently as 1976 two economists could claim "The working woman is a typist, maid, teacher, nurse, cashier, or saleswoman."[84]

The outlook for women in the professions also has not improved a great deal since 1960. Current estimates indicate that although the number of women holding professional and technical jobs has increased, the proportion of women to men in them has changed but slightly. In

1970 women held 14.5 percent of these positions; in 1980 they held 16 percent.[85]

The bulk of middle class women workers are at present found in jobs requiring what Oppenheimer terms "middle quality labor," that is, labor with a fairly high educational level and considerable skills, such as secretarial work, nursing, and teaching. But women tend to predominate *only* in those middle quality occupations that are at a competitive disadvantage in terms of salary scales. And these are the fields that have grown so spectacularly in recent years. Between 1960 and 1970 the number of office workers increased by 45 percent and the number of elementary and high school teachers by 47 percent.[86]

Women can be employed at bargain rates because, in Oppenheimer's words, "the more educated labor in several female occupations is not rewarded by a proportionately higher income." Thus, the segregation of the labor force by gender allows employers to determine wage scales according to the sex of their employees and to disregard education and training in female-dominated fields. Moreover, women tend to be segregated in industries that are less profitable and more competitive than those in which men predominate. According to two economists, women are heavily represented in just those industries that "are not capable of paying higher wages because of the economic environment in which they operate." Men, however, tend to be employed in monopoly sectors that realize higher profits despite paying higher wages because the employer can usually pass on the price increase to consumers. It is no wonder that employers, particularly in the rapidly growing service sector, are wont to hire women. As Oppenheimer notes, "To substitute men to any considerable extent would either require a rise in the price paid for labor, or a decline in the quality of labor, or both."[87]

The availability of relatively low paid but skilled female workers for white collar positions undoubtedly contributes to the sex segregation of the job market. One economist concluded that "employers are not simply looking for cheap labor, but for cheap *female* labor." Some economists have suggested that women's inferior wages are directly linked to the highly sex-segregated structure of the labor market in the United States. "Equal pay for equal work" thus will not result in the elimination of sex differentials in pay scales if the majority of men and women continue to do different kinds of work. And it seems true that the concept of "equal pay for work of comparable value" is still considered revolutionary. A U. S. district court judge recently dismissed a case that raised this issue, commenting, "I am not going to restructure the entire economy of the United States."[88]

As the increase in the need for workers has escalated in several traditionally female fields, the supply of potential female employees has also risen as inflation has put a premium on the second family income. Since about 1965—the start of the great inflation surge—these additional earnings have played a crucial role in maintaining a middle class standard of living. Married women's wages no longer are used just to purchase extras, as was common in the 1950s, but to pay for such critical family expenses as food, mortgage payments, clothing, and medical bills. Moreover, as more wives have gone to work, there has been growing economic pressure on single-income families that are often at a

Courtesy of Michael Kappy, M.D.

Teacher • *The vast majority of women professionals are still found in traditional female fields—teaching, librarianship, nursing, and social work.*

disadvantage in terms of living standards. "Keeping up with the Joneses" has become far more difficult for the family with a single wage earner if the Jones family has two wage earners. In 1978 the median income was $20,900 for dual-earner families compared with $17,200 for families in which only the husband had earnings, and during the 1973–1974 recession the decline in purchasing power because of inflation was 1.3 percent in multiworker families compared to 3.1 percent in families in which the husband was the sole breadwinner.[89]

The two-income family has become the norm rather than the exception. In 1950 both husbands and wives held jobs among only 22 percent of married couples, but by 1979, 51 percent of all husband-wife families had two wage earners. While in the past a typical family's place in the income distribution scale used to depend almost entirely on the husband's earnings, today even if the husband has higher than average wages, the family may have a *below*-average income if the wife is not employed. Another provocative statistic is that nearly 60 percent of the women entering the labor force between 1960 and 1977 were married to men with *above*-average incomes. When these women's wage are added to their husbands' above-average earnings, the result is a widening gap between above-average and below-average income families.[90]

The fact that women with full-time year-round employment contribute an average of 38 percent to their families' incomes underlines the importance of their earnings. It is for this reason that a Department of Labor study concludes that "a significant portion of the rise in overall family income levels is due to the increase in labor force participation by wives in husband-wife families." Moreover, it is widely acknowledged that the two-worker family has helped increase the nation's overall level of consumption. It is little wonder that business magazines rejoice in this development in articles like the one published in 1965—"The Ladies . . . Bless Their Little Incomes."[91]

The importance of women's earnings in making higher levels of consumption possible can also be gauged by the following figures. In 1970 the average annual income of full-time employees was about 1.5 times the average in 1950 (in current dollars), but the average *family* income doubled during these two decades as the labor force participation rate for married women rose from 24 to 41 percent.[92]

Of course, not all women go to work to maintain or improve their families' standard of living. Many women work for economic survival. Today, for example, two-thirds of all women in the labor force either are supporting themselves and their families or are married to men earning less than $15,000 a year.[93]

By the seventies, these realities had forced public opinion into accepting woman's place (albeit a low-paying one) in the job market. Women's employment, however, preceded its wide approval by at least a few years. A 1960 public opinion poll showed that only 34 percent of those sampled approved of the married woman's working; by 1978 the approval rate had jumped to 70 percent, with over 80 percent of the under-thirty age group supporting the idea. Discriminatory policies barring married women from employment fell rapidly in the 1960s as the need for female labor grew. At the start of the decade 65 percent of the companies that still had such policies were reevaluating them. It is not surprising that notions about the appropriateness of employing married women were altered radically as that group came to dominate the female labor force. Some employers even began to indicate decided preferences for hiring wives and older women who, they claimed, were more stable and dependable than single "girls." Oppenheimer evaluates this changed attitude with realism: "The use of married women was not due to a mysterious change of heart, but to the lack of supply of young, unmarried ones."[94]

But not all barriers immediately fell. A number of companies still maintained policies against employing women with young children. As recently as 1970 the Martin-Marietta Company refused to hire women with preschool children. Incredibly, the Fifth Circuit Court of Appeals ruled that this was not a case of sexual discrimination under Title VI since the company's refusal to hire was based on sex *plus* another factor. The Supreme Court later overruled the lower court's decision, vindicating the constitutional right of *all* women to employment.[95]

Nor did the women's magazines of the 1960s immediately reflect the record numbers of wives and mothers taking jobs. The volumes published during the first years of the decade are indistinguishable in tone and attitude from those of the 1950s. For example, a 1960 *Ladies' Home Journal* interview with Debbie Reynolds quotes the actress as saying that she doesn't "actually believe in working mothers" despite her film career. In the same issue of the magazine, Dorothy Thompson protests the then common opinion that higher eduation was "wasted" on women. She argues that education makes women better wives and mothers and leads them to take "a greater interest in their husbands' work."[96]

The first recognition that many married women either had jobs or sought them appeared in a 1963 *Ladies' Home Journal* article entitled "I'm Going to Get a Job." Although the article is aimed entirely at "mature women" with older children, it does contain the first positive note on the subject of wives' employment: children gain in "self-reliance what they miss in maternal attention," the author suggested, and "their children and husbands are proud and excited by their new careers." As the decade progressed, articles such as "One Day Beauty Make-over for Women That Work" and "Twenty Part-time Jobs for Women" became increasingly common. But the issue of jobs for wives and mothers nonetheless

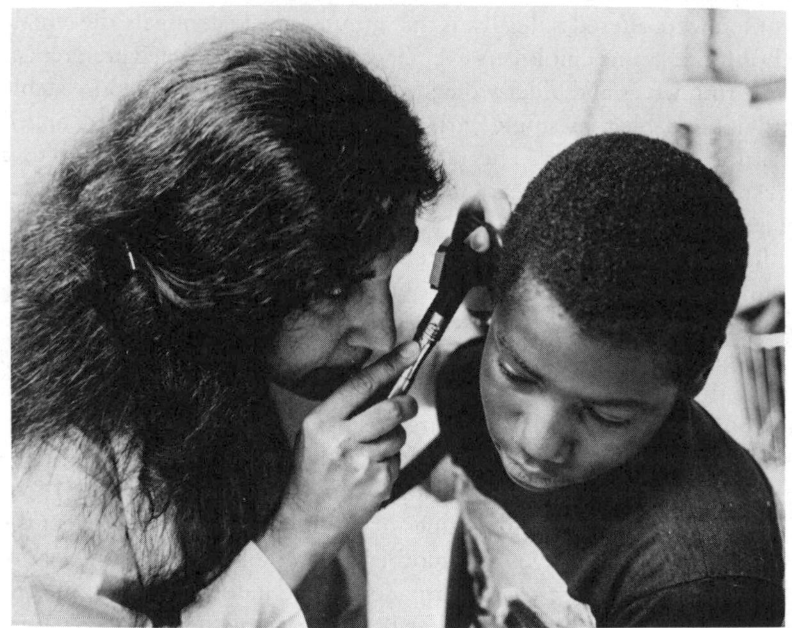

Courtesy of Michael Kappy, M.D.

Woman Physician • *Between 1970 and 1980 the number of women in medical school increased dramatically. This woman is a surgeon at a large teaching hospital.*

encountered some strong dissent in the pages of the *Ladies' Home Journal*. Billy Graham, in a 1970 article on "Jesus and the Liberated Woman," argued that sex roles were divinely ordained; men's natural role was breadwinner while "the appointed destiny of real womanhood . . . [was] wife, mother and homemaker."[97] It is worth noting that the article received a huge response from the magazine's readers, most of it highly critical of Graham's views.

Even the editors of that bastion of domesticity had come to realize, by the mid-1970s, the important role that employment was playing in women's lives. Sylvia Porter's column "Spending Your Money" and Letty Cottin Pogrebin's column "The Working Woman" became regular features of the magazine. Articles with such titles as "Going Back to Work? Helpful Tips from Women Who Have," "How to Ask for a Raise," "Tips on Easing the Morning Crunch for Working Mothers," "Policewomen: How Well Are They Doing in a Man's Job?", "When She Earns More Than He Does," and "Sex and Working Women" appeared with increasing frequency. The magazine also instituted a "Women of the Month" feature that reported on career women of great achievement, only incidentally mentioning their domestic lives. Finally, by 1977, the *Ladies' Home Journal* was advertising itself as a magazine for "the woman who never stands still . . . she's growing a family, an exciting *career*, and a creative way of life that's hers and her's alone."[98] Perhaps full recognition of women's contemporary employment status came in 1976 with the publication of a new mass circulation magazine, *Working Women*, and in 1978 with the first issue of *The Working Mother*.

Thus while the past two decades have witnessed the entry of women, particularly wives and mothers, into the labor force in unprecedented numbers, popular opinion only belatedly noticed the importance of this phenomenon. While the media devoted much space to "bra burning" and other supposed atrocities of the women's movement, little attention was paid to the reality of women's work, which had set the stage for the revival of feminism.

Just When Is Women's Place in the Home?

The ideology that a woman's place is in the home is clearly a temporally limited, class-linked phenomenon that only arises under certain conditions. This ideology could not have existed prior to industrialization because there was little or no distinction between the home and the work place. Such a dictum would have been grossly incompatible with women's productive labor, which was so central to the domestic economy of the day.

Not until the establishment of the factory system in the early nineteenth century was the home separated from the place of work, and at that point the ideology of full-time domesticity developed. Nevertheless, during the first decades of the factory system the employment of women, at least some classes of women, met with little opposition and in fact was widely hailed as important to the nation's economic development. This approval of female industrial labor came at a time when it was generally agreed that male labor should not be diverted from agriculture, the life blood of the young republic.

By the middle of the nineteenth century a change occurred in the labor supply as millions of male immigrants—men who were willing to work for even lower wages than native-born white women—started taking factory jobs. As this cheap source of male labor began to supplant female labor, moralists and opinion makers began decrying the employment of women as an "insidious assault upon the home" which was incompatible with women's "domestic" nature. While women's employment in factories was being condemned, however, a sizable number of educated middle class women were taking jobs in certain "suitable" areas—teaching, nursing, office work, and retail sales. But it was only *unmarried* working women who received grudging approval. With few sources of employment open to them, they could be hired at half the prevailing wage for men with similar skills.

This distinction between jobs for married women and jobs for single women was a constant theme in debates on women and work during most of the first half of the twentieth century. Single "girls" could work briefly at certain approved jobs while they bided their time before marriage, but married women, except under the most dire circumstances, were not even to consider paid employment.

The fear that married women might take jobs away from male breadwinners was most often expressed during periods of high unemployment and tended to subside in times of economic prosperity. Nevertheless, the correlation between unemployment and criticism of married women who work was not a perfect one. Simultaneous high inflation tempered such criticism, for under conditions of rapid price rises a woman's earnings became necessary for the preservation of her family's standard of living. This was certainly the case during the economic downturn of the mid-1970s and early 1980s. Then, too, depressed economic conditions and the concomitant censure of working women did not necessarily lead to an actual reduction in the size of the female labor force. During the depression in the 1930s more women were employed than ever before; out of necessity they ignored their critics and took jobs to replace the lost wages of their male relatives.

The insistence on full-time domesticity for married women was rarely heard during years of national and international conflict. At such times women were told that it was their patriotic duty to take the jobs vacated by men who had left for the fighting front and to staff the industries needed for the war effort. Women responded in record numbers, particularly during World War II. Not only were many more wives and mothers employed than ever before but the traditional barriers to hiring them in a wide variety of occupations fell as the demand for labor in wartime industries grew. Images of the working woman were also modified. The cold, frustrated career woman turned into the pig-tailed, apple-cheeked Rosie the Riveter, a national heroine who was not afraid of getting her fingernails dirty if it helped the war effort.

Traditional ideologies about women and work have gradually been transformed during the postwar era. Consumerism, high inflation, and an increase in the demand for labor in "female" occupations have created a virtual revolution in women's labor force activities. By the 1950s approval of working women had become conditional; not all of them were condemned outright. Employment for older women, for women whose children were grown, was acceptable as long as they had no real career ambitions and were willing to settle for the part-time or temporary, low-paid, dead-end jobs that were opening up in such abundance. But as more and more wives and mothers went to work and as the two-income family became the norm—particularly after the inflation surge of the mid-1960s—there was a great awakening to the fact of women's economic contribution to the family. What historian Carl Degler called "a revolution without ideology" in 1967 now has one.[99] Spurred by the feminist movement, a movement that itself was a response to the reality of work in the lives of women, the popular media belatedly acknowledged that perhaps women's place was *not* in the home.

What of the future? It is clear that women's current position in the job market, along with any continued increase in the female labor force, is going to depend on general economic conditions. Will the cost of living continue to be high, making it difficult for women to choose to stay home without forfeiting the higher standard of living their income makes possible? Will economic forces continue to create a large demand for workers in fields in which women are usually hired? Will the general economic downturn with high rates of unemployment persist and eventually revive the timeworn dogma that women are "pin money workers" who do not really need their jobs as badly as men do? Unless we have a crystal ball to inform us about future economic trends, it is simply not possible to say with any degree of certainty whether women are in the labor force to stay.

7 SHE HAS ONLY HERSELF TO BLAME

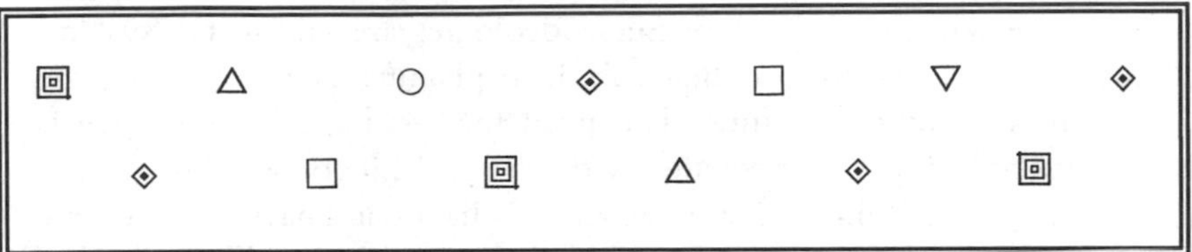

Women are a problem not only as individuals but collectively as a separate group with special functions within the structure of society. As a group, and generally, they are a problem to themselves, to their children and families, to each other, to society as a whole.

Ferdinand Lundberg and Marynia Farnham
Modern Woman: The Lost Sex, 1947

. . . women don't think of themselves as equal to men so they don't act equal; consequently men, employers, relatives, and society do not treat them as equal.

Jean Baer
How to Be an Assertive (Not Aggressive) Woman, 1976

In the spring of 1982 a Wisconsin judge received a lot of publicity when he described a five-year-old victim of a sexual assault as "an extremely promiscuous young lady." Her twenty-four-year-old male assailant, the judge claimed, "didn't know enough to refuse" her purported advances. When his statement caused widespread outrage, the judge said that he did not understand what "all the uproar is about," and went on to explain: "I used the word 'promiscuous,' I believe, and I said that I believed the young lady was the aggressor in this incident. I did not try to see into her mind to determine whether she received sexual gratification from it."[1]

Is there any kind of explanation of a mentality that would *blame* a five-year-old girl for provoking a sexual assault? A psychiatrist might be able to comment on the judge's sanity; as an anthropologist I can only look at the context, and I see an underlying cultural theme in the judge's remarks. It is called "blaming the victim."

Many anthropologists believe that a culture's social, political, and economic institutions produce ideologies that perpetuate or at least do not threaten the status quo. Such ideologies are said to be "system-maintaining" because of their role in explaining or rationalizing the culture's existing structure. The need for ideologies of this type is particularly acute in societies with sharp distinctions along social, ethnic, or racial lines. Divisions between haves and have-nots in these societies always present potential challenges to the established order. For this reason ideologies that explain why certain sectors of the population are more equal or less equal than others can ward off threats to the position of those groups that benefit from the way things are.

Blaming the victim is a system-maintaining ideology. It helps preserve the status quo in the United States and other societies divided along class, ethnic, and racial lines by attributing all sorts of social ills—poverty, delinquency, illegitimacy, low educational attainment—to the behavior and values of the victimized group rather than to the external conditions of inequality and discrimination under which that group lives. William Ryan, who was the first to recognize and label this phenomenon calls blaming the victim a "mythology" consisting of a "set of officially certified non-facts and respected untruths." The ideology's primary function is to obscure the victimizing effects of social forces. In Ryan's words, such an ideology is "an ideal, almost painless evasion" of reality. Instead of analyzing the inequalities caused by social conditions, the ideology focuses on the group or individual that is being victimized. The victims then, are blamed for their misfortune. The effect, writes Ryan, "is always to distract attention from the basic causes [of inequality] and to leave the primary social injustice untouched."[2] Change, says the ideology, involves changing the victims rather than the circumstances under which they live.

The blame-the-victim ideology in American society is most often applied to minority groups, particularly blacks, where it is used to explain low economic status, "aberrant" family structure, and failure to reap the benefits of all—it is said—this society so freely offers. Blaming the victim is also a useful tool in accounting for the underdevelopment of the third world. Poverty and underdevelopment thus derive from some defect in the national character of the nations affected, to their peoples' lack of "achievement motivation" or openness to change.[3]

Blaming the victim has also been widely used to rationalize the economic and social inequality of women in the United States. An excellent example is Jean Baer's statement quoted at the beginning of this chapter. It is *women's fault* that they are not equal. They don't believe themselves equal to men and they therefore don't act equal to them. As an explanation of why women are not treated as equals in our society, Baer's statement completely obscures the real causes of women's inequality in this country by glibly arguing that "they have only themselves to blame."

Tribune Syndicate Company

"Blaming the victim." *This is all too frequently heard in cases of rape and wife abuse.*

Blaming the victim also has a psychological function. In order for individuals to avoid feeling guilt, it is necessary to spin elaborate rationalizations to "explain" why victims are victims, why something they did justified their victimization. Studies have shown that people often seek information that places victims in a bad light so that they can dismiss the victimization by saying "they got what they deserved."[4] In effect, this process allows individuals to relieve themselves of guilt for their lack of compassion for the victims or for their failure to try to stop or prevent victimization.

Women, however, unlike other minority groups, have not until recently regarded themselves as the objects of collective victimization. Moreover, many women have internalized the tenets of victim blaming—they blame themselves and other female victims for their economic, social, and psychological problems. Essentially they ask: "What am I doing to make people discriminate against me?" One consequence of this internalization is that it promotes sexual discrimination because, in the words of two scholars, "the most effective forms of oppression are those with which the victim covertly cooperates."[5] In this sense blaming the victim is not only an ideology that helps support and justify the status quo but it is also a *control mechanism*, for it makes many women accept rather than question their inferior position in a variety of social contexts.

Why women internalize the ideology that ultimately limits their choices and opportunities by allowing discrimination is an important question. The answer in part is that women are socialized to be victims. Susan Brownmiller noted in her book on rape: "The psychic burden under which women function is weighed by a deep belief, borne out by ample evidence, that our attractiveness to men . . . is in direct proportion of our ability to play the victim." Women are encouraged to learn "the art of victimology" through their exposure to novels, motion pictures, popular songs, and television programs that more often portray women as victims than as survivors. A study of television dramas over a six-year period revealed that the most frequent victims of violence were women.[6] Advertisers also sometimes use the "woman as victim" theme. In 1976 Atlantic Records put up a huge billboard overlooking the Sunset Strip in Hollywood. It showed a bruised woman, bound in handcuffs, straddling a record album. The caption read: "I'm black and blue from the Rolling Stones and I love it." Threats to boycott the record company forced the removal of the sign.

As part of the victim-blaming package, women are often held responsible for a host of social ills that strictly speaking only indirectly victimize women themselves. In these cases the victims are their children, their husbands, and their close associates who, it is claimed, are harmed in one way or another by female behavior. The best example of this type of mentality is the allegation that women who work are bad mothers and are therefore wholly at fault for whatever emotional and behavioral problems their children have. This is simply a new twist on the victim-blaming theme—a mere extension of it—because its function is the same: to obscure the role of the social order in creating a variety of problems by automatically placing the blame where it may not be warranted.

It is sometimes difficult to distinguish female victim-blaming from outright misogyny. Is, for example, Philip Wylie's assertion that men and boys are infantilized by their archetypical "Moms"—whom he describes as women who are "twenty-five pounds overweight" with "beady brains behind their beady eyes," who spend their time playing bridge "with the stupid voracity of a hammerhead shark"—simple misogyny or is it victim-blaming? And what about Phyllis Schlafly's recent comment that sexual harassment only occurs "when a non-virtuous woman gives off body language which invites sexual advances"?[7] Does she simply hate women or is it a case of blaming the female victim? The reason why it is difficult to distinguish between the two is clear: it is far easier to victimize a group that is disliked. Defining women as inferior, less trustworthy, less motivated, and more emotional than men justifies mistreatment, or at least unequal treatment, and the status quo goes unchallenged.

This chapter deals with the blaming-the-victim syndrome in the context of employment, psychological and medical diagnosis and treatment, violence, and mother blame.

Blaming the Working Woman

> *It is not particularly important to a great many working women whether or not they earn as much as men, or have equal opportunities for training and promotion.*
>
> Robert W. Smuts, *Women in America,* 1971

Blaming the female victim finds its widest application in the world of work. Here it adopts a variety of guises and is used to "explain" why women are paid less than men and have fewer opportunities for occupational advancement. Women are often said to work only for "pin money" since they have husbands to support them and do not really "need" their jobs. Similarly, it is claimed that women have higher rates of absenteeism and job turnover than men do, along with less interest in moving up the occupational ladder. These purported characteristics of the female labor force are used to rationalize the confinement of women to low-paying, tedious, dead-end positions.

According to the "pin money" argument, men work to provide for their families while women work only to buy "extras." Using this logic, employers rationalize paying women low wages on the grounds that they do not need their earnings to live on. Lest anyone think that this justification for salary discrimination has succumbed to the threat of the Equal Pay Act and the feminist movement, the comments of a county commissioner in Utah should lay such hopes aside. When asked to explain why male employees had received a 22 percent wage increase and female employees a 5 percent increase, he replied, "We felt that with their husbands working, the ladies could stand the squeeze a little better."[8]

This reasoning is specious because it misinterprets why women take jobs. In years past as well as today the reasons have been overwhelmingly economic. During the 1920s and 1930s, for example, a Women's Bureau study indicated that 90 percent of all employed women worked because of economic necessity; they worked in order to support themselves and their families. And the forces that have propelled women into the job market have not changed much in recent years. Of the 44 million women employed in 1980, nearly two-thirds were the sole support of themselves and their families or were married to men whose annual income was under $15,000. Women's median contribution to family income was 38 percent; 12 percent contributed one-half or more. Moreover, according to economic analyst Eliot Janeway, the only reason many families are able to survive today's inflation and maintain a middle class standard of living is that they have two incomes: "Women flocking to work account for the vital margin between solvency and insolvency."[9]

One serious result of the "pin money" myth is the failure of some politicians to take high levels of female unemployment seriously. The belief that women's jobless rates are less worrisome than those of "household heads" is an anachronism that serves economic policy-makers' efforts to downplay the jobless rate. They insist that unemployment figures are artificially inflated by women "secondary workers" and youth who do not represent the "economic backbone" of the labor force. They expressed far less alarm at women's higher rate of unemployment—9.2 percent as opposed to 8 percent for men during the economic recession of the mid-1970s—because women "don't have families to support." Attributing unemployment to women's need and/or desire to work is a classic case of blaming the victim. It also revives the traditional bias that a woman's true place is in the home. One delegate to the 1976 Republican convention expressed this in no uncertain terms: "The unemployment rate tells a dangerously false story for which women are particularly to blame. This is not an economic problem. It's a sociological problem."[10]

Women workers are also accused of higher rates of absenteeism and job turnover than men. These supposed liabilities have been used to justify lower wages as well as failure to promote women to more responsible, better-paying positions. Here it is argued that women are not "attached to the labor force"; they just "up and quit their jobs" to get married or, if already married, to have babies. Why then should employers invest in expensive job-training programs for women or allow them to take on positions of responsibility?

Until the 1930s labor union officials used similar reasoning as a justification for not trying to organize working women. Union officials believed that women were transients in the labor force and not seriously committed to unionization. It was sometimes argued that women would be helped most if union activity secured their husbands, the "bread-winners," a decent wage that would support the whole family. Another argument against admitting women to unions was that they lacked "cohesiveness."[11]

The victimizers have once again ignored the facts. A Department of Labor study of job turnover over one year found that 10 percent of male workers and 7 percent of female workers had changed jobs during the period. The number of women who leave work when they marry or have children has declined in the last two decades, and even with breaks in employment, the average woman now spends 25 years in the labor force. Sex, in fact, does not seem to be the overriding factor affecting the rate at which people quit; not sex but the *type* of job is the most influential factor. As one economist notes: "Women are heavily employed in the kinds of occupations in which women *and* men tend to quit more often, whereas men are more heavily employed in the kinds of jobs in which stability of employment is rewarded." Skilled, professional, and managerial workers have lower job turnover than sales, service, and unskilled workers, and since women are heavily concentrated in the latter job categories it is surprising that their turnover rates are not higher than they are! But even if it were true that on the average women are more likely to quit their jobs than men, this would not be a justification for treating *individual* women as if they conformed to the average rate. Lumping all women together as a distinct class and expecting them all to act in the same preconceived fashion is by definition discrimination on the basis of sex.[12]

Critics of women employees also claim that women miss work more than men do because of "female problems" and are more likely to stay home under the pretext of one minor ailment or another. Here too the facts speak to the contrary. A 1975 survey by the Public Health Service found little difference in male and female absentee rates because of illness and injury; women averaged 5.6 days annually and men averaged 5.2 days annually. Moreover, women over 45 years of age had a lower absentee rate than did men in the same age bracket. Once again, factors other than sex were found to influence absenteeism. A Civil Service Commission study of sick leave noted that as salary and job responsibility increase, the number of days of sick leave taken decreases.[13]

Although ideas have changed since the early days of this century when menstruation, pregnancy, and menopause were viewed as illnesses that disabled women and made them ill-suited for paid employment, many hiring and promotion policies still view women primarily as baby-makers who, if they are not pregnant, will soon become so. This assumption then becomes the employer's rationale for passing over women for promotion. Nor does the situation improve for older women, for the belief that menopausal women suffer emotional disturbances is often used to justify denying them good jobs. Using similar logic, Dr. Edgar Berman, a former member of the Democratic Party's Committee on National Priorities and the late Hubert Humphrey's personal physician, received widespread publicity in 1970 when he questioned women's ability to hold certain responsible positions because of "raging hormonal influences." He estimated that half of all women suffer menstrual difficulties and declared: "Menstruation may very well affect the ability of these women to hold certain jobs. Take a woman surgeon. If she had premenstrual tension—and people with this frequently wind up in a psychiatrist's office—I wouldn't want her operating on me!"[14] Of course, Dr. Berman ignored the research suggesting that men may have four- to six-week cycles that vary predictably and that also seem to be caused by changing hormonal levels.

Victim blamers also assert that women do not get ahead in their jobs because they lack ambition. They claim that women are not interested in promotions, job training, or job changes that add to their work load. "What they seek first in work," wrote the noted sociologist Robert W. Smuts, "is an agreeable job that makes limited demands." "Since they have little desire for a successful career," Smuts continued, "they are likely to drift into traditional women's occupations." This is why "they are willing to take factory and service and clerical jobs that hold little hope for substantial advancement."[15]

Many businessmen also perpetuate these stereotypes of female employees. A National Office Managers Association survey of 1,900 firms found that 65 percent of those responding questioned the wisdom of appointing women to supervisory positions. The reasons? Women would resent having female bosses, men would feel restricted in their language and behavior, women were "too emotional" and, at any rate, uninterested in attaining such positions. The late George Meany offered a similar view in commenting on the lack of women on the thirty-three-member Executive Council of the AFL-CIO: "We have some very capable women in our unions, but they only go up to a certain level. . . . They don't seem to have any desire to go further."[16]

Data regarding lack of ambition in women are difficult to compile because relatively few women have been offered positions of significant responsibility in the business world. Nevertheless, there is no evidence that the 6.5 million women who held professional and technical jobs and the 2.5 million who worked as managers and administrators in 1979 performed any less ably than men in comparable positions.[17] Yet one can see how the internalization of victim-blaming values "takes the heat off" employers when they fail to promote women or pay them what they are worth. In their book *The Managerial Woman* Margaret Hennig and Anne Jardim note that women managers tend to play it safe, that they are reluctant to make bold moves, and that they wait for their work to be recognized. When it is not, they blame themselves.[18]

Yet another assertion made by blaming-the-victim ideologues is that women are "naturally" good at tedious, repetitive tasks. Women are said to be adaptable by nature and ideally suited to carrying out an endless number of routine jobs without complaint. Thus they have an aptitude, if not an affinity, for typing, filing, assembling small items, packaging, labeling, and similar tasks. Once typewriters became permanent office fixtures, some argued that "women seemed to be especially suited as typists . . . because they are tolerant of routine, careful, and manually dextrous." A similar view is spelled out in the pamphlet *The Feminine Touch* issued by Employer's Insurance of Wausau: "The female sex tends to be better suited for the unvarying routine that many individual jobs require. Women are not bored by repetitive work as easily as men. They frequently have a better memory for small details, and are able to concentrate on monotonous tasks." The chief detective in the notorious "Son of Sam" case was quoted in a *New York Magazine* article as saying that he sent two female detectives to the hack bureau to go through tens of thousands of licenses because the women were "judged better able to withstand such drudgery than men."[19]

It is also sometimes suggested that working women are better at being underlings than men. Sociologist Amitai Etzioni, for example, has written that "on the average, women are more amenable to administrative controls than men."[20] That this is a case of victim-blaming is clear. Since there is no evidence that women are naturally more compliant than men, and since in the present job market women often find themselves in positions subordinate to men, one might well interpret women's work behavior, if in fact it differs from men's, as an attempt to deal with the realities of their subject position. Before attributing such behavior to a female psychological quirk, a good analyst would first analyze the structural conditions of women's employment.

Finally, even those women who have broken into formerly male occupations are sometimes blamed for the difficulties they encounter in the work situation. An extreme example is the case of the first woman miner to be killed in a mine accident in this century. Shortly after her death, the safety director of the mine said that if she had been a man "she would have been ten steps away" from the slab of slate that fell from the mine roof and crushed her![21]

All of these notions about the "natural" proclivities of women lack supporting data and are simply rationalizations that allow employers to assign women to certain tasks without guilt. They also help justify the continued segregation of women workers in certain "appropriate" female occupations where their purported aptitude for tedium can be put to good use. It is clear that women are the victims here, as would be any group automatically assigned the low-paying, dead-end, monotonous tasks of society.

Why Are Women Depressed?

> *. . . a study of human behavior requires first and foremost a study of the social contexts within which people move, of the expectations about how they will behave, and of the authority that tells them who they are and what they are supposed to do.*
>
> Naomi Weisstein
> "Psychology Constructs the Female," 1972

The fields of psychiatry and psychology have provided lucrative settings for victim-blaming ideologues. While the majority of psychiatric patients are women, the majority of mental health practitioners are white, middle class, middle-aged men. It is therefore not surprising that the mental health profession has ignored the objective conditions under which female neurosis and depression develop and has sought to explain women's emotional ills in individualistic, victim-blaming terms.

Most psychotherapists, wittingly or unwittingly, help maintain the sexual status quo by suggesting individual rather than collective solutions to female discontent. The patient is encouraged to think that her depression, her neurosis, is unique, that her condition is of her own making. Many mental health professionals view female emotional problems, in Phyllis Chesler's words, as "underhanded domestic tyrannies manufactured by spiteful, self-pitying, and generally unpleasant women whose inability to be happy as women stems from unresolved penis envy. . . . or from general intractable female stubbornness."[22]

Nowhere is the blaming-the-victim syndrome more evident in the profession than in the diagnosis and treatment of female sexual problems. Ferdinand Lundberg and Marynia Farnham in their misogynist tome *Modern Woman: The Lost Sex* asserted that the failure of women to achieve sexual satisfaction is a neurosis stemming from a negative view of child-bearing and attempts to "emulate the male in seeking a sense of personal value by objective exploit." Similarly, the well-known Freudian psychoanalyst Helene Deutsch viewed female sexuality as innately masochistic and passive, and she argued that frigidity in women resulted from nonconformity to the feminine role. More recently, the author of *Psychoanalysis and Female Sexuality* suggested that women who complained of frigidity were actually "in a state of rebellion against the passivity which nature and society forced on them."[23]

Whenever women cross sex-role boundaries and exhibit "masculine" behavioral traits—ambition, aggression, independence—they are labeled neurotic or self-destructive by the psychiatric profession. In her book *Women and Madness*, Phyllis Chesler cites a 1963 study in which the male clinician reported how he "managed" a group of "paranoid" women back to "feminine" health.[24] Given the old Freudian dictum "anatomy is destiny," it is little wonder that women who exhibit "inappropriate" behavior for their sex are automatically labeled "sick."

One element that contributes to the victim-blaming slant in contemporary psychotherapy is the differing standards used to define mental health in men and women. Whereas the behavioral and emotional traits said to characterize healthy males are similar to those said to characterize healthy adults, the experts' clinical picture of the healthy female differs notably from that of the mature male and the mature adult whose sex is unspecified.[25] In essence then psychotherapeutic professionals expect the "well-adjusted" adult female to exhibit behavior and emotions that they themselves define as something less than adult.

Blaming the individual woman for emotional problems that in many cases are related to her fulfillment of traditional, socially accepted, female roles obscures the dilemmas inherent in these roles and relieves society of responsibility for her discontent. Psychiatrist Robert Seidenberg has suggested that the housewife-mother role often produces emotional problems in women. He found that "the trauma of eventlessness"—the absence of stimuli, challenges, choices, and decision making which characterize many women's lives—can threaten their mental well-being as much as physical danger. That married women also have higher rates of mental illness than either unmarried women or married men also suggests that certain strains in women's traditional roles are at least partly to blame for their psychiatric problems. Finally, Dr. Pauline Bart's study of depression in middle-aged married women found that their illnesses were often related to their dutiful fulfillment of the feminine role, a role that was no longer tenable after their children had grown-up.[26]

The Women's Caucus of the American Psychiatric Association has condemned the victim-blaming attitudes of much of the profession and resolved that unequal power relationships between the sexes as well as women's position as "legal domestic" in the home and "exploited worker" in the job market should be recognized as the real source of women's mental problems. The caucus urged psychiatrists "to stop rationalizing the situation of women by labeling its victims neurotic rather than oppressed."[27]

Victim Blaming and the Medical Establishment

> *Many women . . . exaggerate the severity of their complaints to gratify neurotic desires. . . . The woman who is at odds with her biological self develops psychosomatic and gynecologic symptoms.*
>
> J. P. Greenhill, *Office Gynecology*, 1965

Many medical doctors, particularly gynecologists, are preeminent victim blamers. Blaming the female victim is a common and unifying theme in the spheres of childbirth, contraception, abortion, sterilization, menstruation, and menopause. The common thread in all is that women's medical complaints are suspect, that they exaggerate their ills to get attention, and that most female ailments have a psychogenic, not a biogenic, basis. Over the last thirty years all of the following "female problems" at one time or another were said to have a psychological rather than a physical origin: menstrual irregularity, infertility, miscarriage, premature delivery, toxemia in pregnancy, difficult labor, and pelvic pain. One gynecologist, for example, advised his colleagues that when treating women it is often "appropriate to relate the presenting pelvic symptoms to underlying emotional stress rather than to organic disease."[28]

When women are used as guinea pigs—as in the case of the birth control pill and other contraceptive devices—their complaints of side effects are often dismissed as the reaction of neurotic females. Depression, for example, a fairly common side effect of the pill, is discussed in a medical text in the following terms: "Recent evidence suggests that a significant number of these depressive reactions are due to an unrecognized and deeply rooted wish for another child. Other patients who have done poorly on contraceptives are those identified as having primary frigidity." Moreover, some doctors feel that women are best kept in ignorance of other potential side effects of the pill. One doctor testified at congressional hearings that he was opposed to listing the pill's side effects on the package because "if you tell a woman she's going to get a headache, she will."[29]

The development of birth control pills and other contraceptive devices largely aimed at women is the result of a number of assumptions made by the (largely male) research establishment. Not only do researchers believe that conception control is the responsibility of women, they fear the untoward effects of interfering with the male sex drive. Having a healthy supply of sperm is more important psychologically to men than ovulation is to women, claim these authorities; according to Dr. Robert Kistner, a male pill was not developed because "the male is more sensitive to the psychological factors of the sex act than the female."[30]

A similar argument has been used to rationalize the medical preference for female sterilization. According to Dr. Edward Roth, an authority on the subject: "We don't know the long-term effects of vasectomy, and for a man it's more of a blow to the ego. It's more traumatic psychologically for the man to be sterilized . . . women have been getting tubal ligations for a long time, and it's easier for the women to accept." Male doctors' sensitivity in this area is illustrated by their panicky reactions to a study that disclosed the possible harmful side effects of vasectomies in mice.[31]

Although the medical profession has encouraged women to use problematic contraceptive techniques, it has been far more reluctant to permit them to undergo early, medically safe abortions. The reasons often follow victim-blaming logic. A staff physician at a county hospital in Milwaukee compared abortions to such cosmetic procedures as face-lifts and breast enlargements. "Women know what makes them pregnant, and they should have responsibility," he is quoted as saying. At a Right to Life convention another medical practitioner voiced fears of the psychological damage done to women who have abortions, which, he claimed, cause "a loss of previous spontaneous feminine and maternal warmth, tenderness, and ability to love."[32]

Even pregnancy and childbirth have not escaped the net cast by the medical victim blamers. Morning sickness, for example, is described in a 1972 gynecology text as possibly indicating "resentment, ambivalence, and inadequacy in women ill-prepared for motherhood." Thus, a condition that is a well-defined clinical syndrome experienced by 75 to 88 percent of all pregnant women and that seems to be related to higher levels of estrogen during pregnancy is dismissed as a psychosomatic aberration. K. J. Lenanne and R. Lenanne, in objecting to the depiction of women in medical texts, have pointed out that many women experience nausea even *before* they know that they are pregnant and that nausea also occurs among some who use oral contraceptives. Perhaps these latter, the authors have acerbically remarked, "are resentful, ambivalent, and inadequate because they are *not* pregnant."[33]

Some physicians have claimed that many women exaggerate the pain of childbirth. "Exaggeration of the rigors of the process is self-enhancing and at the same time affords a new and powerful means of control over the male," wrote Lundberg and Farnham. The woman who insists that "natural childbirth" methods be used during delivery is particularly suspect: "The intensity of her demands and her uncompromising attitude on the subject are danger signals, frequently indicating severe psychopathology," according to one obstetrician. Finally, a medical opponent of the recent home-birth movement has accused women who opt for home delivery of being "anti-science" and "child abusers."[34]

Menstrual pain has also been treated with skepticism. The author of one gynecology text argues that cramps often "reflect the unhealthy attitude toward femininity that is so predominant in our society." A number of other medical text writers have agreed with this view. One attributes menstrual pain to a "faulty outlook . . . leading to an exaggeration of minor discomfort" which "may even be an excuse to avoid doing something that is disliked," while another states that "the pain is always secondary to an emotional problem so that very little can be done for the patient who prefers to use menstrual symptoms as a monthly refuge from responsibility and effort."[35] Although menstrual pain has been linked to ovulation—a *physical* process—doctors are still suggesting that a condition experienced at one time or another by roughly half of the female population is psychosomatic. The implication is clear: half of all adult women suffer from periodic emotional problems.

Victim blaming by the medical establishment reached a crescendo during the 1977 Senate subcommittee hearings on unnecessary surgical procedures. The highest ranking staff physician of the American Medical Association argued that hysterectomy was justified, even in the case of a healthy uterus, in a woman who feared pregnancy or cancer. This suggestion has the same ring as a remark made by a gynecologist in 1892 who said he would rather take his chances as a "moonshiner in the mountains of East Tennessee than be a uterus in New York." Residents in gynecology are following the AMA's lead when they tell women, "Think of the uterus as a cradle. After you've had all your babies there's no reason to keep the cradle." The chief of obstetrics and gynecology at a Rhode Island hospital agreed: "The uterus is just a muscle and it's a liability after children are born because it's a cancer site." The illustrious doctor added that this reasoning "ideally" applied to breasts as well, but "this would be a hard concept to sell in this society." A little-noted fact in these discussions is that while a hysterectomy eliminates the possibility of later uterine cancer, the death rate from uterine cancer is less than the mortality rate from hysterectomies.[36]

Menopause has also drawn the attention of victim blamers. The common medical depiction of menopausal women as neurotics suffering from hot flashes and severe depression has been adopted by the public at large. A judge in Toronto, for example, dismissed the testimony of a forty-eight-year-old woman, stating: "There comes a certain age in a woman's life . . . when the evidence is not too reliable." This stereotype overlooks the fact that only 20 to 30 percent of the female population has such symptoms.[37] Moreover, it is usually assumed that depression is caused by the loss of reproductive capacity, while little attention is paid to the objective life conditions of many middle-aged women—their "empty nests," their husbands' inattention, their lack of challenging employment opportunities, and society's glorification of feminine youth and beauty. But rather than question traditional sex roles or the unequal distribution of power between men and women, the medical establishment appeals to the "empty uterus" as the source of female discontent.

These beliefs and practices are grounded in medicine's view of women. A 1971 gynecology text states that "the traits that compose the core of the female personality are feminine narcissism, masochism, and passivity." If women are naturally passive, one wonders why doctors find it necessary to prescribe for them so many mood-altering drugs—particularly tranquilizers. It is estimated that about 45 percent of American women use psychotropic drugs on a regular basis—more than twice the percentage of men who use them—and that doctors are twice as likely to prescribe such drugs for women as for men. Drug companies encourage and profit from this high usage. A 1974 ad for a sedative in *Medical World News* reads: "When you see the same patient over and over with functional complaints . . . consider Bellergal Spacetabs. Most doctors have a number of patients who complain of *vague symptoms* such as menopausal disorders . . . premenstrual tension . . . palpitations . . ."[38] The patient in the ad is a woman.

Victim-blaming in the medical field is partly rooted in medical school training that urges doctors to look for personality factors in diagnosing women's complaints. The tendency of many male physicians to view their female patients as hysterical, emotionally unstable children lends support to the notion that most female ailments have a psychogenic basis. These attitudes serve a common function: they infantilize the female patient and maintain a hierarchical relationship between her and her physician. In this sense, blaming the victim in the medical realm is simply another instance of the efficacy of this ideology as a control mechanism that perpetuates the status quo.

"Good Girls" Don't Get Raped or Abused or Battered

In a way the victim is always the cause of the crime.
Menachem Amir, *Patterns in Forcible Rape*, 1971

Whether they like it or not, a woman's a sex object, and they're the ones that turn the men on.
Judge Archie Simonson
Dane County, Wisconsin

Nowhere is victim-blaming more pernicious than when it is used to rationalize sexual and physical aggression against girls and women. The recent courtroom statements cited above and at the beginning of this chapter clearly show that blaming the victim is still too often the norm in the perception of rape and sexual assault and in the treatment of its victims. This is also true of wife beating. In fact, attitudes toward abused wives and rape victims are strikingly similar. Just as the rape victim is supposedly a seductive temptress who asked for what she got, the abused wife purportedly provoked her husband into beating her. It is also said that women secretly enjoy being beaten, just as they are supposed to be "turned on" by rape.[39]

Although what is considered "proper female behavior" has changed considerably over the last hundred years, the view that women who are harassed or abused invite such treatment is not a new one. In 1886, for example, a judge in Ohio discharged a prisoner who had been arrested for "insulting" a woman, on the ground that "no honest woman has occasion to be out alone on the streets . . . after half past ten o'clock at night." Nor are such views limited to our own society. A judge in Minas Gerais, Brazil, on acquitting a man of charges of seducing a minor, commented:

> In today's world it is the women not the men who are doing the seducing. Reality shows us that the real seducers are the daughters of Eve who sashay their way through God's world with their miniskirts, low-cut and see-through blouses . . . for the sole purpose of exhibiting their curvaceous bodies to attract the eyes of men.[40]

Victim-blaming as a rationalization for rape has two components. First, it is assumed that all women covertly desire rape and second it is argued that no woman can be raped against her will, so forcible rape does not really exist. The conclusion is then that if a woman is raped, she is at fault. As Susan Brownmiller has written: " 'She was asking for it' " is the classic rapist's remark as he shifts the burden of blame from himself to his victim."[41]

Victim precipitation, a concept in criminology often used in rape cases, tries to determine if the victim's behavior contributed in any way to the crime. The argument is that although an unlawful act has occurred, if the victim had acted differently—had not walked alone at night or allowed a stranger to enter the house—the crime might not have taken place. A court case in California in which the judge overturned the conviction of a man who had picked up a female hitchhiker and raped her is illustrative. The ruling read, in part:

> The lone female hitchhiker, in the absence of an emergency . . . advises all who pass by that she is willing to enter the vehicle with anyone who stops, and in doing so advertises she has less concern for the consequences than the average female. Under such circumstances, it would not be unreasonable for the man in the position of the defendant . . . to believe that the female would consent to sexual relations.

A similar line of reasoning caused a recent uproar in Great Britain. When a judge was asked to explain why he let off a convicted rapist with a fine but no jail sentence, he replied: "I am not saying that a girl hitching home late at night should not be protected by the law, but she was guilty of a great deal of contributory negligence." Another case of so-called victim precipitation involved a twenty-two-year-old woman cab driver in San Francisco who was raped at gunpoint and then fired from her job. According to her boss, she was dismissed for her own good because she was "so young and didn't screen her fares carefully."[42] An even more horrifying example of this type of thinking is the minister who wrote to "Dear Abby" that a young girl whose father had sexually abused her had "tempted him" by "wearing tight-fitting, revealing clothes."

It is not surprising that rapists echo these sentiments, believing that women are responsible for avoiding rape and condoning their acts by saying that their victims "provoked" them or "led them on." One convicted rapist put it this way:

> . . . by the body language or unconsciously they flirt—sometimes the way that they dress—their minds say one thing—their bodies say another—or some come on with their seduction type overall tone—that says one thing but could possibly mean something else. *Or they put themselves in the position of being alone.*[43]

And, the Rutgers University police seem to agree that it is a woman's fault if she is raped. Campus police issued "warning cards" to women in "dangerous" situations which read: "If I was a rapist, you'd be in trouble."

Two criminologists have described the thinking behind the concept of victim precipitation in rape cases as "the personification and embodiment of the rape mythology cleverly stated in academic-scientific terms."[44] Whether popular or academic, the deeply ingrained notion that women precipitate rape by their behavior or dress is so widespread that rape victims often agonize over what they did to cause themselves to be raped.

These attitudes are also evident in the way rape victims are handled by the courts; the victim is more often treated like the criminal than is the rapist. Some states still permit testimony about the victim's prior sexual experience and general moral demeanor, and juries in rape cases are notorious for taking such evidence into account in determining a verdict. One study of the jury system reported that in cases of rape "the jury scrutinizes the female complainant and weighs the conduct of the victim in judging the guilt of the defendant."[45]

Police often look askance at rape charges. A California police manual states that "forcible rape is the most falsely reported crime," and Brownmiller notes that policemen assume that rape complaints are made by prostitutes who "didn't get paid." If a woman is raped by a stranger the police usually take the charge more seriously than if she is raped by a man she knows. The latter, they claim, is a woman who "changed her mind." The police also tend to discount sexual assault if the woman lacks a "good reputation"; given this belief, they claim that only virgins can be raped. "A slice from a cut cake is never missed" is a common refrain in police stations. The attitudes of many police officers toward rape were summarized by the warden of San Quentin, who argued that women "invite" rape by going to bars, accepting pick-ups from strangers, and wearing tight sweaters and skirts. "When it happens," he said, "they have nobody to blame but themselves." What is completely ignored here is that almost half of all reported rapes occur in the homes of the victims—not on the street—and are committed by men unknown to the victims.[46]

No matter how a woman behaves when she is raped, she is still held responsible for the outcome. While popular opinion denies the possibility of forcible rape, a judge in England suggested that a woman who was seriously injured fighting off a rapist only had herself to blame for being hurt. She should have "given in" to the rapist, said the judge. The *London Times* editorialized: "This almost suggests that refusing to be raped is a kind of contributory negligence." (The accused rapist, a soldier in the Coldstream Guards was freed pending appeal on the grounds that he had a "promising career.")[47]

All of this rationalizing suggests that women, by their virtue, can control the behavior of others. This makes about as much sense as saying that a good child will never be bullied or an honest man will never be mugged!

Blaming the victim is a theme in the treatment of rape in much of the media. Susan Brownmiller did a survey of "true confessions" type magazines and found that nearly all contained stories on rape, near rape, and rape fantasies. She summarized her findings: "Taken in toto [the magazines] promulgated a philosophy of submission in which the female victim was often to blame, whereas the men in her life—husband, boyfriend, or rapist—emerged as persons of complex emotion deserving of sympathy." One story, entitled "I Was the Victim of a Gang Rape," ended with the victim saying: "I learned a lesson I hope other girls will remember. When you look for trouble—as I did—you can be sure you'll get it." In another article, "I Was the Victim of a Sex Gang," the blurb read "Gang Raped by Seven Boys—Because I Led Their Girls into a Women's Lib Club."[48] The recent spate of Grade B movies with scene after scene of semiclothed women shrieking in terror as they are stalked by deranged killers or rapists contains the same implicit message: women who are independent, women who are living on their own, are "asking for it."

In dealing with sexual abuse the victim blamers characteristically ignore the facts. According to the National Commission on the Causes and Prevention of Violence, only 4 percent of reported rapes involved any "precipitant behavior" on the part of the victim—a far lower figure than for victims of other kinds of violent crimes. Nor are the majority of rape charges brought by women who "changed their mind." A study showed that only 2 percent of rape complaints proved to be false, about the same rate as for other felonies. Finally, the idea that women secretly "enjoy" rape is too preposterous to be taken seriously. Since rape has been shown to be a crime of violence, not a crime of passion, how can women be termed seducers? As Ruth Herschberger has remarked, "The notion that a victim of sexual aggression is forced into an experience of sensory delight should be relegated to the land where candy grows on trees."[49]

Since the evidence negates the widespread belief that rape victims are responsible for what happens to them, it is senseless to argue that if women took special precautions in their dress and behavior the problem would disappear. Moreover, why should the burden of rape prevention be forced on women? Why should women restrict their lives because of the criminal behavior of some men? One certainly has to agree with Brownmiller's statement that "there can be no private solutions to the problem of rape."[50] Yet these attitudes persist since by viewing rape as a "women's problem" brought on by the victims themselves the social forces that lead to violence against women can be ignored, relieving men and society of guilt.

The treatment of wife abuse is remarkably similar to that of rape, and the victim is blamed just as pointedly. Police, who are notoriously loath to intervene in domestic disputes, too often take the attitude that if a woman's husband beat her, she probably deserved it. In courtroom after courtroom, said one lawyer, "it remains the responsibility of the battered woman to convince the judge that she is truly a victim." Family court judges are no more sympathetic; they frequently ask the woman what she did to provoke the husband's attack. A family court judge in Columbus, Ohio, advised a battered woman to study the Bible, attend a fundamentalist church, and learn how to be a good wife. He then dismissed the charges against her husband. Furthermore, the police and courts often assume that women who accuse their husbands of beating them are vindictive and will only prosecute if they are convinced that the wife is a "worthy victim."[51]

Prone to Violence, a recent book published in England, claims that some women are "violence prone," that they are addicted to pain because of their own violent childhoods. These women, insist the authors, should be distinguished from "genuine" battered wives who are not accomplices in their husbands' violent behavior.[52] It is interesting that the authors of the book have nothing whatsoever to say about some men's apparent predilection for inflicting pain.

The attitude that some women deserve or enjoy being beaten is sometimes shared by members of the abused woman's family. A woman whose husband beat her while she was pregnant got no support from her relatives or her doctor:

> My mother said I must be doing things to make him mad, and my sister said it was all right for a man to beat his own wife. I told my gynecologist that my husband was extremely violent, and I was mortally afraid of him. Guess what he said? I should relax more. He prescribed tranquilizers.[53]

Victim blamers have had a field day looking for culprits in wife abuse cases. A member of the New Hampshire Commission on the Status of Women, for example, held the women's liberation movement responsible for the increased incidence of wife beating and rape. Moreover, individuals in modern society are sometimes so inured to blaming the victim when it comes to wife abuse that they are not aware that they are doing it. A recent scholarly conference on D. H. Lawrence is a case in point. It considered the question of whether Lawrence despised women or venerated them. Most of those present agreed that "the fact that Lawrence used to beat his wife, Frieda, had nothing to do with the case; she was a singularly difficult woman."[54]

The victim of wife beating, like the rape victim, is often perceived as having instigated the attack. The old but still common notion that some women are masochistic and receive gratification from their husband's violent behavior effectively shifts the responsiblity for the abuse from the assailant to the victim. This is certainly suggested in one study of wife beating which concludes: "A husband's behavior may serve to fill a wife's needs even though she protests it."[55] Given such a view, it is not surprising that the authors of the study ignore remedial measures for the offender and suggest ways for the victim to change *her* behavior. The result of this bias is that many of the experts who have dealt with the problem of wife beating pay far more attention to the victim than to the victimizer.

It is known that even the most innocuous remark made by a woman married to a battering husband may be perceived by him as "whining" or "nagging" and then used to justify his violent behavior. Family counselors agree that such men are usually obsessive people who have learned how to trigger themselves emotionally. According to Del Martin, author of *Battered Wives*, this places wives in a "no-win situation. If they are passive, they are doormats that invite abuse. If they are aggressive, they invite the beatings to put them in their place."[56]

Many who are otherwise sympathetic to the battered wife are perplexed as to why she takes the abuse. The reasons are not that difficult to discern. Not only are many women economically dependent on their husbands but they have also been socialized to be victims. Here is a classic case of the internalization of victim-blaming values. Marjory Fields, a lawyer involved in battered wives cases, has observed that abused wives "not only take the beatings, they tend to feel responsible for them."[57]

A mere 2 percent of battering husbands are ever prosecuted, a fact clearly related to these attitudes, as is the cavalier treatment by the police of what they term "domestic spats." Police officers are advised by their superiors to make arrests only when severe injuries have occurred and to try to get the parties involved to "reason" with each other. Martin has pointedly remarked that "it is hard to imagine any other situation in which police would be officially advised to encourage a victim to 'reason' with an attacker."[58]

While assault and battery are quickly punished when they occur between strangers, punitive action is rare when abuse takes place within a marital relationship. The extreme to which this reluctance can be carried is evidenced in a court decision in England. A man who killed his wife and pleaded guilty to "manslaughter" was sentenced to only three years probation on the grounds that his wife had "nagged him constantly for 17 years." The judge commented: "I don't think I have ever come across a case where provocation has gone on so long."[59]

Even the reaction to recent attempts to provide shelters for battered women shows a victim-blaming mentality among so-called "pro-family" elements. Witness the bizarre statement of Senator Gordon Humphrey of New Hampshire, who predicted that such shelters would be "anti-family indoctrination centers"; Senator Jesse Helms of North Carolina warned that such refuges would lead to "the disintegration of the family." On a more rational level other critics have pointed out that establishing shelters for battered women is extremely unfair to the woman. As a lawyer in wife abuse cases has stressed: "It is clearly a denial of a woman's civil rights to remove her from the home because her husband has broken the law. We already have shelters for criminals: they are called jails, and in any rational system of justice the perpetrator would be harassed, not the victim."[60]

And That Old Standby: Mother Blame

> *Should anything go wrong, as in the production of a Hitler, a woman is said to be at the root of the trouble—in this case, Hitler's mother.*
>
> Ruth Herschberger, *Adam's Rib,* 1970

Those who blame the victim have devoted much time and rhetoric to "mother blame." In this category of victim-blaming, it is not women themselves who are said to be adversely affected by their behavior but their children and ultimately society at large. The psychiatric profession, in particular, has been responsible for popularizing the view that the "lack of or superabundance of mother love causes neurotic, criminal . . . and psychopathic children."[61] Yet the absent or cold father and other forms of deprivation are rarely blamed for problem children and problem adults.

Mother blame is a natural outgrowth of the traditional, socially approved sexual division of labor that sees child rearing as exclusively "women's work." If something goes wrong, it must be the mother's fault.

Mothers are not only blamed for their children's psychological and behavioral problems but sometimes for their physical problems as well. Infant colic has been attributed to maternal insecurity, anxiety, tension, and conflicts about accepting the feminine or maternal role. Although colic is a physical condition affecting about 23 percent of all newborns, it is listed under "psychological disorders" in one widely used pediatric text.[62] The assumption is that the baby's disturbed behavior is caused by the mother's anxiety. It never occurs to the mother blamers that it could be the baby's crankiness, stemming from a physical ailment, that causes the mother's anxiety!

Women are held responsible for their children's psychological and behavioral problems, no matter what the mother does. If she works, she is accused of child neglect; if she stays home and devotes herself to child care, she is berated for smothering her offspring. Mother blamers have long attributed juvenile delinquency to women's employment. During World War II working mothers were lambasted for rearing "latch key" children who got into trouble because of lack of supervision. At the same time, however, women were accused of overprotecting their children. According to Dr. David Levy, author of *Maternal Overprotection*, first published in 1943, some women had "made maternity into a disease." According to Levy, many women were both rejecting *and* overprotecting, behavior that made for unhappy, neurotic children.[63]

Mother blame reached a crescendo shortly after the war with the publication of *Modern Woman: The Lost Sex*. Ferdinand Lundberg and Marynia Farnham estimated that between 40 and 50 percent of all mothers were either "rejecting, over-solicitous, or dominating" and that they produced "the delinquents, the behavior problem children, and some substantial portion of criminals and persons who are a trouble to themselves, to close associates, and often to society." Speaking of the Freudian influence in the postwar years, Betty Friedan has written that "it was suddenly discovered that the mother could be blamed for everything." She added: "In every case history of a troubled child; alcoholic, suicidal, schizophrenic, psychopathic, neurotic adult; impotent, homosexual male; frigid promiscuous female; ulcerous, asthmatic, and otherwise disturbed American, could be found a mother."[64]

Somewhat less shrill than Lundberg and Farnham, well-known psychiatrist Abram Kardiner wrote that "motherhood is a full-time job" and that "children reared on a part-time basis will show the effects of such care in the distortions of character that inevitably result." Lest it be thought that mother blame is merely an artifact of the 1950s feminine mystique, a 1977 newspaper editorial adopted the philosophy in an attempt to explain the high crime rate:

> Let's speculate that the workday grind makes Mom more inaccessible, irritable . . . and spiteful, thereby rendering family life less pleasant . . . than the good old days when she stayed in the kitchen and baked apple pies. What could that be doing to . . . the rising crime rate? Say, fellows, could it be Mom's fault?

In a similar vein the "Pro-Family Caucus" at a recent White House Conference on Families distributed a pamphlet that averred: "Ninety percent of problems with children are probably the result of a mother who (1) has failed to learn how to really love her man and submit to him, (2) has tried to escape staying at home, or (3) has hindered her husband in the discipline of the children."[65]

These views, of course, ignore studies indicating that absent and low-profile fathers are probably more responsible for delinquency in their children than are working mothers. Moreover, the most comprehensive study of maternal employment, *The Employed Mother in America*, effectively rebuts the myths concerning the supposed ill effects of working mothers on their offspring. One of the book's contributors concludes, for example, that "maternal employment per se cannot be considered an index of maternal deprivation having consequent detrimental effects on the development of children," while another states that "maternal employment . . . is not the overwhelming influential factor in children's lives that some have thought it to be."[66]

What of the woman who stays home and devotes herself full-time to child raising? She too is the target of mother blamers who hold her accountable for an extensive variety of social problems. In his book *Generation of Vipers* Philip Wylie characterized such women as "Moms" who led empty lives and preyed on their offspring, keeping them tied to their proverbial apron strings. This theme was echoed by Edward Strecker, a psychiatric consultant to the Army and Navy Surgeons General. In an attempt to account for the emotional disorders of 600,000 men unable to continue their military service, Strecker wrote: "In the vast majority of case histories, a Mom is at fault." And the cause of "Moms": "In most cases, a Mom is a Mom because she is the immature result of a Mom."[67]

E. E. LeMasters, a family sociologist, explains mother blame succinctly: "If you are convinced that the American mother is what's wrong in our society, then you do not need to look for other possible explanations of the problem under consideration."[68]

If it weren't for Martha, there'd have been no Watergate.
Richard Nixon, in interview with
David Frost, September 1977

Richard Nixon's statement holding Martha Mitchell responsible for Watergate is an illustration of the extremes to which victim blamers go.

According to Nixon, Watergate occurred because "John Mitchell wasn't minding the store," because he was preoccupied with his wife's mental and emotional problems. This claim is particularly malicious given the all-male cast of the Watergate affair. A similar kind of remark was made during the "Son of Sam" episode when a New York psychiatrist was quoted in *Time* magazine as saying that the killer "must have been terribly provoked by a woman."[69]

While an assertion such as Nixon's was widely viewed as self-serving, the opinions of psychiatrists and other authoritative victim blamers are often taken seriously by the general public, including women. Women not only participate in this ideology, they sometimes internalize it, blaming themselves and other women for a host of problems. In fact, the very persistence of victim-blaming is partly a result of the implicit and explicit participation of its targets, strong evidence of the ideology's effectiveness in rationalizing subordination. Blaming the female victim is certainly not a male monopoly. Phyllis Schlafly's vitriolic claim that "*virtuous* women are seldom accosted by unwelcome sexual propositions" could have been made by any number of her male counterparts.[70]

Although I have termed blaming the victim a "system-maintaining" ideology that preserves or at least does not challenge the established order, I would be naive to suggest that employment discrimination, psychiatric and medical misdiagnosis, rape, wife beating, and other areas in which female victims are blamed are purely social phenomena. Although social attitudes make these abuses possible, the behavior of individuals translates them into practice. But I contend that the psychology of individuals deserves less emphasis than the material conditions under which victim-blaming occurs. What makes a particular male a rapist or a wife beater is less important than the economic, social, and political circumstances in which rape and battering are found. The present structure of American society plays the crucial role in perpetuating the victimization of women—and then justifying it by blaming it on the very group that is being victimized.

A timely illustration is the ideology's usefulness as an explanation for the failure of women to make significant advances in employment. The explanation wholly ignores structural inequities and ongoing discrimination in the labor market. Despite the feminist movement and a plethora of equal opportunity laws, it is well known that women overwhelmingly remain in low-paid, low-prestige, female job ghettos. But, aver the victim blamers, undaunted, the cause is women's lack of interest in getting ahead, their fear of success, and their reluctance to assume the added responsibility that comes with advancement.

Blaming the victim also has been a clever tactic for explaining why the Equal Rights Amendment has not passed. As journalist Ellen Goodman has observed, the claim that the ERA did not pass because of the "pushy, strident and/or militant style" of its proponents has great appeal. It permits people to claim that they are "in favor of equal rights for women" while blaming women themselves for the failure to achieve them.[71]

The goal of the victim blamers in these contexts is to conveniently mask the reality of continued discrimination on the basis of sex. But I want to emphasize that although blaming the victim does distort reality by obscuring the inequalities in American life, it is not the cause of these deeply rooted social and economic inequalities—it is a rationalization for them.

EPILOGUE

Where Do We Go From Here?

One cannot rule out the possibility of a backlash, a sense that things have already gone too far.

Joann Vanek
"Household Work, Wage Work, and Sexual Equality," 1980

Has there been a basic revolution in the roles of American women? Has the material base of American society changed to the extent that I have claimed and can it account for changes in the work women do and the way it is perceived? There is some disagreement on these issues. Some insist that in most ways social life has continued to follow traditional patterns. This view can be summarized as follows: The family is "here to stay" and women's position in it as primary nurturer and domestic laborer continues essentially unaltered. Women are having fewer children, but in time the birthrate will probably rise again. At most, women with jobs are secondary and impermanent breadwinners; primary family income always has been and remains dependent on male wages. This mystification of what is happening in the United States today appears to me an empty variant of the philosophy *plus ça change, plus c'est la même chose.*[1]

Such claims ignore the vast numbers of married women who now work outside the home, the current lowest birthrate in American history, and the skyrocketing incidence of single-parent households. Have these trends really had so little influence on women's traditional roles? Given the massive changes in the foundations of American society, this conservative philosophy may be comforting, but it is also naive to suppose that women's roles and their ideological supports have remained in some inviolate time warp.

There is no doubt that the domestic and nondomestic lives of American women have been transformed in important ways. But what of the future? Will there be a backlash? Have things gone too far in the restructuring of the roles of American women? Does the antifeminism of the Schlaflys and Falwells portend a wave of reaction against women and some of their new-found gains? Once again, from the perspective of cultural materialism, the answer must be: It depends on a variety of infrastructural conditions. If this book is to be a consistent analysis based on a particular set of theoretical principles rather than on reassurance or wishful thinking, then this answer is the only one possible.

Despite this cheerless statement, I do not see a return to the traditional family of earlier decades. It is unlikely that we will go back to the scenario of some bygone era when Mom was a full-time housewife and Dad brought home the bacon. The wages of married women are simply too important to family income, too crucial to maintaining any semblance of a middle class standard of living, to be readily or willingly forgone. In addition, the even more critical financial needs of the growing number of single-parent households will increase the reliance on the wages of females. No, I do not believe that the inroads that women have made into the labor force will be reversed. Any major shift presupposes a broad range of prior economic and social changes, changes that I do not believe can be brought about by even the most vociferous antifeminist rhetoricians.

Nevertheless, as I write this in early 1983, the unemployment rate has been at a forty-year high—over 10 percent—for months and predictions that it will remain at this level are not being dismissed out of hand by spokesmen (I use the masculine intentionally) of the Reagan administration. Past experience tells us that as the jobless rate climbs, the "pin money" argument is dusted off and used as a rallying point against working women, who are blamed for taking jobs away from male breadwinners. Reagan, in fact, has said that the recession is not the only cause of high unemployment under his administration. "Ladies, I'm not picking on anyone," he opined at a news conference, but "the increase in women who are working today and two-worker families" are partly responsible for unemployment.[2] The "pin money" diatribe, however, is unlikely to fly anymore for the simple reason that, as millions of Americans are aware, women are *not* earning "pin money"; they are not working just to buy "extras." They are working to pay for food, health care, and education and most important of all to help defray the hefty monthly installments now required for most home mortgages.

The tendency to take female unemployment less seriously than male unemployment is still strong. This is evident in the jobs bills being proposed in Congress: they are actually *men's* job bills. When Congress suggests funding jobs to repair the nation's roads, bridges, and mass transit systems, they are talking about *men's* jobs since men hold over 98 percent of all construction jobs in this country. Today, as in the depression, the solution to hard times is to create jobs for family (read: male) "breadwinners." But at a time when 52 percent of all women are in the labor force, when one out of six families depends exclusively on women's wages, and when untold numbers of households survive only because of two incomes, the failure to address *female* joblessness ignores economic reality.

Still, one might argue that since the rate of inflation has recently come down, the cost of living will eventually decline, making women's contribution to family income less critical than it was during the great inflation surge of the 1970s. First, it is still far too early to know whether the decline in the inflation rate is a mere blip in the long-term trend toward higher and higher prices. Second, with the present high cost of education, utilities, and housing, most single income families are unlikely to be able to make ends meet, even if the rate of inflation continues to decline.

Whatever the future rates of inflation and joblessness, women's employment will also be affected by the demand for female labor. Because the labor market is still highly segregated by sex and because women are still overwhelmingly employed in the low-paying service sector of the economy, a distinct demand for female labor persists. This makes it improbable that women will be cast out of the job market. In fact, service jobs are likely to continue to grow at the expense of manufacturing jobs. In the 1980 census, clerks surpassed factory workers in numbers, and it is estimated that during the 1980s, 700,000 new secretarial positions will be created, more than in any other job category. There is also no question that many public and private employers are saving billions of dollars by hiring women rather than men. In 1979 wages in the private service sector, an area of the economy dominated by women, averaged $9,583 while in the private industrial sector, which is primarily male, wages averaged $23,433. Since women comprised 41 percent of all wage earners in that year, employers' savings were considerable.[3] Women not only need their jobs but many employers need women to fill them.

For this reason I believe that the anti-union stance of a company like J. P. Stevens will pale in comparison to the resistance of large banks, insurance companies, and other employers of cheap female labor if serious attempts are made to unionize women. A good example is the current intransigence of Nationwide Insurance in the face of efforts by the office workers' union "9 to 5" to organize the company's clerks, typists, and secretaries. Of course, there is the possibility that if cheap and docile female labor becomes less cheap and less docile it will be replaced by machines. In fact, women now fill 90 percent or more of the jobs targeted for automation—file clerk, bookkeeper, secretary, typist,

Courtesy of Michael Kappy, M.D.

Tillie the Teller • *Many of women's traditional jobs in banks and offices are slated for automation. This bank's 24 hour deposit and withdrawal service is called "Tillie the All-Time Teller."*

and bank teller. The U.S. Department of Labor predicts that clerical workers will be more affected by widespread office automation than any other white collar workers.[4]

But why the far right's attack on working women? Political scientist Zillah R. Eisenstein has suggested that the ultimate goal of the antifeminist ideologues of the New Right is to remove married women from the labor force because women with jobs are a threat to the patriarchal family. Eisenstein argues that whether women demand equality at home or not, they do so in the marketplace; no working woman opposes the demand for equal pay for equal work. This insistence on equality has the potential of not only disrupting the current patriarchal structure of the job market with its female ghettos and its 59 cents to the dollar wages but of making women question the sexual division of labor at home. There is evidence that the families of the majority of New Right activists themselves are organized along traditional lines: mother stays home and father supports the family, a model they would like to see imposed on everyone else.[5]

I doubt that the forces of the New Right will be successful in imposing their dependent female/working male version of the family on the population at large. The economic conditions for it are simply not present. Married women's wages are too important to their families' well-being for them to opt out of the job market and adopt the life-style that America's most reactionary elements deem the only appropriate one for wives and mothers. In addition, the dependence on cheap female labor by major sectors of the American economy should not be underestimated. While the forces of the right and the interests of business and industry may be united in their common opposition to affirmative action and the radical new concept of equal pay for work of comparable value, women's labor is far too important to many segments of the economy to permit the right-wing ideology of *Kinder, Kuchen,* and *Kirche* to prevail.

What about the New Right's attempt to limit a woman's reproductive choices? I think that these attempts are punitive; beneath all the rhetoric, the right-to-lifers really want women to pay a price for their new-found sexual freedom. This also reflects the fear of loss of male control; here I agree with Eisenstein that the women's movement in general and its call for reproductive choice in particular threatens the foundations of the traditional patriarchal family.[6] Whatever the hidden agenda of the right-wing ideologues, I seriously doubt their future success. While it is true that they have managed to get legislation passed—the federal ban on Medicaid payments for abortion—which curtails the reproductive freedom of poor women, I think it unlikely that the Congress will adopt a general prohibition on reproductive choice, either through a Human Life Amendment or some other form of legislation.

Abortion will remain legal for the same reasons that we will not return to the day when the family with three or four children was the norm. Given the current cost of living, children are expensive to raise, particularly if a woman gives up her job in order to care for them. The recent and much heralded baby boomlet should not be misconstrued as the resurrection of the era of the 3.2-child family. The slight increase in the birthrate is the result of that cohort of women who, having delayed producing children until their thirties, are now having one or two. The average number of children per woman is not increasing. The "procreative imperative" has been broken, and the protestations of the right wing alone are not about to revive it.[7]

Today women's completed fertility rate is lower than it has ever been, and more married women than ever before have jobs. What does this mean for the mother role? There has been a marked turn-around in the child-rearing literature on the necessity of an omnipresent mother for a child's proper growth and development. An exclusive mother-child bond is no longer seen as absolutely necessary for healthy offspring, and Dad has finally reentered the child-rearing picture. The myth that children are seriously damaged by alternative forms of child care, including day-care centers, has finally been laid to rest.

Could the current dicta of the child-rearing experts be only a fad that in time will be supplanted by a revival of the call for full-time maternal care and renewed invectives against the working mother? Once again, I doubt it, given women's present commitment to the labor force and the high cost of rearing children—phenomena that give no indication of being reversed. Since my entire analysis in this book suggests that the ideological buttresses for women's roles are largely reflective of the productive and reproductive conditions that prevail during the period they are espoused, the maternal ideal of an earlier era cannot be resurrected without major changes in the foundations of American society.

What about housework? Hasn't it remained largely unchanged despite the record number of married women holding jobs and the

1.8-child family? It is true that the sexual division of labor in the home does not yet reflect the reality of women's employment; most married women still have two jobs (at work and at home) and labor under the burden of the double day. It is also true that as long as most people live in small nuclear families, housekeeping tasks will continue to be the individual household's responsibility.

Nevertheless, changes both in the definition of good housekeeping and in the time devoted to it have taken place. The day is past when the pages of the women's magazines are routinely filled with a mind-boggling array of make-work activities. The emphasis is now on time-*saving*, not time-*spending* hints. Women's domestic advisors no longer insist on "eat off the floor" standards of cleanliness and seem to feel that a little dust never hurt anyone. Moreover, because the double day has become routine for many employed women, they are indeed spending less time on housekeeping tasks. Nowhere is this more evident than in meal preparation. Not only are there more convenience foods on the market than ever before but the suggestion "Let's go out to eat" is no longer reserved for special occasions. In 1981 Americans spent $75 billion in restaurants, and the number of fast-food franchises has doubled in less than 10 years to 60,000. There are predictions that by the year 2000, one out of every two meals will be eaten away from home.[8]

The reasons why women are spending fewer hours on housework are not altogether clear. Are they using more outside services? Are they receiving more help from their husbands and children? Are they working more efficiently? Are their housekeeping standards less lofty? Or are their labor-saving devices really saving labor for the first time? Whatever the cause, it is reasonable to suppose that if present employment and fertility trends continue, the time spent on housework will decline still further.

Finally, will women continue to be blamed for being victims, despite their gains in other areas? Will women still be blamed for their employment in low-paying, female ghettos? If the majority of women remain in the dead-end, low-wage sector of the job market, it is almost certain that victim-blaming ideologues will continue to be heard: "It is their own fault that the ladies don't get ahead." "If they don't get paid as much as men it's because they don't work as hard and aren't really serious about their jobs. After all, equal pay for equal work is the law of the land." Reagan's statement about unemployment is concrete evidence that victim-blaming is still a popular tactic. It is also true, however, that this sort of obfuscation may begin to be challenged since millions of men as well as women know full well the necessity of two family incomes. More and more men are bound to become aware that their wives' 59 cents on the dollar wages make it more difficult to make ends meet. Nevertheless, this kind of rhetoric will surely continue as long as it is useful, that is, as long as the present structure of the labor market remains the same and as long as women are victimized by it. It is certainly easier and less threatening to blame women, than it is to blame the inequities inherent in the structure of the economy itself.

Some will be disturbed that I have not emphasized the role of the women's movement in the transformation of women's roles in this country. Common wisdom has it that a feminist ideology influenced women to take jobs, led to the demand for a more equitable division of labor in child care and housework, and raised the cry against blaming the female victim in employment, rape, spouse abuse, and other areas. I do not mean to diminish the importance of the women's movement in these protests against the status quo, and I do not doubt the power and influence of feminist ideology. Feminism has indeed made women question the low pay and segregation of female labor, the unfairness of the double day, and the vitriolic victim-blaming directed against them. Nevertheless, I argue that women's consciousness was raised on these and other issues by the material conditions of their lives, by the disjunctions between ideology and reality, the very disjunctions that also led to the feminist revival. Viewed from this perspective, the women's movement is ultimately a *result* rather than a cause of women's discontent.

As a cultural materialist I believe that a feminist ideology neither caused the changes in women's roles in this country nor that a conservative ideology will return those roles to what some view as "the good old days." Perhaps the folly of an idealist interpretation of the roles of American women will be clearer if we imagine the following scenario. Paraphrasing the words of anthropologist Marvin Harris, let us suppose that there is a large and influential group of American men conspiring for a return to nineteenth-century sex roles. They vehemently assert that a woman's place is in the home, that the loss of full-time mother care lies at the root of the nation's problems, and that the women's movement is a dire threat to "traditional family values" and must be expunged at all costs. Can any informed person seriously believe that such a group of individuals could succeed in imposing their program on large numbers of women? The strength of their convictions will do nothing to change the series of material factors that are the basis for the revolution in women's roles and the renewal of feminism.[9]

Where then do we go from here? Despite my occasional pessimism about the future roles of American women, I am not arguing that "the more things, change, the more they remain the same." I find that philosophy deeply conservative for it seeks reassurance, not illumination about the transformations that have taken place in American society. The soothing claims that the family will always be with us, that it *really* has not changed much, and that women will always take primary responsibility for child care and housework because it is in the nature of things are ideological stances based more on wishful thinking and uneasiness about the current order than on close analysis. Such reassurances neither seriously consider the major changes that have occurred in women's roles in this country nor do they seek to explain them. They are basically conservative attempts to obscure what is taking place in American society today, attempts that should remind feminists of the truism that in order to change the world we first have to understand it.

NOTES

1. The Anthropological Perspective

1. Robert Asahina, "Social Science Fiction," *New York Times Book Review*, 16 August 1981.
2. Marvin Harris, *Cultural Materialism: The Struggle for a Science of Culture* (New York, 1979), p. ix. The cultural materialist approach in anthropology has its roots in the theories of Karl Marx and Friedrich Engels, but it is a materialism shorn of the Hegelian dialectic. In Engels's words:

   > According to the materialist conception, the determining factor in history is, in the final instance, the production and reproduction of the immediate essentials of life. This, again, is of a twofold character. On the one side, the production of the means of existence, of articles of food and clothing, dwellings, and of the tools necessary for that production; on the other side, the production of human beings themselves, the propagation of the species. The social organization under which the people of a particular epoch and a particular country live is determined by both kinds of production. (Friedrich Engels, *The Origin of the Family, Private Property, and the State* [New York, 1964; orig. ed. 1884], p. 5)

3. Examples of a cultural materialist approach to sex roles include Ernestine Friedl, *Women and Men: An Anthropologist's View* (New York, 1975); M. Kay Martin and Barbara Voorhies, *The Female of the Species* (New York, 1975); William T. Divale and Marvin Harris, "Population, Warfare, and the Male Supremacist Complex," *American Anthropologist* 78 (September 1976): 521–538.
4. Betty Friedan, *The Feminine Mystique* (New York, 1974).
5. William Goode, *World Revolution and Family Patterns* (New York, 1963), p. 56.
6. Friedan, *The Feminine Mystique*; Simone de Beauvoir, *The Second Sex* (New York, 1952).
7. Mary Beth Norton and Carol Ruth Berkin, "Women and American History," in *Women of America: A History*, ed. Carol Ruth Berkin and Mary Beth Norton (Boston, 1979), pp. 3–15.
8. For discussions of some of the problematic aspects of prescriptive literature, see Michael Zuckerman, "Dr. Spock: The Confidence Man," in *The Family in History*, ed. Charles E. Rosenberg (Philadelphia, 1975), pp. 179–207; Jay Mechling, "Advice to Historians on Advice to Mothers," *Journal of Social History* 9 (1975): 44–63; and Mary Beth

Norton, "The Paradox of Women's Sphere," *Women of America: A History*, ed. Carol Ruth Berkin and Mary Beth Norton (Boston, 1979), pp. 139–149.

9. Norton, "The Paradox of Women's Sphere," p. 145. In fact, women were as prolific advice givers as men. Of the ninety-three books, manuals, and popular articles on motherhood and child rearing used in my research for chapters 2 and 3 of this book, women wrote forty-seven, or nearly half of them.
10. John B. Watson, *Psychological Care of Infant and Child* (New York, 1928).
11. Carl N. Degler, *At Odds: Women and the Family in America from the Revolution to the Present* (New York, 1980), pp. 49, 82–83.

2: Putting Mothers on the Pedestal

1. Jessie Bernard, *The Future of Motherhood* (New York, 1974), p. 7; Marvin Harris, *America Now: The Anthropology of a Changing Culture* (New York, 1981), p. 84.
2. Thomas Weisner and Ronald Gallimore, "My Brother's Keeper: Child and Sibling Caretaking," *Current Anthropology* 18 (June 1977): 170. For information on cross-cultural differences in child-rearing values see Wallace E. Lambert, Josiane F. Hamers, and Nancy Frasure-Smith, *Child Rearing Values: A Cross-national Study* (New York, 1979).
3. Weisner and Gallimore, "My Brother's Keeper," p. 173.
4. Judith K. Brown, "A Note on the Division of Labor by Sex," *American Anthropologist* 72 (October 1970): 1073–1078; Wanda Minge-Klevana, "Does Labor Time Increase with Industrialization? A Survey of Time Allocation Studies," *Current Anthropology* 21 (June 1980): 279–298.
5. Leigh Minturn and William W. Lambert, *Mothers of Six Cultures* (New York, 1964), pp. 95–97, 100–101, 112–113. This study does not measure the actual amount of time mothers spent with their infants, only whether mothers had primary or exclusive care of them.
6. This is what has been called "the most important confidence trick that society plays on the individual—to make appear as necessary what is in fact a bundle of contingencies" (Peter L. Berger and Thomas Luckmann, *The Social Construction of Reality* [New York, 1966], p. 135).
7. Jay Mechling, "Advice to Historians on Advice to Mothers," *Journal of Social History* 9 (Fall 1975): 44, 53.
8. Quoted in Ruth H. Bloch, "Untangling the Roots of Modern Sex Roles: A Survey of Four Centuries of Change," *Signs* 4 (Winter 1978): 242; quoted in Nancy F. Cott, *The Bonds of Womanhood: "Woman's Sphere" in New England, 1780–1835* (New Haven, 1977), p. 58.
9. Phillipe Aries, *Centuries of Childhood* (New York, 1965); Kathryn Kish Sklar, "Introduction," in Catherine E. Beecher, *A Treatise on Domestic Economy* (New York, 1977; first published, 1841), p. vi.

10. Carl N. Degler, *At Odds: Women and the Family in America from the Revolution to the Present* (New York, 1980), p. 5; Philip J. Greven, Jr., "Family Structure in Seventeenth Century Andover, Massachusetts," in *The American Family in Socio-Historical Perspective*, ed. Michael Gordon (New York, 1973), pp. 77–99; John Demos, *A Little Commonwealth: Family Life in Plymouth Colony* (New York, 1970); Bloch, "Untangling the Roots of Modern Sex Roles."
11. Demos, *A Little Commonwealth*, pp. 57–58; Cotton Mather, *Ornaments of the Daughters of Zion*, 3d ed. (Delmar, N.Y., 1978; 3d ed. first published, 1741), pp. 108–109; Benjamin Wadsworth, "The Well-ordered Family, or, Relative Duties," in *The Colonial American Family: Collected Essays* (New York, 1972; first published, Boston, 1712).
12. Demos, *A Little Commonwealth*, p. 141; Arthur W. Calhoun, *A Social History of the American Family: The Colonial Period* (New York, 1960; first published, 1917), p. 87.
13. Peter Gregg Slater, *Children in the New England Mind* (Hamden, Conn., 1977), p. 16; Mather, *Ornaments of the Daughters of Zion*, p. 108.
14. John F. Walzer, "A Period of Ambivalence: Eighteenth Century American Childhood," in *The History of Childhood*, ed. Lloyd de Mause (New York, 1974), pp. 351–382; Wadsworth, "The Well-ordered Family, or, Relative Duties," p. 46; quoted in Edmund S. Morgan, *The Puritan Family*, rev. ed. (New York, 1966), p. 45.
15. Margaret W. Masson, "The Typology of the Female as a Model for the Regenerate: Puritan Teaching, 1690–1730," *Signs* 2 (Winter 1976): 304–315; J. William Frost, *The Quaker Family in Colonial America: A Portrait of the Society of Friends* (New York, 1973); Laurel Thatcher Ulrich, "Vertuous Women Found: New England Ministerial Literature, 1668–1735," in *A Heritage of Her Own*, ed. Nancy F. Cott and Elizabeth H. Pleck (New York, 1979), pp. 58–80; Ruth H. Bloch, "American Feminine Ideals in Transition: The Rise of the Moral Mother, 1785–1815," *Feminist Studies* 4 (1978): 106. I am indebted to Bloch's two articles for the sources contained in this and the next section of the chapter. They are the most thorough research on the prescriptive literature of the colonial period and early nineteenth century that I have found.
16. Mather, *Ornaments of the Daughters of Zion*, p. 105; Mary Beth Norton, *Liberty's Daughters: The Revolutionary Experience of American Women* (Boston, 1980), pp. 90, 94; Bloch, "American Feminine Ideals in Transition," p. 105.
17. Mary P. Ryan, *Womanhood in America: From Colonial Times to the Present* (New York, 1975), p. 60; Bloch, "Untangling the Roots of Modern Sex Roles," p. 242; Bloch, "American Feminine Ideals in Transition," p. 107; Alice Kessler-Harris, *Women Have Always Worked* (Westbury, N.Y., 1981), p. 29.
18. Bloch, "American Feminine Ideals in Transition," pp. 101, 103–104.

19. Hugh Smith, *Letters to Married Women on Nursing and the Management of Children*, 2d ed. (Philadelphia, 1796), p. 58; Cott, *The Bonds of Womanhood*, p. 24; W. Elliot Brownlee, *Dynamics of Ascent: A History of the American Economy* (New York, 1974), p. 77; Ryan, *Womanhood in America*, p. 91.
20. Quoted in Degler, *At Odds*, p. 361.
21. Bloch, "Untangling the Roots of Modern Sex Roles," p. 251; Bloch, "American Feminine Ideals in Transition," p. 114; Degler, *At Odds*, pp. 69, 179; Philip J. Greven, Jr., *Four Generations: Population, Land, and Family in Colonial Andover, Massachusetts* (Ithaca, N.Y., 1970).
22. Cott, *The Bonds of Womanhood*, p. 57.
23. Frost, *The Quaker Family in Colonial America*, p. 87; Smith, *Letters to Married Women*, p. 108; Slater, *Children in the New England Mind*, p. 148.
24. Slater, *Children in the New England Mind*, p. 73.
25. Ibid., pp. 93–94; Bloch, "American Feminine Ideals in Transition," pp. 112–113.
26. Quoted in Frost, *The Quaker Family in Colonial America*, p. 72; Smith, *Letters to Married Women*, pp. 54, 57.
27. Jane West, *Letters to Young Ladies* (New York, 1974; orig. ed., London, 1806), pp. 190, 208–209, 211–212, emphasis in original.
28. William Buchan, *Advice to Mothers*, reprinted in *The American Physician and Child Rearing: Two Guides 1809–1894* (New York, 1972; first published, 1809), pp. 3, 77.
29. An American Matron, *The Maternal Physician* (New York, 1972; reprint of orig. ed., Philadelphia, 1811), pp. 8, 17–18.
30. Quoted in Cott, *The Bonds of Womanhood*, p. 86; quoted in Bloch, "American Feminine Ideals in Transition," p. 112; Cott, *The Bonds of Womanhood*, p. 86.
31. Barbara Sicherman, "American History," *Signs* 1 (Winter 1975): 496.
32. Bloch, "Untangling the Roots of Modern Sex Roles," p. 250.
33. Arthur W. Calhoun, *A Social History of the American Family: From Independence through the Civil War* (New York, 1960; first published, 1918), p. 52; Reverend John S. C. Abbott, *The Mother at Home* (New York, 1833), p. 152; Ryan, *Womanhood in America*, p. 126.
34. Mary P. Ryan, "Femininity and Capitalism in Antebellum America," in *Capitalist Patriarchy and the Case for Feminist Socialism*, ed. Zillah R. Eisenstein (New York, 1979), p. 153; Brownlee, *Dynamics of Ascent*, pp. 87, 89, 116.
35. Cott, *The Bonds of Womanhood*, p. 36; Barbara Ehrenreich and Deirdre English, *For Her Own Good: 150 Years of the Experts' Advice to Women* (New York, 1978), p. 129; quoted in Degler, *At Odds*, p. 376.
36. Roger Thompson, *Women in Stuart England and America* (Boston, 1974), p. 75.
37. Kessler-Harris, *Women Have Always Worked*, p. 34; Philip J. Greven, Jr., "The Average Size of Families and Households in the Province of Mas-

sachusetts in 1764 and in the United States in 1790: An Overview," in *Household and Family in Time Past*, ed. Peter Laslett (London, 1972), p. 551.

38. Slater, *Children in the New England Mind*, p. 149; Bernard Wishy, *The Child and the Republic: The Dawn of Modern American Child Nurture* (Philadelphia, 1968), p. 40; Degler, *At Odds*, p. 69.
39. Degler, *At Odds*, pp. 72–73; Catherine Beecher, *A Treatise on Domestic Economy*, (New York, 1977; first published, 1841).
40. Kessler-Harris, *Women Have Always Worked*, p. 34; Degler, *At Odds*, p. 181; Harris, *America Now*, p. 81.
41. Although the fear of "race suicide" is usually associated with the very late nineteenth and early twentieth centuries and with the figure of Theodore Roosevelt, there were in fact references to it prior to the Civil War. See Linda Gordon, *Woman's Body, Woman's Right* (New York, 1977), chapter 7, and Arthur W. Calhoun, *A Social History of the American Family: Since the Civil War* (New York, 1960; first published, 1919), chapter 11.
42. James C. Mohr, *Abortion in America: The Origins and Evolution of National Policy 1800–1900* (New York, 1978), pp. 50, 20; Gordon, *Woman's Body, Woman's Right*, pp. 52, 57n.
43. "Maternity," *The Ladies' Museum* 1 (September 1825): 31; Robert Sunley, "Early Nineteenth Century American Literature on Child Rearing," in *Childhood in Contemporary Cultures*, ed. Margaret Mead and Martha Wolfenstein (Chicago, 1963), p. 152.
44. Philip J. Greven, Jr., *Child Rearing Concepts, 1628–1861* (Itasca, Ill., 1973).
45. Lydia Sigourney, *Letters to Mothers* (Hartford, 1838), p. 10; William Thayer, "The Era for Mothers," *The Mother's Assistant* 16 (May 1851): 141.
46. Edward Mansfield, *The Legal Rights, Liabilities, and Duties of Women* (Salem, Mass., 1845), p. 105, emphasis in original.
47. William Dewees, *A Treatise on the Physical and Medical Treatment of Children*, 10th ed. (Philadelphia, 1847), pp. 64–65; Sigourney, *Letters to Mothers*, pp. 28, 82, 87; Abbott, *The Mother at Home*, p. 169.
48. Lydia Maria Child, *The Mother's Book* (New York, 1972; first published, 1831), p. 4; Sigourney, *Letters to Mothers*, pp. 16, 32, 87; "The Responsibility of Mothers," *Parents Magazine* 1 (March 1841): 156.
49. Abbott, *The Mother at Home*, pp. 155–156; Sunley, "Early Nineteenth Century American Literature on Child Rearing," p. 152.
50. Quoted in Barbara Welter, "The Cult of True Womanhood: 1820–1860," in *The American Family in Socio-Historical Perspective*, ed. Michael Gordon (New York, 1973), p. 240; John S. C. Abbott, "Paternal Neglect," *Parents Magazine* 2 (March 1842): 148; Abbott, *The Mother at Home*, pp. 76–79.
51. *Ladies' Literary Cabinet* 5 (January 1822): 5.
52. Abigail J. Stewart, David G. Winter, and A. David Jones, "Coding Categories for the Study of Child Rearing from Historical Sources," *Journal of Interdisciplinary History* 5 (1975): 701.

53. George C. Beckwith, "The Fate of Nations Dependent on Mothers," *The Mother's Assistant* 15 (January 1850): 4; Abbott, *The Mother at Home*, p. 153; quoted in Anne L. Kuhn, *The Mother's Role in Childhood Education: New England Concepts 1830–1860* (New Haven, 1947), p. 34. Somewhat later the British sociologist Herbert Spencer, who was widely read in the United States, propounded a similar idea when he wrote that "Children . . . had to be long nurtured by female parents" for "social progress" to take place (quoted in Lorna Duffin, "Prisoners of Progress: Women and Evolution," in *The Nineteenth Century Woman*, ed. Sara Delmont and Lorna Duffin [New York, 1978], p. 78).
54. Abbott, *The Mother at Home*, p. 11, emphasis in original; "Religion Is the Strength of Women," *Ladies' Magazine* 7 (May 1834): 226; Sigourney, *Letters to Mothers*, p. 15.
55. Jabez Burns, *Mothers of the Wise and Good* (Boston, 1851); Abbott, *The Mother at Home*, pp. 11–12.
56. Quoted in Kuhn, *The Mother's Role in Childhood Education*, p. 67, emphasis in original; Elizabeth S. Hall, "A Mother's Influence," *The Mother's Assistant* 1 (February 1849): 25.
57. Catherine Beecher, *Suggestions Respecting Improvements in Education* (New York, 1829), p. 54; Sigourney, *Letters to Mothers*, pp. 13, 16; "Influence of Women—Past and Present," *Ladies' Magazine* 13 (1840): 246.
58. Sigourney, *Letters to Mothers*, pp. 2, 24; Child, *The Mother's Book*, p. 9; "Children," *Godey's Ladies Book* 60 (January–June 1860): 272; quoted in Calhoun, *A Social History of the American Family: From Independence through the Civil War*, pp. 84–85.
59. Degler, *At Odds*, p. 55; Ryan, *Womanhood in America*, p. 84; Ann Dally, *Inventing Motherhood* (London, 1982), p. 17; Cott, *The Bonds of Womanhood*, p. 84.
60. Emma Marwedel, *Conscious Motherhood: The Earliest Unfolding of the Child in the Cradle, Nursery, and Kindergarten* (Boston, 1887), p. 78; Wishy, *The Child and the Republic*, pp. 104, 107.
61. John Brisben Walker, "Motherhood as a Profession," *The Cosmopolitan* 25 (May 1898): 89; Marwedel, *Conscious Motherhood*, p. 34; quoted in Glenn Davis, *Childhood and History in America* (New York, 1976), p. 99.
62. Ehrenreich and English, *For Her Own Good*, pp. 180–181; Marwedel, *Conscious Motherhood*, pp. 41, 47.
63. Russell Thacher Trall, *The Mother's Hygienic Handbook* (New York, 1874), p. 5; quoted in Ryan, *Womanhood in America*, p. 195.
64. Quoted in Aileen S. Kraditor, ed., *Up from the Pedestal* (Chicago, 1968), pp. 194–196; quoted in William J. O'Neill, *Everyone Was Brave* (Chicago, 1971), p. 36.
65. Lois Scharf, *To Work and to Wed* (Westport, Conn., 1980), p. 17.
66. Catherine Beecher, *Woman Suffrage and Woman's Profession* (Boston, 1871), p. 4; quoted in Degler, *At Odds*, p. 197; Trall, *The Mother's Hygienic Handbook*, p. 5.

67. Daniel Scott Smith, "Family Limitation, Sexual Control, and Domestic Feminism in Victorian America," in *Clio's Consciousness Raised*, ed. Mary Hartman and Lois W. Banner (New York, 1974), p. 122; Mohr, *Abortion in America*, pp. 230, 242–243; Gordon, *Woman's Body, Woman's Right*, p. 167; Margaret Gibbons Wilson, *The American Woman in Transition: The Urban Influence, 1870–1920* (Westport, Conn., 1979), p. 52.
68. Marvin Harris, *America Now*, p. 81.
69. Quoted in Gordon, *Woman's Body, Woman's Right*, p. 150.
70. Ellen Key, *The Renaissance of Motherhood* (New York, 1914), p. 119; Ehrenreich and English, *For Her Own Good*, p. 165.
71. Peter Gabriel Filene, *Him/Her/Self* (New York, 1976), p. 41.
72. Ryan, *Womanhood in America*, p. 243.
73. Degler, *At Odds*, p. 81; quoted in Scharf, *To Work and to Wed*, p. 17; Ellen Key, *The Century of the Child* (New York, 1909), pp. 101, 87.
74. Filene, *Him/Her/Self*, p. 37; Wilson, *The American Woman in Transition*, p. 58.
75. G. Stanley Hall, *Adolescence*, vol. 2 (New York, 1904), pp. 607, 610, 634; Key, *The Renaissance of Motherhood*, pp. 115, 110.
76. Theodore Roosevelt, "The American Woman as Mother," address before the National Congress of Mothers reprinted in *Ladies' Home Journal* 22 (July 1905): 4.
77. Quoted in Filene, *Him/Her/Self*, p. 36.
78. Nathan Maccoby, "The Communication of Childrearing Advice to Parents," in *Selected Studies in Marriage and the Family*, 3d ed., ed. Robert F. Winch and Louis Wolf Goodman (New York, 1968), p. 255. The three women's magazines analyzed in the study were the *Ladies' Home Journal*, *Woman's Home Companion*, and *Good Housekeeping*.
79. L. Emmett Holt, *The Care and Feeding of Infants* (New York, 1896); G. Stanley Hall, *Youth: Its Education, Regimen and Hygiene* (New York, 1911; first published, 1904).
80. Hall, *Youth: Its Education, Regimen and Hygiene*, pp. 304–305, 297, 283, 307, 304, 319.
81. An American Mother, "Is a College Education Best for Our Girls?" *Ladies' Home Journal* 17 (July 1900): 15; Anne E. Randolph, "Is the American Girl Being Miseducated?" *Ladies' Home Journal* 27 (September 1910): 67.
82. Roosevelt, "The American Woman as Mother," pp. 3–4; Key, *The Century of the Child*, p. 84.
83. Ehrenreich and English, *For Her Own Good*, p. 172; Edward Bok, editorial, *Ladies' Home Journal* 27 (June 1910): 5; Key, *The Century of the Child*, p. 100. For a more complete discussion of the "woman question" see Ehrenreich and English, *For Her Own Good*, chapter 1.
84. Dorothy Fisher Canfield, *Mothers and Children* (New York, 1914), pp. 180, 182; Key, *The Century of the Child*, p. 102.
85. Barnetta Brown, "Mothers' Mistakes, Fathers' Failures," *Ladies' Home Journal* 17 (February 1900): 32; Edward Bok, editorial, *Ladies' Home Journal* 32

(September 1915): 5.

86. Key, *The Renaissance of Motherhood*, pp. 167, 135; Key, *The Century of the Child*, p. 86; Key, *The Renaissance of Motherhood*, p. 136.

87. John B. Watson, *Psychological Care of Infant and Child* (New York, 1928), p. 87; Sheila N. Rothman, *Woman's Proper Place: A History of Changing Ideals and Practices, 1870 to the Present* (New York, 1978), p. 212.

88. Watson, *Psychological Care of Infant and Child*, pp. 7–9.

89. Ibid., pp. 78, 80–82.

90. Ibid., pp. 84–85.

91. D. A. Thom, *Child Management*, Children's Bureau Publication no. 143 (Washington, D.C., 1925), pp. 3–4; *Are You Training Your Child to Be Happy?*, Children's Bureau Publication no. 202 (Washington, D.C., 1930), p. 54; Arthur H. Sutherland and Myron M. Stearns, "Never Too Young to Learn Responsibility," *Ladies' Home Journal* 44 (March 1927): 27, 228.

92. Ernest R. Groves and Gladys Hoagland Groves, *Parents and Children* (Philadelphia, 1928), pp. 116, 119.

93. Mrs. Max West, *Infant Care*, Children's Bureau Publication no. 8, reprinted in *Children and Youth in America: A Documentary History*, vol. 2 (Cambridge, 1971; first published, 1914), p. 37; Martha M. Eliot, *Infant Care*, 3d rev. ed., Children's Bureau Publication no. 8 (Washington, D.C., 1929), p. 3.

94. *Are You Training Your Children to Be Happy?*, p. 1, emphasis in original; Mary McCarthy, *The Group* (New York, 1963), p. 228.

95. Eliot, *Infant Care*, p. 57; *Infant Care*, 5th rev. ed., Children's Bureau Publication no. 8 (Washington, D.C., 1938), p. 6. By 1980 *Infant Care* had gone through thirteen editions and was still the best-seller of the U.S. government's 24,000 publications.

96. Sir Frederick Truby King, *Feeding and Care of Babies* (London, 1913).

97. Harry Braverman, *Labor and Monopoly Capitalism* (New York, 1974), pp. 90, 107, 118.

98. Nancy Pottishman Weiss, "Mother, the Invention of Necessity: Dr. Spock's *Baby and Child Care*," *American Quarterly* 29 (Winter 1977): 531; Ryan, *Womanhood in America*, p. 347.

99. Quoted in Rothman, *Woman's Proper Place*, p. 215; Groves and Groves, *Parents and Children*, pp. 120–121.

100. Groves and Groves, *Parents and Children*, pp. 140, 132, 148, emphasis added; Children's Bureau, *Infant Care*, 5th rev. ed. (Washington, D.C., 1938), p. 6, emphasis in original.

101. Rothman, *Woman's Proper Place*, p. 217; John B. Watson, "The Weakness of Women," *The Nation* 125 (July 6, 1927): 10.

102. Quoted in Scharf, *To Work and to Wed*, p. 31; Eliot, *Infant Care*, p. 2; quoted in Filene, *Him/Her/Self*, p. 132; quoted in Leila J. Rupp, *Mobilizing Women for War* (Princeton, N.J., 1978), p. 63.

103. William H. Chafe, *The American Woman, Her Changing Social, Economic, and Political Roles, 1920–1970* (New York, 1972), p. 56; Degler, *At Odds*, p. 181.

3: Mothers Descend

1. Philip Slater, *Pursuit of Loneliness*, rev. ed. (Boston, 1976), p. 72; Barbara Ehrenreich and Deirdre English, *For Her Own Good: 150 Years of the Experts' Advice to Women* (New York, 1978), p. 191.
2. Marvin Harris, *America Now: The Anthropology of a Changing Culture* (New York, 1981), pp. 90, 41.
3. *Perspectives on Working Women: A Databook*, Bureau of Labor Statistics Bulletin 2080 (Washington, D.C., 1980), p. 27; Judy Klemesrud, "Mothers Who Shift Back from Jobs to Homemaking," *New York Times*, 19 January 1983, pp. 13, 16.
4. Leo Kanner, *In Defense of Mothers* (Springfield, Ill., 1941), p.7; Sibylle Escalona, "A Commentary upon Some Recent Changes in Child Rearing Practices," in *Selected Studies in Marriage and the Family*, ed. Robert F. Winch and Robert McGinnis (New York, 1953), p. 211; cited in Glenn Davis, *Childhood and History in America* (New York, 1976), p. 135; Celia B. Stendler, "Sixty Years of Child Training Practices," *Journal of Pediatrics* 36 (1950): 122–134; Josephine Kenyon, "Less Rigid Schedules for Babies," *Good Housekeeping* 110 (February 1940): 92.
5. Margaret A. Ribble, *Rights of Infants* (New York, 1943), p. 63; Arnold Gessell and Frances L. Ilg, *Infant and Child in the Culture of Today* (New York, 1943), p. 57; Josephine Kenyon, "Tired Mothers," *Good Housekeeping* 110 (January 1940): 63; Ehrenreich and English, *For Her Own Good*, pp. 94–95.
6. Kanner, *In Defense of Mothers*, pp. 102, 5, 7, 166; Michael Zuckerman, "Dr. Spock: The Confidence Man," in *The Family in History*, ed. Charles E. Rosenberg (Philadelphia, 1975), pp. 179–207; Benjamin Spock, *Baby and Child Care*, rev. ed. (New York, 1968; first published, 1946), p. 155. By the mid-1970s the various editions of Spock's *Baby and Child Care* had sold 28 million copies, making it the best-selling child-care manual of all time. I am using the 1968 edition of Spock's manual here because it includes the same topics as the earlier editions. Not until the 1976 revised edition, discussed in a later section of this chapter, did Spock introduce significant changes in his views of the mother and father roles.
7. Martha Wolfenstein, "Fun Morality: An Analysis of Recent American Child Training Literature," in *Childhood in Contemporary Cultures*, ed. Margaret Mead and Martha Wolfenstein (Chicago, 1955), pp. 168–178; *Infant Care*, 7th rev. ed., Children's Bureau Publication no. 8 (Washington, D.C., 1942), p. 41; Wolfenstein, "Fun Morality," p. 173.
8. Escalona, "A Commentary upon Some Recent Changes in Child Rearing

Practices," p. 212; Ribble, *Rights of Infants*, pp. 10, 12, 21, emphasis added.

9. John Bowlby, *Child Care and the Growth of Love*, 2d ed. (Baltimore, 1965; first published, 1951 as *Maternal Care and Mental Health*), pp. 13–14, 77. John Bowlby, who was the Dr. Spock of British child care, based his research about maternal deprivation on orphaned and otherwise institutionalized children living apart from their parents. A member of the British upper class, Bowlby never included in his studies members of his own class or their traditional child-rearing methods—including the hiring of governesses and the sending of boys to boarding school at an early age. See also Ann Dally, *Inventing Motherhood: The Consequences of an Ideal* (London, 1982), chapter 7.
10. Nancy Pottishman Weiss, "Mother, the Invention of Necessity: Dr. Spock's *Baby and Child Care*," *American Quarterly* 29 (Winter 1977): 531; Slater, *Pursuit of Loneliness*, pp. 70–71.
11. Ribble, *Rights of Infants*, p. 108; Weiss, "Mother, the Invention of Necessity," p. 543.
12. Spock, *Baby and Child Care*, pp. 63–64; Ehrenreich and English, *For Her Own Good*, pp. 243, 245, emphasis in original.
13. Philip Wylie, *Generation of Vipers* (New York, 1942), p. 185; David M. Levy, *Maternal Overprotection* (New York, 1943), pp. 3, 161.
14. Edward A. Strecker, *Their Mothers' Sons* (Philadelphia, 1946), pp. 14, 21, 31, 147; Geoffrey Gorer, *The American People*, rev. ed. (New York, 1964), p. 64n.
15. Kanner, *In Defense of Mothers*, pp. 40–41; Mollie Stevens Smart and Russell Cook Smart, *It's a Wise Parent* (New York, 1946), p. 8.
16. E. E. LeMasters, *Parents in Modern America: A Sociological Study* (Homewood, Ill., 1970), pp. 121–124; Ehrenreich and English, *For Her Own Good*, p. 202.
17. Ribble, *Rights of Infants*, pp. 67, 101–102; Anna W. M. Wolf, *The Parents' Manual* (New York, 1941), pp. 46, 222, 218.
18. Bowlby, *Child Care and the Growth of Love*, p. 15.
19. Spock, *Baby and Child Care*, pp. 31, 321; David Goodman, *A Parent's Guide to the Emotional Needs of Children* (New York, 1959), p. 35.
20. Dan Gillmor, "The Care and Feeding of Spock-marked Fathers," *Parents' Magazine* 29 (July 1954): 36–37.
21. Urie Bronfenner, "The Study of Identification through Interpersonal Perception," in *Person Perception and Interpersonal Behavior*, ed. R. Tagiuri and L. Petrullo (Stanford, Calif., 1958), pp. 110–130; Levy, *Maternal Overprotection*; Goodman, *A Parent's Guide to the Emotional Needs of Children*, pp. 54–55.
22. Margaret Mead, "The Job of the Children's Mother's Husband," *New York Times Magazine*, 10 May 1959, p. 66.
23. Robert Sears et al., *Patterns in Child Rearing* (Evanston, Ill., 1957), p. vi;

Daniel R. Miller and Guy E. Swanson, *The Changing American Parent* (New York, 1958); Gorer, *The American People*, p. 54.

24. Robert F. Winch, *The Modern Family*, 3d rev. ed. (New York, 1971), pp. 163, 167; Adrienne Germaine, "Status and Roles of Women as Factors in Fertility Behavior: A Policy Analysis," *Studies in Family Planning* 6 (1975): 192–200; Carl N. Degler, *At Odds: Women and the Family in America from the Revolution to the Present* (New York, 1980), p. 81.
25. Peter Gabriel Filene, *Him/Her/Self* (New York, 1976), p. 69; quoted in Leila J. Rupp, *Mobilizing Women for War* (Princeton, N.J., 1976), p. 139.
26. Betty Friedan, *The Feminine Mystique* (New York, 1974); Goodman, *A Parent's Guide to the Emotional Needs of Children*, p. 35; Agnes Meyer, "Children in Trouble," *Ladies' Home Journal* 72 (March 1955): 205.
27. Degler, *At Odds*, p. 432; Spock, *Baby and Child Care*, p. 566.
28. Sidonie M. Gruenberg and Hilda S. Krech, *The Modern Mother's Dilemma*, Public Affairs Pamphlet No. 247 (New York, 1957), pp. 1–4.
29. Ibid., pp. 12, 14, 17.
30. Ibid., pp. 24–25.
31. Ibid., pp. 18–20.
32. Alicia Patterson, address to the Radcliffe Alumnae Association, November 1961, reprinted in *Harper's Magazine* 225 (October 1962): 123; Bruno Bettelheim, "Growing Up Female," *Harper's Magazine* 225 (October 1962): 124.
33. Edith De Rham, *The Love Fraud* (New York, 1965), pp. 132, 158, 160–161.
34. René A. Spitz, *The First Year of Life* (New York, 1965), p. 206.
35. *Infant Care*, 11th rev. ed., Children's Bureau Publication no. 8 (Washington, D.C., 1963), p. 11; Margaret A. Ribble, *Rights of Infants*, rev. ed. (New York, 1965), pp. 101, 141, 143, emphasis added; Ribble, *Rights of Infants* (New York, 1943), p. 109; Haim G. Ginnott, *Between Parent and Child* (New York, 1965), p. 169.
36. F. Ivan Nye and Lois Wladis Hoffman, *The Employed Mother in America* (Chicago, 1963), pp. 196–202. See also, Lois M. Stolz, "Effects of Maternal Employment on Children: Evidence from Research," *Child Development* 31 (1960): 749–782.
37. Ribble, *Rights of Infants*, rev. ed. (1965), p. 141, emphasis added; De Rham, *The Love Fraud*, p. 162.
38. Margaret Mead, "A Cultural Anthropologist's Approach to Maternal Deprivation," in *Deprivation of Maternal Care: A Reassessment of Its Effects* (Geneva, 1962), pp. 55–56; Bettelheim, "Growing Up Female," p. 127.
39. Friedan, *The Feminine Mystique*, p. 332; Alice S. Rossi, "Equality between the Sexes: An Immodest Proposal," in *Roles Women Play: Readings Towards Women's Liberation*, ed. Michele Hoffnung Garskof (Belmont, Calif., 1971; first published, 1965), pp. 163–164.
40. Benjamin Spock, *Baby and Child Care*, rev. ed. (New York, 1976), p. xix;

Rudolph Schaffer, *Mothering* (Cambridge, Mass., 1977), pp. 100, 106.

41. Rochelle P. Wortis, "The Acceptance of the Concept of the Maternal Role by Social Scientists: Its Effects on Women," in *Family in Transition*, 2d ed., ed. Arlene S. Skolnick and Jerome H. Skolnick (Boston, 1977), p. 363; Julius Segal and Herbert Yahraes, *A Child's Journey: Forces That Shape the Lives of Our Young* (New York, 1978), p. 119.
42. Schaffer, *Mothering*, p. 103, emphasis in original; Segal and Yahraes, *A Child's Journey*, pp. 119, 122; Schaffer, *Mothering*, p. 104.
43. Wortis, "The Acceptance of the Concept of the Maternal Role," pp. 365–366.
44. Schaffer, *Mothering*, p. 100; quoted in Beatrice Marden Glickman and Nesha Bass Springer, *Who Cares for the Baby?* (New York, 1978), pp. 165–166; quoted in Maureen Green, *Fathering* (New York, 1976), pp. 207–208, emphasis in original.
45. Nancy Choderow, *The Reproduction of Mothering* (Berkeley, Los Angeles, London, 1978), p. 74, emphasis in original; Wortis, "The Acceptance of the Concept of the Maternal Role," p. 369.
46. Segal and Yahraes, *A Child's Journey*, p. 74; Slater, *Pursuit of Loneliness*, pp. 72–73.
47. Helen L. Bee, "The Effect of Maternal Employment on the Development of the Child," in *Social Issues in Development Psychology*, ed. Helen L. Bee (New York, 1974), p. 104; Segal and Yahraes, *A Child's Journey*, p. 95, emphasis in original; quoted in Sally Werkos Olds, *The Mother Who Works Outside the Home* (New York, 1975), p. 15.
48. Schaffer, *Mothering*, p. 105; Segal and Yahraes, *A Child's Journey*, p. 95; Bee, "The Effect of Maternal Employment on the Development of the Child," p. 104.
49. Spock, *Baby and Child Care*, rev. ed. (1976), p. 37.
50. Sidney Cornelia Callahan, *The Working Mother* (New York, 1972), p. 23; Olds, *The Mother Who Works Outside the Home*, p. 58; Letty Cottin Pogrebin, "The Working Woman: Working Mothers," *Ladies' Home Journal* 91 (August 1974): 60.
51. Dava Sobel, "Children of Working Mothers," *New York Times* 13 December 1981, p. 14E; both quoted in Glickman and Springer, *Who Cares for the Baby?*, pp. 172, 180, emphasis in original; Choderow, *The Reproduction of Mothering*, p. 74.
52. Some of the books on fatherhood and fathering published between 1970 and 1980 are David B. Lynn, *The Father: His Role in Child Development* (Belmont, Calif., 1974); Michael E. Lamb, ed., *The Role of the Father in Child Development* (New York, 1976); Maureen Green, *Fathering* (New York, 1976); Marshall L. Hamilton, *Father's Influence on Children* (Chicago, 1977); and William Reynolds, *The American Father* (New York, 1978). Quoted in James Levine, *Who Will Raise the Children?* (Philadelphia, 1976), p. 28.

53. Helen L. Bee, "On the Importance of Fathers," in *Social Issues in Developmental Psychology*, ed. Helen L. Bee (New York, 1974), pp. 369, 371, emphasis in original; Levine, *Who Will Raise the Children?*, p. 29, emphasis in original.
54. Milton Kotelchuck, "The Nature of a Child's Ties to His Father," Ph.D. diss., Harvard University, 1972; quoted in Vivian Gornick, "Here's News: Fathers Mother as Much as Mothers," *Village Voice*, 13 October 1975, pp. 10–11.
55. Martin Greenberg and Norman Morris, "Engrossment: The Newborn's Impact upon the Father," *American Journal of Orthopsychiatry* 44 (July 1974): 526–527, 529, 522–523.
56. Gary Mitchell, William K. Redican, and Jody Gomber, "Lesson from a Primate: Males Can Raise Babies," *Psychology Today* 7 (April 1974): 64, 67–68. Studies of primate behavior, like studies of humans, have concentrated on maternal rather than paternal behavior. In a review of the literature on fathering among primates, Gary Mitchell and Edna M. Brandt wrote that although "in some species of New World monkeys, the father assumes the total burden of care for an infant, while the mother's only contacts with it involve nursing and cleaning for short periods of time . . . paternal behavior in nonhuman primates has been largely ignored by primatologists, who have meanwhile extensively and intensively studied maternal behavior." See Gary Mitchell and Edna M. Brandt, "Paternal Behavior in Primates," in *Primate Socialization*, ed. Frank Poirier (New York, 1972), p. 173.
57. Segal and Yahraes, *A Child's Journey*, pp. 128, 106–107; Gilbert W. Kliman and Albert Rosenfeld, *Responsible Parenthood* (New York, 1980), pp. 282–283; Marshall L. Hamilton, *Father's Influence on Children* (Chicago, 1977), pp. 140–141.
58. Schaffer, *Mothering*, p. 105; Benjamin Spock, "Women and Children: Male Chauvinist Spock Recants—Almost," in *The Future of the Family*, ed. Louise Kapp Howe (New York, 1972), pp. 154–155.
59. Spock, *Baby and Child Care*, rev. ed. (1976), pp. 46–47.
60. T. Berry Brazelton, "On Becoming a Family," *Redbook* 156 (February 1981): 56; Burton L. White, *The First Three Years of Life* (Englewood Cliffs, N.J., 1975), p. 256; Myron Brenton, "The Paradox of the American Father," in *The Future of the Family*, ed. Louise Kapp Howe (New York, 1972), p. 126, emphasis in original; Virginia Held, "The Equal Obligations of Mothers and Fathers," in *Having Children*, ed. Onora O'Neill and William Ruddick (New York, 1979), p. 236, emphasis in original.
61. Virginia Barber and Merrill Skaggs Maguire, *The Mother Person* (New York, 1975), p. 89; Letty Cottin Pogrebin, "A Partnership Plan for Parents Who Work (or: How to Bring Dad More into the Act and Give Mom a Break)," *Ladies' Home Journal* 97 (October 1980): 152.
62. Barber and Maguire, *The Mother Person*, p. 48; Shirley Radl, *Mother's Day Is*

Over (New York, 1973), pp. 3, 6; Angela Barron McBride, *The Growth and Development of Mothers* (New York, 1973), p. 121, emphasis in original.

63. Jane Lazarre, *The Mother Knot* (New York, 1976), p. 85; Barber and Maguire, *The Mother Person*, p. 114; Radl, *Mother's Day Is Over*, p. 19; Barber and Maguire, *The Mother Person*, p. 217.

64. Didi Moore, "The Only-Child Phenomenon," *New York Times Magazine*, 18 January 1981, p. 26; Maya Pines, "Only Isn't Lonely (or Spoiled or Selfish)," *Psychology Today* 15 (March 1981): 15–16.

65. Alvin Toffler, *Future Shock* (New York, 1970), p. 242; Betty Rollin, "Motherhood: Who Needs It?" in *The Future of the Family*, ed. Louise Kapp Howe (New York, 1972), pp. 82, 77; Jeanne Binstock, "Motherhood: An Occupation Facing Decline," *The Futurist* 6 (June 1972): 102. A number of antinatalist books have appeared over the last decade: Anna Silverman and Arnold Silverman, *The Case against Having Children* (New York, 1971); Ellen Peck, *The Baby Trap* (New York, 1971); Ellen Peck and Judith Senderowitz, eds., *Pronatalism: The Myth of Mom and Apple Pie* (New York, 1974); Katherine Harper, *The Childfree Alternative* (Brattleboro, Vt., 1980); Diana Burgwyn, *Marriage Without Children* (New York, 1981).

66. Geraldine Carro, "How to Raise Happy, Healthy Children," *Ladies' Home Journal* 97 (October 1980): 90.

67. Selma Fraiberg, *Every Child's Birthright: In Defense of Mothering* (New York, 1977), pp. 56, 84–88.

68. Erna Wright, *Common Sense in Child Rearing* (New York, 1973), pp. 214–215, 217; *Infant Care*, 13th rev. ed. (Washington, D.C. 1980), p. 54. Wright was also out of step with the times in her claim that the "only-child is a lonely child . . ." She urged women to have at least two children (p. 76).

69. Ibid., p. 222; quoted in Mary P. Ryan, *Womanhood in America: From Colonial Times to the Present* (New York, 1975), p. 408.

70. Elaine Heffner, *Mothering: The Emotional Experience of Motherhood after Freud and Feminism* (Garden City, N.Y., 1978), pp. 14, 12, 10, 169, emphasis added.

71. Wright, *Common Sense in Child Rearing*, pp. 69–70.

72. Gornick, "Here's News: Fathers Mother as Much as Mothers," p. 11; Levine, *Who Will Raise the Children?*, p. 17.

73. Zelda S. Klapper, "The Impact of the Women's Liberation Movement on Child Development Books," *American Journal of Orthopsychiatry* 41 (October 1971): 728.

74. Hans Sebald, *Momism: The Silent Disease of America* (Chicago, 1976), pp. 1–2, 169–170, 243, 246, 249, 261.

75. *Perspectives on Working Women*, p. 27; Friedan, *The Feminine Mystique*, chapter 1.

76. Olds, *The Mother Who Works Outside the Home*, p. 2; *Perspectives on Working Women*, p. 27.

77. Joan D. Mandle, *Women and Social Change in America* (Princeton, N.J., 1979), p. 115; Ryan, *Womanhood in America*, p. 400; Daniel Yankelovich, "New Rules in American Life," *Psychology Today* 15 (April 1981): 60, 69.
78. Cited in Moore, "The Only-Child Phenomenon," p. 26; cited in Ryan, *Womanhood in America*, p. 401.
79. Gornick, 'Here's News: Fathers Mother as Much as Mothers," p. 11; Ehrenreich and English, *For Her Own Good*, p. 26; Kotelchuck, "The Nature of a Child's Ties to His Father"; Gornick, "Here's News: Fathers Mother as Much as Mothers," p. 11.
80. Margaret Mead, "Some Theoretical Considerations on the Problem of Mother-Child Separation," *American Journal of Orthopsychiatry* 24 (July 1954): 477.
81. Slater, *Pursuit of Loneliness*, p. 70.
82. Elizabeth Janeway, "Who Is Sylvia? On the Loss of Sexual Paradigms," *Signs* 5 (Summer 1980): 574.

4: Good Housekeeping

1. Charlotte Perkins Gilman, *Women and Economics* (Boston, 1898), p. 237; see William F. Ogburn and M. F. Nimkoff, *Technology and the Changing Family* (Cambridge, 1955), p. 153, for an example of the conventional wisdom regarding technology and the time spent on housework.
2. Valerie Oppenheimer, *The Female Labor Force in the United States* (Berkeley, Los Angeles, London, 1970), pp. 29–39.
3. E. P. Thompson, "Time, Work Discipline, and Industrial Capitalism," *Past and Present* 38 (December 1967): 56–97.
4. Margaret Benston, "The Political Economy of Women's Liberation," in *The Politics of Housework*, ed. Ellen Malos (London, 1980), pp. 119–129.
5. Ann Oakley, *Woman's Work: The Housewife, Past and Present* (New York, 1976), p. 9; see, for example, Marshall Sahlins, *Stone Age Economics* (Chicago, 1972).
6. Leonore Davidoff, "The Rationalization of Housework," in *Dependence and Exploitation in Work and Marriage*, ed. Diana Leopold Barker and Sheila Allen (London, 1976), pp. 121–151; Margaret Mead, *Male and Female* (New York, 1955); George Peter Murdock, "Comparative Data on the Division of Labour by Sex," *Social Forces* 15 (1937): 553. The obvious exception to Murdock's statement is the occupation of wet nurse.
7. Quoted in Alice Morse Earle, *Homelife in Colonial Days* (New York, 1898), p. 252; quoted in Rolla Milton Tryon, *Household Manufactures in the United States, 1640–1860* (Chicago, 1917), pp. 96–97.
8. Quoted in Tryon, *Household Manufactures in the United States*, pp. 43–44.
9. Mary Beth Norton, *Liberty's Daughters: The Revolutionary Experience of American Women, 1750–1800* (Boston, 1980), pp. 21–22; Earle, *Homelife in Colonial Days*, p. 150; Julia C. Spruill, *Women's Life and Work in the Southern*

Colonies (Chapel Hill, N.C., 1938), p. 74; Earle, *Homelife in Colonial Days*, p. 166; quoted in Earle, *Homelife in Colonial Days*, p. 158.

10. Earle, *Homelife in Colonial Days*, pp. 212—213.
11. Ibid., p. 103.
12. Norton, *Liberty's Daughters*, p. 11; Earle, *Homelife in Colonial Days*, p. 255.
13. William A. Alcott, *The Young Housekeeper: or, Thoughts on Food and Cookery* (Boston, 1838), p. 32; Tryon, *Household Manufactures in the United States*, pp. 42—43; Victor Selden Clark, *History of Manufactures in the United States, 1860—1914*, vol. 1 (Washington, D.C., 1929), p. 438.
14. Tryon, *Household Manufactures in the United States*, pp. 244—247.
15. Margaret Reid, *Economics of Household Production* (New York, 1934), pp. 44—47.
16. Tryon, *Household Manufactures in the United States*, p. 276.
17. Ibid., pp. 303, 370—372.
18. H. I. Harwell, *The Domestic Manual: Or Family Directory, Containing Receipts in Arts, Trade, and Domestic Economy* (New London, Conn., 1816), p. 1.
19. John J. Aikin, *The Arts of Life: 1. Providing Food 2. Providing Clothing 3. Providing Shelter*, 1st U.S. ed. (Boston, 1830; orig. published, 1803), p. 2.
20. Lydia Maria Child, *The Frugal Housewife* (Boston, 1831), pp. 3—6, 92—96.
21. Sarah Josepha Hale, *The Good Housekeeper; Or the Way to Live Well and to Be Well While We Live* (Boston, 1839), p. 1.
22. Eliza Farrar, *The Young Lady's Friend* (New York, 1974; first published, 1836), p. 33; Mrs. A. J. Graves, *Woman in America: Being an Examination into the Moral and Intellectual Condition of American Female Society* (New York, 1843), p. 24; Eliza Leslie, *The House Book or, A Manual of Domestic Economy for Town and Country*, 8th ed. (Philadelphia, 1845), p. 4.
23. Catherine Beecher, *A Treatise on Domestic Economy* (New York, 1977; first published, 1841), p. 30; Alcott, *The Young Housekeeper*, p. 31; Beecher, *A Treatise on Domestic Economy*, pp. 44, 46.
24. "Learning vs. Housewifery," *Godey's Lady's Book* 18 (August 1839): 95.
25. Farrar, *The House Book*, pp. 90, 35; Mrs. L. G. Abele, *Woman in Her Various Relations: Containing Practical Rules for American Females* (New York, 1853), p. 11; Beecher, *A Treatise on Domestic Economy*, p. 148.
26. Alcott, *The Young Housekeeper*, p. 18; Lydia Sigourney, *Letters to Young Ladies*, 6th ed. (New York, 1841), p. 80; Beecher, *A Treatise on Domestic Economy*, p. 144.
27. Graves, *Woman in America*, p. 29; Alcott, *The Young Housekeeper*, pp. 37, 24—25, 52.
28. Beecher, *A Treatise on Domestic Economy*, p. 143; Alcott, *The Young Housekeeper*, p. 38.
29. Farrar, *The Young Lady's Friend*, p. 37; Alcott, *The Young Housekeeper*, p. 42; Beecher, *A Treatise on Domestic Economy*, pp. 39—40; Graves, *Woman in America*, p. 28.
30. Alcott, *The Young Housekeeper*, pp. 37, 39—40.

31. Ibid., p. 43; Graves, *Woman in America*, pp. 41–42, 55.
32. Alcott, *The Young Housekeeper*, p. 33; Graves, *Woman in America*, pp. 47–48.
33. Alcott, *The Young Housekeeper*, p. 52; Leslie, *The House Book*, pp. 227, 3.
34. Graves, *Woman in America*, pp. 70, 75, 77; Alcott, *The Young Housekeeper*, p. 28; Beecher, *A Treatise on Domestic Economy*, pp. 27–28.
35. Alcott, *The Young Housekeeper*, p. 76; Mrs. L. G. Abele, *The Mother's Book of Daily Duties* (New York, 1853), p. 192.
36. Beecher, *A Treatise on Domestic Economy*, pp. 147–148.
37. Graves, *Woman in America*, pp. xiv–xv.
38. Mary P. Ryan, "Femininity and Capitalism in Antebellum America," in *Capitalist Patriarchy and the Case for Socialist Feminism*, ed. Zillah R. Eisenstein (New York, 1979), p. 166; Susan M. Strasser, "An Enlarged Human Existence? Technology and Household Work in Nineteenth Century America," in *Women and Household Labor*, ed. Sarah Fenstermaker Berk (Beverly Hills, Calif., 1980), pp. 30–31.
39. Berk, *Women and Household Labor*, pp. 32–3, 45.
40. Ibid., p. 44; Ross M. Robertson, *History of the American Economy*, 2d ed. (New York, 1964), p. 337.
41. Strasser, "An Enlarged Human Existence?" pp. 33–35.
42. Ibid., pp. 36–37; Siegfried Giedion, *Mechanization Takes Command* (New York, 1948), p. 553.
43. Alice Kessler-Harris, *Women Have Always Worked* (Old Westbury, N.Y., 1981), 41–42; Strasser, "An Enlarged Human Existence?," p. 41.
44. Strasser, "An Enlarged Human Existence?," pp.40–41; Kessler-Harris, *Women Have Always Worked*, p. 41.
45. Barbara Ehrenreich and Deidre English, "The Manufacture of Housework," *Socialist Revolution* 26 (October–December 1975): 18; Helen Campbell, *The Easiest Way in Housekeeping and Cooking* (New York, 1881), p. 35.
46. Campbell, *The Easiest Way in Housekeeping and Cooking*, p. 36; Catherine E. Beecher and Harriet Beecher Stowe, *The American Woman's Home; or Principles of Domestic Science* (New York, 1869), p. 333.
47. Strasser, "An Enlarged Human Existence?" p. 43.
48. Beecher and Stowe, *The American Woman's Home*, pp. 15, 13; Campbell, *The Easiest Way in Housekeeping and Cooking*, p. 35.
49. William D. Andrews and Deborah C. Andrews, "Technology and the Housewife in Nineteenth Century America," *Women's Studies* 2 (1974): 317; quoted in Andrews and Andrews, "Technology and the Housewife," p. 317.
50. Quoted in Ann D. Gordon, Mari Jo Buhle, and Nancy E. Schrom, "Women in American Society: An Historical Contribution," *Radical America* 5 (1971): 32.
51. Jean Gardener, "Women's Domestic Labor," in *Capitalist Patriarchy and the*

Case for Socialist Feminism, ed. Zillah R. Eisenstein (New York, 1979), pp. 173–189; Gerda Lerner, "The American Housewife: An Historical Perspective," in *Feminist Perspectives on Housework and Child Care*, ed. Amy Swerdlow (transcript of a conference sponsored by Sarah Lawrence College, 1978), pp. 22–34. There is considerable Marxist literature on the nature of the housewife's work under capitalism and its hidden benefits to the capitalist system. See, for example, Wally Seccombe, "The Housewife and Her Labor under Capitalism," *New Left Review* 83 (January–February, 1974): 3–24 and *Radical America* 7 (July–October 1973). The entire volume deals with women's labor.

52. Gordon, Buhle, and Schrom, "Women in American Soiety," p. 51; *Ladies' Home Journal* 22 (January 1905): 31. See Ruth Schwartz Cowan, "A Case Study of Technological and Social Change: The Washing Machine and the Working Wife," in *Clio's Consciousness Raised*, ed. Mary Hartman and Lois W. Banner (New York, 1974), pp. 245–253, for a full discussion of the conventional wisdom about labor-saving devices.
53. Richard A. Berk and Sarah Fenstermaker Berk, *Labor and Leisure at Home: Content and Organization of the Household Day* (Beverly Hills, Calif., 1979); Hazel Kyrk, *Economic Problems of the Family* (New York, 1933), p. 52.
54. John Kenneth Galbraith, *Economics and the Public Purpose* (New York, 1973), p. 29.
55. Ibid., p. 33
56. Mead, *Male and Female*, p. 248.
57. Heidi I. Hartmann, "Capitalism and Women's Work in the Home, 1900–1930," Ph.D. dissertation, Yale University, 1974, p. 112.
58. Ibid., p. 87; Stuart Ewen, *Captains of Consciousness: Advertising and the Social Roots of Consumer Culture* (New York, 1976), p. 164.
59. Margaret Gibbons Wilson, *The American Woman in Transition: The Urban Influence, 1870–1920* (Westport, Conn., 1979), p. 83; Hartmann, "Capitalism and Women's Work in the Home," pp. 157, 166.
60. Ruth Schwartz Cowan, "Two Washes in the Morning and a Bridge Party at Night: The American Housewife between the Wars," *Women's Studies* 3 (1976): 159; idem, "The 'Industrial Revolution' in the Home: Household Technology and Social Change in the 20th Century," *Technology and Culture* 17 (January 1976): 4–5.
61. Cowan, "The 'Industrial Revolution' in the Home," p. 7; Hartmann, "Capitalism and Women's Work in the Home," p. 151.
62. Strasser, "An Enlarged Human Existence?," p. 39; Cowan, "The 'Industrial Revolution' in the Home," p. 7.
63. Quoted in Wilson, *The American Woman in Transition*, p. 84; Hartmann, "Capitalism and Women's Work in the Home," p. 154.
64. Hartmann, "Capitalism and Women's Work in the Home," pp. 109, 112.
65. Theodore Caplow, *The Sociology of Work* (Minneapolis, 1954), p. 266.

66. Hartmann, "Capitalism and Women's Work in the Home"; Jane Davison, *The Fall of a Doll's House* (New York, 1980), p. 81; Wilson, *The American Woman in Transition*, p. 77.
67. Mary L. Wade, "Refined Life on Small Incomes; Or, The Woman Who Does Her Own Work," *Proceedings of the Third Lake Placid Conference on Home Economics* (Lake Placid, N.Y., 1901), p. 101; Maria Parloa, "How I Plan a Week's Work Without a Servant," *Ladies' Home Journal* 22 (January 1905): 31.
68. Cowan, "A Case Study of Technological and Social Change," p. 247.
69. Reid, *Economics of Household Production*, p. 65.
70. Davison, *The Fall of a Doll's House*, p. 77; Maria Parloa, "How I Keep My House Clean and Sweet," *Ladies' Home Journal* 22 (February, 1905): 40; Helen Campbell, *Household Economics* (New York, 1907), p. 206; Ellen Swallow Richards, *The Cost of Cleanness* (New York, 1914), frontispiece.
71. Mrs. Julian Heath, "The New Kind of Housekeeping," *Ladies' Home Journal* 32 (January 1915): 2.
72. Karl Marx, *Capital* (New York, 1936; orig. published, 1867), p. 405.
73. Gilman, *Women and Economics*, pp. 14–15, 247, 257.
74. Thorstein Velben, *The Theory of the Leisure Class* (New York, 1912), pp. 55, 128.
75. Davison, *The Fall of a Doll's House*, p. 85.
76. Quoted in William D. Jenkins, "Housewifery and Motherhood: The Question of Role Change in the Progressive Era," in *Woman's Being, Woman's Place*, ed. Mary Kelley (Boston, 1979), pp. 146–147; quoted in Carol Lopate, "Ironies of the Home Economics Movement," *Edcentric: A Journal of Educational Change* 31–32 (November 1974): 56.
77. Anna M. Cooley, *Domestic Art in Woman's Education* (New York, 1911), p. viii.
78. Ibid., pp. 4, 67–69.
79. Helen Kinne and Anna M. Cooley, *The Home and the Family* (New York, 1919), p. 103.
80. Lydia May Balderston, *Housewifery* (Philadelphia, 1919).
81. Cooley, *Domestic Art in Woman's Education*, pp. 247, 251–252.
82. Henrietta I. Goodrich, "Suggestions for a Professional School of Home and Social Economics," *Proceedings of the Second Lake Placid Conference on Home Economics* (Lake Placid, N.Y., 1900), p. 39.
83. Editorial, *Ladies' Home Journal* 22 (January 1905): 22.
84. Wade, "Refined Life on Small Incomes," p. 97; Edward Bok, editorial, *Ladies' Home Journal* 28 (October 1911): 6.
85. Heath, "The New Kind of Housekeeping," p. 2.
86. Christine Frederick, *The New Housekeeping: Efficiency Studies in Home Management* (Garden City, N.Y., 1913), pp. ix, 11–12, 22.
87. Ibid., pp. 10, 103.

88. Ibid., p. 63; titles cited in Lopate, "Ironies of the Home Economics Movement," 56; quoted in Jenkins, "Housewifery and Motherhood," p. 145.
89. Christine Frederick, *The New Housekeeping*, pp. 25, 30—31.
90. Ibid., pp. 127, 131, 142.
91. Frederick, *Household Engineering: Scientific Management of the Home* (Chicago, 1919), p. 380; Frederick, *The New Housekeeping*, p. 70.
92. Frederick, quoted in Hartmann, "Capitalism and Women's Work in the Home," pp. 195—196; Frederick, *The New Housekeeping*, pp. 101, 233, emphasis in original.
93. Caplow, *The Sociology of Work*, p. 260.
94. Frederick, *The New Housekeeping*, p. 191.

5. House Beautiful

1. Letty Cottin Pogrebin, "Rethinking Housework," in *Feminist Perspectives on Housework and Child Care*, ed. Amy Swerdlow (transcript of a conference sponsored by Sarah Lawrence College, 1978), p. 52; Ruth Schwartz Cowan, "Two Washes in the Morning and a Bridge Party at Night: The American Housewife between the Wars," *Women's Studies* 3 (1976): 152.
2. Staffan Burenstam Linder, *The Harried Leisure Class* (New York, 1970), p. 40.
3. Benjamin R. Andrews, "The Home Woman as Buyer and Controller of Consumption," *Annals of the American Academy of Political and Social Sciences* 143 (May 1929): 41; Betty Friedan, *The Feminine Mystique* (New York, 1974), p. 197; Anna E. Richardson, "The Woman Administrator in the Modern Home," *Annals of the American Academy of Political and Social Sciences* 143 (May 1929): 25; Christine Frederick, *Selling Mrs. Consumer* (New York, 1929), p. 250; Loring A. Schuler, editorial, *Ladies' Home Journal* 45 (January 1928): 32.
4. Stuart Ewen, *Captains of Consciousness: Advertising and the Social Roots of Consumer Culture* (New York, 1976), pp. 115—116; Heidi I. Hartmann, "Capitalism and Women's Work in the Home, 1900—1930", Ph.D. diss., Yale University, 1974, pp. 96, 159.
5. Hartmann, "Capitalism and Women's Work in the Home," pp. 346—349.
6. Cowan, "Two Washes in the Morning," pp. 159, 161—162; Hartmann, "Capitalism and Women's Work in the Home," pp. 161—162.
7. Cowan, "Two Washes in the Morning," p. 159; Jane Davison, *The Fall of a Doll's House* (New York, 1980), p. 82. By 1930 the icebox and kitchen range were standard equipment even in working class homes (Cowan, "Two Washes in the Morning," pp. 164).
8. Cowan, "Two Washes in the Morning," p. 162; Siegfried Giedion, *Mechanization Takes Command* (New York, 1948), p. 570.

9. Hartmann, "Capitalism and Women's Work in the Home," p. 166; Ross M. Robertson, *History of the American Economy*, 2d ed. (New York, 1964), p. 336; Robert Lynd and Helen Lynd, *Middletown* (New York, 1929), p. 155.
10. Lynd and Lynd, *Middletown*, p. 165.
11. Ibid., pp. 169–170.
12. Cowan, "Two Washes in the Morning," pp. 148–149.
13. *Saturday Evening Post*, 18 February 1928, p. 60; Loring A. Schuler, editorial, *Ladies' Home Journal* 46 (February 1929): 30; Frederick, *Selling Mrs. Consumer*, p. 169.
14. John Kenneth Galbraith, *Economics and the Public Purpose* (New York, 1973), pp. 31–33; Ewen, *Captains of Consciousness*, pp. 35–36, 167.
15. Davison, *The Fall of a Doll's House*, p. 93.
16. Galbraith, *Economics and the Public Purpose*, pp. 30–31.
17. Theodore Caplow, *The Sociology of Work* (Minneapolis, 1954), p. 268.
18. Loring A. Schuler, editorial, *Ladies' Home Journal* 46 (March 1929): 34; Mildred Maddocks Bently, "Household Engineering Applied," *Ladies' Home Journal* 42 (April 1925): 12, 145; *Ladies' Home Journal* (August 1924).
19. Andrews, "The Home Woman as Buyer and Controller of Consumption," p. 41; Silas Bent, "Woman's Place Is in the Home," *Century* 116 (June 1929): 211; Loring A. Schuler, editorial, *Ladies' Home Journal* 45 (January 1928): 32; Frederick, *Selling Mrs. Consumer*, p. 247; Loring A. Schuler, editorial, *Ladies' Home Journal* 46 (January 1929): 22.
20. Ruth Schwartz Cowan, "The 'Industrial Revolution' in the Home: Household Technology and Social Change in the 20th Century," *Technology and Culture* 17 (January 1976): 21; Clara H. Zillessen, "When Housework Is Not Drudgery," *Ladies' Home Journal* 44 (January 1927): 127, 133.
21. Andrews, "The Home Woman as Buyer and Controller of Consumption," p. 41; Ewen, *Captains of Consciousness*, p. 168.
22. Cowan, "Two Washes in the Morning," p. 155; quoted in Ewen, *Captains of Consciousness*, pp. 173–174, 170.
23. Quoted in Lynd and Lynd, *Middletown*, p. 173; quoted in Ewen, *Captains of Consciousness*, p. 161.
24. Benjamin R. Andrews, *Economics of the Household* (New York, 1923), p. 409; Elizabeth Cook, "The Kitchen Sink Complex," *Ladies' Home Journal* 48 (September 1931): 12; Poppy Cannon, "Pin Money Slaves," *Forum* 84 (August 1930): 99.
25. Frederick, *Selling Mrs. Consumer*, p. 251.
26. Ibid., p. 180, emphasis in original; Ewen, *Captains of Consciousness*, pp. 166–167.
27. Bently, "Household Engineering Applied," p. 36; Lillian M. Gilbreth, *The Home-maker and Her Job* (New York, 1928), pp. vii, 85.
28. Gilbreth, *The Home-maker and Her Job*, pp. 87, 92.
29. Ibid., pp. 93, 97–98, 106.

30. Lynd and Lynd, *Middletown*, p. 171; Gove Hambridge and Dorothy Cooke Hambridge, "Leisure to Live," *Ladies' Home Journal* 46 (May 1930): 30.
31. Andrews, *Economics of the Household*, pp. 408, 55.
32. Bell Wiley, *So You're Going to Get Married!* (Philadelphia 1938), pp. 110–111, 115, 118–119; Cannon, "Pin Money Slaves," p. 101.
33. Hartmann, "Capitalism and Women's Work in the Home," pp. 158, 160; Lynd and Lynd, *Middletown*, p. 175n.
34. Ruth Lindquist, *The Family in the Present Social Order* (Chapel Hill, N.C., 1931), pp. 37–39.
35. Richardson, "The Woman Administrator in the Modern Home," p. 22; Margaret Reid, *Economics of Household Production* (New York, 1934), pp. 91–92.
36. Richardson, "The Woman Administrator in the Modern Home," p. 23; Lindquist, *The Family in the Present Social Order*, p. 42.
37. Nona Glazer, "Everyone Needs Three Hands: Doing Unpaid and Paid Work," in *Women and Household Labor*, ed. Sarah Fenstermaker Berk (Beverly Hills, Calif., 1980), p. 259.
38. Ruth Milkman, "Women's Work and Economic Crisis: Some Lessons of the Great Depression," *Review of Radical Political Economics* 8 (1976): 81–82; Cowan, "Two Washes in the Morning," pp. 167–168; Jean Gardner, "Women's Domestic Labor," in *Capitalist Patriarchy and the Case for Socialist Feminism*, ed. Zillah R. Eisenstein (New York, 1979), pp. 186–187.
39. Cowan argues that the feminine mystique first arose in the 1920s, not in the late 1940s, as Friedan would have it (Cowan, "Two Washes in the Morning"; Friedan, *The Feminine Mystique*).
40. Ewen, *Captains of Consciousness*, p. 165.
41. Barbara Ehrenreich and Deidre English, "The Manufacture of Housework," *Socialist Revolution* 26 (October–December 1975): 36; Frederick, *Selling Mrs. Consumer*, pp. 171, 22, 43; quoted in Hartmann, "Capitalism and Women's Work in the Home," p. 378.
42. Davison, *The Fall of a Doll's House*, p. 179; Friedan, *The Feminine Mystique*, p. 231; Joann Vanek, "Household Technology and Social Status: Rising Living Standards and Status and Residence Differences in Housework," *Technology and Culture* 19 (July 1978): 394.
43. Helena Z. Lopata, *Occupation: Housewife* (New York, 1971), p. 173; quoted in Giedion, *Mechanization Takes Command*, p. 619.
44. Lee Rainwater, Richard P. Coleman, and Gerald Handel, *Workingman's Wife* (New York, 1959), p. 215; quoted in Friedan, *The Feminine Mystique*, pp. 206, 208.
45. John P. Robinson, "Housework Technology and Household Work," in *Women and Household Labor*, ed. Sarah Fenstermaker Berk (Beverly Hills, Calif., 1980), p. 54; Joann Vanek, "Time Spent on Housework," *Scientific American* 231 (May 1974): 116–120.

46. Joann Vanek, "Housewives as Workers," in *Women Working*, ed. Ann H. Stromberg and Shirley Harkess (Palo Alto, Calif., 1978), p. 400; Katherine E. Walker and Margaret E. Woods, *Time Use: A Measure of Household Production of Family Goods and Services* (Washington, D.C., 1976), pp. 32, 43; Vanek, "Time Spent in Housework," pp. 117, 119; J. N. Morgan, I. Sirageldin, and N. Baerwaldt, *Productive Americans* (Ann Arbor, Mich., 1966), p. 111. The twelve country time-use survey is Alexander Szalai, ed., *The Use of Time: Daily Activities of Urban and Suburban Populations in Twelve Countries* (The Hague, 1972), p. 125.
47. Vanek, "Time Spent on Housework," p. 118; Vanek, "Housewives as Workers," p. 402.
48. C. Northcote Parkinson, *Parkinson's Law and Other Studies in Administration* (Boston, 1957), p. 2.
49. Friedan, *The Feminine Mystique*, pp. 227, 229, emphasis in original.
50. Source: King Features, New York. The hints from Heloise are taken from those published in her newspaper column in the early 1970s and from her book *Heloise All Around the House* (New York, 1967). For an analysis of the time saving vs. time spending nature of Heloise's hints see, Maxine L. Margolis, "In Hartford, Hannibal, and (New) Hampshire, Heloise Is Hardly Helpful," *Ms. Magazine* 9 (June 1976): 28–36.
51. Davison, *The Fall of a Doll's House*, p. 196.
52. Ann Oakley, *The Sociology of Housework* (New York, 1974), pp. 51, 53.
53. Quoted in Davison, *The Fall of a Doll's House*, p. 183.
54. Oakley, *The Sociology of Housework*, p. 104; Margaret Mead, *Male and Female* (New York, 1955), p. 247. This phenomenon is not limited to the United States. After a time-use survey of twelve countries, Szalai concluded: "One of the most curious cross-national findings with regard to housewives' use of time is the fact that they tend to extend their housework more or less in proportion to their husbands' working hours. In social groups and strata where employed men work longer hours, there is a distinct tendency for housewives to put more hours into their own daily housework" (Szalai, *The Use of Time*, p. 20).
55. Rainwater, Coleman, and Handel, *Workingman's Wife*, p. 214; quoted in Friedan, *The Feminine Mystique*, p. 207.
56. Oakley, *Woman's Work*, p. 93, emphasis in original; Oakley, *The Sociology of Housework*, pp. 104, 111.
57. Nona Glazer-Malbin, "Housework," *Signs* 1 (Summer 1976): 920; Philip Slater, *Earthwalk* (New York, 1974), p. 180. See Glazer, "Everyone Needs Three Hands," for a discussion of the shoddiness of goods manufactured for the home.
58. Quoted in Russell Lynes, *The Domesticated Americans* (New York, 1963), pp. 271–272; quoted in Friedan, *The Feminine Mystique*, p. 207.
59. Ferdinand Lundberg and Marynia Farnham, *Modern Woman: The Lost Sex* (New York, 1947), p. 369; Mirra Komarovsky, *Women in the Modern World*

(Boston, 1953), p. 116.

60. Edith De Rham, *The Love Fraud* (New York, 1965), p. 156; Robinson, "Household Technology and Household Work," pp. 57, 59; Frank Stafford and Greg Duncan, "The Use of Time and Technology by Households in the United States," manuscript, Department of Economics, University of Michigan, Ann Arbor, 1977, p. 36. In Robinson's study, once women's higher employment status, lower marriage rate, fewer children, younger age, higher education, and higher income were taken into account, the 1975 sample of women still spent 22 minutes less a day in family care than did the 1965 sample of women. This came to an average decrease of 2.5 hours per week spent on housework ("Household Technology and Household Work," p. 61). In this and the other time budget studies cited, although national samples were used, uniform definitions of housework were not established. Some included child care while others did not.

61. Lawrence Van Gelder, "Time Spent on Housework Declines," *New York Times*, 22 May 1979, section 3, p. 10; Heidi I. Hartmann, "The Family as the Locus of Gender, Class, and Political Struggle: The Example of Housework," *Signs* 6 (Spring 1981): 385; Robinson, "Household Technology, and Household Work," p. 55; Berk and Berk, *Labor and Leisure at Home*, p. 232.

62. Joann Vanek, "Household Work, Wage Work, and Sexual Equality," in *Women and Household Labor*, ed. Sarah Fenstermaker Berk (Beverly Hills, Calif., 1980), p. 279; Martin Meissner et al., "No Exit for Wives: Sexual Division of Labor and the Cumulation of Household Demands," *Canadian Review of Sociology and Anthropology* 12 (November 1975): 433; Hartmann, "The Family as the Locus of Gender, Class, and Political Struggle," p. 383.

63. Nadine Brozan, "Men and Housework: Do They or Don't They," *New York Times*, 1 November 1980, p. 52.

64. Robinson, "Household Technology and Household Work," pp. 55–56. The use of commercial food services—restaurants, fast-food establishments, school cafeterias—is more widespread than in the past and may partially explain the reduction in hours devoted to housework.

65. Ibid., p. 62.

66. Ibid., p. 65.

67. Alice Skelsey, *The Working Mother's Guide to Her Home, Her Family and Herself* (New York, 1970), pp. 9, 13, 23–24, emphasis in original.

68. Sally Werdkos Olds, *The Mother Who Works Outside the Home* (New York, 1975), pp. 72, 74–75.

69. Mary Ellen Pinkham and Pearl Higginbotham, *Mary Ellen's Best of Helpful Hints* (New York, 1979).

70. Skelsey, *The Working Mother's Guide*, pp. 18, 44, 49.

71. Olds, *The Mother Who Works Outside the Home*, p. 71; Heloise, *Hints from*

Heloise (New York, 1981), pp. xi—xii; Pinkham and Higginbotham, *Mary Ellen's Best of Helpful Hints.*

72. Arlene Rossen Cardozo, *Women at Home* (New York, 1976), pp. 38, 32.
73. Marabel Morgan, *The Total Woman* (New York, 1975), pp. 31, 28.
74. Rae André, *Homemakers: The Forgotten Workers* (Chicago, 1981), p. 44.
75. Glazer, "Everyone Needs Three Hands," p. 257.
76. Brozan, "Men and Housework," p. 52.
77. André, *Homemakers*, pp. 44, 61.
78. Glazer, "Everyone Needs Three Hands," p. 256; Ismail Sirageldin, *Non-market Components of National Income* (Ann Arbor, 1969).

6. When is Women's Place in the Home?

1. Ann Oakley, *Woman's Work: The Housewife, Past and Present* (New York, 1976); Valerie Oppenheimer, *The Female Labor Force in the United States* (Berkeley, Los Angeles, London, 1970).
2. William H. Chafe, *The American Woman: Her Changing Social, Economic, and Political Roles, 1920–1970* (New York, 1972), p. 54.
3. Jessie Bernard, *Women, Wives and Mothers* (Chicago, 1975).
4. M. Kay Martin and Barbara Voorhies, *The Female of the Species* (New York, 1975).
5. Robert W. Smuts, *Women and Work in America* (New York, 1971), p. 137.
6. Roger Thompson, *Women in Stuart England and America* (Boston, 1974), p. 103.
7. Elizabeth Abbott, *Women in Industry* (New York, 1910), pp. 18–20.
8. Elizabeth Anthony Dexter, *Colonial Women of Affairs* (Boston, 1924); Julia C. Spruill, *Women's Life and Work in the Southern Colonies* (Chapel Hill, N.C., 1938); Richard Morris, *Studies in the History of American Law* (New York, 1930).
9. Gerda Lerner, *The Majority Finds Its Past* (New York, 1979), p. 22; W. Elliot Brownlee and Mary M. Brownlee, *Women in the American Economy* (New Haven, 1976), pp. 41–42.
10. Benjamin Wadsworth, "The Well-Ordered Family, or, Relative Duties," in *The Colonial American Family: Collected Essays* (New York, 1972; first published, 1712, Boston), p. 29; Cotton Mather, *Ornaments of the Daughters of Zion*, 3d ed. (Delmar, N.Y., 1978; first published, 1741), p. 7; Nancy F. Cott, *The Bonds of Womanhood: Woman's Sphere in New England, 1780–1835* (New Haven, 1977), p. 22.
11. Elizabeth Faulkner Baker, *Technology and Women's Work* (New York, 1964).
12. Quoted in Alice Kessler-Harris, *Women Have Always Worked* (Westbury, N.Y., 1981), p. 8.
13. Carl N. Degler, *At Odds: Women and the Family in America from the Revolution to the Present* (New York, 1980), p. 368.
14. Quoted in Baker, *Technology and Women's Work*, pp. 5–6; Alice Kessler-

Harris, "Stratifying by Sex: Understanding the History of Working Women," in *Labor Market Segmentation*, ed. Richard C. Edwards, Michael Reich, and David M. Gordon (Lexington, Mass., 1975), p. 220; Abbott, *Women in Industry*, pp. 55–56.

15. Kessler-Harris, "Stratifying by Sex"; Brownlee and Brownlee, *Women in the American Economy*, pp. 16–17; Baker, *Technology and Women's Work*, p. 52.
16. Abbott, *Women in Industry*, p. 360.
17. Ibid.
18. Brownlee and Brownlee, *Women in the American Economy*, pp. 212–213.
19. Ibid., pp. 197, 213–214; quoted in Baker, *Technology and Women's Work*, p. 84.
20. I am indebted to Kessler-Harris, "Stratifying by Sex," for the ideas expressed in this paragraph.
21. Baker, *Technology and Women's Work*, pp. 59–60.
22. Brownlee and Brownlee, *Women in the American Economy*, p. 22.
23. Dee Garrison, "The Tender Technicians: The Feminization of Public Librarianship, 1876–1905," in *Clio's Consciousness Raised*," ed. Mary Hartman and Lois W. Banner (New York, 1974), pp. 158–178.
24. Karen O. Mason, Maris A. Vinovskis, and Tamara K. Hareven, "Women's Work and the Life Course in Essex County, Massachusetts, 1880," in *Transitions: The Family and the Life Course in Historical Perspective*, ed. Tamara K. Hareven (New York, 1978), pp. 187–216.
25. Smuts, *Women and Work in America*, pp. 113–122; Azel Ames, *Sex in Industry* (Boston, 1875); quoted in Margery Davies, "Women's Place Is at the Typewriter: The Feminization of the Clerical Labor Force," in *Labor Market Segmentation*, ed. Edwards, Reich, and Gordon.
26. Smuts, *Women and Work in America*, p. 119.
27. Oakley, *Woman's Work*, p. 45.
28. Brownlee and Brownlee, *Women in the American Economy*, p. 3; Degler, *At Odds*, p. 384.
29. Smuts, *Women and Work in America*, p. 23.
30. Ibid., p. 141.
31. Peter Gabriel Filene, *Him/Her/Self* (New York, 1976), p. 25.
32. Quoted in Baker, *Technology and Women's Work*, p. 81.
33. See Thomas F. Gossett, *Race: The History of an Idea in America* (New York, 1965), chapter 12, for a discussion of early twentieth-century views on immigrant labor. Abbott, *Women in Industry*, p. 323; cited in Smuts, *Women and Work in America*, p. 131.
34. Sophonisba Breckinridge, *Women in the Twentieth Century* (New York, 1933); Davies, "Women's Place Is at the Typewriter," p. 292.
35. Cited in Breckinridge, *Women in the Twentieth Century*, p. 100.
36. Chafe, *The American Woman*, p. 52.
37. Quoted in ibid., p. 53.
38. In Friedan's words, "Fulfillment as a woman had only one definition for

American women *after 1949*—the housewife-mother" (*The Feminine Mystique* [New York, 1974], p. 38, emphasis added). Her error is in claiming that this attitude only dates from 1949; Oppenheimer, *The Female Labor Force in the United States*, p. 3; Chafe, *The American Woman*, pp. 54, 79.

39. Chafe, *The American Woman*, p. 64; Lorine Pruette, *Women and Leisure* (New York, 1972; first published, 1924), pp. 100–101.
40. Oppenheimer, *The Female Labor Force in the United States*, p. 130; *The New York Times*, 16 December 1928.
41. Pruette, *Women and Leisure*, p. 62; Filene, *Him/Her/Self*, p. 126.
42. Chafe, *The American Woman*.
43. Quoted in Leila J. Rupp, *Mobilizing Women for War* (Princeton, 1978), p. 61.
44. Cited in Kessler-Harris, *Women Have Always Worked*, p. 126. The primary identification of career women with their domestic role is still with us; newswriters questioned Paula Hawkins at her first press conference after her election to the United States Senate about who did the family laundry (*Gainsville Sun*, 11 November 1980).
45. Anonymous, "I Wish I Had Married and Found Life," *Good Housekeeping* 77 (November 1923): 141; quoted in Chafe, *The American Woman*, p. 105.
46. Quoted in Filene, *Him/Her/Self*, p. 155.
47. Chafe, *The American Woman*, pp. 56–57.
48. Degler, *At Odds*, p. 415; Ruth Milkman, "Women's Work and Economic Crisis: Some Lessons from the Great Depression," *Review of Radical Political Economics* 8 (1976): 73–97, 81.
49. Chafe, *The American Woman*, p. 108; Oppenheimer, *The Female Labor Force in the United States*, pp. 127–132; Filene, *Him/Her/Self*, p. 155; Degler, *At Odds*, p. 414.
50. Rose Wilder Lane, "Women's Place Is in the Home," *Ladies' Home Journal* 53 (October 1936): 18; Dorothy Thompson, "If I Had a Daughter," *Ladies' Home Journal* 56 (September 1939): 4; Maureen Honey, "Images of Women in the *Saturday Evening Post*, 1931–1936," *Journal of Popular Culture* 10 (1976): 252–258.
51. Chafe, *The American Woman*, pp. 91–94.
52. Milkman, "Woman's Work and Economic Crisis, pp. 73–97; Jean Collier Brown, *The Negro Woman Worker* (Washington, D.C. 1938), p. 3.
53. Hadley Cantril, *Public Opinion, 1935–1946* (Princeton, 1951), pp. 1044–1075. Employed women were not the only scapegoats during the 1930s. The rabid anti-Semitism of Father Coughlin and others who blamed the depression on an "international conspiracy of Jewish bankers" also sought to "explain" the disastrous economic conditions through the age-old practice of creating a scapegoat.
54. United States Department of Labor, *Handbook on Women Workers* (Washington, D.C., 1975), pp. 15, 18; Smuts, *Women and Work in America*, p. 145; Glen C. Cain, *Married Women in the Labor Force* (Chicago, 1966),

p. 1; Chafe, *The American Woman*, p. 57.

55. Dorothy Thompson, "It's a Woman's World," *Ladies' Home Journal* 57 (July 1940): 25; Oppenheimer, *The Female Labor Force in the United States*, p. 92; Chafe, *The American Woman*, p. 283.
56. Quoted in Rupp, *Mobilizing Women for War*, p. 97.
57. Quoted in ibid., p. 96.
58. Quoted in ibid., p. 242.
59. Filene, *Him/Her/Self*, p. 169.
60. Carl N. Degler, "Revolution Without Ideology: The Changing Place of Women in America," in *The American Woman*, ed. Robert J. Lifton (Boston, 1967), pp. 140–141.
61. Cantril, *Public Opinion*, p. 1045.
62. Ibid., p. 1047; Chafe, *The American Woman*, pp. 180–186; Rupp, *Mobilizing Women for War*.
63. A. G. Mazerik, "Getting Rid of the Women," *Atlantic Monthly* 176 (June 1945): 79–83.
64. Quoted in Chafe, *The American Woman*, p. 177; quoted in Karen Beck Skold, "The Job He Left Behind: American Women in the Shipyards During World War II," in *Women, War and Revolution*, ed. Carol R. Berkin and Clara M. Lovett (New York, 1980), p. 67; Constance Roe, "Can the Girls Hold Their Jobs in Peacetime?," *Saturday Evening Post* 216 (September 1944): 28–39.
65. Ferdinand Lundberg and Marynia Farnham, *Modern Woman: The Lost Sex* (New York, 1947).
66. Chafe, *The American Woman*, p. 190; Smuts, *Women and Work in America*, p. 146.
67. Cited in Friedan, *The Feminine Mystique*, p. 53.
68. Degler, "Revolution Without Ideology," p. 205; United States Department of Labor, *Handbook of Women Workers*, p. 17; Chafe, *The American Woman*, p. 218.
69. Quoted in Kessler-Harris, *Women Have Always Worked*, pp. 143–144.
70. Oppenheimer, *The Female Labor Force in the United States*, pp. 97–107.
71. Ibid., p. 156–157.
72. Marvin Harris, *America Now: The Anthropology of a Changing Culture* (New York, 1981), p. 44.
73. Juanita M. Kreps, *Sex in the Marketplace* (Baltimore, 1971), p. 34.
74. Oppenheimer, *The Female Labor Force in the United States*, p. 171.
75. Ibid., p. 131.
76. Filene, *Him/Her/Self*, p. 174; Smuts, *Women and Work in America*, pp. 64, 146–148.
77. Friedan, *The Feminine Mystique*, p. 46; Ryan, *Womanhood in America*, p. 332.
78. Helene Deutsch, *The Psychology of Women* (New York, 1944); Chafe, *The American Woman*, p. 210; Florida Scott-Maxwell, "Should Mothers of Young Children Work?" *Ladies' Home Journal* 75 (November 1958): 158.

79. Florida Scott-Maxwell, "Women Know They Are Not Men," *Ladies' Home Journal* 75 (November 1958): 60; Agnes E. Meyer, "Women Aren't Men," *Atlantic Monthly* 186 (February 1950): 28–29; quoted in Carol Hymowitz and Michaele Weissman, *A History of Women in America* (New York, 1978), p. 325.
80. Ashley Montagu, "The Triumph and Tragedy of American Women," *Saturday Review*, 27 September 1958, p. 34.
81. Oppenheimer, *The Female Labor Force in the United States*, p. 104.
82. Degler, *At Odds*, p. 432; John Kenneth Galbraith, *Economics and the Public Purpose* (New York, 1973).
83. United States Department of Labor, *Perspectives on Working Women: A Databook* (Washington, D.C., 1980), p. 4; United States Department of Labor, Bureau of Labor Statistics, unpublished marital and family statistics, January 1983. In 1950 only 12 percent of women with preschool children were in the labor force. The participation rate for this group has increased more than fourfold in thirty years.
84. United States Department of Labor, *Employment in Perspective: Working Women* (Washington, D.C., 1982); Nancy S. Barrett, "Women in the Job Market: Occupations, Earnings, and Career Opportunities," in *The Subtle Revolution: Women at Work*, ed. Ralph E. Smith (Washington, D.C., 1979), pp. 31–61; Juanita M. Kreps and R. John Leaper, "Home Work, Market Work and the Allocation of Time," in *Women in the American Economy*, ed. Juanita M. Kreps (Englewood Cliffs, N.J., 1976), p. 70.
85. Joan Klein, "Sneak Preview: the 1980 Census," *Working Woman* 5 (September 1980): 73.
86. Oppenheimer, *The Female Labor Force in the United States*; United States Department of Commerce, *A Statistical Portrait of Women in the United States* (Washington, D.C., 1976), p. 35.
87. Oppenheimer, *The Female Labor Force in the United States*, p. 99; Mary Stevenson, "Women's Wages and Job Segregation," in *Labor Market Segmentation*, ed. R. C. Edwards, Michael Reich, and David M. Gordon (Lexington, Mass., 1975), p. 250; Barbara Deckard and Howard Sherman, "Monopoly Power and Sex Discrimination," *Politics and Society* 4 (1974): 475–482; Oppenheimer, *The Female Labor Force in the United States*, p. 100.
88. Kreps, *Sex in the Marketplace*, p. 38 emphasis in original; Stevenson, "Women's Wages and Job Segregation," p. 253; quoted in the *Gainesville Sun*, 7 October 1980.
89. Kristin Moore and Isabel Sawhill, "Implications of Women's Employment for Home and Family," in *Women and the American Economy*, ed. Juanita M. Kreps (Englewood Cliffs, 1976), pp. 102–122; United States Department of Labor, *Perspectives on Working Women: A Databook* (Washington, D.C., 1980), p. 53.
90. United States Department of Labor, *Perspectives on Working Women*, pp.

20–22; Ralph E. Smith, "The Movement of Women into the Labor Force," in *The Subtle Revolution*, ed. Ralph E. Smith (Washington, D.C., 1979), pp. 1–29; Paul Ryscavage, "More Wives in the Labor Force Have Husbands with 'Above-Average' Incomes," *Monthly Labor Review* 102 (June 1979): 40–42.

91. United States Department of Labor, *Handbook on Women Workers*, p. 137; cited in Barbara Ehrenreich and Deirdre English, *For Her Own Good: 150 Years of the Experts' Advice to Women* (New York, 1978), p. 257.
92. Clair Vickery, "Women's Economic Contribution to the Family," in *The Subtle Revolution*, ed. Ralph E. Smith (Washington, D.C., 1979), pp. 159–200.
93. *National Now Times* 16 (March 1983): 2.
94. Degler, *At Odds*, p. 433; *Ms. Magazine* 9 (June 1981): 45; Oppenheimer, *The Female Labor Force in the United States*, pp. 50. 181.
95. Catherine East, "The Current Status of the Employment of Women," in *Women in the Work Force*, ed. Mildred E. Katzell and William C. Byham (New York, 1972), pp. 7–14.
96. Dorothy Thompson, "It's All the Fault of Women," *Ladies' Home Journal* 77 (May 1960): 16.
97. Betty Hannah Hoffman, "I'm Going to Get a Job," *Ladies' Home Journal* 80 (July 1963): 107; Billy Graham, "Jesus and the Liberated Woman," *Ladies' Home Journal* 87 (December 1970): 42.
98. *New York Times*, 19 January 1977, emphasis added.
99. Degler, "Revolution Without Ideology."

7. She Has Only Herself to Blame

1. Ferdinand Lundberg and Marynia Farnham, *Modern Women: The Lost Sex* (New York, 1947), p. 1; Jean Baer, *How to Be an Assertive (Not Aggressive) Woman* (New York, 1976), p. 12; quoted in *Ms. Magazine*, April 1982.
2. William Ryan, *Blaming the Victim* (New York, 1971), pp. xiii, 9, 24.
3. See, for example, Daniel Patrick Moynihan, *The Negro American Family* (Washington, D.C., 1965); Janice E. Perlman, *The Myth of Marginality: Urban Poverty and Politics in Rio de Janeiro* (Berkeley, Los Angeles, London, 1976).
4. Elliot Aronson, "The Rationalizing Animal," *Psychology Today* 6 (December 1973): 46–52.
5. For discussions of the characteristics of minority groups and women as a minority group see Louis Wirth, "The Problems of Minority Groups," in *Man in the World Crisis*, ed. Ralph Linton (New York, 1945), pp. 347–350; Helen M. Hacker, "Women as a Minority Group," *Social Forces* 30 (1951): 60–69; William Chafe, *Women and Equality* (New York, 1977); Ellen Keniston and Kenneth Keniston, "An American Anachronism: The Image of Women and Work," *American Scholar* 33 (1964): 335.

6. Susan Brownmiller, *Against Our Will: Men, Women and Rape* (New York, 1976), p. 373; Arthur S. Fleming, *Window Dressing on the Set: Women and Minorities in TV* (Washington, D.C.: 1977).
7. Philip Wylie, *Generation of Vipers* (New York, 1942), chapter 11; quoted in the *Gainesville Sun*, 26 April 1981.
8. Robert W. Smuts, *Women and Work in America* (New York, 1971), p. 108. Quoted in *Ms. Magazine* 3 (December 1975). Early in this century a physiological argument was used against women. When a library official was asked why women librarians were paid so much less than their male counterparts, he replied: "Women are hampered by their delicate physique and inability to endure continued mental strain" (Quoted in Gena Corea, *The Hidden Malpractice* [New York, 1977], p. 89). The "pin money" argument was also used by the opponents of the Equal Pay Act passed in 1963.
9. William H. Chafe, *The American Woman: Her Changing Social, Economic and Political Roles, 1920–1970* (New York, 1972), p. 63; Nancy Kreiter, "Closing the Wage Gap," *Spokeswoman* 10 (October 1980): 6; United States Department of Labor, *Perspectives on Working Women* (Washington, D.C. 1980), p. 1; Eliot Janeway, "Reviving the Economy," *Working Women* 2 (October 1977): p. 66.
10. *Time* magazine, 18 October 1976; quoted in Sylvia Porter, "Women Swell Jobless Rolls," *Gainesville Sun*, 19 August 1976. A similar pattern of victim blaming is evident in Canada. There the finance minister blamed "terrible unemployment" on "two forces outside government control—the baby boom and the influx of women into the work force."
11. See Chafe, *The American Woman*, chapter 2, for a further discussion of these points.
12. Joy F. Sokeitus and Kathy McFadden, *Myths about Working Women* (Pittsburgh, n.d.); United States Department of Labor, *The Myth and the Reality* (Washington, D.C., 1975); Barbara R. Bergman, "The Economics of Women's Liberation," *Challenge* 16 (1973): 14.
13. United States Department of Labor, *The Myth and the Reality*; Esther Peterson, "Working Women," in *The Woman in America*, ed. Robert Jay Lifton (Boston, 1967), pp. 144–172.
14. Quoted in Corea, *The Hidden Malpractice*, pp. 98–99.
15. Smuts, *Women and Work in America*, p. 108.
16. Peterson, "Working Women," p. 166; quoted in *Ms. Magazine*, July 1977.
17. United States Department of Labor, *Perspectives on Working Women*, p. 2.
18. Margaret Hennig and Anne Jardim, *The Managerial Woman* (New York, 1977).
19. Elizabeth Faulkner Baker, *Technology and Women's Work* (New York, 1964), p. 74; quoted in *Ms. Magazine*, April 1975; quoted in Robert Daley, "The Search for Sam: Why It Took So Long," *New York Magazine*, 22 August 1977.

20. Amitai Etzioni, *The Semi-professions and Their Organizations* (New York, 1969), p. xv.
21. *New York Times*, 11 November 1979.
22. Naomi Weisstein, "Psychology Constructs the Female," in *Women in Sexist Society*, ed. Vivian Gornick and Barbara K. Moran (New York, 1972), p. 217; Phyllis Chesler, "Patient and Patriarch: Women in the Psychotherapeutic Relationship," in *Women in Sexist Society*, ed. Gornick and Moran, p. 379.
23. Lundberg and Farnham, *Modern Women: The Lost Sex*, p. 265; Helen Deutsch, *The Psychology of Women* (New York, 1944); Hendrick M. Ruitenbeek, *Psychoanalysis and Female Sexuality* (New Haven, 1966), p. 17.
24. Phyllis Chesler, *Women and Madness* (New York, 1972), p. 70.
25. I. K. Broverman et al., "Sex Role Stereotypes and Clinical Judgements in Mental Health," *Journal of Consulting and Clinical Psychology* 34 (1970): 1–4.
26. Dusty Sklar, "The Trauma of Eventlessness," *Family Weekly*, (January 1976); Walter R. Gove, "The Relationship between Sex Roles, Marital Status, and Mental Health," *Social Forces* 51 (1972): 34–44; Pauline Bart, "Depression in Middle Aged Women," in *Women in Sexist Society*, ed. Gornick and Moran, pp. 163–186.
27. Quoted in Jessie Bernard, "The Paradox of a Happy Marriage," in *Women in Sexist Society*, ed. Gornick and Moran, p. 158.
28. J. P. Greenhill, *Office Gynecology* (Chicago, 1965), pp. 158, 154; Howard J. Osofsky, "Women's Reactions to Pelvic Examinations," *Obstetrics and Gynecology* 30 (July 1967): 146.
29. Edward Ciriacy and Lowell Hughes, "Contraceptive Counseling," in *Family Practice*, ed. Howard F. Conn (Philadelphia, 1973), p. 300; quoted in Barbara Ehrenreich, "Gender and Objectivity in Medicine," *International Journal of Health Services* 4 (1974): 621.
30. Quoted in Corea, *The Hidden Malpractice*, p. 159.
31. Quoted in the *News Record of New Jersey*, 1975; Ehrenreich, "Gender and Objectivity in Medicine", p. 621.
32. Quoted in the *Milwaukee Sentinel*, 1976; quoted in *Ms. Magazine*, July 1977.
33. Quoted in Corea, *The Hidden Malpractice*, p. 77; K. J. Lenanne and R. Lenanne, "Alleged Psychogenic Disorders in Women—A Possible Manifestation of Sexual Prejudice," *New England Journal of Medicine* 288 (1973): 298.
34. Lundberg and Farnham, *Modern Woman: The Lost Sex*, p. 294; quoted in Barbara Ehrenreich and Deidre English, *For Her Own Good* (New York, 1978), p. 251; quoted in the *Gainesville Sun*, 24 August 1977.
35. Greenhill, *Office Gynecology*, p. 154; quoted in Lenanne and Lenanne, "Alleged Psychogenic Disorders in Women," p. 288.
36. *Gainesville Sun*, 8 June 1977; quoted in Julia Graham Lear, "Women's Health: The Side Effects of Bias," in *The Victimization of Women*, ed. Jane

Roberts Chapman and Margaret Gates (Beverly Hills, Calif., 1978), p. 233; quoted in Corea, *The Hidden Malpractice*, p. 239; quoted in *Ms. Magazine*, November 1977.

37. Quoted in *Ms. Magazine*, July 1977; Corea, *The Hidden Malpractice*, p. 236.
38. Quoted in Ehrenreich, "Gender and Objectivity in Medicine," p. 620; Corea, *The Hidden Malpractice*, p. 80, emphasis in original.
39. Menachem Amir, *Patterns in Forcible Rape* (Chicago, 1971), p. 259; quoted in *Ms. Magazine*, February 1976.
40. Quoted in Smuts, *Women and Work in America*, p. 118; quoted in *Ms. Magazine*, June 1975.
41. Brownmiller, *Against Our Will*, p. 374. Lending support to the notion that women secretly desire rape is Helene Deutsch's assertion in *The Psychology of Women* that all women have rape fantasies that are symbolically found in dreams. She also claims that these rape fantasies are evidence of women's innate masochism.
42. Quoted in the *New York Times*, 10 July 1977; quoted in the *New York Times*, 24 January 1982; quoted in "Rape Victim," *Civil Rights Update* (Washington, D.C., 1979), p. 6.
43. Quoted in Donna D. Schram, "Rape," in *The Victimization of Women*, ed. Chapman and Gates p. 65, emphasis added.
44. Kurt Weis and Sandra S. Borges, "Victimology and Rape: The Case of the Legitimate Victim," in *Rape Victimology*, ed. Leroy G. Schultz (Springfield, Ill., 1975), p. 112.
45. Quoted in Brownmiller, *Against Our Will*, pp. 419, 408.
46. Quoted in Jill Tweedy, "Why Are Women Always to Blame for Rape?" *Washington Post*, 26 March 1972; quoted in Brownmiller, *Against Our Will*, p. 447; Susan Griffin, "Rape: The All-American Crime," in *Rape Victimology*, ed. Leroy Schultz, pp. 19–39.
47. Quoted in *Ms. Magazine*, November 1977.
48. Brownmiller, *Against Our Will*, pp. 282–283, 286.
49. Cited in Griffin, "Rape: The All-American Crime," p. 23; cited in Brownmiller, *Against Our Will*, p. 410; Ruth Herschberger, *Adam's Rib* (New York, 1970), p. 24.
50. Brownmiller, *Against Our Will*, p. 449.
51. Beverly Jacobson, "Battered Women," *Civil Rights Digest* 9 (1977): 10; Rita Henley Jensen, "Battered Women and the Law," *Victimology* 2 (1977–78): 589; Judith Gingold, "One of These Days—Pow—Right in the Kisser," *Ms. Magazine* 5 (February 1976).
52. Erin Pizzey and Jeffrey Shapiro, *Prone to Violence* (London, 1982).
53. Quoted in the *Gainesville Sun*, 5 September 1977.
54. Reported on the *Today Show*, 16 September 1977; *New York Times*, 1980.
55. J. E. Snell, R. J. Rosenwald, and A. Robey, "The Wifebeater's Wife," *Archives of General Psychiatry* 2 (1964): 107–112.
56. Del Martin, "Battered Women: Society's Problem," in *The Victimization of*

Women, ed. Chapman and Gates, p. 125.
57. Quoted in Gingold, "One of These Days—Pow—Right in the Kisser," p. 52.
58. Martin, "Battered Women: Society's Problem," p. 117.
59. Quoted in the *Independent Florida Alligator*, 20 October 1977.
60. Quoted in Ellen Goodman, "Broken Wives Battered Bill," *Spokeswoman* 10 (October 1980): 16; Jacobson, "Battered Women," p. 11.
61. Herschberger, *Adam's Rib*, p. 16; Chessler, "Patient and Patriarch," p. 278.
62. Lenanne and Lenanne, "Alleged Psychogenic Disorders in Women," p. 290.
63. David Levy, *Maternal Overprotection* (New York, 1943), p. 213.
64. Lundberg and Farnham, *Modern Woman: The Lost Sex*, pp. 304–305; Betty Friedan, *The Feminine Mystique* (New York, 1974), p. 189.
65. Abram Kardiner, *Sex and Morality* (Indianapolis, 1954), p. 224; *Gainesville Sun*, 25 March 1977; quoted in Gloria Steinem, "The Nazi Connection: Authoritarianism Begins at Home," *Ms. Magazine* 9 (May 1980): 21.
66. For data suggesting that absent fathers may be responsible for much juvenile delinquency, see Nancy Choderow, "Being and Doing: A Cross-cultural Examination of Males and Females," in *Women in Sexist Society*, ed. Gornick and Moran, pp. 259–291; F. Ivan Nye and Lois Wladis, *The Employed Mother in America* (Chicago, 1963); Lee G. Burchinal, "Personality Characteristics in Children," in *The Employed Mother in America*, ed. Nye and Wladis, p. 118; Alberta Engvall Siegal et al., "Dependence and Independence in Children," in *The Employed Mother in America*, ed. Nye and Wladis, p. 80.
67. Wylie, *Generation of Vipers*; Edward A. Strecker, *Their Mothers' Sons* (Philadelphia, 1946), pp. 23, 70.
68. E. E. LeMasters, *Parents in America* (Homewood, Ill., 1970), p. 127.
69. Quotes from *Time* magazine, 8 September 1977 and 11 July 1977.
70. Quoted in the *New York Times*, 26 April 1981, emphasis added.
71. Ellen Goodman, "It's Not a Question of Style," *Spokeswoman* 9 (July–August 1979): 16.

Epilog: Where Do We Go From Here?

1. Joann Vanek, "Household Work, Wage Work, and Sexual Equality," in *Women and Household Labor*, ed. Sarah Fenstermaker Berk (Beverly Hills, Calif., 1980), p. 285. For examples of this view see Carl N. Degler, *At Odds: Women and the Family in America from the Revolution to the Present* (New York, 1980) and Mary Jo Bane, *Here to Stay: American Families in the Twentieth Century* (New York, 1976).
2. Editorial, *New York Times*, 16 May 1982.
3. María Patricia Fernández Kelly, "Contemporary Production: Seven

Features and One Puzzle," paper presented at the Conference on the Americas in the New International Division of Labor, Center for Latin American Studies, University of Florida, Gainesville, Florida, April 1983; Zillah R. Eisenstein, "The Sexual Politics of the New Right: Understanding the 'Crisis of Liberalism' for the 1980s," *Signs* 7 (Spring 1982): 579.

4. Reported on "All Things Considered," National Public Radio, 4 February 1983; "Automation Is Threatening Office Work," *Gainesville Sun*, 20 May 1982.
5. Eisenstein, "The Sexual Politics of the New Right"; David W. Brady and Kent L. Tedin, "Ladies in Pink: Religion and Political Ideology in the Anti-ERA Movement," *Social Science Quarterly* 56 (March 1976): 564–575.
6. Eisenstein, "The Sexual Politics of the New Right."
7. Marvin Harris, *America Now: The Anthropology of a Changing Culture* (New York, 1981).
8. Moira Hodgson, "We Are Where We Eat," *Gainesville Sun*, 8 April 1982.
9. Marvin Harris, *Cultural Materialism: The Struggle for a Science of Culture* (New York, 1979), p. 73.

BIBLIOGRAPHY

Abbott, Edith

1910 *Women in Industry*. New York: D. Appleton.

Abbott, John S. C.

1833 *The Mother at Home*. New York: American Tract Society.

1842 "Paternal Neglect." *Parent's Magazine* 2 (March).

Abele, Mrs. L. G.

1853 *The Mother's Book of Daily Duties*. New York: R. T. Young.

1853 *Woman in Her Various Relations: Containing Practical Rules for American Females*. New York: R. T. Young.

Aikin, John J.

1830 (orig. 1803) *The Arts of Life: 1. Providing Food. 2. Providing Clothing. 3. Providing Shelter*. 1st Amer. ed. Boston: Carter & Hendee, and Waitt & Dow.

Alcott, William A.

1838 *The Young Housekeeper; or, Thoughts on Food and Cookery*. Boston: George W. Light.

American Matron, An

1972 (orig. 1811) *The Maternal Physician: A Treatise on the Management of Infants, From Their Birth until Two Years Old*. New York: Arno.

American Mother, An

1900 "Is a College Education Best for Our Girls?" *Ladies' Home Journal* 17 (July): 15.

Ames, Azel

1875 *Sex in Industry: A Plea for the Working-Girl*. Boston: J. R. Osgood.

Amir, Menachem

1971 *Patterns of Forcible Rape*. Chicago: University of Chicago Press.

André, Rae

1981 *Homemakers: The Forgotten Workers*. Chicago: University of Chicago Press.

Andrews, Benjamin R.

1923 *Economics of the Household*. New York: Macmillan.

1929 "The Home Woman as Buyer and Controller of Consumption." *Annals of the American Academy of Political and Social Sciences* 143 (May): 41–48.

Andrews, William D., and Deborah C. Andrews

1974 "Technology and the Housewife in Nineteenth Century America." *Women's Studies* 2 (3): 309–328.

Anonymous
1923 "I Wish I Had Married and Found Life." *Good Housekeeping* 77 (November): 141.

Aries, Philippe
1965 *Centuries of Childhood*. New York: Vintage.

Aronson, Elliot
1973 "The Rationalizing Animal." *Psychology Today* 6 (December): 46–52.

Asahina, Robert
1981 "Social Science Fiction." *New York Times Book Review* (August 16).

Baer, Jean
1976 *How to Be An Assertive (Not Aggressive) Woman*. New York: New American Library.

Baker, Elizabeth Faulkner
1964 *Technology and Women's Work*. New York: Columbia University Press.

Balderston, Lydia May
1919 *Housewifery*. Philadelphia: J. B. Lippincott.

Bane, Mary Jo
1976 *Here to Stay: American Families in the Twentieth Century*. New York: Basic Books.

Barber, Virginia, and Merrill Skaggs Maguire
1975 *The Mother Person*. New York: Bobbs Merrill.

Barrett, Nancy S.
1979 "Women in the Job Market: Occupations, Earnings, and Career Opportunities." In *The Subtle Revolution*. Ed. Ralph E. Smith, pp. 31–61. Washington D.C.: The Urban Institute.

Bart, Pauline
1972 "Depression in Middle Aged Women." In *Women in Sexist Society*. Ed. Vivian Gornick and Barbara K. Moran, pp. 163–186. New York: New American Library.

Beauvoir, Simone de
1952 *The Second Sex*. New York: Alfred A. Knopf.

Beckwith, George C.
1850 "The Fate of Nations Dependent on Mothers." *The Mother's Assistant* 15 (January): 4–5.

Bee, Helen L.
1974 "On the Importance of Fathers." In *Social Issues in Developmental Psychology*. Ed. Helen L. Bee, pp. 367–377. New York: Harper and Row.
1974 "The Effect of Maternal Employment on the Development of the Child." In *Social Issues in Developmental Psychology*. Ed. Helen L. Bee, pp. 97–106. New York: Harper and Row.

Beecher, Catherine E.
1829 *Suggestions Respecting Improvements in Education*. New York: Hartford, Packard, and Butler.
1977 (orig. 1841) *A Treatise on Domestic Economy*. New York: Schocken.
1871 *Woman Suffrage and Woman's Profession*. Boston: Hartford, Brown and Gross.
Beecher, Catherine E., and Harriet Beecher Stowe
1869 *The American Woman's Home; or Principles of Domestic Science*. New York: J. B. Ford.
Benston, Margaret
1980 (orig. 1969) "The Political Economy of Women's Liberation." In *The Politics of Housework*. Ed. Ellen Malos, pp. 119–129. London: Allison and Busby.
Bent, Silas
1929 "Woman's Place Is in the Home." *Century* 116 (June): 204–213.
Bently, Mildred Maddocks
1925 "Household Engineering Applied." *Ladies' Home Journal* 42 (April): 36, 145–147.
Berger, Peter L., and Thomas Luckmann
1966 *The Social Construction of Reality*. Garden City, N.Y.: Doubleday.
Bergman, Barbara R.
1973 "The Economics of Women's Liberation." *Challenge* 16: 11–17.
Berk, Richard A., and Sarah Fenstermaker Berk
1979 *Labor and Leisure at Home: Content and Organization of the Household Day*. Beverly Hills, Calif.: Sage.
Bernard, Jessie
1972 "The Paradox of the Happy Marriage." In *Women in Sexist Society*. Ed. Vivian Gornick and Barbara K. Moran, pp. 145–162. New York: New American Library.
1974 *The Future of Motherhood*. New York: Penguin.
1975 *Women, Wives, and Mothers*. Chicago: Aldine.
Bettelheim, Bruno
1962 "Growing Up Female." *Harper's* 225 (October): 120–128.
Binstock, Jeanne
1972 "Motherhood: An Occupation Facing Decline." *The Futurist* 6 (June): 99–102.
Bloch, Ruth H.
1978 "American Feminine Ideals in Transition: The Rise of the Moral Mother, 1785–1815." *Feminist Studies* 4 (2): 101–126.
1978 "Untangling the Roots of Modern Sex Roles: A Survey of Four Centuries of Change." *Signs* 4 (2): 237–252.
Bok, Edward
1910 Editorial. *Ladies' Home Journal* 27 (June): 5.
1911 "Why the Wife Alone." *Ladies' Home Journal* 32 (September): 5.

Bowlby, John
1965 *Child Care and the Growth of Love*. 2d ed. Baltimore: Penguin.
Brady, David W., and Kent L. Tedin
1976 "Ladies in Pink: Religion and Political Ideology in the Anti-ERA Movement." *Social Science Quarterly* 56 (March): 564–575.
Braverman, Harry
1974 *Labor and Monopoly Capitalism*. New York: Monthly Review Press.
Brazelton, T. Berry
1981 "On Becoming a Family." *Redbook* 156 (February): 53–60.
Breckinridge, Sophonisba
1933 *Women in the Twentieth Century*. New York: McGraw-Hill.
Brenton, Myron
1972 "The Paradox of the American Father." In *The Future of the Family*. Ed. Louise Kapp Howe, pp. 125–136. New York: Simon and Schuster.
Bronfenner, Urie
1958 "The Study of Identification through Interpersonal Perception." In *Person Perception and Inter-personal Behavior*. Ed. R. Tagiuri and L. Petrullo, pp. 110–130. Stanford: Stanford University Press.
Broverman, Inge K., Donald M. Broverman, Frank E. Clarkson, Paul S. Rosenkranz, and Susan R. Vogel
1970 "Sex Role Stereotypes and Clinical Judgements in Mental Health." *Journal of Consulting and Clinical Psychology* 34 (1): 1–4.
Brown, Barnetta
1900 "Mothers' Mistakes and Fathers' Failures." *Ladies' Home Journal* 17 (February): 32.
Brown, Jean Collier
1938 *The Negro Woman Worker*. Women's Bureau Bulletin 165. Washington, D.C.: Government Printing Office.
Brown, Judith K.
1970 "A Note on the Division of Labor by Sex." *American Anthropologist* 72 (5): 1073–1078.
Brownlee, Elliot W.
1974 *Dynamics of Ascent: A History of the American Economy*. New York: Alfred A. Knopf.
Brownlee, Elliot W., and Mary M. Brownlee
1976 *Women in the American Economy*. New Haven: Yale University Press.
Brownmiller, Susan
1976 *Against Our Will: Men, Women and Rape*. New York: Bantam.
Brozan, Nadine
1980 "Men and Housework: Do They or Don't They." *New York Times* (November 1): 52
Buchan, William
1972 (orig. 1809) *Advice to Mothers*. Reprinted in *The Physician and Child-*

rearing: Two Guides 1809–1894. New York: Arno Press.

Burchinal, Lee G.

1963 "Personality Characteristics of Children." In *The Employed Mother in America*. Ed. F. Ivan Nye and Lois Wladis Hoffman, pp. 106–121. Chicago: Rand McNally.

Burenstam Linder, Staffan

1970 *The Harried Leisure Class*. New York: Columbia University Press.

Burgwyn, Diana

1981 *Marriage Without Children*. New York: Harper and Row.

Burns, Jabez

1851 *Mothers of the Wise and Good*. Boston: Gould and Lincoln.

Cain, Glen C.

1966 *Married Women in the Labor Force*. Chicago: University of Chicago Press.

Calhoun, Arthur W.

1960 (orig. 1917) *A Social History of the American Family: The Colonial Period*. Vol. 1. New York: Barnes and Noble.

1960 (orig. 1918) *A Social History of the American Family: From Independence through the Civil War*. Vol. 2. New York: Barnes and Noble.

1960 (orig. 1919) *A Social History of the American Family: Since the Civil War*. Vol. 3. New York: Barnes and Noble.

Callahan, Sidney Cornelia

1972 *The Working Mother*. New York: Warner.

Campbell, Helen

1881 *The Easiest Way in Housekeeping and Cooking*. New York: Fords, Howard, and Hubert.

1907 *Household Economics*. New York: G. P. Putnam.

Canfield, Dorothy Fisher

1914 *Mothers and Children*. New York: Henry Holt.

Cannon, Poppy

1930 "Pin Money Slaves." *Forum* 84 (August): 98–103.

Cantril, Hadley

1951 *Public Opinion, 1935–1946*. Princeton: Princeton University Press.

Caplow, Theodore

1954 *The Sociology of Work*. Minneapolis: University of Minnesota Press.

Cardozo, Arlene Rossen

1976 *Women at Home*. New York: Doubleday.

Carro, Geraldine

1980 "How to Raise Happy, Healthy Children." *Ladies' Home Journal* 97 (October): 90–92.

Chafe, William H.

1972 *The American Woman: Her Changing Social, Economic, and Political Roles, 1920–1970*. New York: Oxford University Press.

1977 *Women and Equality: Changing Patterns in American Culture*. New York:

Oxford University Press.

Chesler, Phyllis

1972 "Patient and Patriarch: Women in the Psychotherepeutic Relationship." In *Women in Sexist Society*. Ed. Vivian Gornick and Barbara K. Moran, pp. 362–392. New York: New American Library.

1972 *Women and Madness*. New York: Doubleday.

Child, Lydia Maria

1831 *The Frugal Housewife*. 6th ed. Boston: Carter, Hendee, and Babcock

1972 (orig. 1831) *The Mother's Book*. New York: Arno Press.

"Children"

1860 *Godey's Lady's Book* 60 (January–June): 272.

Children's Bureau

1930 *Are You Training Your Child to Be Happy?* Children's Bureau Publication 202. Washington, D.C.: Government Printing Office.

1938 *Infant Care*. 5th rev. ed. Children's Bureau Publication 8. Washington: D.C.: Government Printing Office.

1942 *Infant Care*. 7th rev. ed. Children's Bureau Publication 8. Washington, D.C.: Government Printing Office.

1963 *Infant Care*. 11th rev. ed. Children's Bureau Publication 8. Washington, D.C.: Government Printing Office.

1980 *Infant Care*. 13th rev. ed. U.S. Department of Health and Human Services Publication (OHDS) 80-30015. Washington, D.C.: Government Printing Office.

Choderow, Nancy

1972 "Being and Doing: A Cross-Cultural Examination of Males and Females." In *Women in Sexist Society*. Ed. Vivian Gornick and Barbara K. Moran, pp. 259–291. New York: New American Library.

1978 *The Reproduction of Mothering*. Berkeley, Los Angeles, London: University of California Press.

Ciriacy, Edward, and Lowell Hughes

1973 "Contraceptive Counseling." In *Family Practice*. Ed. Howard F. Conn, pp. 298–309. Philadelphia: Saunders.

Clark, Victor Selden

1929 *History of Manufactures in the United States, 1860–1914*. Vol. 1. Washington, D.C.: Carnegie Institution.

Coale, Ansley J., and Melvin Zelnik

1963 *New Estimates of Fertility and Population in the United States*. Princeton: Princeton University Press.

Cook, Elizabeth

1931 "The Kitchen Sink Complex." *Ladies' Home Journal* 48 (September): 14, 148.

Cooley, Anna M.

1911 *Domestic Art in Woman's Education*. New York: Charles Scribner.

Corea, Gena
1977 *The Hidden Malpractice: How American Medicine Treats Women as Patients and Professionals.* New York: William Morrow.
Cott, Nancy F.
1977 *The Bonds of Womanhood: Women's Sphere in New England, 1780–1835.* New Haven: Yale University Press.
Cowan, Ruth Schwartz
1974 "A Case Study of Technological and Social Change: The Washing Machine and the Working Wife." In *Clio's Consciousness Raised.* Ed. Mary Hartmann and Lois W. Banner, pp. 245–253. New York: Harper and Row.
1976 "The 'Industrial Revolution' in the Home: Household Technology and Social Change in the Twentieth Century." *Technology and Culture* 17 (January): 1–23.
1976 "Two Washes in the Morning and a Bridge Party at Night: The American Housewife between the Wars." *Women's Studies* 3 (2): 147–172.
Daley, Robert
1977 "The Search for Sam: Why It Took So Long." *New York Magazine* (August 22).
Dally, Ann
1982 *Inventing Motherhood: The Consequences of an Ideal.* London: Burnett Books Ltd.
Davidoff, Leonore
1976 "The Rationalization of Housework." In *Dependence and Exploitation in Work and Marriage.* Ed. Diana Leopold Barker and Sheila Allen, pp. 121–151. London: Longman.
Davies, Margery
1975 "Women's Place Is at the Typewriter: The Feminization of the Clerical Labor Force." In *Labor Market Segmentation.* Ed. Richard C. Edwards, Michael Reich, and David M. Gordon, pp. 279–296. Lexington, Mass.: D. C. Heath.
Davis, Glenn
1976 *Childhood and History in America.* New York: Psychohistory Press.
Davison, Jane
1980 *The Fall of a Doll's House: Three Generations of American Women and the Houses They Lived In.* New York: Holt, Rinehart and Winston.
Deckard, Barbara, and Howard Sherman
1974 "Monopoly Power and Sex Discrimination." *Politics and Society* 4 (4): 475–482.
Degler, Carl N.
1967 "Revolution Without Ideology: The Changing Place of Women in America." In *The Woman in America.* Ed. Robert Jay Lifton,

pp. 163–210. Boston: Beacon.
1980 *At Odds: Women and the Family in America from the Revolution to the Present.* New York: Oxford University Press.

Demos, John
1970 *A Little Commonwealth: Family Life in Plymouth Colony.* New York: Oxford University Press.

De Rham, Edith
1965 *The Love Fraud: Why the Structure of the American Family Is Changing and What Women Must Do to Make It Work.* New York: Clarkson N. Potter.

Deutsch, Helene
1944 *The Psychology of Women.* New York: Grove and Stratton.

Dewees, William
1847 *A Treatise on the Physical and Medical Treatment of Children.* 10th ed. Philadelphia: Blanchard and Lea.

Dexter, Elizabeth Anthony
1924 *Colonial Women of Affairs.* Boston: Houghton Mifflin.

Divale, William T., and Marvin Harris
1976 "Population, Warfare, and the Male Supremacist Complex," *American Anthropologist* 78 (September): 521–528.

Duffin, Lorna
1978 "Prisoners of Progress: Women and Evolution." In *The Nineteenth Century Woman.* Ed. Sara Delamont and Lorna Duffin, pp. 57–91. New York: Barnes and Noble.

Earle, Alice Morse
1898 *Homelife in Colonial Days.* New York: Macmillan.

East, Catherine
1972 "The Current Status of the Employment of Women." In *Women in the Work Force.* Ed. Mildred E. Katzell and William C. Byham, pp. 7–14. New York: Behavioral Publications.

Ehrenreich, Barbara
1974 "Gender and Objectivity in Medicine." *International Journal of Health Services* 4 (4): 617–623.

Ehrenreich, Barbara, and Deirdre English
1975 "The Manufacture of Housework." *Socialist Revolution* 26 (October–December): 5–40.
1978 *For Her Own Good: 150 Years of the Experts' Advice to Women.* New York: Anchor.

Eisenstein, Zillah R.
1982 "The Sexual Politics of the New Right: Understanding the 'Crisis of Liberalism' for the 1980s." *Signs* 7 (Spring): 567–588.

Eliot, Martha M.
1929 *Infant Care.* 3d rev. ed. Children's Bureau Publication 8. Washington, D.C.: Government Printing Office.

Engels, Friedrich
1964 (orig. 1884) *Origin of the Family, Private Property, and the State*. New York: International Publishers.

Escalona, Sibylle
1953 "A Commentary upon Some Recent Changes in Child Rearing Practices." In *Selected Studies in Marriage and the Family*. Ed. Robert F. Winch and Robert McGinnis, pp. 208–214. New York: Henry Holt.

Etzioni, Amitai
1969 *The Semi-professions and Their Organizations*. New York: Free Press.

Ewen, Stuart
1976 *Captains of Consciousness: Advertising and the Social Roots of Consumer Culture*. New York: McGraw-Hill.

Farrar, Eliza
1974 (orig. 1836) *The Young Lady's Friend*. New York: Arno Press.

Fernández Kelly, María Patricia
1983 "Contemporary Production: Seven Features and One Puzzle." Paper presented at the Conference on the Americas in the New International Division of Labor, Center for Latin American Studies, University of Florida, April 1983.

Filene, Peter Gabriel
1976 *Him/Her/Self*. New York: New American Library.

Fleming, Arthur S.
1977 *Window Dressing on the Set: Women and Minotiries in TV*. Washington, D.C.: U.S. Commission on Civil Rights.

Fraiberg, Selma
1977 *Every Child's Birthright: In Defense of Mothering*. New York: Basic Books.

Frederick, Christine
1913 *The New Housekeeping: Efficiency Studies in Home Management*. Garden City, N.Y.: Doubleday.
1919 *Household Engineering: Scientific Management in the Home*. Chicago: American School of Home Economics.
1929 *Selling Mrs. Consumer*. New York: The Business Bourse.

Friedan, Betty
1974 (orig. 1963) *The Feminine Mystique*. New York: Dell.

Friedl, Ernestine
1975 *Women and Men: An Anthropologist's View*. New York: Holt, Rinehart and Winston.

Frost, J. William
1973 *The Quaker Family in Colonial America: A Portrait of the Society of Friends*. New York: St. Martin's Press.

Galbraith, John Kenneth
1973 *Economics and the Public Purpose*. New York: New American Library.

Gardener, Jean
1979 "Women's Domestic Labor." In *Capitalist Patriarchy and the Case for Socialist Feminism*. Ed. Zillah R. Eisenstein, pp. 173–189. New York: Monthly Review Press.
Garrison, Dee
1974 "The Tender Technicians: The Feminization of Public Librarianship, 1876–1905." In *Clio's Consciousness Raised*. Ed. Mary Hartmann and Lois W. Banner, pp. 158–178. New York: Harper and Row.
Germaine, Adrienne
1975 "Status and Roles of Women as Factors in Fertility Behavior: A Policy Analysis." *Studies in Family Planning* 6: 192–200.
Gesell, Arnold, and Frances L. Ilg
1943 *Infant and Child in the Culture of Today*. New York: Harper and Brothers.
Giedion, Siegfried
1948 *Mechanization Takes Command*. New York: Oxford University Press.
Gilbreth, Lillian M.
1928 *The Home-maker and Her Job*. New York: D. Appleton.
Gillmor, Dan
1954 "The Care and Feeding of Spock-marked Fathers." *Parents' Magazine* 29 (July): 36–37, 92–93.
Gilman, Charlotte Perkins
1898 *Women and Economics*. Boston: Small, Maynard.
Gingold, Judith
1976 "One of These Days—Pow—Right in the Kisser." *Ms. Magazine* 5 (February): 51–4, 94.
Ginott, Haim G.
1965 *Between Parent and Child*. New York: Macmillan.
Glazer, Nona
1980 "Everyone Needs Three Hands: Doing Unpaid and Paid Work." In *Women and Household Labor*. Ed. Sarah Fenstermaker Berk, pp. 249–273. Beverly Hills, Calif.: Sage.
Glazer-Malbin, Nona
1976 "Housework." *Signs* 1 (Summer): 905–922.
Glickman, Beatrice Marden, and Nesha Bass Springer
1978 *Who Cares for the Baby?* New York: Schocken.
Goode, William
1963 *World Revolution and Family Patterns*. New York: Free Press.
Goodman, David
1959 *A Parents' Guide to the Emotional Needs of Children*. New York: Hawthorne.
Goodman, Ellen
1979 "It's Not a Question of Style." *Spokeswoman* 9 (July–August): 16.

1980 "Broken Wives Battered Bill." *Spokeswoman* 10 (October): 16
Goodrich, Henrietta I.
1900 "Suggestions for a Professional School of Home and Social Economics." *Proceedings of the Second Lake Placid Conference on Home Economics*. Pp. 26–40. Lake Placid, N.Y.
Gordon, Ann D., Mari Jo Buhle, and Nancy E. Schrom
1971 "Women in American Society: An Historical Contribution." *Radical America* 5 (4): 3–66.
Gordon, Ann D., Mari Jo Buhle, and Nancy Schrom Dye
1976 "The Problem of Women's History." In *Liberating Women's History*. Ed. Berenice A. Carroll, pp. 75–92. Urbana: University of Illinois Press.
Gordon, Linda
1977 *Woman's Body, Woman's Right: Birth Control in America*. New York: Penguin.
Gorer, Geoffrey
1964 *The American People*. Rev. ed. New York: Norton.
Gornick, Vivian
1975 "Here's News: Fathers Mother as Much as Mothers." *Village Voice* (October 13): 10–11.
Gossett, Thomas F.
1965 *Race: The History of an Idea in America*. New York: Schocken.
Gove, Walter R.
1972 "The Relationship between Sex Roles, Marital Status and Mental Illness." *Social Forces* 51 (1): 34–44.
Graham, Billy
1970 "Jesus and the Liberated Woman." *Ladies' Home Journal* 87 (December): 40–44.
Graves, Mrs. A. J.
1843 *Woman in America: Being an Examination into the Moral and Intellectual Condition of American Female Society*. New York: Harper and Brothers.
Green, Maureen
1976 *Fathering*. New York: McGraw-Hill.
Greenberg, Milton, and Norman Morris
1974 "Engrossment: The Newborn's Impact upon the Father." *American Journal of Orthopsychiatry* 44 (July): 520–531.
Greenhill, J. P.
1965 *Office Gynecology*. 8th rev. ed. Chicago: Yearbook Medical Publications.
Greven, Jr., Philip J.
1970 *Four Generations: Population, Land and Family in Colonial Andover, Massachusetts*. Ithaca: Cornell University Press.
1972 "The Average Size of Families and Households in the Province of Massachusetts in 1764 and in the United States in 1790: An

Overview." In *Household and Family Life in Past Time*. Ed. P. Laslett, pp. 545–560. London: Cambridge University Press.

1973 *Child Rearing Concepts, 1628–1861*. Itasca, Ill.: Peacock.

1973 "Family Structure in Seventeenth Century Andover, Massachusetts." In *The American Family in Socio-Historical Perspective*. Ed. Michael Gordon, pp. 77–99. New York: St. Martin's Press.

Griffin, Susan

1975 "Rape: The All-American Crime." In *Rape Victimology*. Ed. Leroy G. Schultz, pp. 19–39. Springfield, Ill.: Charles C. Thomas.

Groves, Ernest R., and Gladys Hoagland Groves

1928 *Parents and Children*. Philadelphia: J. B. Lippincott.

Gruenberg, Sidonie M., and Hilda S. Krech

1957 *The Modern Mother's Dilemma*. Public Affairs Pamphlet 247. New York.

Hacker, Helen M.

1951 "Women as a Minority Group." *Social Forces* 30 (1) 60–69.

Hale, Sarah Josepha

1839 *The Good Housekeeper; or the Way to Live Well and to Be Well While We Live. Containing Directions for Choosing and Preparing Food, in Regard to Health, Economy, and Taste*. Boston: Weeks, Jordan.

Hall, Elizabeth S.

1849 "A Mother's Influence." *The Mother's Assistant* 14 (February): 25–29.

Hall, G. Stanley

1904 *Adolescence*. Vol. 2. New York: D. Appleton.

1911 (orig. 1904) *Youth: Its Education, Regimen, and Hygiene*. New York: D. Appleton.

Hambridge, Gove, and Dorothy Cooke Hambridge

1930 "Leisure to Live." *Ladies' Home Journal* 46 (May): 30, 141.

Hamilton, Marshall L.

1977 *Father's Influence on Children*. Chicago: Nelson-Hall.

Harper, Katherine

1980 *The Childfree Alternative*. Brattleboro, Vt.: Stephen Greene.

Harris, Marvin

1979 *Cultural Materialism: The Struggle for a Science of Culture*. New York: Random House.

1981 *America Now: The Anthropology of a Changing Culture*. New York: Simon and Schuster.

Hartmann, Heidi I.

1974 "Capitalism and Women's Work in the Home, 1900–1930." Ph.D. Dissertation, Yale University.

1981 "The Family as the Locus of Gender, Class, and Political Struggle: The Example of Housework." *Signs* (Spring): 366–394.

Harwell, H. I.

1816 *The Domestic Manual: or Family Directory. Containing Receipts in Arts,*

Trade, and Domestic Economy. New London: Conn.: Samuel Green.

Heath, Mrs. Julian
1915 "The New Kind of Housekeeping." *Ladies' Home Journal* 32 (January): 2.

Heffner, Elaine
1978 *Mothering: The Emotional Experience of Motherhood after Freud and Feminism*. Garden City, N.Y.: Doubleday.

Held, Virginia
1979 "The Equal Obligations of Mothers and Fathers." In *Having Chidren*. Ed. Onora O'Neill and William Ruddick, pp. 228–239. New York: Oxford University Press.

Heloise
1967 *Heloise All Around the House*. New York: Pocket Books.
1981 *Hints from Heloise*. New York: Avon.

Hennig, Margaret and Anne Jardim
1977 *The Managerial Woman*. New York: Anchor.

Herschberger, Ruth
1970 *Adam's Rib*. New York: Har/Row.

Hill, Joseph Adna
1978 (orig. 1929) *Women in Gainful Occupations 1870 to 1920*. Westport, Conn.: Greenwood.

Hodgson, Moira
1982 "We Are Where We Eat." *Gainesville Sun* (April 8).

Hoffman, Betty Hannah
1963 "I'm Going to Get a Job." *Ladies' Home Journal* 80 (July): 107.

Holt, L. Emmett
1896 *The Care and Feeding of Infants*. New York: D. Appleton.

Honey, Maureen
1976 "Images of Women in the *Saturday Evening Post*, 1931–1936." *Journal of Popular Culture* 10 (2): 352–358.

Hymowitz, Carol, and Michaele Weissman
1978 *A History of Women in America*. New York: Bantam.

"Influence of Women-Past and Present"
1840 *Ladies' Magazine* 13:245–46.

Jacobson, Beverly
1977 "Battered Women." *Civil Rights Digest* 9 (4): 2–11. Washington, D.C.: U.S. Commission on Civil Rights.

Janeway, Eliot
1977 "Reviving the Economy: If Women Can't Do It No One Can." *Working Woman* 2 (October): 66–67.

Janeway, Elizabeth
1980 "Who Is Sylvia? On the Loss of Sexual Paradigms." *Signs* 5 (Summer): 573–589.

Jenkins, William D.
1979 "Housewifery and Motherhood: The Question of Role Change in the Progressive Era." In *Woman's Being, Woman's Place*. Ed. Mary Kelley, pp. 142–153. Boston: G. K. Hall.

Jenson, Rita Henley
1977–78 "Battered Women and the Law." *Victimology* 2 (3–4): 585–590.

Kanner, Leo
1941 *In Defense of Mothers*. Springfield, Ill.: Charles C. Thomas.

Kardiner, Abram
1954 *Sex and Morality*. Indianapolis: Bobbs-Merrill.

Keniston, Ellen, and Kenneth Keniston
1964 "An American Anachronism: The Image of Women and Work." *American Scholar* 33 (3): 355–375.

Kenyon, Josephine
1940 "The Tired Mother." *Good Housekeeping* 110 (January): 63, 77.
1940 "Less Rigid Schedules for Babies." *Good Housekeeping* 110 (February): 92.

Kessler-Harris, Alice
1975 "Stratifying by Sex: Understanding the History of Working Women." In *Labor Market Segmentation*. Ed. Richard C. Edwards, Michael Reich, and David M. Gordon, pp. 217–242. Lexington, Mass.: D. C. Heath.
1981 *Women Have Always Worked*. Old Westbury, N.Y.: The Feminist Press.

Key, Ellen
1909 *The Century of the Child*. New York: G. P. Putnam.
1914 *The Renaissance of Motherhood*. New York: G. P. Putnam.

King, Sir Frederick Truby
1913 *Feeding and Care of Baby*. London: Oxford University Press.

Kinne, Helen, and Anna M. Cooley
1919 *The Home and the Family*. New York: Macmillan.

Klapper, Zelda S.
1971 "The Impact of the Women's Liberation Movement on Child Development Books." *American Journal of Orthopsychiatry* 41 (October): 725–732.

Klein, Joan
1980 "Sneak Preview: The 1980 Census." *Working Woman* 5 (September): 72–74.

Klemesrud, Judy
1983 "Mothers Who Shift Back From Jobs to Homemaking." *New York Times*, January 19, pp. 13, 16.

Kliman, Gilbert W., and Albert Rosenfeld
1980 *Responsible Parenthood*. New York: Holt, Rinehart and Winston.

Komarovsky, Mirra
1953 *Women in the Modern World*. Boston: Little, Brown.
Kotelchuck, Milton
1972 "The Nature of a Child's Ties to His Father." Ph.D. Dissertation, Harvard University.
Kraditor, Aileen S., ed.
1968 *Up from the Pedestal*. Chicago: Quadrangle.
Kreps, Juanita M.
1971 *Sex in the Marketplace*. Baltimore: Johns Hopkins University Press.
Kreps, Juanita M., and R. John Leaper
1976 "Home Work, Market Work, and the Allocation of Time." In *Women and the American Economy*. Ed. Juanita M. Kreps, pp. 61–81. Englewood Cliffs, N.J.: Prentice-Hall.
Kuhn, Anne L.
1947 *The Mother's Role in Childhood Education: New England Concepts 1830–1860*. New Haven: Yale University Press.
Kyrk, Hazel
1933 *Economic Problems of the Family*. New York: Harper and Row.
Lamb, Michael E., ed.
1976 *The Role of the Father in Child Development*. New York: John Wiley.
Lambert, Wallace E., Josiane F. Hamers, and Nancy Frasure-Smith
1979 *Child-rearing Values: A Cross-national Study*. New York: Praeger.
Lane, Rose Wilder
1936 "Women's Place Is in the Home." *Ladies' Home Journal* 53 (October): 18.
Lazarre, Jane
1976 *The Mother Knot*. New York: McGraw-Hill.
Lear, Julia Graham
1978 "Women's Health: The Side Effects of Bias." In *The Victimization of Women*. Ed. Jane Roberts Chapman and Margaret Gates, pp. 225–250. Beverly Hills, Calif.: Sage.
"Learning vs Housewifery"
1839 *Godey's Lady's Book* 28 (August): 95.
LeMasters, E. E.
1970 *Parents in America: A Sociological Analysis*. Homewood, Ill.: Dorsey.
Lenanne, K. J., and R. Lenanne
1973 "Alleged Psychogenic Disorders in Women—A Possible Manifestation of Sexual Prejudice." *New England Journal of Medicine* 288 (6): 288–292.
Lerner, Gerda
1978 "The American Housewife: An Historical Perspective." In *Feminist Perspectives on Housework and Child Care*. Ed. Amy Swerdlow, pp. 22–34. Transcript of a conference sponsored by Sarah

Lawrence College, 22 October, 1977.
1979 *The Majority Finds Its Past*. New York: Oxford University Press.

Leslie, Eliza
1845 *The House Book: or, A Manual of Domestic Economy for Town and Country*. 8th ed. Philadelphia: Carey and Hart.

Levine, James
1976 *Who Will Raise the Children?* Philadelphia: J. B. Lippincott.

Levy, David M.
1943 *Maternal Overprotection*. New York: Columbia University Press.

Lindquist, Ruth
1931 *The Family in the Present Social Order*. Chapel Hill: University of North Carolina Press.

Lopata, Helena Z.
1971 *Occupation: Housewife*. New York: Oxford University Press.

Lopate, Carol
1974 "Ironies of the Home Economics Movement." *Edcentric: A Journal of Educational Change* 31–32 (November): 40–42, 56.

Lundberg, Ferdinand, and Marynia Farnham
1947 *Modern Woman: The Lost Sex*. New York: Harper and Brothers.

Lynd, Robert, and Helen Merrill Lynd
1929 *Middletown*. New York: Harcourt, Brace.

Lynes, Russell
1963 *The Domesticated Americans*. New York: Harper and Row.

Lynn, David B.
1974 *The Father: His Role in Child Development*. Belmont, Calif.: Wadsworth.

McBride, Angela Barron
1973 *The Growth and Development of Mothers*. New York: Harper and Row.

McCarthy, Mary
1963 *The Group*. New York. Harcourt, Brace, and World.

Maccoby, Nathan
1968 "The Communication of Child Rearing Advice to Parents." In *Selected Studies in Marriage and the Family*. 3d ed. Ed. Robert F. Winch and Louis Wolf Goodman, pp. 254–259. New York: Holt, Rinehart and Winston.

Mandle, Joan D.
1979 *Women and Social Change in America*. Princeton: Princeton University Press.

Mansfield, Edward
1945 *The Legal Rights, Liabilities, and Duties of Women*. Salem, Mass.: John P. Jewett.

Margolis, Maxine L.
1976 "In Hartford, Hannibal, and (New) Hampshire, Heloise Is Hardly Helpful." *Ms. Magazine* 9 (June): 28–36.

Martin, Del

1978 "Battered Women: Society's Problem." In *The Victimization of Women*. Ed. Jane Roberts Chapman and Margaret Gates, pp. 111–141. Beverly Hills, Calif.: Sage.

Martin, M. Kay, and Barbara Voorhies

1975 *Female of the Species*. New York: Columbia University Press.

Marwedel, Emma

1887 *Conscious Motherhood: The Earliest Unfolding of the Child in the Cradle, Nursery, and Kindergarten*. Boston: D. C. Heath.

Marx, Karl

1936 (orig. 1867) *Capital*. New York: Modern Library.

Mason, Karen O., Maris A. Vinovskis, and Tamara K. Hareven

1978 "Women's Work and the Life Course in Essex County, Massachusetts, 1880." In *Transitions: The Family and the Life Course in Historical Perspective*. Ed. Tamara K. Hareven, pp. 187–216. New York: Academic Press.

Mason, Margaret W.

1976 "The Typology of the Female as a Model for the Regenerate: Puritan Teaching, 1690–1730." *Signs* 2 (Winter): 304–315.

"Maternity"

1825 *The Ladies' Museum* 1 (September 17): 31.

Mather, Cotton

1978 (orig. 1741) *Ornaments for the Daughters of Zion*. 3d ed. Delmar, N.Y.: Scholars Facsimiles and Reprints.

Mazerik, A. G.

1945 "Getting Rid of the Women." *Atlantic Monthly* 176 (June): 79–83.

Mead, Margaret

1954 "Some Theoretical Considerations on the Problem of Mother-child Separation." *American Journal of Orthopsychiatry* 24 (July): 471–483.

1955 *Male and Female*. New York: Mentor.

1959 "The Job of the Children's Mother's Husband." *New York Times Magazine* (May 10): 7, 66–67.

1962 "A Cultural Anthropologist's Approach to Maternal Deprivation." In *Deprivation of Maternal Care: A Reassessment of Its Effects*. Ed. Mary D. Ainsworth, pp. 45–62. Geneva: World Health Organization.

Mechling, Jay

1975 "Advice to Historians on Advice to Mothers." *Journal of Social History* 9 (1): 44–63.

Meissner, Martin, Elizabeth W. Humphreys, Scott M. Meis, and William J. Scheu

1975 "No Exit for Wives: Sexual Division of Labor and the Cumulation of Household Demands." *Canadian Journal of Sociology and Anthropology* 12 (November): 424–439.

Meyer, Agnes E.
1950 "Women Aren't Men." *Atlantic Monthly* 186 (February): 28–29.
1955 "Children in Trouble." *Ladies' Home Journal* 72 (March): 68–69, 204–216.
Milkman, Ruth
1976 "Women's Work and Economic Crisis: Some Lessons of the Great Depression." *Review of Radical Political Economics* 8 (1): 73–97.
Miller, Daniel R., and Guy E. Swanson
1958 *The Changing American Parent*. New York: John Wiley.
Minge-Klevana, Wanda
1980 "Does Labor Time Increase with Industrialization? A Survey of Time Allocation Studies." *Current Anthropology* 21 (June 1980): 279–298.
Minturn, Leigh, and William W. Lambert
1964 *Mothers of Six Cultures*. New York: John Wiley.
Mitchell, Gary, and Edna M. Brandt
1972 "Paternal Behavior in Primates." In *Primate Socialization*. Ed. Frank Poirier, pp. 173–206. New York: Random House.
Mitchell, Gary, William K. Redican, and Jody Gomber
1974 "Lessons from a Primate: Males Can Raise Babies." *Psychology Today* 7 (April): 63–68.
Mohr, James C.
1978 *Abortion in American: The Origins and Evolution of National Policy, 1800–1900*. New York: Oxford University Press.
Montagu, Ashley
1958 "The Triumph and Tragedy of American Women." *Saturday Review* (September 27): 13–15, 34–35.
Moore, Didi
1981 "The Only-Child Phenomenon." *New York Times Magazine* (January 18): 26–27, 45–48.
Moore, Kristi, and Isabel Sawhill
1976 "Implications of Women's Employment for Home and Family." In *Women in the American Economy*. Ed. Juanita M. Kreps, pp. 102–122. Englewood Cliffs, N.J.: Prentice-Hall.
Morgan, Edmund S.
1966 *The Puritan Family*. Rev. ed. New York: Harper and Row.
Morgan, J. N., I. Sirageldin, and N. Baerwaldt
1966 *Productive Americans*. Ann Arbor, Mich.: Institute for Social Research.
Morgan, Marabel
1975 *The Total Woman*. New York: Pocket Books.
Morris, Richard Brandon

1930 *Studies in the History of American Law*. New York: Columbia University Press.

Moynihan, Daniel Patrick

1965 *The Negro American Family*. Office of Policy Planning and Research, U.S. Department of Labor. Washington, D.C.: Government Printing Office.

Murdock, George Peter

1937 "Comparative Data on the Division of Labor by Sex." *Social Forces* 15 (4): 551–553.

National Now Times 16 (March 1983): 2.

Norton, Mary Beth

1979 "The Paradox of Women's Sphere." In *Women in America: A History*. Ed. Carol Ruth Berkin and Mary Beth Norton, pp. 139–149. Boston: Houghton Mifflin.

Nye, F. Ivan, and Lois Wladis Hoffman

1963 *The Employed Mother in America*. Chicago: Rand McNally.

Oakley, Ann

1974 *The Sociology of Housework*. New York: Pantheon.

1976 *Woman's Work: The Housewife, Past and Present*. New York: Vintage.

Ogburn, William F., and Meyer Francis Nimkoff

1955 *Technology and the Changing Family*. Boston: Houghton Mifflin.

Olds, Sally Werdkos

1975 *The Mother Who Works Outside the Home*. New York: Child Study Press.

O'Neill, William J.

1971 *Everyone Was Brave*. Chicago: Quadrangle.

Oppenheimer, Valerie

1970 *The Female Labor Force in the United States*. Population Monograph 5. Berkeley, Los Angeles, London: University of California Press.

Osofsky, Howard J.

1967 "Women's Reactions to Pelvic Examinations." *Obstetrics and Gynecology* 30 (July): 146–151

Parkinson, C. Northcote

1957 *Parkinson's Law and Other Studies in Administration*. Boston: Houghton Mifflin.

Parloa, Maria

1905 "How I Plan a Week's Work Without a Servant." *Ladies' Home Journal* 22 (January): 31.

1905 "How I Keep My House Clean and Sweet." *Ladies' Home Journal* 22 (February): 40.

Patterson, Alicia

1962 Address to the Radcliffe Alumnae Association. Reprinted in *Harper's* 225 (October): 123.

Peck, Ellen
1971 *The Baby Trap*. New York: Bernard Geis.
Peck, Ellen, and Judith Senderowitz, eds.
1974 *Pronatalism: The Myth of Mom and Apple Pie*. New York: Thomas Y. Crowell.
Perlman, Janice E.
1976 *The Myth of Marginality: Urban Poverty and Politics in Rio de Janeiro*. Berkeley, Los Angeles, London: University of California Press.
Peterson, Esther
1967 "Working Women." In *The Woman in America*. Ed. Robert Jay Lifton, pp. 144–172. Boston: Beacon.
Pines, Maya
1981 "Only Isn't Lonely (or Spoiled or Selfish)." *Psychology Today* 15 (March): 15–19.
Pinkham, Mary Ellen, and Pearl Higginbotham
1979 *Mary Ellen's Best of Helpful Hints*. New York: Warner.
Pizzey, Erin, and Jeffrey Shapiro
1982 *Prone to Violence*. London.
Pogrebin, Letty Cottin
1974 "The Working Woman: Working Mothers." *Ladies' Home Journal* 91 (August): 60–62.
1978 "Rethinking Housework." In *Feminist Perspectives on Housework and Child Care*. Ed. Amy Swerdlow, pp. 49–60. Transcript of a conference sponsored by Sarah Lawrence College, 22 October, 1977.
1980 "A Partnership Plan for Parents Who Work (or: How to Bring Dad More into the Act and Give Mom a Break)." *Ladies' Home Journal* 97 (October): 152–154.
Porter, Sylvia
1976 "Women Swell Jobless Roles." *Gainesville Sun* (August 19).
Pruette, Lorine
1972 (orig. 1924) *Women and Leisure: A Study of Social Waste*. New York: Arno.
Radl, Shirley
1973 *Mother's Day Is Over*. New York: Charterhouse.
Rainwater, Lee, Richard P. Coleman, and Gerald Handel
1959 *Workingman's Wife*. New York: Oceana.
Randolph, Ann E.
1910 "Is the American Girl Being Mis-educated?" *Ladies' Home Journal* 27 (September): 67.
Reid, Margaret
1934 *Economics of Household Production*. New York: John Wiley.
Reynolds, William
1978 *The American Father*. New York: Paddington.

Ribble, Margaret A.
1943 *Rights of Infants*. New York: Columbia University Press.
1965 *Rights of Infants*. Rev. ed. New York: Columbia University Press.

Richards, Ellen Swallow
1914 *The Cost of Cleanness*. New York: John Wiley.

Richardson, Anne E.
1929 "The Woman Administrator in the Modern Home." *Annals of the American Academy of Social Sciences* 143 (May): 21–32.

Robertson, Ross. M.
1964 *History of the American Economy*. 2d ed. New York: Harcourt, Brace and World.

Robinson, John P.
1980 "Housework Technology and Household Work." In *Women and Household Labor*. Ed. Sarah Fenstermaker Berk, pp. 53–67. Beverly Hills, Calif.: Sage

Roe, Constance
1944 "Can the Girls Hold Their Jobs in Peacetime?" *Saturday Evening Post* 216 (September): 28–39.

Rollin, Betty
1972 "Motherhood: Who Needs It?" In *The Future of the Family*. Ed. Louise Kapp Howe, pp. 69–82. New York: Simon and Schuster.

Roosevelt, Theodore
1905 "The American Woman as Mother." Address before the National Congress of Mothers. Reprinted in the *Ladies' Home Journal* 22 (July): 3–4.

Rossi, Alice S.
1971 (orig. 1964) "Equality Between the Sexes: An Immodest Proposal." In *Roles Women Play: Readings Toward Women's Liberation*. Ed. Michele Hoffnung Garskof, pp. 145–164. Belmont, Calif.: Brooks/Cole.

Rothman, Sheila M.
1978 *Woman's Proper Place: A History of Changing Ideals and Practices, 1870 to the Present*. New York: Basic Books.

Ruitenbeek, Henrik M.
1966 *Psychoanalysis and Female Sexuality*. New Haven: Yale University Press.

Rupp, Leila J.
1978 *Mobilizing Women for War: German and American Propaganda, 1939–1945*. Princeton: Princeton University Press.

Ryan, Mary P.
1975 *Womanhood in America: From Colonial Times to the Present*. New York: New Viewpoints.
1979 "Femininity and Capitalism in Antebellum America." In *Capitalist Patriarchy and the Case for Socialist Feminism*. Ed. Zillah R. Eisenstein, pp. 151–168. New York: Monthly Review Press.

Ryan, William
1971 *Blaming the Victim*. New York: Vintage.
Ryscavage, Paul
1979 "More Wives in the Labor Force Have Husbands with 'Above-Average' Incomes." *Monthly Labor Review* (102 (June): 40–42
Sahlins, Marshall
1972 *Stone Age Economics*. Chicago: Aldine.
Schaffer, Rudolph
1977 *Mothering*. Cambridge: Harvard University Press.
Scharf, Lois
1980 *To Work and to Wed*. Westport, Conn.: Greenwood.
Schram, Donna D.
1978 "Rape." In *The Victimization of Women*. Ed. Jane Roberts Chapman and Margaret Gates, pp. 52–79. Beverly Hills, Calif.: Sage.
Schuler, Loring A.
1928 "Homebuilders." *Ladies' Home Journal* 45 (January): 32.
1929 "Home Catches Up." *Ladies' Home Journal* 46 (January): 22.
1929 "Experience." *Ladies' Home Journal* 46 (February): 30.
1929 Editorial. *Ladies' Home Journal* 46 (March): 34.
Scott-Maxwell, Florida
1958 "Should Mothers of Young Children Work?" *Ladies' Home Journal* 75 (November): 58–59, 158–160.
1958 "Women Know They Are Not Men." *Ladies' Home Journal* 75 (November): 60–61, 166.
Sears, Robert R., Eleanor E. Maccoby, and Harry Levin
1957 *Patterns of Child Rearing*. Evanston, Ill.: Row, Peterson.
Sebald, Hans
1976 *Momism: The Silent Disease of America*. Chicago: Nelson Hall.
Seccombe, Wally
1974 "The Housewife and Her Labour under Capitalism." *New Left Review* 83 (January–February): 3–24.
Segal, Julius, and Herbert Yahraes
1978 *A Child's Journey: Forces That Shape the Lives of Our Young*. New York: McGraw-Hill.
Sicherman, Barbara
1975 "American History." *Signs* 1 (Winter): 461–485.
Siegal, Alberta Engvall, Lois Meek Stolz, Ethel Alice Hitchcock, and Jean Adamson
1963 "Dependence and Independence in Children." In *The Employed Mother in America*. Ed. F. Ivan Nye and Lois Wladis Hoffman, pp. 67–81. Chicago: Rand McNally.
Sigourney, Lydia
1838 *Letters to Mothers*. Hartford: Hudson and Skinner.

1841 *Letters to Young Ladies*. 6th ed. New York: Harper and Brothers.

Silverman, Anna, and Arnold Silverman
1971 *The Case Against Having Children*. New York: David McKay.

Sirageldin, Ismail
1969 *Non-Market Components of National Income*. Survey Research Center. Ann Arbor: University of Michigan Press.

Skelsey, Alice
1970 *The Working Mother's Guide to Her Home, Her Family and Herself*. New York: Random House.

Sklar, Dusty
1976 "The Trauma of Eventlessness." *Family Weekly* (January 11).

Sklar, Kathryn Kish, ed.
1977 "Introduction." In Catherine E. Beecher, *A Treatise on Domestic Economy*, pp. v–xviii. New York: Schocken; orig. ed. 1841.

Skold, Karen Beck
1980 "The Job He Left Behind: American Women in the Shipyards during World War II." In *Women, War, and Revolution*. Ed. Carol R. Berkin and Clara M. Lovett, pp. 55–75. New York: Holmes and Meier.

Slater, Peter Gregg
1977 *Children in the New England Mind*. Hamden, Conn.: Archon.

Slater, Philip
1974 *Earthwalk*. New York: Anchor.
1976 *Pursuit of Loneliness*. Rev. ed. Boston: Beacon.

Smart, Mollie Stevens, and Russell Cook Smart
1946 *It's a Wise Parent*. New York: Charles Scribner's Sons.

Smith, Daniel Scott
1974 "Family Limitation, Sexual Control, and Domestic Feminism in Victorian America." In *Clio's Consciousness Raised*. Ed. Mary Hartmann and Lois W. Banner, pp. 119–136. New York: Harper and Row.

Smith, Hugh
1796 *Letters to Married Women on Nursing and the Management of Children*. 2d ed. Philadelphia: Mathew Carey.

Smith, Ralph E.
1979 "The Movement of Women into the Labor Force." In *The Subtle Revolution: Women at Work*. Ed. Ralph E. Smith, pp. 1–29. Washington, D.C.: The Urban Institute.

Smuts, Robert W.
1971 *Women and Work in America*. New York: Schocken.

Snell, J. E., R. J. Rosenwald, and A. Robey
1964 "The Wifebeater' Wife." *Archives of General Psychiatry* 2 (8): 107–112.

Sobel, Dava

1981 "Children of Working Mothers." *New York Times* (December 13): p. 14E.

Sokeitus, Joy F., and Kathy McFadden

n.d. *Myths about Working Women*. Pittsburgh: Know Inc.

Spitz, René

1965 *The First Year of Life: A Psychoanalytic Study of Normal and Deviant Development of Object Relations*. New York: International Universities Press.

Spock, Benjamin

1968 (orig. 1946) *Baby and Child Care*. Rev. and enlarged ed. New York: Pocket Books.

1972 "Women and Children: Male Chauvinist Spock Recants—Almost." In *The Future of the Family*. Ed. Louise Kapp Howe, pp. 151–158. New York: Simon and Schuster.

1976 *Baby and Child Care*. Rev. and updated ed. New York: Pocket Books.

Spruill, Julia C.

1938 *Women's Life and Work in the Southern Colonies*. Chapel Hill: University of North Carolina Press.

Stafford, Frank, and Greg Duncan

1977 "The Use of Time and Technology by Households in the United States." Manuscript, Department of Economics, University of Michigan, Ann Arbor.

Stendler, Celia B.

1950 "Sixty Years of Child Training Practices." *Journal of Pediatrics* 36: 122–134.

Steinem, Gloria

1980 "The Nazi Connection: Authoritarianism at Home." *Ms Magazine* 9 (May): 14–24.

Stevenson, Mary

1975 "Women's Wages and Job Segregation." In *Labor Market Segmentation*. Ed. Richard C. Edwards, Michael Reich, and David M. Gordon, pp. 243–255. Lexington, Mass.: D. C. Heath.

Stewart, Abigail J., David G. Winter, and A. David Jones

1975 "Coding Categories for the Study of Child Rearing from Historical Sources." *Journal of Interdisciplinary History* 5 (4): 687–701.

Stolz, Lois M.

1960 "Effects of Maternal Employment on Children: Evidence from Research." *Child Development* 31:749–782.

Strasser, Susan M.

1980 "An Enlarged Human Existence? Technology and Household Work in Nineteenth Century America." In *Women and Household Labor*. Ed. Sarah Fenstermaker Berk, pp. 29–51. Beverly Hills, Calif.: Sage.

Strecker, Edward A.
1946 *Their Mothers' Sons*. Philadelphia: J. B. Lippincott.

Sunley, Robert
1963 "Early Nineteenth Century American Literature on Child Rearing." In *Childhood in Contemporary Cultures*. Ed. Margaret Mead and Martha Wolfenstein, pp. 150–167. Chicago: University of Chicago Press.

Sutherland, Arthur H., and Myron M. Stearns
1927 "Never Too Young to Learn Responsibility." *Ladies' Home Journal* 44 (March): 27, 228.

Szalai, Alexander, ed.
1972 *The Use of Time: Daily Activities of Urban and Suburban Populations in Twelve Countries*. The Hague: Mouton.

Thayer, William
1851 "The Era for Mothers." *The Mother's Assistant* 16 (May): 129–146.

Thom, D. A.
1925 *Child Management*. Children's Bureau Publication 143. Washington, D.C.: Government Printing Office.

Thompson, Dorothy
1939 "If I Had a Daughter." *Ladies' Home Journal* 56 (September): 4.
1940 "It's a Woman's World." *Ladies' Home Journal* 57 (July): 25.
1960 "It's All the Fault of Women." *Ladies' Home Journal* 77 (May): 11–19.

Thompson, E. P.
1967 "Time, Work Discipline, and Industrial Capitalism." *Past and Present* 38 (December): 56–97.

Thompson, Roger
1974 *Women in Stuart England and America*. Boston: Routledge & Kegan Paul.

Toffler, Alvin
1970 *Future Shock*. New York: Random House.

Trall, Russell Thacher
1874 *The Mother's Hygienic Handbook*. New York: S. R. Wells.

Tryon, Milton Rolla
1917 *Household Manufactures in the United States, 1640–1860*. Chicago: University of Chicago Press.

Tweedy, Jill
1972 "Why Are Women Always to Blame for Rape?" *Washington Post*, March 26.

Ulrich, Laurel Thatcher
1979 "Vertuous Women Found: New England Ministerial Literature, 1668–1735." In *A Heritage of Her Own*. Ed. Nancy F. Cott and Elizabeth H. Pleck, pp. 58–80. New York: Touchstone.

United States Commission on Civil Rights
1979 "Rape Victim." *Civil Rights Update.* Washington, D.C.: Government Printing Office.
United States Department of Commerce
1976 *A Statistical Portrait of Women in the United States.* Special Studies Series 58, Washington, D.C.: Government Printing Office.
United States Department of Labor
1975 *Handbook on Women Workers.* Women's Bureau Bulletin 297. Washington, D.C.: Government Printing Office.
1975 *The Myth and the Reality.* Women's Bureau, Employment Standards Administration. Washington, D.C.: Government Printing Office.
1980 *Perspectives on Working Women: A Databook.* Washington, D.C.: Government Printing Office.
1982 *Employment in Perspective: Working Women.* Washington, D.C.: Government Printing Office.
Vanek, Joann
1974 "Time Spent on Housework." *Scientific American* 231 (May): 116–120.
1978 "Household Technology and Social Status: Rising Living Standards and Status and Residence Differences in Housework." *Technology and Culture* 19 (July): 361–375.
1978 "Housewives as Workers." In *Women Working.* Ed. Ann H. Stromberg and Shirley Harkess, pp. 392–414. Palo Alto, Calif.: Mayfield.
1980 "Household Work, Wage Work, and Sexual Equality." In *Women and Household Labor.* Ed. Sarah Fenstermaker Berk, pp. 275–291. Beverly Hills, Calif.: Sage.
Van Gelder, Lawrence
1979 "Time Spend on Housework Declines." *New York Times* (May 22), part 3, p. 10.
Veblen, Thorstein
1912 *The Theory of the Leisure Class.* New York: Viking.
Vickery, Clair
1979 "Women's Economic Contribution to the Family." In *The Subtle Revolution: Women at Work.* Ed. Ralph E. Smith, pp. 159–200. Washington, D.C.: The Urban Institute.
Wade, Mary L.
1901 "Refined Life on Small Incomes; or, The Woman Who Does Her Own Work." *Proceedings of the Third Lake Placid Conference on Home Economics,* pp. 95–102. Lake Placid, N.Y.
Wadsworth, Benjamin
1972 (orig. 1712) "The Well-ordered Family, or, Relative Duties." In *The Colonial American Family: Collected Essays,* pp. 1–121. New York: Arno.

Walker, John Brisben
1898 "Motherhood as a Profession." *The Cosmopolitan* 25 (May): 89–93.

Walker, Katherine E., and Margaret E. Woods
1976 *Time Use: A Measure of Household Production of Family Goods and Services.* Washington, D.C.: American Home Economics Association.

Walzer, John F.
1974 "A Period of Ambivalence: Eighteenth Century American Childhood." In *The History of Childhood.* Ed. Lloyd de Mause, pp. 351–382. New York: The Psychohistory Press.

Watson, John B.
1927 "The Weakness of Women." *The Nation* 125 (July 6): 9–10.
1928 *Psychological Care of Infant and Child.* New York: Norton.

Weis, Kurt, and Sandra S. Borges
1975 "Victimology and Rape: The Case of the Legitimate Victim." In *Rape Victimology.* Ed. Leroy G. Schultz, pp. 91–141. Springfield Ill.: Charles C. Thomas.

Weisner, Thomas, and Ronald Gallimore
1977 "My Brother's Keeper: Child and Sibling Caretaking." *Current Anthropology* 18 (2): 169–190.

Weiss, Nancy Pottishman
1977 "Mother, the Invention of Necessity: Dr. Benjamin Spock's *Baby and Child Care.*" *American Quarterly* 29 (Winter): 519–546.

Weisstein, Naomi
1972 "Psychology Constructs the Female." In *Women in Sexist Society.* Ed. Vivian Gornick and Barbara K. Moran, pp. 207–224. New York: New American Library.

Welter, Barbara
1973 "The Cult of True Womanhood: 1820–1860." In *The American Family in Socioo-historical Perspective.* Ed. Michael Gordon, pp. 224–250. New York: St. Martin's.

West, Jane
1974 (orig. 1806) *Letters to a Young Lady.* Vol. 3. New York: Garland.

West, Mrs. Max
1971 (orig. 1914) *Infant Care.* Children's Bureau Bulletin 8. Reprinted in *Children and Youth in America: A Documentary History.* Vol. 2. 1866–1932, pp. 37–38. Cambridge: Harvard University Press.

White, Burton L.
1975 *The First Three Years of Life.* Englewood Cliffs, N.J.: Prentice Hall.

Wiley, Bell
1938 *So You're Going to Get Married!* Philadelphia: J. B. Lippincott.

Wilson, Margaret Gibbons
1979 *The Ameican Woman in Transition: The Urban Influence,* 1870–1920. Westport, Conn.: Greenwood.

Winch, Robert F.
1971 *The Modern Family*. 3d ed. New York: Holt, Rinehart and Winston.

Wirth, Louis
1945 "The Problem of Minority Groups." In *Man in the World Crisis*. Ed. Ralph Linton, pp. 347–350. New York: Columbia University Press.

Wishy, Bernard
1968 *The Child and the Republic: The Dawn of Modern American Child Nurture*. Philadelphia: University of Pennsylvania Press.

Wolf, Anna W. M.
1941 *The Parents' Manual*. New York: Simon and Schuster.

Wolfenstein, Martha
1955 "Fun Morality: An Analysis of Recent American Child Training Literature." In *Childhood in Contemporary Cultures*. Ed. Margaret Mead and Martha Wolfenstein, pp. 168–178. Chicago: University of Chicago Press.

Wortis, Rochelle
1977 "The Acceptance of the Concept of the Maternal Role by Behavioral Scientists: Its Effects on Women." In *Family in Transition*. Ed. Arlene S. Skolnick and Jerome H. Skolnick, pp. 362–378. Boston: Little, Brown.

Wright, Erna
1973 *Common Sense in Child Rearing*. New York: Hart.

Wylie, Philip
1942 *Generation of Vipers*. New York: Farrar and Rinehart.

Yankelovich, Daniel
1981 "New Rules in American Life." *Psychology Today* 15 (April): 35–91.

Zillessen, Clara H.
1927 "When Housework Is Not Drudgery." *Ladies' Home Journal* 44 (January): 127, 133.

Zuckerman, Michael
1975 "Dr. Spock: The Confidence Man." In *The Family in History*. Ed. Charles E. Rosenberg, pp. 179–207. Philadelphia: University of Pennsylvania Press.

INDEX

Designer:	Kitty Maryatt
Compositor:	Trend Western
Printer:	Vail-Ballou
Binder:	Vail-Ballou
Text:	11 pt. Weiss
Display:	Weiss